WealthWatch

WealthWatch

A Study of Socioeconomic Conflict in the Bible

MICHAEL S. MOORE

With a Foreword by Baruch A. Levine

PICKWICK *Publications* · Eugene, Oregon

WEALTHWATCH
A Study of Socioeconomic Conflict in the Bible

Pickwick Publications
An Imprint of Wipf and Stock Publishers
199 W. 8th Ave., Suite 3
Eugene, OR 97401

www.wipfandstock.com

ISBN 13: 978-1-61097-296-3

Cataloging-in-Publication data:

Moore, Michael S.

Weathwatch : a study of socioeconomic conflict in the Bible / Michael S. Moore ; foreword by Baruch A. Levine.

xvi + 304 p. ; 23 cm. Includes bibliographical references and indexes.

ISBN 13: 978-1-61097-296-3

1. Economics in the Bible. 2. Economics—Moral and ethical aspects. 3. Middle Eastern literature—Relation to the Old Testament. 4. Gilgamesh—Criticism, interpretations, etc. 5. Atrahasis (Old Babylonian epic) 6. Bible. O.T. Pentateuch. 7. Maccabees. 8. Bible. N.T. Luke—Parables. I. Levine, Baruch A. II. Title.

BS670 M66 2011

Manufactured in the U.S.A.

Contents

Foreword

THERE IS AN ANECDOTE I remember from my youth which came to mind as I was studying the present, in-depth work by Michael Moore, *WealthWatch*. The applicability of the anecdote will soon be evident. It goes like this:

In Hebrew religious school, a young student is being taught the Torah (the Five Books of Moses), and is reading the narrative in Exodus, chapter 16, about manna from heaven. At one point, we are told that the manna tasted like "*tsappiḥit* in honey" (v. 31). The student asks the teacher: "How do you translate *tsappiḥit*?" Now, this word occurs only here in all of Scripture (*hapax legomenon*), and there has always been a lingering uncertainty about its derivation, although we assume that it refers to a kind of cake, something like baklava.

The teacher's answer to the student is most telling. "You see, the Israelites were in bondage to Pharaoh in Egypt, until the LORD liberated them under the leadership of Moses, bringing them into the wilderness. There was no food to eat, so the LORD in His kindness brought down manna from heaven, which tasted like *tsappiḥit* in honey. Now do you understand?" The student shook his head, and persisted in his query, ultimately forcing the teacher to retrace the biblical narrative all the way back to Abraham, as he set out for the Land of Canaan, without ever actually translating *tsappiḥit*! And yet, the student now realized, it is hoped, that though it mattered little how the manna was concocted, it mattered greatly how it fit into the overall narrative of Israel's liberation and formation as a people. One could write a paper entitled: "*Tsappiḥit* and Israel's *Heilsgeschichte*."

This anecdote epitomizes the situation of the contemporary student of Scripture, who is often left with a sense of uncertainty as to the meaning of the biblical text, and who persists in the effort to probe it in ever greater depth, often without ultimate satisfaction. There is a sense that understanding the relevance of Scripture, in particular, is somehow dependent on subtlety of language and form, not to speak of the unspoken context. To return to the anecdote, we must not only place a particular scene in biblical context, as the teacher sought to do, but extend our search into the surrounding cultures of the ancient Near East so as to comprehend fully what the Hebrew Bible has to say. This is what Michael has accomplished in excellent form.

In reviewing the history of biblical interpretation we encounter a paradox of sorts: The text of the Hebrew Bible, most notably the Torah, has over the centuries been regarded by its interpreters as sacred, constituting a divine revelation. One might think that acknowledging the authority of Scripture would suffice, yet virtually every generation of believers since antiquity has sought to probe the biblical message as if it required updating. More recently, however, biblical scholarship has deepened and expanded further the search for meaning in real time and contemporary relevance, supported by rich discoveries and by the urge to get back to the unfiltered message, a goal shared by believers and non-believers, alike, and Jews and Christians alike.

Underlying most efforts at biblical interpretation has, after all, been a concern with relevance. What does the Bible have to say about the great issues of our time? In the Jewish and Christian traditions, pre-modern interpreters mostly took Scripture out of historical context in an effort to relate it to their contemporary concerns. They applied what the Bible says about Pharaoh to Caesar, as an example. As is true in most of modern scholarship, and in literature and the arts, engagement of cultural context, not flight from it, has become the key to unveiling relevance. At some point, great artists stopped portraying biblical characters dressed as Venetians of the seventeenth century, and attempted, at least, to imagine how they really looked, conscious that they didn't look like themselves.

Michael Moore has given us a broadly based contextual study of wealth as an issue of consequence in the Hebrew Bible, with added discussion of inter-testamental Judaism and early Christianity. His method of getting to core-issues is to study conflict, which is arguably the most reliable index of what was most important in life. One can hardly argue against the conclusion that what people often fought over, condemned, or extolled, was wealth. What is more, it should be emphasized that rhetorically, it is conflict that moves narrative. Moore has written an expansive treatment of wealth as an issue of conflict in ancient Israel. He has enlightened us through learned exegesis, has explored massive ancient

Near Eastern materials, and has shown how much we must know, and how clearly we must think, if we seek more than a superficial notion of relevance. At a time when the Hebrew Bible is the referent of debate on a plethora of contemporary issues, it is refreshing to have a study of its deeper relevance.

Baruch A. Levine
Skirball Professor, Emeritus, of Bible and Ancient Near Eastern Studies
New York University

Abbreviations

ABD	*The Anchor Bible Dictionary*. 6 vols. Edited by David Noel Freedman. New York: Doubleday, 1992
AfO	*Archiv für Orientforschung*
AhW	*Akkadischer Handworterbuch*. 3 vols. Edited by Wolfram von Soden. Wiesbaden: Otto Harrassowitz, 1965–81
AJES	*American Journal of Economics and Sociology*
AJS	*Association of Jewish Studies*
AJSLL	*American Journal of Semitic Languages and Literatures*
Akk	Akkadian
AJT	*Asia Journal of Theology*
ANET	*Ancient Near Eastern Texts Relating to the Old Testament*. 3rd ed. Edited by James B. Pritchard. Princeton: Princeton University Press, 1969
Arab	Arabic
Aram	Aramaic
ARS	*Annual Review of Sociology*
ASOR	American Schools of Oriental Research
ASR	*American Sociological Review*
Atr	*Atrahasis*
BA	*Biblical Archaeologist*
BASOR	*Bulletin of the American Schools of Oriental Research*
BBR	*Bulletin of Biblical Research*
BCE	before the common era
BI	*Biblical Interpretation*
Bib	*Biblica*
BibInt	*Biblical Interpretation*
BiOr	*Bibliotheca Orientalis*
BJS	*British Journal of Sociology*

BWL	*Babylonian Wisdom Literature.* W. G. Lambert. Oxford: Clarendon, 1960
BZ	*Biblische Zeitschrift*
CAD	*Chicago Assyrian Dictionary.* 20 vols. Edited by Martha T. Roth, et al. Chicago: Oriental Institute of the University of Chicago, 1921–2011
CANE	*Civilizations of the Ancient Near East.* 4 vols. Edited by Jack M. Sasson. Peabody, MA: Hendrickson, 2000
CAT	*The Cuneiform Alphabetic Texts from Ugarit, Ras Ibn Hani and Other Places.* Edited by Manfred Dietrich, et al. Münster: Ugarit, 1995
CBQ	*Catholic Biblical Quarterly*
CD	Damascus Document
CE	common era
CML	*Canaanite Myths and Legends.* Edited by John C. L. Gibson. Edinburgh: T. & T. Clark, 1977
CSEL	*Corpus scriptorium ecclesiasticorum latinorum*
CTH	*Catalogue des texts hittites.* Edited by Emmanuel Laroche. Paris: Klinksieck, 1971
DDD	*Dictionary of Deities and Demons.* Edited by Karel van der Toorn, et al. Leiden: Brill, 1999
DSD	*Dead Sea Discoveries*
EA	*Die El Amarna Tafeln.* 2 vols. Translated by Jørgen A. Knudtzon. Aalen: Zeller, 1964
EBio	*Encyclopedia of Bioethics.* 5 vols. Edited by Stephen G. Post. New York: MacMillan Reference, 2004
ECI	*Encyclopedia of Communication and Information.* 3 vols. Edited by Jorge Reina Schement. New York: Macmillan, 2002
EDSS	*Encyclopedia of the Dead Sea Scrolls.* 2 vols. Edited by Lawrence H. Schiffman. New York: Oxford University Press, 2000
Ee	*Enūma elish*
EESH	*Encyclopedia of European Social History.* 6 vols. Edited by Peter N. Stearns. Detroit: Scribner, 2001
Eg	Egyptian

EHJ	*Encyclopedia of the Historical Jesus.* Edited by Craig A. Evans. London: Routledge, 2008
EJ	*Encyclopedia Judaica.* 22 vols. Edited by Michael Berenbaum and Fred Skolnick. Detroit: MacMillan Reference, 2007
EMA	*Encyclopedia of Modern Asia.* 6 vols. Edited by Karen Christensen and David Levinson. Scribner's Sons, 2003
EoA	*Encyclopedia of Apocalypticism.* 3 vols. Edited by John J. Collins, et al. New York: Continuum, 2000
ER	*The Encyclopedia of Religion.* 16 vols. Edited by Mircea Eliade. New York: Macmillan, 1987
Erra	*Epic of Erra*
ESTE	*The Encyclopedia of Science, Technology, and Ethics.* 4 vols. Edited by Carl Mitcham. Detroit: Macmillan Reference, 2005
EWB	*Encyclopedia of World Biography.* 23 vols. Edited by Paula K. Byers. Detroit: Gale, 2004
FC	*Fathers of the Church.* 118 vols. Washington, DC: Catholic University of America, 1947–
GE	*Gilgamesh Epic*
GEM	*The Gale Encyclopedia of Medicine.* 5 vols. Edited by Deirdre S. Blanchfield and Jacqueline L. Longe. Detroit: Gale, 2002
Gk	Greek
GKC	*Gesenius' Hebrew Grammar.* Edited by E. Kautzsch. Translated by A. E. Cowley. 2nd ed. Oxford: Oxford University Press, 1910
GNT	*Greek New Testament*
HAL	*Hebräisches und aramäisches Lexikon zum Alten Testament.* 5 vols. Edited by Ludwig Koehler et al. Leiden: Brill, 1967–95
HTR	*Harvard Theological Review*
HUCA	*Hebrew Union College Annual*
IDB	*Interpreter's Dictionary of the Bible.* 5 vols. Edited by George A. Buttrick. Nashville: Abingdon, 1962–76
Int	*Interpretation*
JAAR	*Journal of the American Academy of Religion*

JAOS	*Journal of the American Oriental Society*
JBE	*Journal of Business Ethics*
JBL	*Journal of Biblical Literature*
JBQ	*Jewish Bible Quarterly*
JCS	*Journal of Cuneiform Studies*
JDR	*Journal of Divorce and Remarriage*
JESHO	*Journal of the Economic and Social History of the Orient*
JETS	*Journal of the Evangelical Theological Society*
JJS	*Journal of Jewish Studies*
JLEO	*Journal of Law, Economics, and Organization*
JNES	*Journal of Near Eastern Studies*
JQR	*Jewish Quarterly Review*
JRE	*Journal of Religious Ethics*
JSNT	*Journal for the Study of the New Testament*
JSOT	*Journal for the Study of the Old Testament*
JSP	*Journal for the Study of the Pseudepigrapha*
JSS	*Journal of Semitic Studies*
KAI	*Kanaanäische und aramäische Inschriften.* 2 vols. Edited by Herbert Donner and Wolfgang Röllig. Wiesbaden: Harrassowitz, 2002
KUB	*Keilschrifturkunden aus Boghazköi*
Lat	Latin
LB	Late Babylonian
LSJ	*A Greek-English Lexicon.* Edited by H. G. Liddell, R. Scott, and H. S. Jones. Oxford: Oxford University Press, 1996
LXX	The Septuagint
Maq	*Die assyrische Beschwörungssammlung Maqlû.* Translated by Gerhard Meier. Horn, Austria: Berger, 1937
MB	*Monde de la Bible*
MT	Masoretic Text
NCE	*New Catholic Encyclopedia.* 15 vols. Edited by Janet Halfmann. Detroit: Gale, 2002
NDHI	*New Dictionary of the History of Ideas.* 6 vols. Edited by Maryanne Cline Horowitz. Detroit: Scribner, 2005
NT	*Novum Testamentum*

NTS	*New Testament Studies*
NZSTR	*Neue Zeitschrift für Systematische Theologie und Religionsphilosophie*
OB	Old Babylonian
OED	*Oxford English Dictionary.* 20 vols. Oxford: Oxford University Press, 2010
Or	*Orientalia*
OTE	*Old Testament Essays*
OTP	*Old Testament Pseudepigrapha.* 2 vols. Edited by James Charlesworth. Garden City, NY: Doubleday, 1983–1985
RA	*Revue d'assyrologie*
RB	*Revue biblique*
RBL	*Review of Biblical Literature*
REJ	*Revue des études juives*
ResQ	*Restoration Quarterly*
RevQ	*Revue de Qumran*
RHA	*Revue hittite et asianique*
RlA	*Reallexicon der Assyriologie.* Edited by Erich Ebeling et al. Berlin: de Gruyter, 1928–
SAA Gilg	*The Standard Babylonian Epic of Gilgamesh.* Edited by Simo Parpola. State Archives of Assyria 1. Helsinki: Neo-Assyrian Text Corpus Project, 1997
Sam	Samaritan Pentateuch
SB	Standard Babylonian
SEJ	*Southern Economic Journal*
SJOT	*Scandinavian Journal of Theology*
Sum	Sumerian
Syr	Syriac
TDNT	*Theological Dictionary of the New Testament.* 10 vols. Edited by G. Kittel and G. Friedrich. Grand Rapids: Eerdmans, 1964–76
TDOT	*Theological Dictionary of the Old Testament.* 14 vols. Edited by G. Johannes Botterweck et al. Grand Rapids: Eerdmans, 1978–2004
TuL	*Tod und Leben nach die Vorstellungen der Babylonier.* Edited by Erich Ebeling. Berlin: de Gruyter, 1931
TZ	*Theologische Zeitschrift*

UF	*Ugarit Forschungen*
Ug	Ugaritic
UNP	*Ugaritic Narrative Poetry.* Edited by Simon B. Parker, et al. Atlanta: Society of Biblical Literature, 1997
USQR	*Union Seminary Quarterly Review*
UT	*Ugaritic Textbook.* 3 vols. Edited by Cyrus Gordon. Rome: Pontificium Instititum Biblicum, 1965
Vg	Vulgate
VT	*Vetus Testamentum*
VTSup	*Vetus Testamentum Supplements*
WA	*World Archaeology*
WTJ	*Westminster Theological Journal*
ZA	*Zeitschrift für Assyriologie*
ZABR	*Zeitschrift für Altorientalische und Biblische Rechtsgeschichte*
ZAVA	*Zeitschrift für Assyriologie und vorderasiatische Archäologie*
ZAW	*Zeitschrift für die alttestamentliche Wissenschaft*
ZTK	*Zeitschrift für Theologie und Kirche*

1

Introduction

I T'S A FAMILIAR STORY.

A young lady graduates near the top of her class, enrolls in her favorite university, and falls in love with a fellow student. The honeymoon quickly ends, however, when the first fight between them uncovers a Grand Canyon separating their worldviews about *money*—how to earn it, how to spend it, how to save it, how to manage it. Ten years, two moves, and three children later, things really hit a wall when one of them tries to seize unilateral control of the family checkbook. The other resists, of course, but to no avail. Convinced their differences are irreconcilable, they cave in to the pressure and choose litigation over listening.[1]

Confiding her pain to a friend she learns of a class at her friend's church entitled "God and Your Money—A Biblical Perspective." Worried about the future of her children and anxious to get out of debt she registers for this class with great expectations.

The first night of class utterly shatters those expectations.

Having learned at university that ancient texts divorced from their literary-historical contexts can be made to say anything—anything at all—she quickly realizes within the first five minutes of class that the instructor's approach to the Bible, however zealous and well-intentioned, completely ignores the literary-historical context out of which it originally comes to life.[2] What she hears instead is a polished "3-step" formula:

1. Aleksandr Solzhenitsyn manipulates this contrast in a speech to the Harvard graduating class of 1978 in order to describe what he perceives to be one of the fundamental weaknesses of Western culture (go to www.columbia.edu/cu/augustine/arch/solzhenitsyn/harvard1978.html).

2. This composite adjective refers to interpretative approaches which try to give balanced attention to the synchronic (literary) as well as the diachronic (historical)

1

- *Step 1*— Shallow overview of selected prooftexts about wealth and possessions divorced from their literary-historical contexts;
- *Step 2*— Selective economic prejudices laid over these prooftexts designed to champion the instructor's preconceived bias; finally leading up to
- *Step 3*— "Authoritative" religious instruction on "what the Bible says" about wealth and possessions.

Frustrated by this experience she decides to drop the class. Not only that, she begins to wonder why so many of her "church friends" read the Bible through such a shallow lens.[3] She wonders whether the historical claims of the Bible are genuine, not to mention its claim to religious authority.[4] Finding our office through another friend, she bravely comes in to talk about this stuff in spite of the "friendly warning" from one of our secretaries: "Watch out—he's writing a book about this stuff."

ANOTHER BOOK ABOUT THIS STUFF?

Well, that warning was on-target. I *was* "writing a book about this stuff"—the book you now hold in your hands—and the experience of helping this young lady climb out of her "money pit"[5] helped contribute greatly to its final shape. Weekly meetings with this soccer mom helped me—yea, forced me—to re-examine the Bible from a wholly different perspective as *her* socioeconomic questions fought for more and more attention. Witnessing her struggle to (re)connect with *her* "sacred text" helped me understand why so many others struggle to (re)connect with

---

dimensions of ancient texts, whether written by Homer or Shakespeare or Isaiah or Kabti-ilāni-marduk (Klein, *Interpretation*; Tate, *Interpretation*; Jonker, *Exclusivity*).

3. Stendahl ("Bible," 5) states his opinion clearly: "It is as Holy Scripture, Holy Writ, that the Bible has become a classic in the West," adding his "doubts that it—or substantial parts of it, at least—would have ever become a classic were it not for its status as Holy Scripture."

4. In Gunton's words (*Revelation*, ix), "the doctrine of revelation has been in recent times at once neglected and overused." Still, "no credible person today seriously believes that the Bible fell out of heaven fully bound in its current state with gilded edges" (McDonald, *Canon*, 5).

5. *The Money Pit* is a Richard Benjamin film released by Universal Pictures in 1986.

their "sacred texts," especially those which have been "desacralized"[6] and/ or "despiritualized."[7]

The purpose of this book is to help postmodern Westerners understand what the Bible has to say about wealth and possessions. Its major presuppositions are (a) that nobody can "understand themselves" apart from some recognition of their "spiritual roots,"[8] and (b) that these roots sink deeper into the pages of the Bible than most people realize. Positioning itself within definable boundaries, however, the following book focuses only upon that part of the Bible most recognized to be its ideological core; i.e., the part called *Torah* by some, *Pentateuch* by others.[9] Further, the approach adopted here attempts to interpret *this* "great text"[10] against other "great texts" in its literary-historical context, including (a) some epic poems from Mesopotamia,[11] (b) some Jewish texts from Syria-Palestine,[12] and (c) some Nazarene parables.[13] Choosing *which* epic poems, *which* Jewish texts, and *which* Nazarene parables will

6. Eliade ("Preface," x–xi) uses this term to describe what he sees as one of the major by-products of secularization. Of course, reading the Bible as "sacred text" does not automatically lead to belief in its "divine inspiration," but it does not negate the fact that "no one in the English-speaking world can be considered literate without a basic knowledge of the Bible" (Hirsch, "Bible," 1).

7. Solzhenitsyn prefers this word to "secularized" because he believes the foundations of Western culture to be profoundly spiritual (cited in Moore, *Faith*, 258).

8. Kluger, *Gilgamesh*, 13.

9. Both terms (one Hebrew, one Greek) refer to the first five books of the Bible—*Genesis, Exodus, Leviticus, Numbers*, and *Deuteronomy*—the foundational section revered by all three monotheistic faiths (Blenkinsopp, *Pentateuch*; Zucker, *Torah*; Karabell, *Peace*; Kramer, "Traditions").

10. Though the present study distinguishes between "literary texts" and "non-literary" texts, the boundaries between the two are not always easy to define. Reiner ("Literatur") includes in the category of "literary texts" the following: myths, epics, autobiographies, propaganda literature, poetry (including hymns and prayers), love lyrics, laments, elegies, wisdom literature (both philosophical and didactic), humorous literature, and some prose texts. Foster ("Literature") basically agrees with this taxonomy.

11. The *Epic of Gilgamesh*, the *Atrahasis Epic*, and the *Epic of Erra* (Dalley, *Myths*, 50–125, 9–35, 285–312).

12. Evans, *Texts*; Murphy, *Wealth*.

13. The context provided by the Greek New Testament is historically relevant to Jewish and Muslim *as well as* Christian study (Sabbath, "Introduction," 1–12). Khalidi shows that where the Qur'an and hadiths depict Jesus as "a somewhat distant figure of no immediate or pragmatic moral relevance to Muslim piety," populist Muslim stories portray him as "a living moral force" (*Jesus*, 26; see Achtemeier, *New Testament*; Johnson, *Possessions*).

doubtless seem arbitrary to some readers, yet *interpretation against some context is preferable to interpretation against no context.*[14] Before beginning, however, we first need to define our terms, identify our presumptions, and try to distinguish what makes this study different from other studies.

How, for example, should "wealth" be defined? Where some define it as "the spontaneous production of the earth or the result of labor employed in the cultivation of the earth,"[15] others reject the notion that "wealth . . . is an end in itself, or that the accumulation of as much wealth as possible is an appropriate end for politics to pursue."[16] Still others link "wealth" closely to the term "money," defining it as a "useful or agreeable thing possessing exchangeable value," especially when used as an "instrument of . . . public (or) private purpose."[17] Unwittingly mirroring one of the ideological triads of the Dead Sea Scrolls—"wealth," "fornication," "defilement"[18]—a wealthy heiress warns her readers not to give in to wealth's "pitfalls, bounties, and perils."[19]

Where some focus on "know-how, technology, and skills" as wealth's *assets*, others identify it in terms of *liabilities.*[20] Often associated with the name of Thomas Malthus,[21] this "glass-half-empty" approach presumes that all economic systems operate as "zero-sum games" in which "one person's prosperity comes at another's expense," so that "viewed in this way, talk about profit sounds obscene."[22] Eric Beinhocker rejects this approach, proposing instead that "the origin of wealth is *knowledge,* [and]

14. Polaski, *Authorizing*, 45–49; Moore, Review of *Authorizing*, 294–96.

15. Bentham, *Reward*, 237.

16. Nussbaum, "Aristotle," 105.

17. Mill, *Economy,* 1.8, 10.

18. CD 4:17–18 (the "three nets of Belial"). Murphy (*Wealth*, 40), argues that Belial's second "net," whether transcribed הין ("arrogance") or הון ("wealth"), refers to "a specific kind of arrogance . . . associated with the abuse of wealth," a conclusion reached earlier by Tournay ("À propos").

19. Willis, *Navigating*, 10. Neusner defines "economics" as a discipline comprised of "systematic doctrines on rational action in regard to scarcity, encompassing a definition of wealth and systematically rational rules on the increase and disposition of wealth" (*Economics*, 5).

20. McGurn, "Economics," 22.

21. Malthus (*Essay*) is best known for his doomsday predictions.

22. McGurn, "Economics," 23. Brueggemann calls this the "myth of deprivation" (*Memory*, 69–76).

rather than treating knowledge as an assumption, an exogenous input, [or] a mysterious process outside the bounds of economics . . . [in actuality it's] the endogenous heart of the economy."[23]

Question: Does "wealth" mean one thing to pre-moderns and something else to postmoderns?[24] *Answer:* Many seem to think so. In fact, one historian believes that "the ancients have no word for our modern concept of economics . . . [though] they do have definite ideas about how society should be ordered—for instance, whether there should be private property or not. They also understand the connections between the availability of commodities and price fluctuations. They speculate on why money is valuable and the connections between monetary value and societal conventions. What they do not do is link this all together into a coherent view of economic phenomena and their behavior."[25]

Many challenge this assessment,[26] yet few challenge whether

> the social institution upon which most Americans focus their attention, interests, and concerns is *economics*. When the average U.S. family is in difficulty (for example), it is invariably due to the fact that the U.S. provisioning system—the system of jobs, goods and services, production, and consumption—is in trouble . . . Within this framework, the organizing principle of American life is instrumental mastery—the individual's ability to control his or her environment, personal and impersonal, in order to at-

23. Beinhocker, *Wealth,* 317.

24. Euben pursues this question in greater depth ("Premodern"), but this study will not pursue it here, in part because "no history of taxation over the course of antiquity has been written, to say nothing of a satisfactory general economic history" (Hudson, "Antiquity," 3).

25. Gonzalez, *Faith,* xiv. Polanyi (*Livelihood*) thinks that ancient Near Eastern urban economies possess temple/state administrations, but not price-setting markets. North disagrees (*Structure*), as does Silver ("Polanyi," 795–829).

26. Opinions remain divided, for example, over the "theoretical" nature of Xenophon's (d. 354 BCE) famous essay, *Oeconomicus*. Finley, for example, finds in *Oeconomicus* "not one sentence that expresses an economic principle or offers an economic analysis" (*Economy,* 19), but Pomeroy rejects this opinion as "an anachronistic view of economic theory which excludes, by definition, much of what the Greeks themselves regard as the economy" (*Xenophon,* 43). Neusner argues that in "Christianity, down to the . . . seventh century (CE), economics as a matter of theory enjoys no position whatsoever" (*Economics,* 4).

tain quantity-oriented success: wealth, ownership, "good looks,"
proper grades, and all other measurable indications of success.[27]

Question: Why begin *another* book on "money and the Bible" by re-
hearsing such well-worn questions? *Answer:* Because anyone who's ever
read the Bible *and* balanced an online checking account knows that a
massive Grand Canyon separates the contemporary postmodern global
economy from the ancient Near Eastern economy out of which the Bible
originates,[28] and any interpreter who tries to ignore the "gorilla-in-the-
middle-of-the-room" existence of this Canyon risks not only commit-
ting the venal sin of historical irrelevancy,[29] but also the mortal sin of
intellectual dishonesty.[30]

   Another term in need of clarification is the slippery word "Western."
Some believe, for example, that Western culture "derives from two sources: Israelite prophecy and revelation, on the one hand, as a source of ethics and religion, and Greek philosophy and reasoning, on the other."[31] A
few argue that "the Islamic tradition also claims to be based on the same
two sources: the prophets of Israel and the philosophers of Greece,"[32] but
whatever the merits of these assertions,[33] "Western" remains a nebulous

27. Malina, *World,* 29.

28. Pointing to the growing "rift" between "the biblical world and our own," Oakman
suggests that the "social sciences" can help chart more "persuasive directions for translating meaning across centuries and cultures" ("Hermeneutics," 267).

29. "History" is "the intellectual form in which a civilization renders account to itself
of its past" (Huizinga, "Definition," 14).

30. Serious interpretation of ancient literature involves learning (a) the *language* in
which it is written, (b) the *context* in which it is produced, and (c) the *structure* within
which it is preserved. Levenson warns against the kind of extremism which "widens
the gap between past and present in the name of uncompromising historical honesty"
("Liberation," 229–30).

31. Ernst, *Muhammad,* 5.

32. Ibid., 6. The accuracy of this claim, of course, is hotly debated. Grafton feels that
critics like Ernst too simplistically label "colonialists" and "Orientalists" as "the primary
Western villains prompting radical Islamic responses" (Review of *Muhammad,* 529).
Ohrenstein and Gordon, however, trace the history of modern Western economics to
the writings of "Greek philosophers, Islamic scholars, medieval Schoolmen, and the
Mercantilists of the sixteenth and seventeenth centuries" (*Economic,* xvi).

33. Arguing that "the organizing principles of an economy should be individual liberty and limited government" and that "our material aspirations, not to mention many
of our nonmaterial needs, are best served by a free economic order—one that accords
individuals broad freedoms to produce, consume, negotiate, and exchange according to
their own preferences, expectations, and abilities," Kuran questions whether traditional-

term for many readers. Some try to define it as something only difficultly corralled between antithetical poles, imagining East-West relations as a "clash of culture and cultural identities . . . shaping the patterns of cohesion, disintegration, and conflict in the post-Cold War world."[34] Others more inclusively define it as an umbrella term for the ideological "salad bowl" making up the bulk of contemporary Euro-American culture.[35]

Arguments can be advanced on both sides of this debate. The point here is simply to note how difficult it is to draw absolute boundaries between "East" and "West," especially when trying to define slippery terms like "wealth" and "possessions." Historians tend to frown on sweeping generalizations,[36] yet the fact remains that *the ancient Near Eastern library commonly called the Bible*[37] *is the oldest and most influential contributor to Western economic values.*[38] In spite of its Eastern origins (and the West's "moral decay"),[39] nothing else explains why so many people, like the soccer mom outside my office door, turn to the Bible for socioeconomic help instead of Xenophon's *Oeconomicus*,[40] Kautilya's

---

ist Muslim economies can succeed "in a domain modern civilization has secularized" (*Islam*, 53). Other Muslim leaders warn against the problem of over-dependence on the West (i.e., "Westoxification"; Esposito and Mogahed, *Billion*, 42).

34. Huntington, *Clash*, 20–21.

35. Hobson, *Origins*, 2. Nussbaum suggests that "the real 'clash of civilizations' is not between 'Islam' and 'the West,' but within all modern nations—between people who are prepared to live on terms of equal respect with others who are different, and those who seek the protection of homogeneity and the domination of a single 'pure' religious and ethnic tradition" ("Democracy," B6).

36. Bernal goes too far when he argues that Greek culture is impossible to conceive apart from the cultural contributions of ancient Egypt (*Athena*), but even Bernal's harshest critics concede his larger point (Lefkowitz and Rogers, *Athena*; Levine, Review of *Athena*).

37. "Bible" is the traditional English translation of the plural Greek noun τὰ βίβλια, "the scrolls." The Christian church is the institution most responsible for transforming this plural noun into a singular one.

38. The present study is hardly alone in this presumption (see ApRoberts, *Web*; Jeffrey, *People*; Frye and Macpherson, *Myths*).

39. Brzezinski strongly criticizes the "permissive cornucopia" he sees poisoning contemporary Western culture (*Control*, 64–74).

40. Written in c. 362 BCE (Pomeroy, *Oeconomicus*).

Arthashastra,[41] Ibn Sīnā's *Kitab al-Siyāsa,*[42] or Marx's *Das Kapital.*[43] Nothing else explains why *this* "sacred text" exercises so much influence on so many, regardless of geographic location, ethnic identity, religious belief, and/or socioeconomic status.[44]

WHAT ABOUT THE ECONOMISTS?

The following pages put before this "great text" some pointed socio-economic questions. Such a study is easier to imagine than implement, however, because socioeconomic approaches to the Bible are still in their infancy.[45] Many factors contribute to this *status quo,* not least the widespread acceptance of "3-step" approaches in lieu of serious research.[46] Nevertheless, the following pages do not attempt to analyze every Hebrew text about wealth,[47] nor do they attempt to outline the unabridged history of Western economics.[48] What they *do* try to do is survey the basic character and development of the ancient Near Eastern

41. *Arthashastra* is a compendium of Indian writings on wealth and property compiled in the fourth century BCE by a Hindu sage named Kautilya. Rangarajan provides an English translation (*Arthashastra*).

42. L. Ma'lūf (*Traités,* 1–17) edits this essay by Ibn Sīnā (ابن سينا, latinized as "Avicenna," d. 1037 CE).

43. Marx, *Kapital.*

44. Wachlin calls the Bible "the world's all-time best-seller ... a book that has influenced Western culture as much as any other single work, the one piece of American literature that has affected American lives more than any other" ("Bible," 31). Study of the Bible, of course, does not equate to the study of theology. In fact, to quote Bloom (*Closing,* 259), "one need only read Adam Smith's classic economic treatise *Wealth of Nations* on education (Book V), to observe how the reform of universities, particularly the marginalizing of theological influence in universities, was essential to the emergence of modem political economy and the regime founded on it."

45. Exceptions only prove the rule, one of the more intriguing being Stansell's attempt to explain the Hebrew economy via three models: the "patron-client" model, the "limited wealth" model, and the "honor-shame" model ("Abraham," 92–110).

46. Other factors include the ideological and methodological biases permeating the scholarly guild, a situation which generates another set of problems (Tate, *Interpretation,* 4).

47. To my knowledge no one has yet attempted to write such an introduction, though some have begun to lay the foundations; e.g., Gottwald (*Tribes*), and Gerstenberger (*Theologies*). Arnold explores the developmental similarities between Babylonian and Israelite economies ("Nebuchadnezzar," 330–55), and Lemche tries to explain these similarities from the archaeological record ("Bones," 121–39).

48. On this challenging task see the histories of Ferguson, *Ascent*; O'Brien, *Classical*; Ahiakpor, *Macroeconomics*; Levy, *Dismal*; Eltis, *Classical*; Perelman, *Capitalism.*

library most responsible for establishing and reinforcing the most fundamental Western values about wealth and possessions.

Contemporary economists offer only marginal help toward this kind of examination because (a) the level of disagreement within the discipline is high,[49] and (b) most economists—like most mathematicians or biologists—presume the Bible to be a unitary document like any modern "book."[50] "Classical" and "neo-classical" theorists, for example, tend to define economics as "the science of human choice among scarce alternative resources,"[51] a definition which presumes (a) that all people can and do make free-will choices about their economic lives, and (b) that the consequences of these choices are qualitatively (and in some cases quantitatively) measurable.[52] Not only are such presumptions questionable, however, but too often they presume the existence of a hypothetical world in which incredibly smart people have only to deal with simple situations, when in fact the world is a rather complex place in which average people have to deal with some rather difficult economic situations.[53] Thus the neo-classical approach often tends to be simplistic, anecdotal, and hyper-individualistic,[54] especially when proponents focus all their attention on individual wealth to the exclusion of the "social or-

49. Posner ("Primitive," 1–3) rehearses the major point of disagreement within the discipline as the "formalist" vs. "substantivist" debate, the former too narrowly defining "economics" as something focusing only on the marketplace, the latter too narrowly rejecting all attempts to apply contemporary economic categories to ancient cultures.

50. More on this below, but a classic illustration is Ginzberg's rejection of the "higher critics" because of "certain very serious shortcomings in the philological approach to an interpretation of the Scriptures" (*Economics*, 7), a "criticism" Wallis justifiably skewers as speciously uninformed (Review of *Economics*, 270).

51. North, *Scholarship*, 79 (citing Robbins, *Science*, 15).

52. The most recognizable source of "classical" economic theory is Adam Smith, *Wealth of Nations* (see Davis, *Theory*, 1–17). Where Brueggemann rejects the "classical" theory as the "myth of deprivation" (*Memory*, 69–76), Kasper argues (*Macroeconomic*, 1–5) that the Great Depression in the U.S. brought "institutionalist" economists to power because of their ability to do what the neo-classicists could not: engage the problems of unused labor and unused natural resources. When the American economy overheated in the 1960s, however, policy-makers turned back to the classicists with a vengeance. Riding this wave, Friedman proposed that the best way to replace the centralized, bureaucratized social welfare system created by New Deal institutionalists was to create a "negative income tax" (*Capitalism*, 191–94).

53. Beinhocker, *Wealth*, 52 (citing Swedish economist A. Leijonhufvud).

54. Weber argues against any view which reduces human beings to passive objects instead of active subjects (*Social*, 72).

ganization, transformation, distribution, and consumption of the objects of nature" needed to insure the "satisfaction of subsistence needs."[55]

Question: Is there more than one way to conceptualize the discipline of economics? *Answer:* Yes. Theorists resistant to "individual-vs.-society" continuums sometimes overreact by conceptualizing the discipline merely in terms of issues "close to people's lives."[56] Critics of this definition, however, find it much too simplistic to be taken seriously, to the point that some go out of their way to denigrate the discipline as a whole, calling it "the dismal science,"[57] "the pig philosophy,"[58] and/ or (my personal favorite) a "futile and pettifogging scholasticism."[59] Others gravitate to the other extreme, subcategorizing the discipline into ever-smaller divisions like "institutional economics,"[60] "information economics,"[61] "computational economics,"[62] "Keynesian economics,"[63] "Marxist economics,"[64] and the like. Frustrated and perplexed, some question (a) whether any definition can effectively distinguish socioeconomic *form* from *substance*,[65] or (b) whether economics can truly be defined *as a discipline.* John Stuart Mill (d. 1873) comes close to this

55. Mann, *Social,* 1:24. Copeland is a good example of a "heterodox" institutionalist (*Economics*).

56. Galbraith, *Affluent,* 3.

57. Carlyle, *Chartism,* 17.

58. Ibid., 17.

59. Laughland, Review of *Frozen,* 54–55. Keynes insists that while economics may be difficult to define, to label it "undefinable" is ultimately counterproductive (*Theory,* cited in Stiglitz, "Information," 462).

60. Veblen (*Absentee*) rejects the idea that people are independent makers of economic decisions, arguing instead that individual decisions are constantly subject to changing institutions. The primary value for economic systems, from Veblen's perspective, is to make money, not produce goods.

61. Stiglitz, "Information."

62. Mirowski (*Machine*) sharply challenges American neo-classical economic theory because he sees it as something fundamentally unable to incorporate the impact of the computer and its ability to manage multiple markets simultaneously.

63. Keynes, *Theory.*

64. Marx and Engels, *Manifesto.* This is not an exhaustive list.

65. According to Stanfield (*Economic,* 1–7) Polanyi distinguishes between the study of the allocation of scarce means for competing ends (*formalist* economics) vs. the study of how human groups actually solve problems of production and distribution (*substantivist* economics). Beinhocker, on the other hand (*Origin,* 97), draws five distinctions between "traditional economics" and what he calls "complexity economics":

kind of skepticism when he argues that "economic phenomena depend on (too) many causal factors . . . left out of economic theories . . . [so that] when the factors left out are of particular importance, the predictions of the theories may be completely mistaken."[66]

Question: How does the phenomenon of globalization affect this debate? *Answer:* Radically, yet uncertainly. Some theorists, for example, define globalization as "a catch-all word for growing world trade, the growing linkages between financial markets in different countries, and the many

	Complexity Economics	Traditional Economics
Dynamics	Open, dynamic, nonlinear systems, far from equilibrium	Closed, static, linear systems in equilibrium
Agents	Modeled individuality; use inductive rules of thumb to make decisions; have incomplete information; are subject to errors and biases; learn and adapt over time	Modeled collectivity; use complex deductive calculations to make decisions; have complete information; make no errors and have no biases; have no need for learning or adaptation (are already perfect)
Networks	Explicitly model interactions between individual agents; networks of relationships change over time	Assume agents only interact indirectly through market mechanisms (e.g., auctions)
Emergence	No distinction between micro- and macroeconomics; macro patterns are emergent result of micro-level behaviors and interactions	Micro- and macroeconomics remain separate disciplines
Evolution	The evolutionary process of differentiation, selection, and amplification provides the system with novelty and is responsible for its growth in order and complexity	No mechanism for endogenously creating novelty, or growth in order and complexity

66. Mill, "Economy," 4:323.

other ways in which the world is becoming a smaller place."[67] Others define it much more broadly; e.g., as "a multi-dimensional set of social processes which create, multiply, stretch, and intensify worldwide social interdependencies ... while at the same time fostering in people a growing awareness of deepening connections between the local and the distant."[68] Where the first definition focuses on economics *per se,* the second confines itself to the parameters of general sociology.

Others view the phenomenon of globalization as little more than a faddish trend promoted by an idealistic group of academics ("globalists") whose only desire is to see "the process of globalization continue, and indeed intensify."[69] Opposing them, however, stands another group of idealists ("localists") who "seek to escape or overcome the problems posed by globalization through small-scale forms of economic and cultural development and political organization."[70] Niall Ferguson reconfigures this debate onto a broader historical grid when he points out that "economies which combine all the institutional innovations— banks, bond markets, stock markets, insurance and property-owning democracy—perform better over the long run than those which do not ... [Thus] it is not wholly surprising that the Western financial model tends to spread around the world, first in the guise of imperialism, then in the guise of globalization."[71]

Whatever the parameters or goals or implications of this debate, suffice it to say here, with Alex MacGillivray, that "globalization" immediately and most obviously connotes "a genuine uncertainty about what we're experiencing."[72]

WHAT ABOUT THE BIBLE?

This "genuine uncertainty" often makes it difficult to imagine how any of the foregoing theoretical discussions might help postmodern readers comprehend the socioeconomic character of the Bible, especially when (a) contemporary economic theory stands embroiled in a "state

67. Krugman, *Unraveling,* 365.

68. Steger, *Globalization,* 13.

69. Kitching, "Globalism," 874.

70. Mandle, *Globalization* (cited in Kitching, "Globalism," 874).

71. Ferguson, *Ascent,* 341–42.

72. MacGillivray, *Globalization,* 5.

of turmoil";[73] (b) the structures and ideologies of ancient Near Eastern socioeconomic institutions are so difficult to reconstruct;[74] and (c) the structure and development of the Bible itself remains unclear. This last assertion may catch some readers off guard, but it is important to recognize here, at the outset of this study, that the ancient Near Eastern library commonly called the Bible is not a "book" in the modern sense of the word.[75] Whereas most ancient Near Eastern literature comes straight out of the ground, raw and unedited,[76] the Bible is a layered tapestry of texts gathered together over many centuries by predominantly Hebrew-speaking peoples living in "canonical communities"[77] dedicated to the preservation of an "official" religious ideology—monotheistic Yahwism.[78] Those who believe its pages to contain the Word of God find little reason, in spite of this developmental history, to question its historicity or integrity,[79] yet most critical historians wrestle with two basic questions; viz., (a) What material in the Hebrew Bible is recognizably, evidently, and authentically "historical?"; and (b) How can Israel's socioeconomic history be reconstructed from such a source?[80]

Attempts to engage these questions honestly often generate a great deal of discussion over (a) how much weight to assign to the biblical-

73. Hausman, "Economics."

74. The International Scholars Conference on Ancient Near Eastern Economies has tried to work on this problem (Hudson and Levine, *Privatization*); one of the more provocative interpreters is Morris Silver (*Structures of the Ancient Near East, Economic Structures of Antiquity, Prophets and Markets*).

75. Schniedewind reminds us that "we not only tend to think of the Bible as a single book, but we also read the Bible as if it came from a world of texts, books, and authors ... Yet the Bible was written before there were books" (*Bible*, 3).

76. Richard, *Archaeology*; Gittlen, *Sacred*.

77. Sanders, *Canon*; Childs, *Introduction*; Brueggemann, *Theology*, 61–89.

78. We say "official" because mounting archaeological evidence reveals a much less monotheistic picture of "Israel" than that championed by the biblical authors (Smith, *Memoirs*, 87–88). With regard to content, Gunkel's *fin de siècle* question still remains relevant: "Is the Old Testament a system in which there can be no contradiction, or does it not contain a varied plenitude of records of a great religio-historical process in which there have actually been all sorts of different positions?" (*Israel*, 20).

79. One of the best discussions on this point is the carefully-written chapter on "Revelation and Inspiration" in LaSor et al., *Survey*, 591–97).

80. Davies states the problem clearly: "Canons lie uneasily with historical investigation" (*Scribes*, 5), and Sherwood challenges any who would try to "take the text back, through some kind of seductive academic striptease, to a pure and naked original state" (*Biblical*, 2).

vs.-non-biblical evidence;[81] (b) how much attention to focus on the entire Bible vs. its various sub-sections (e.g., prophecy vs. apocalyptic; law vs. wisdom; Gospels vs. Epistles);[82] and/or (c) how to evaluate the characteristics of the socioeconomic institutions to which it refers (e.g., Is slavery acceptable or unacceptable? Is the monarchy progressive or regressive? How do "work" and "rest" interrelate?).[83] Serious engagement with such questions does not require the putting of Hebrew economics "on hold" until the historians can figure everything out (hardly!), yet no serious interpreter can afford to pretend (a) that these questions are not important, or (b) that they are not legitimate.[84]

WHAT ABOUT THE THEOLOGIANS?

While the economists and historians labor at *their* questions, teachers face the daily task of explaining to students how this "great text" impacts everyday life. Like no other library on earth the Bible exercises tremen-

81. Hurvitz criticizes Davies for failing to appreciate sufficiently the external controls provided by non-biblical Hebrew and Aramaic texts ("Quest," 301–15) and McDonald voices similar criticism against those who try to over-simplify the canonical process (*Canon*, 3–19, 401–30).

82. Hoppe's approach, for example, works well with the prophetic, but not the wisdom literature (*Poor*, 42–121). Recognizing many of the blind spots within the scholarly guild, Duchrow suggests three models "by which the people of God respond to their economic and political contexts": (a) the *prophetic* model of revolution/reform; (b) the *torah republic* model (as "Israel" adjusts to life in the Persian empire); and (c) the *apocalyptic resistance* model (as "Israel" hunkers down in small groups to preserve its identity from contamination and annihilation ("Perspectives," 21).

83. Following Otto's contention that the paradise story in Gen 2–3 most likely preserves a "sapiential dialogue with the priestly creation narrative" ("Paradieserzählung," 188), Waschke argues that the work-rest polarity impacts a number of Hebrew texts, so that where Exod 20:11 focuses on human *rest* as a reflection of divine *rest* (נוח), the rationale for sabbath-keeping in Deut 5:15 finds its deepest roots in the language of redemption from obligatory *work* (עבד; "Ruhe," 76–81). Alt ("Königtum") explains the gap between rich and poor in monarchical Israel in terms of two factors: (a) monarchies by their very nature give rise to bureaucracies, and (b) ancient Near Eastern bureaucracies are often populated by foreigners. Loretz ("Rentenkapitalismus") argues that the changes perpetrated by these bureaucracies are predominantly economic in nature, but Kessler (*Statt*) gives attention to both socioeconomic and political factors. Chaney ("Bitter") adapts the theories of Lenski (*Power*) to identify the socioeconomic contours of life in ancient Israel, but his approach gives more attention to trends than texts.

84. Schniedewind, *Bible*, 195–214. It's indefensible to assert, with Frye, that "if anything historically true is in the Bible, it is there not because it is historically true ... but for ... reasons (which) have presumably something to do with spiritual profundity or significance" (*Code*, 40).

dous power and influence on contemporary life,[85] and though critical historians may never agree on the size of its "historical kernel,"[86] its impact on the global economy is too significant to be ignored.[87] No one, for example, can understand the character and development of modern Western democracies apart from some understanding of the core religious texts upon which they are based, chief among which stands the Bible.[88] In Gerd Theissen's opinion, the Bible is important for everyone to understand—for "atheists, so that they might better understand the religious self-conception of others; and for Christians, so that they might better understand themselves."[89]

That such facts need highlighting today is more than a little ironic. The world in which our grandparents lived was "largely self-contained in a far simpler system."[90] The world in which *we* live, however, is religiously pluralistic, spiritually abstruse, secularly entrenched, and blissfully ignorant of its own history, and this in spite of the fact that

> economy, trade, and business have become increasingly interdependent and transnational. In the 1990s, with the advancement of computers, telecommunications, and media, we experienced daily "wake-up calls," events occurring half-way around the world that immediately affected us at home. What happened in Germany or Japan directly changed the game in America and caused us to think and act outside our own area of control. Now we have a single global banking system connected by high-tech networks for the rapid transfer of funds and a global stock and commodities market open 24 hours a day, seven days a week.[91]

85. Newman, *Religion,* 14. Goodblatt underlines the powerful role the Hebrew Bible plays in the formation of national Jewish identity (*Nationalism,* 28–48).

86. Murphy's assessment of *Esther* might be cited via illustration: "There is reason to speak of a 'kernel' of historical fact lying behind the story, but it is almost impossible to determine" (*Wisdom,* 154).

87. Even so convicted an unbeliever as William Blake can describe "the stolen and perverted writings of Homer and Ovid, of Plato and Cicero" as "artifice" compared to "the sublime of the Bible" (*Writings,* 480).

88. Petersen, "Genesis," 5.

89. Theissen, *Bible,* 15.

90. Cohen, *Resilience,* 19; see Friedman, *Consequences*; Theissen, *Bible,* 1–15; Williamson et al., *Democracy.*

91. McFarland et al., *Leadership,* 40.

Beinhocker's analysis of this history is wonderfully concise: "For a very, very, very long time not much happened; then all of a sudden, all hell broke loose."[92] To assess its accuracy one need only consider the fact that every person now reading these lines awoke to a world this morning very different from the one in which he or she awoke a few short years ago. The technological revolution driving the development of the contemporary global economy, in other words, is forcing every one of us to re-imagine how we think, what we consume, and yes, how we assess the resource most responsible for the basic values upon which we make our daily economic decisions.[93]

Our grandparents' questions do not engage this world because *this* world generates an entirely new set of questions: "What does globalization mean for labor markets and fair wages? How does it affect chances for real jobs and reliable rewards? What does it say to the ability of nations to determine the economic futures of their populations? What is the hidden dowry of globalization? Christianity? Cyber-proletariatization? New forms of structural adjustment? Americanization disguised as human rights (or as MTV)?"[94] The following pages, at any rate, do not attempt to chart the history of globalization, but they do assume it to be the primary context against which most of us attempt to define (a) the socioeconomic changes hurdling at us from so many directions, as well as (b) the increasingly irrelevant ways in which so many interpreters of the Bible respond to them.

This latter point is easily illustrated by comparing the questions upon which televangelists focus[95] with the questions upon which critical scholars focus.[96] Engaging the latter, for example, one quickly learns how difficult it is for South Americans to engage, much less agree with their North American colleagues over what kind of slavery occurs in

92. Beinhocker, *Wealth*, 11.

93. Bloxham defines "economic value management" as "an integrated approach to managing any organization that is based on the principle of stewardship," emphasizing that the "foundation" of this approach is "a set of principles or beliefs" (*Management*, 4).

94. Appadurai, "Grassroots," 1–2.

95. Johns, *Televangelism*; Schultze, *Televangelism*; Frankl, *Televangelism*.

96. The American Academy of Religion, for example, produces a quarterly journal called the *Journal of the American Academy of Religion*, and the Society of Biblical Literature produces the quarterly *Journal of Biblical Literature*.

the book of *Exodus*.[97] One sees how difficult it is for South Africans to engage North Americans over the Tower of Babel story in *Genesis* (pro-apartheid or anti-apartheid?),[98] not to mention how difficult it is for West Africans to talk to Euro-Americans about *Ezra* and *Nehemiah* apart from the latter's focus on the "problem of polygamy."[99]

Some find these discussions exhilarating. Others find them exhausting and tiresome, even threatening, often because they refuse to recognize the depth of the Grand Canyon separating *this* world from the ancient world. Whatever the reasons, such responses generate a never-ending parade of "3-step" approaches,[100] not to mention the "Bible as literature" courses perennially offered by many public universities.[101] Whatever the accomplishments of either camp, both tend to marginalize or ignore the following questions: (a) How does globalization affect the economic values of contemporary Westerners? (b) Do materialistic ideas like "client satisfaction" and "market share" complement or replace the Judeo-Christian ideas of "fellowship" and "community?"[102] (c) Does the "global-markets + government-deregulation = prosperity" equation produce greater prosperity or greater inequality?[103]

Whatever one's attitude toward these questions, they are not simply going to go away. In fact, the *really* tough question is not whether anyone wants to "hike the Canyon" today, but whether anyone will want to hike it thirty or forty years from now. Few Westerners believe that

97. See, e.g., the spirited debate between Pixley, Levenson, and Collins (Ogden Bellis and Kaminsky, *Hebrew*, 215–75).

98. Hiebert applies Gen 11 to this socio-political Grand Canyon ("Babel," 142–43), to which Lapsley positively responds ("Exegesis," 23).

99. Levison, *Return*; Segovia, *Teaching*; Achcar, *Barbarisms*; Bediako, "Mbiti."

100. Note, for example, Schippe's resistance to historical criticism (*Influence*). Appadurai points to *media* and *migration* as the two factors most responsible for this shallowness (*Modernity*, 3). Roseberry uses the phrase "political economy" to describe "how political behavior evolves, shapes, and is shaped by the institutions of production, consumption, and distribution" ("Political," 181). With Murphy, the following study presumes that economic symbols are much easier to analyze than economic systems (*Wealth*, 22–24).

101. Gabel argues that a purely literary approach ought to have "nothing to do with whether or not the words correspond to an objective reality" (*Literature*, 4), but Stendahl argues that "there is something artificial in the idea of 'the Bible as literature.'" Why? Because "it is as Holy Scripture that the Bible is a classic in our culture" ("Classic," 6).

102. Schultze thinks this is already happening (*Communicating*).

103. Appadurai, "Grassroots," 1.

wealth and possessions are less important to pre-moderns than they are to postmoderns, yet how are the divergent worldviews just described to be assessed in the future, and by whose yardstick?[104] Few Westerners believe that "personal reality" is easily separated from "authentic histori-cal experience,"[105] yet how are *my* memories to be gauged against *your* memories—particularly if the two of us no longer share a common worldview?[106] What role will the Bible play in *that* discussion, if any?[107]

Contemporary theologians resist such questions, in part,[108] because another one obstinately stands in their way; viz., How can the words in-scribed on an ancient tablet dug out of a temple in Syria or palace in Iraq *mean anything at all* to a secretary in Seattle or a toolmaker in Toledo?[109] Even among those who *do* recognize the value of historical inquiry, of what *real* importance is the socioeconomic world of early Christianity[110] or early Judaism,[111] not to mention the ancient Near Eastern world out of which both religions come to life?[112]

104. One reviewer tries to bridge the gap by suggesting that "Xenophon's discus-sion of use value and exchange value is worth xeroxing and circulating to introductory economics students" (Lowry, Review of *Xenophon,* 828).

105. Smith, *Memoirs,* 126, 166. Mendelsohn puts the matter bluntly when he asserts that "the 'ancient' Near Eastern world is becoming with each new excavation increas-ingly 'modern'" (*Slavery,* v).

106. Collins, *Babel,* 27–52.

107. Stendahl raises this question in his 1983 presidential address to the Society of Biblical Literature ("Classic"), and William Safire addresses it in his study of the book of *Job* (*Dissident,* xvii).

108. Notable exceptions include Long, *Economy;* Rasmussen, *Anxiety;* Meeks, *Economist;* Ruppel, *Theologie;* McFague, *Abundant.*

109. Vanhoozer explains why this question is so persistent: "Paraphrasing Marx, we might say that the point of postmodern thought is not to interpret the text, but to *situ-ate* it. Postmodern exegesis is always 'situated': always 'from below,' never 'from above'" ("Scripture," 160).

110. Notable exceptions include Gonzalez, *Faith,* xi; Deist, *Material;* Hengel, *Judaism,* 1.6–57; Bassler, *Mammon;* Hanson and Oakman, *Palestine.*

111. Notable exceptions include Neusner, *Mishnah;* Ohrenstein and Gordon, *Analysis.*

112. In Cahill's words, "to appreciate the Bible properly we cannot begin with it" (*Gifts,* 8). In the words of Fox-Genovese, "history cannot simply be reduced—or elevat-ed—to a collection, theory, and practice of reading texts . . . For historians, the text exists as a function, or articulation, of context. In this sense historians work at the juncture of the symbiosis between text and context, with context understood to mean the very conditions of textual production and dissemination" ("Literary," 85).

The proverb attributed to George Santayana remains the most appropriate response to these questions: "Those who cannot remember the past are condemned to repeat it."[113] Some people understand this proverb better than others, of course, because some know from bitter personal experience what historical amnesia can do to a culture when its leaders arrogantly "deny the uniformity of . . . human behavior and the behavior of social institutions."[114] It's not necessary to travel all the way back to the Bronze Age to see the power of historical amnesia at work. Indeed, only a few decades ago in central Europe a determined cadre of highly-educated "Christians" perpetrated unspeakable atrocities against their neighbors, all in the name of God and country.[115]

For these and other reasons the following pages focus on two questions: (a) How can a study of ancient Near Eastern socioeconomic conflict motifs help Westerners understand what the Bible has to say about wealth and possessions? and (b) How can such a study help Westerners understand the influence of the Bible on their daily economic decisions? The second question, of course, predicates itself upon careful investigation of the first, yet neither is addressable apart from another one; viz., Why do so many of the books about wealth and possessions sold in contemporary religious bookstores so blithely champion the "3-step" approach?[116]

113. Santayana, *Life*, 284. Perdue defines "postmodernism" as "an extensive array of evocative modulations" determined to construct an epistemology that "places the source of understanding within the interaction of the mind of the interpreter, his or her multiple locations, networks of identities, and the linguistic-cultural expressions of the text" (*Reconstructing*, 240). Himmelfarb makes pertinent application: "Postmodernism amounts to the denial of the fixity of any 'text,' of the authority of the author over the interpreter, of any 'canon' that 'privileges' great books over comic books" ("Telling," 158).

114. Cameron and Neal, *Concise*, 4.

115. Haas argues that the European holocaust of the 1930s and 40s cannot be "tamed" as merely the work of sadists or barbarians, but resulted from the systematic application of a Nazi-adopted "ethic" which still poses a challenge (*Morality*). On Sept 24, 2007, for example, the president of Columbia University (Lee Bollinger) accused the president of Iran (Mahmoud Ahmadinajad) not simply of denying the reality of the "holocaust," but of "defying historical truth and making all of us who continue to fear humanity's capacity for evil shudder at this closure of memory" (www.youtube.com/watch?v=tACSopIZVdk). *Question:* Why do leaders like Ahmadinajad continue to find their way to power? *Answer:* Because "revisionists are found in all right-wing groups" (Lange, *Rechten*, 22).

116. By "religious bookstore" we refer not to legitimate booksellers, but the propagandizing marketplaces dedicated to the selling of populist pablum to religionists

While it's true that the "monetary theology" of Jesus "resists the dull pressure of events and the sameness of human thought,"[117] many contemporary writers tend to marginalize and dismiss what Walter Brueggemann calls the "Dominant Reality" of Western life—*narcissistic consumerism*.[118] Granted, some observe (a) that the Bible devotes "twice as many verses to money (as) to faith and prayer combined,"[119] and (b) that "not one of Jesus' parables does not have deep stewardship implications."[120] Yet few dare to criticize the culture responsible for creating this Dominant Reality, and this is what causes many to conclude that all Westerners are crass materialists more interested in *profits* than *prophets*.[121]

Yet the prophets still speak.[122] They speak in strange, dead languages, to be sure, but their voices remain clear and their arguments remain cogent.[123] The question is whether anyone wants to listen to what they have to say; i.e., whether the heirs of the Judeo-Christian tradition want to understand the primary documents responsible for creating their socio-economic value system.[124] Christian evangelicals, to cite only one group of constituent Westerners, wrestle mightily with this question

---

brainwashed by the "3-step" approach. Ron Sider sounded a warning about this in his 1977 landmark study, *Rich Christians in an Age of Hunger*, but many others have since joined "the resistance." See Van Drimmelen, *Global*; Hoffman, *Global*; Comor, *Global*; Hesselbein, *Community*; Cobb, *Sustaining*; Went, *Enigma*; Heslam, *Globalization*.

117. Buchan, *Frozen*, 107.

118. Brueggemann defines this Dominant Reality as a "matrix of military consumerism" enveloped by "a sophisticated mixture of violence and repression disseminated through a calloused media to numbed believers," its core value being "the conviction that well-being, security, and happiness are the results of getting, having, using, and consuming—activities which may be done without restraint or limit, even at the expense of others" (*Theology*, 718).

119. Alcorn, *Money*, 16.

120. Vallet, *Stones*, 5.

121. As Fort puts it, "religion and business have had an uneasy relationship throughout history. Religious belief may sanction business activity, but it may also condemn it … The relationship between money and virtue tends to be ambivalent" (*Prophets*, 4).

122. Stendahl's classic insight remains sound: one cannot understand what the Bible *means* until one first understands what it *meant* ("Biblical," 418–32), and Corn reminds us that "biblical texts are the cornerstone of our customs, our laws, our literature and art, our family structure, and our notion of romantic love" (*Incarnation*, xii–xiii).

123. Klay, "Evangelicalism," 32–37.

124. Mangum argues that a less-than-generous income support system combines with a less-than-progressive tax structure in the U.S. to produce an economy character-

through their practice of stewardship, their critique of self-in-
dulgence, and their emphasis on moderation, offering substantial
resistance to the consumption ethic which modern advertising
presents so enticingly. Nevertheless, they often fail to recognize,
or at least respond to three things: The *first* is the power of advertising to shape people's perceptions, desires, and lifestyles
... *Second*, most evangelicals ignore the fact that millions of
working-class people do not share many of the benefits of the
new culture ... [and] this ... leads to a *third* shortcoming: most
evangelicals do not seem to understand that social and economic
forces are making it very hard for all Americans to practice biblical stewardship, to tithe, to forsake covetousness, and to avoid
extolling money and possessions.[125]

Our grandparents engage *their* questions in a world shaped by the
post-war polarities of the Cold War (most simplistically put, "capitalism"
vs. "communism").[126] Our generation, however, faces a Reality much more
difficult to define, much less critique.[127] How tempting it is in this brave
new world to hide our heads in the sand[128]—to label market consumerism a "biblical principle,"[129] and the socialist pablum so often formulated

---

ized by the highest per capita income in the world right alongside the highest level
of poverty among developed nations (*Persistence*, 48–77). See Kermally, *Economics*;
Jorgensen and Stiroh, *Raising*; Cohen and Rutsky, *Consumption*.

125. Smith, "Capitalism," 78. Brown blames the "iconography of consumption" for
creating "an infinite array of competing images circulating for our personal entertainment, fulfillment, and ultimately our enslavement" (*Psalms*, 13).

126. Ray argues that "the fall of communism appears to offer further evidence of the
exhaustion of modernity" ("Post-Communism," 543).

127. The Hebrew prophet Amos challenges the consumerism corrupting Israel: "Alas
for those who lie on beds of ivory, and lounge on their couches, and eat lambs from the
flock, and calves from the stall; who sing idle songs to the sound of the harp, and like
David improvise on instruments of music; who drink wine from bowls, and anoint
themselves with the finest oils, but grieve not for the ruin of Joseph!" (Amos 6:4–6), but
Stearns argues that "full-blown consumerism is a modern product" (*Consumerism*, 1).

128. Smart (*Silence*) points to biblical illiteracy as the major contributor to contemporary apathy, but Suter thinks *greed* is the "big problem": "The question is whether the
labor and resources of the Third World nations should contribute more to the opulence
of America's cats and dogs than to the elementary good health of Third World humans"
("Christians," 649). See Clapp, *Passion*.

129. Moe-Lobeda refutes many "market-myths" now permeating the Western
Church; i.e., (1) that global economic growth benefits all; (2) that human freedom and
market freedom are inseparably linked; (3) that human beings are essentially economic
beings with the "right" to consume whatever they want without regard to the welfare
of others; and (4) that corporate globalization is inevitable, even though Adam Smith

in response to it as "the biblical principle of liberation."[130] How tempting it is to argue, with the pharaoh of *Exodus*, that "private gifts from Yahweh can be had at the expense of community."[131]

THE APPROACH OF THIS BOOK

Addressing such questions is not going to be easy. The following pages do not attempt to explain every text about money,[132] nor do they try to analyze every factor responsible for the turmoil in contemporary socioeconomic theory.[133] This book makes no attempt to examine the rationale behind every ancient Near Eastern ledger notation,[134] nor does it try to investigate all the factors responsible for creating the ancient Near Eastern cultures responsible for giving the Bible its distinctive shape and substance.[135] Instead, it merely attempts to identify the "socioeconomic DNA"[136] embedded in a representative sample of "great texts," then reconstruct from this analysis the literary-historical trajectory against which the primary socioeconomic conflict motifs animating the *torah/*

---

envisioned a capitalist economy bounded by a non-market-oriented societal ethic ("False," 16–21).

130. Pinnock notes how easily Marxist economic rhetoric neutralizes legitimate concern for the poor ("Pursuit," 5–14).

131. Brueggemann, *Theology*, 646. Wuthnow argues that "the economic crisis in America's churches . . . (is) both structural and spiritual" (*Crisis*, 12).

132. This book does not focus, for example, on non-literary texts like the "law of the atonement shekel" (Exod 30:11–16) or the "laws of the votive offerings" (Lev 27), though each has a contribution to make to our overall understanding (Baker, *Tight*, 305–15). Similarly, though the GNT is saturated with socioeconomic motifs ("What does it profit" a man to gain the whole world?" "I give my life as a ransom for many," "Friend, lend me three loaves," "Give for alms the things which are within," "You will be repaid at the resurrection of the righteous," etc.), the following pages focus only upon the stewardship parables of *Luke's Gospel*.

133. Hausman, "Economics"; Dasgupta, *Economics*; Sklair, *Globalization*.

134. Snell points out that "the ancient Near East is the time and place where something like modern money" is first invented ("Methods," 1487), but the present study makes no attempt to duplicate his work (see, especially, *Life*).

135. Note instead the work of the International Scholars Conference on Ancient Near Eastern Economies (Hudson and Levine, *Privatization*).

136. Hudson uses the DNA metaphor ("Reconstructing," 7), and Walls focuses on the "ancient cultural codes and meanings" embedded in ancient literary texts (*Desire*, 6). The approach taken by Liverani (*Prestige*) resembles that which previous generations used to call *geisteskulturlich* ("spirit of the culture"; e.g., Jeremias, *Handbuch*).

pentateuch find position and meaning.[137] Just as geneticists use DNA analysis to analyze the basic traits of a given organism, so also can the basic socioeconomic character of *torah* be made more understandable.

The "Achilles heel" of this approach, of course, is that few Westerners know much about the "great literature" of the ancient Near East,[138] not to mention the "great literatures" of ancient Greece,[139] ancient Rome,[140] medieval Europe,[141] modern Europe,[142] modern Russia,[143] or even North America.[144] Rather than listing all the reasons for this problem, however, it seems best here simply to illustrate it. In Max Weber's classic study, for example, *The Protestant Ethic and the Spirit of Capitalism*,[145] one of the greatest minds of the twentieth century lays out an attractive, yet profoundly Eurocentric explanation for the origins of capitalism (i.e., that it results from a dialectical clash between Catholics and Protestants over the nature and meaning of wealth and work).[146] Weber argues, in the words of one biographer, that when "industriousness and self-discipline

137. Working within literary categories developed by Talmon, Fields defines a "motif" as an "encapsulation of a basic principle or societal experience with which the authors of narratives are concerned" (*Sodom*, 20), and Hendel argues that "motifs" are "essential semantic units of biblical narrative," and that "to elucidate them adequately requires knowledge of language, literary and religious traditions, and cultural context, as well as an eye for intertextuality and the nuances of literary style" (Review of *Sodom*, 127).

138. Wasserman (*Style*) points out that there are several levels of "literariness" in "literary texts," an insight which helps explain why Lambert and Millard can find so little of "literary merit" in *Atrahasis* (*Atra-Hasis*, 7, 13) in spite of von Soden's objections ("Götter," 419). Mugerauer is right, however, to insist that the primary function of "great literature" is to challenge entrenched value systems, especially when they become corrupt ("Literature," 407–15).

139. Rostovtzeff, *Economic*; Michell, *Economics*; Kallet, *Money*; Lowry, *Economic*; Seaford, *Greek*. To quote Snell, "students of the history of freedom have tended to search for the roots of Western freedom in the ancient history of Greece and Rome and argue that Greece gave birth to a unique set of attitudes that led to, and to a great extent, were identical to our own . . . the so-called Greek miracle" (*Flight*, 1–2).

140. Bowditch, *Horace*; Safrai, *Roman*. Gunkel sees Westerners as "Israelites in religion, Greeks in art, and Romans in law" (*Israel*, 60).

141. Pounds, *Economic*; Hodges, *Towns*; Ekelund, *Sacred*.

142. Taylor, *Society*; Lachmann, *Capitalists*.

143. Carr, *Soviet*; Friedberg, *Euphoria*; Lewin, *Undercurrents*; Jha, *Perilous*.

144. Veitch, *Superrealism*; Spindler, *American*.

145. Weber, *Ethic*.

146. Weber's influence continues as several scholars attempt to extend his thinking to neighboring disciplines (e.g., Chalcraft, *Sectarianism*).

become expressions of Protestant values in the secular realms of labor and domestic life … (then) financial success comes to be understood as visible evidence of election to grace, thereby forming an ideological link between capitalism, individualism, and religion."[147] Occasionally Weber buttresses this argument with references to this or that primary text from Greece, Rome, China, India, and the Arab world, *yet never does he attempt to interpret the primary biblical texts in their literary-historical contexts.*[148] This astonishing fact rather single-handedly explains the primary rationale behind the present study.[149] However brilliantly argued or widely accepted, no analysis of Western economic history can afford to ignore (a) the original texts of the Bible in their original contexts,[150] (b) the twentieth and twenty-first century revolution in literary criticism (particularly the rise of inter- and intra-textual literary analysis);[151] and/

147. Machacek, "Prosperity," 561.

148. Weber is not to be entirely faulted for this because, as Johnson points out, the modern discipline of biblical studies does not come into its own until "biblical theology cuts loose from its moorings to dogmatic theology to become an enterprise seeking its own methods and categories" (*Sharing,* ix), and Friedman documents how the "early stages of research on the Bible" have "less material evidence to go on," a fact which inevitably makes "our forerunners' arguments more theoretical" ("Essay," 3). MacKinnon denounces Weber's methods and conclusions ("Calvinism"; "Explanation"), but Zaret defends them ("Use," 246–49). Like Weber, Mauss also ignores the ancient Near Eastern literature, focusing instead on the literature of the Romans, Indians, and Germans (*Gift,* 46–62).

149. Ginzberg puts the matter clearly as early as 1932: "It is desirable, of course, to utilize the best that critical anthropology and economic history has to offer, but real progress is only to be made through an intensive study of the texts" ("Economics," 344–45).

150. In addition to the "great texts" examined below see Moran, *Amarna*; Pettinato, *Ebla*; Dietrich, *Cuneiform*; Wise, *Scrolls*. Recent studies of Syro-Palestinian economics include Bell, *Evolution*; Feldman, *Diplomacy*; Monroe, *Scales*; Schloen, *House*; McGeough, *Exchange.*

151. Interpreters are slowly coming around to the fact that "the meaning of meaning is meaningless apart from the concept of intertextuality" (Tate, *Interpretation,* xv). As early as the 1970s Moran challenges his colleagues in Assyriology to practice "more comprehensive critical strategies of … contemporary literary criticism" (Review of *Altorientalischen,* 189–90).

or (c) the corollary revolution in historiography,[152] particularly Israelite historiography.[153]

Thus guided by the foregoing definitions, presumptions, methods, and delimitations, chapter 2 attempts to isolate and identify the predominant socioeconomic conflict motifs animating a representative sample of three "great texts" from Abraham's world—the *Epic of Gilgamesh*, the *Epic of Atrahasis*, and the *Epic of Erra*. Chapter 3 then examines several primeval stories in the *torah/pentateuch* in order to discover how much the socioeconomic conflict motifs identified in chapter 2 resonate with those animating the "Old Testament of the Old Testament."[154] Chapter 4 builds on this by analyzing a representative sample of Hebraic texts from the Second Temple period in order to trace the development of this socioeconomic trajectory into the Hellenistic period,[155] after which chapter 5 tries to show how this trajectory contributes to the development of several "stewardship parables" preserved within the sect of the Nazarenes. Chapter 6 then concludes the book with a few "so what?" questions, all in the hope of applying the wisdom of the ancients to the questions of the soccer mom sitting patiently outside my office.[156]

152. Momigliano argues that the "principles of historical research need not be different from the criteria of common sense," particularly in light of "the serious problems we all have to face because of the current devaluation of the notion of evidence and of the corresponding over-appreciation of rhetoric and ideology" (*Essays*, 3).

153. Kofoed, *Text*; van Seters, *Search*; Halpern, *Historians*; Long, *Israel*; Grabbe, *Moses*.

154. Moberly (*Testament*) argues that the material in *Genesis* is so primeval the relationship it sustains to the rest of the Hebrew Bible resembles that between the Old and New Testaments.

155. According to Neusner, the Jews do not have "a single history, unitary, continuous, internally cogent, and they have not formed a single economy," nor does Judaism possess a "single, unitary, linear, and harmonious economic history" (*Mishnah*, xii–xiii).

156. Holman insists that "poverty and wealth are never purely academic. Human need and affluence have been treated as moral issues across most cultures throughout history" (*Wealth*, 9).

2

Socioeconomic Conflict Motifs
in Ancient Near Eastern Epics

A NCIENT NEAR EASTERN SCRIBES are justifiably famous for creating the world's oldest literature.[1] So much information appears on their billboards,[2] stamp-seals,[3] laws,[4] correspondence,[5] and other *administrative* texts, it is difficult to catalogue it all,[6] much less interpret it to a postmodern audience.[7] So much *incantational* literature has come to light, moreover, it is impossible to imagine any other "system of Western or Near Eastern magic so highly developed."[8] However, investigators seeking to understand the socioeconomic DNA of this culture are far more

---

1. Dandamaev exhaustively describes Mesopotamian scribal practice (*Vavilonskie*); Schams exhaustively describes Jewish scribal practice (*Scribes*). For translations of the major primary texts, see Cogan, *Raging*; Dalley, *Myths*; Donner and Röllig, *Kanaanische*; Parker, *Ugaritic*; Matthews and Benjamin, *Parallels*; Foster, *Muses*; Dietrich, *Cuneiform*; Gibson, *Syrian*; Pritchard, *Texts* (this list is not exhaustive).

2. Pertinent examples include the Merneptah stele (1213–1203 BCE), the Black Obelisk of Shalmeneser III (858–824 BCE), the Behistun Inscription of Darius III (see Polaski, "Stones," 37–48); the plaster texts from Deir Alla (Hackett, *Balaam*; Moore, *Balaam*).

3. Keel, *Stempelsiegel*; Omura, "Stamp"; Michèle-Daviau, *Jawa*, 84–89.

4. Wilcke, *Law*; Sallaberger, "Prolog."

5. Parpola, *Letters*; Heimpel, *Letters*; Roberts, "Mari."

6. Wilcke, *Law*. Galil analyzes the socioeconomic lives of 447 families, focusing on legal transactions, administrative records, court decisions, and letters (*Families*, 19–46).

7. Major attempts, however, include van de Mieroop, *History*; Bottéro, *Mesopotamia*; Snell, *Life*; Kuhrt, *Ancient*; von Soden, *Orient*; Nemet-Nejat, *Mesopotamia*; Oppenheim, *Mesopotamia*.

8. Geller, "Freud," 1. Major introductions to the incantation literature include Abusch, *Witchcraft*; Cryer, *Divination*; Nunn, *Egyptian*; Kammenhuber, *Orakelpraxis*.

likely to find what they seek in the "great texts,"[9] particularly the mytho-poeic epics.[10] Pursuant to this analysis the following pages presume:

- that the authors of these myths "imagine their gods in their own image";[11]

- that the divine society portrayed in these myths "is nothing else than the human world";[12]

- that myth reflects "economic processes in human society . . . trans-ferred to the realm of divine beings";[13]

- that pantheons often "change in response to different economic systems and new socioeconomic realities";[14]

- that myth "explores important social issues"[15] and "engages vital issues of human concern";[16]

- that the structure of a given myth reflects the structure of the so-ciety responsible for producing it;[17]

- that myth is the most likely place to find "statements critical of kings [and] royal policies";[18]

9. Attempts to define the "great literature" appear in Reiner, "Akkadische," 151–210, and Groneberg, "Definition," 59–84. Hudson uses the DNA metaphor ("Reconstructing," 7), and Yoffee, while appreciative of the newer economic research based more or less exclusively on administrative texts, warns that "culture history cannot afford to exclude the indigenous interpretations of events and behavior that are provided in myths and epics" ("Economy," 283).

10. Mesopotamian scribes often describe their "great texts" as *iškaru* ("series"; see Lambert, Review of *Evolution*, 116). George significantly updates Lambert's taxonomi-cal reflections ("Genre," 46–51).

11. *BWL* 7.

12. Komoróczy, "Work," 37. Handy observes that the Canaanite pantheon mir-rors a tiered bureaucracy quite typical in ancient Near Eastern monarchies (*Heaven*, 169–79).

13. Lemche, "Sovereign," 109. Kirk points out that all myths have the same basic ele-ments: "gods, heroes, relations of men and gods, relation of mortality and immortality, origin of evils, family stresses, fertility, and eschatology" (*Myth*, 205).

14. Frymer-Kensky, *Goddesses,* 11. Wilcke recognizes the "analogy between the or-ganization of human society and the pantheon" (*Law*, 30).

15. Clifford, *Creation*, vii.

16. Bottéro, "Akkadian," 2301.

17. Lévi-Strauss, *Anthropology,* 17. Walls conditions this by observing that myth "may work to reinforce, invert or subvert social practices" (*Desire*, 5–6).

18. Launderville, *Piety,* 40.

- that "the social functions of ancient myths" are identifiable from clues embedded in "the literary and symbolic complexity of ancient mythological literature";[19]

- that myth "provides a template or blueprint for the organization of social and psychological processes much as genetic systems provide blueprints for the organization of organic processes";[20]

- that economic values are reflected less by "lists of prices at different markets" than by the socioeconomic conflict motifs embedded in "the great masterpieces of literature";[21]

- that the "great literature" of the ancient Near East demonstrates a remarkable "inter-connectedness of themes, motifs and expressions";[22]

- that "great literature" is distinguished by "its mimetic reflection of social conditions and its regenerative force in constituting reality";[23]

- that Mediterranean myth is the product of "a long and complicated process" involving the transmission of material originating in the ancient Near East;[24]

- that myth "is one of the chief mediums by which writers do their theologizing";[25]

- that "monotheism and myth are neither mutually exclusive nor incompatible."[26]

Thorkild Jacobsen's observation still holds true: "Sumerians and Akkadians picture their gods as human in form, governed by human emotions, and living in the same type of world . . . In almost every par-

19. Walls, *Desire*, 6.
20. Geertz, *Interpretation*, 216.
21. Buchan, *Frozen*, 84.
22. Bodi, *Ezekiel*, 19.
23. Iser, "Staging," 887.
24. Moran, "Ovid," 122.
25. Batto, *Slaying*, 1; see George, *Babylonian*, 28–33. This assertion is as true for George Lucas' *Star Wars* as it is for Sîn-lēqi-unninni's *Gilgamesh*.
26. Fishbane, *Myth*, 16.

ticular the world of the gods is . . . a projection of terrestrial conditions."[27] So do his presuppositions:

> The theocratic mode of experience sees through to the ground of events, to the forces that ultimately cause and shape them . . . Decisive events, or stages of events, are therefore most naturally recorded as experienced theocratically [and] at this point the historian faces a dilemma . . . Do we try to convey things the way they appear to the ancients, or do we rely only on sources in the secular mode or translatable into it . . . ? Irrespective of *what* the Sumerians believed, the fact *that* they so believed makes it proper historical material commanding the historian's full attention.[28]

THE EPIC OF GILGAMESH

Among the most famous myths preserved by ancient Near Eastern scribes the *Epic of Gilgamesh* stands as "one of the greatest literary compositions ever written in cuneiform Akkadian."[29] Sometimes dubbed "the Babylonian *Odyssey*,"[30] this "great text" melds the "tragedy of the *Iliad* with the wanderings and marvels of the *Odyssey*."[31] A "masterpiece of world literature,"[32] *Gilgamesh* combines a "subtlety of style" with a "grandeur of vision"[33] so robust, first-time readers sometimes find it a

27. Jacobsen, "Democracy," 167.

28. Jacobsen, "Historian," 148–49. On the other side of the mythopoeic coin Harris warns readers that "epics and myths may incorporate ideals and stereotypes far different from the realities of human life" and "must therefore be checked against other sources" ("Conflict," 622).

29. Dalley, *Myths*, 39. Postgate calls *Gilgamesh* "the jewel in the crown of Mesopotamian literature" (Review of *L'Épopée*, 575).

30. Heidel, *Gilgamesh*, 1; see Jacobsen, *Treasures*, 195–96.

31. Abusch, "Development," 614.

32. George, *Babylonian*, 13. Contemporary interpreters compare *Gilgamesh* to the Hebrew books of *Ecclesiastes* (Savignac, "Sagesse," 318–23; Shields, "Seek," 129–46) and *Daniel* (Parpola, "Esoteric," 318–27). Van der Toorn frowns on such attempts ("Ecclesiastes," 22–30), but Damrosch emphasizes *Gilgamesh's* ability to "interweave a whole series of themes in a synoptic exploration of the limits and meaning of culture" (*Narrative*, 88).

33. Jager, "Birth," 132. Some translations are more literal and others are more dynamic, the former exemplified by Speiser (*ANET* 72–99), the latter by Maul (*Gilgamesch*).

bit "overwhelming."[34] Although several versions are known to exist,[35] the longest and most complete comes from a scribe named Sîn-lēqi-unnini,[36] who structures his poem as a literary chiasm[37] written in Standard Babylonian (SB):

- Gilgamesh abuses his subjects[38]
  - The gods create Gilgamesh's "double"
    - Gilgamesh invades the Cedar Forest to plunder its treasure and slaughter its Guardian (Humbaba)
    - Ishtar "invades" Gilgamesh to plunder his "fruit/treasure" and slaughter him with her Cosmic Weapon (the Bull of Heaven)
  - The gods un-create Gilgamesh's "double"
- Gilgamesh abuses himself.[39]

34. Rilke uses the German word *ungeheuer* to describe his reaction to *Gilgamesh* in a letter written on December 11, 1916 (cited in Moran, "Rilke," 208–9). Non-specialists are just as attracted to *Gilgamesh* as specialists (Mitchell, *Gilgamesh*, 2). In fact, one doctoral dissertation chronicles *Gilgamesh's* impact on the English-speaking world over a period of 150 years (Nilson, "Gilgamesh," 2). Nilson also sees "chiastic movement" in the poem.

35. Dalley translates the OB and SB versions into twenty-first-century English (*Myths*, 39–153). Foster et al. (*Gilgamesh*) translate the Babylonian and Hittite versions as well as the Sumerian legends. Tigay analyzes most of these versions in his groundbreaking diachronic study (*Evolution*). The standard critical edition is *The Babylonian Gilgamesh Epic* by Andrew George. The present study works mostly with the SB version of tablets 1–11, tablet 12 being an appendix added only after tablets 1–11 "freeze" into their "canonical form" (Abusch, "Development," 620).

36. An Assyrian curriculum list names Sîn-lēqi-uninni as the *āšipu*-priest responsible for the Gilgamesh "series" (*iškaru*). See Lambert, "Catalogue," 59–77.

37. Chiasms are literary devices used by ancient writers to arrange a text's main ideas into concentric circles in order to spotlight a "key idea" at the center (Cross, "Prose," 3). Abusch sees a chiasm in the way the fruits and animals are laid out on *GE* 6 ("Ishtar," 175–76), and Moran recognizes several chiasms in *Atrahasis* ("Creation," 48–49). Breck lays out four of the basic elements found in most chiasms: (a) framing by inclusion, (b) pivoting at the center, (c) progressive heightening of parallel elements, and (d) dynamic spiraling from the periphery to the center (*Chiasmus*). Each of these occurs in SB *Gilgamesh*.

38. George thinks the name "Gilgamesh" means "father/hero" (*Babylonian*, 71–90).

39. This is hardly the first attempt to define the literary structure of this "great text" (see Foster, *Gilgamesh*, xi; Abusch, "Development," 614–22).

Like all "great literature," this chiastic poem preserves much more than mere literary accomplishment.[40] This poem is rather a "cultural text" designed to critique a "big problem" threatening the welfare of the riverine economy of Babylonia.[41]

Gilgamesh Abuses His Subjects

Following several preliminaries, the plotline begins when a "hunter/ trapper"[42] (named Shangashu in the Hittite version)[43] complains to Gilgamesh, king of Uruk,[44] that a "wild man" has invaded his territory and disrupted his business.[45] Endowed with superhuman strength (lit., like a "shooting star of Anu")[46] this "wild man" "constantly roams the hill country. Constantly he eats vegetation alongside the cattle. Constantly he puts his feet in the watering hole . . ."[47] He keeps filling in the pits I dig. He keeps pulling out the traps I set. He releases from my grasp the herds, the beasts of the field. He prevents me from 'engaging in fieldcraft.'"[48] Like other "wild men," this undisciplined creature (whom the gods call "Enkidu")[49] not only disrupts Shangashu's business, he threatens the welfare of Babylonian "civilization."[50] Disrupting commerce in and around

---

40. Jarman sees several themes in Gilgamesh: friendship, justice, hubris, death, immortality, wisdom, love ("Light," 330), and Walls reads the poem as a commentary on "the meaning of life, the mystery of love, the fragility of desire, and the relentlessness of the grave" (*Desire*, 9–10).

41. Polanyi distinguishes minor issues from "big problems" (*Livelihood,* xli; see Harris, *Gender,* 32), and Davenport reads SB *Gilgamesh* as a subtle, yet focused example of anti-imperialist critique ("Anti-Imperialist," 1–23).

42. *GE* 1:113 (*sa-a-a-du . . . ḫa-bi-lu*).

43. Beckman, "Gilgamesh," 158.

44. Boehmer, "Uruk," 465–78.

45. Mobley compares Enkidu with other "wild men" like Samson, Elijah and John the Baptist ("Wild," 217–33; *Empty,* 19–74). Henze reflects on the process by which "Nebuchadnezzar" becomes a "wild man" in Dan 4:33 (*Madness*).

46. *GE* 1:152 (*ki-iṣ-ri ša ᵈa-nim*). Heidel's translation, "[his strength] is like [that of] the host of heaven" (*Gilgamesh*, 20), is preferable to George's "mighty as a lump of rock from the sky" (*Babylonian*, 547).

47. *GE* 1:153–55.

48. *GE* 1:157–60 (*e-pe-[eš] ṣēri* (this is Speiser's translation, *ANET* 75).

49. Sum ᵈen.ki.du probably means "lord of the field" (Akk *bēl kidu*; see Langdon, *Sumerian*, 178), but can also possibly mean "creation of Enki" (ᵈ*Enki.du*; see Parpola, *Prophecies,* xciii), or "lord of the netherworld" (see Zimmern, *Bibliothek* 6:1:571–2).

50. Westenholz and Koch-Westenholz, "Enkidu," 437–51.

"Sheepfolded Uruk,"[51] he encourages the "beasts of the field" to tear down the hegemonic walls of "human oppression."[52] Like the monster Grendel in *Beowulf*, he challenges all the boundaries so carefully erected to protect "civilized folk" from everything lurking in the dark "wilderness."[53] Alarmed by this "invasion," Gilgamesh therefore commands that a prostitute be found to "civilize" Enkidu as soon as possible.[54]

That Mesopotamia's greatest epic poem begins with a socioeconomic conflict between a "businessman" and a "wild man" is no accident. *Gilgamesh* begins with a "livelihood severely threatened"[55] because this is the kind of crisis to which every reader can relate.[56] The primary function of myth is to articulate the "universal imperative" of the culture responsible for producing it,[57] and *Gilgamesh's* "universal imperative" is deep enough to challenge a hero's mettle, yet broad enough to challenge

---

51. Van de Mieroop (*City*) and Benjamin (*Deuteronomy*) discuss the prerogatives and peculiarities of ancient cities, and Leemans examines the Babylonian business world in a pioneering study (*Merchant*).

52. Enkidu's status changes as the *Gilgamesh* legend grows and develops over time. In the Sumerian stories (*Gilgamesh and Akka*; *Gilgamesh, Enkidu, and the Netherworld*), for example, he is Gilgamesh's human servant (Foster et al., *Gilgamesh*, 99–104, 129–43). In both OB and SB *Gilgamesh*, however, he mutates into Gilgamesh's quasi-divine companion, fellow-warrior, and erstwhile rival (Blenkinsopp, *Treasures*, 93).

53. No less a critic than J. R. R. Tolkien points out this parallel ("Beowulf," 1–32). For Moorey, "civilization" results from the "emergence of complex urban societies" (*Mesopotamian*, v), and Jacobsen emphasizes the persistence of these socioeconomic distinctions in his earlier work ("Conflict").

54. Ovid sings of the power of love to civilize wild beasts (*Amatoria* 2:467–80). Kamionkowski compares the civilizing of Enkidu with the civilizing of Israel ("Savage," 176–81). Though they rarely hold "official" titles, Mesopotamian prostitutes do own land and run their own businesses (de la Fuye, *Documents*, 587).

55. Jacobsen, *Treasures*, 197.

56. Abusch ("Development," 617) sees three levels of conflict in the Akkadian *Gilgamesh* tradition: "hero-vs.-man" (OB version); "hero-vs.-king" (eleven-tablet SB version); and "hero-vs.-god" (twelve-tablet SB version).

57. Burkert, *Structure*, 16–22. Walls' attempt to read Gilgamesh through a lens ground by "queer theory" is problematic for this very reason—because it delimits itself to the preoccupation of a very small minority within a mainstream audience far removed from the world of the original text (*Desire*, 13–17), thereby making it difficult to see how "a text which depicts the relationship between Gilgamesh and Enkidu in terms that . . . are, at least to some degree, homoerotic, can also be a text in which Gilgamesh and Enkidu are represented as equals, given that an egalitarian sexual relationship is not conceivable within the cultural context in which the *Gilgamesh Epic* is generated" (Ackerman, *Heroes*, 87).

a popular audience.[58] Where *Atrahasis* portrays Babylon's management-vs.-labor conflict as a heavenly war between "divine slaves"-vs.-"divine citizens,"[59] and the *Creation Epic* (*enūma elish*) portrays the problem of overpopulation as a generational conflict between older-vs.-younger deities,[60] *Gilgamesh* focuses on the perennial socioeconomic conflict between those who are "civilized" vs. those who run "wild."

Like all good storytellers, Sîn-lēqi-unnini knows his audience. Realizing that this audience expects its heroes to be "heroic,"[61] he introduces the poem's protagonist through a series of heroic epithets—the "support of his brothers," "a goring wild bull," "a raging flood-wave," the "king superior to all other kings."[62] After this, though, he abruptly shifts their attention away from the king's noble exterior to his darkly troubled interior: "In Sheepfolded Uruk[63] he paces back and forth, A wild bull preening, his head held high[64] . . . The young men of Uruk he 'oppresses.'[65] He lets no son stay with his father. Day and night his behavior waxes 'ar-

---

58. In Kramer's words, "what gives these episodes lasting significance is their *human* quality," i.e., the fact that "they revolve about forces and problems common to human beings everywhere" ("Gilgamesh," 8).

59. Lambert and Millard, *Atra-Hasis*.

60. Talon, *Creation*; Kilmer, "Overpopulation," 160–77; Heidel, *Babylonian*; Moran, "Flood," 51–61; Bodi, *Ezekiel*, 66. As noted below, Akkadian myth often symbolizes pre- and extra-creational chaos-forces via the technical terms *rigmu* and *ḫubūru* ("noise" and "tumult," *CAD* R:328–34). Further, *Erra* 1:79 voices a concern that the land "in its entirety" (*nap-ḫar-ša*) might "overwhelm us" (*ir-bu-ú e-li-ni*).

61. Mobley, *Empty*, 19–74. Rouland ("Sociological," 90–99) defines heroism as a sociological expectation in *Beowulf*, *Gilgamesh*, and the *Odyssey*, and Schein (*Mortal*, 69–70) stresses that what makes mortal heroes "heroic" is that, unlike the gods, they risk something which can be permanently lost—their lives. The present study presumes, with Jason (*Ethnopoetry*) and Berlin ("Ethnopoetry," 18), that *Gilgamesh* is a "heroic epic."

62. *GE* 1:29–35. Sum *Gilgamesh and Akka* refers to Gilgamesh as "the grain-giver" (Kramer and Jacobsen, "Gilgamesh," 18).

63. Oft-repeated in *Gilgamesh*, this epithet might be translated "Impregnable Uruk" or "Citadel of Uruk."

64. Humanity's darker, bestial nature is not, of course, a theme unique to Gilgamesh. "From Homer on the Greeks (to cite another example) are preoccupied with the problem of defining what makes man a civilized being and what sets off the human world from the non-human world which surrounds it and sometimes bids fair to engulf it" (Segal, "Raw," 289). Lévi-Strauss explores this tension at great length (*Raw*).

65. *GE* 1:65 (*adāru*). See *CAD* A/1:102–7, and note Enlil's "oppression" (*adāru*) in *Atr* 1:355.

rogant"[66] ... Allowing no maiden to stay with [her spouse], no warrior's daughter, no young man's bride.[67] Anu often hears their complaints."[68]

Where older interpretations of this arrogance imagine it to be an "extension" of the king's "manly vigor,"[69] more recent interpreters read this paragraph as a thinly-veiled critique of "domestic service or corvée,"[70] as a sustained reflection on the theme "valor carried to excess becomes vicious,"[71] as "a warning to tyrants in the same tradition as the great Aeschylean and Shakespearean tragedies,"[72] or as aligning "the tragic tradition in literature" with "the disastrous misuse of the world's resources."[73] Many see in these lines the motif of the "restless young king";[74] i.e., just as the restless young kings Saul (1 Sam 14:24–46) and Rehoboam (1 Kgs 12:1–15) abuse *their* subjects, so this restless young

66. *GE* 1:67 (*kadāru*). N.B. the alliteration created by the word-pair *adāru* // *kadāru*.

67. Some interpret these lines as a veiled reference to *prima noctis* ("first night"), a custom in which kings and other nobles lay sexual claim to virgin brides on their wedding night (OB *GE* 2:149–63; see Davenport, "Anti-Imperialist," 3–9). Whatever the possibilities, Mesopotamian wives run households and make independent contracts as early as the third millennium (Wilcke, *Law*, 52–53).

68. *GE* 1:63–72. Should sufficient weight be given to the Sum *Gilgamesh* tradition (particularly *Gilgamesh, Enkidu, and the Netherworld*, much of which is duplicated on SB tablet 12), this passage may allude to a polo-like game called *pukku*, a game the king always wins (*GE* 1:66; 12:57–58; see Klein, "Oppression," 187–201).

69. Jacobsen, *Treasures*, 196. Others see here only unbridled sexual lust (e.g., Kilmer, "Overlooked," 128–29; Held, "Parallels," 137).

70. Klein, "Oppression," 197. Gilgamesh also oppresses his subjects in Sumerian myth (Foster et al., *Gilgamesh*, 134–35; Komoróczy, "Work," 30–32), and the suffering created by corvée ("forced") labor is documented as early as the twenty-third century BCE (Wilcke, *Law*, 21, 35).

71. Foster, "Sex," 24.

72. Vulpe, "Irony," 279. Davenport notes that "despite the obvious differences between the Sumerian sources and the Akkadian epic ... both versions present Gilgamesh as an abuser of the social norms governing Mesopotamian society" ("Anti-Imperialist," 8).

73. Meeker opposes "the assumption that nature exists for the benefit of humankind, the belief that human morality transcends natural limitations, and humanism's insistence upon the supreme importance of the individual personality" (*Comedy*, 42, 59), but George lists other options (*Babylonian*, 449).

74. Abusch finds this "restlessness" on all levels of the Akkadian tradition ("Development," 618–20).

king abuses *his* subjects.[75] Like Saul, he "troubles the land."[76] Like David (2 Sam 11:1–5), he "takes" things that should not be "taken."[77]

Creating Gilgamesh's "Double"

Royal misbehavior like this often leads to grave repercussions because when the strong trample on the weak and the weak cry out, the gods usually respond, albeit on their own timetable.[78] In the Hebrew Bible Yahweh often responds to such situations by sending prophets to challenge the violators of *his* "universal imperative."[79] Mesopotamian deities, however, are rarely so direct.[80] Rather than send a prophet to Gilgamesh, for example, they create a "double"[81] of his bestial self and throw it across

---

75. Vulpe, "Irony," 279. The seer Samuel warns his audience about the dangers associated with royal arrogance (1 Sam 8:11–13), and Abusch argues that, "Gilgamesh is unable to rule successfully because of the very energy that makes him a successful hero" ("Development," 619).

76. In 1 Sam 14:29 Jonathan says of Saul, "my father troubles the land."

77. Grillet and Lestienne (*Regnes*, 196) point out that the verb לקח ("to take") in the "law of the king" (1 Sam 8:11) first appears in the "law of the priest" (1 Sam 2:14). The poet Sîn-lēqi-unnini similarly repeats the phrase *ul ú-maš-šar* ("he will not leave alone") in order to highlight Gilgamesh's "big problem" (*GE* 1:68, 72, 76, 85, 91).

78. Vulpe believes that "the gods in *Gilgamesh* are neither wise nor just," and that "heaven is organized as is life on earth" where "the strong always manage to crush the weak" ("Irony," 279; citing Garelli, *L'Assyrologie*, 99), but Shipp denounces such cynicism (*Dead*, 11–12). The problem of "delayed" divine response is the subject of the Mesopotamian "Poem of the Righteous Sufferer" (*Ludlul bēl nēmeqi*; see Annus and Lenzi, *Ludlul*, 3–44), the Egyptian "Protests of the Eloquent Peasant" (*ANET* 407–10), and the Hebrew book of *Job* (see Sitzler, *Vorwurf*).

79. Where Hebrew prophets often state this imperative directly (through doom-oracles), they can also state it indirectly (through parables; see Moore, *Faith*, 111–38).

80. Mesopotamian prophets appear to be more covert than their Hebrew colleagues, as a general rule (Nissinen et al., *Prophets*, 13–178).

81. In *The Descent of Ishtar* Enki makes an image called "Aṣušunamir" to distract Ereshkigal's attention away from Ishtar's invasive presence (Dalley, *Myths*, 158, translates "good-looking playboy"). In the Kirta myth El creates a "double" to save Kirta (*UNP* 38–39), and Baal creates a "double" of himself to trick Mot into thinking he has died (*CML* 16). As van den Hout shows, the Anatolians gravitate to the use of royal doubles in many of their rituals (*Purity*), a practice George observes in a few Babylonian sources (*Babylonian*, 456).

his path,[82] their intention being to make him "refocus his energies"[83] by "contending" with Enkidu for the "peace of Uruk."[84]

To ask which kind of intervention is more "effective"—direct vs. indirect; Hebrew vs. Babylonian—is relatively unimportant to the present discussion.[85] Suffice it to say here that where Yahweh does what he does to bring leaders like David and Naaman to repentance,[86] Babylonian deities do what they do to restore silence to the universe;[87] i.e., to create mechanisms strong enough to absorb the "chaotic noise" and "anarchic restlessness" threatening to disturb the tranquility of the cosmos.[88] Thus the gods send Enkidu into Gilgamesh's life not to elicit repentance, but to force him, by looking into their custom-made "mirror,"[89] to ask, How can I replace the politics of "oppression" and "arrogance" with the politics of "prudence" and "wisdom?"[90]

---

82. Note the morphological pun in *GE* 1:96 ("male" [*zikaru*] // "double" [*zikru*]). George thinks the third person masculine suffix in this line refers not to Gilgamesh, but to Enki (*Babylonian*, 788).

83. Moran, "Gilgamesh," 2328; Jacobsen, *Treasures*, 196. Similar dynamics shape other "dual-hero" stories—like the Castor-Pollux story in Roman legend and the David-Jonathan story in the Hebrew Bible (Harris, *Heavenly*; Eliade, *Quest*, 127–75).

84. *GE* 1:98 reads *liš-ta-a-na-nu-ma*, "Let them contend with each other," the verb *šanānu* often denoting the king-vs.-deity rivalry (*CAD* Š/1:366–9). Magnanini thinks of Enkidu as Gilgamesh's "foil" ("Foils," 167–96), but Damrosch wonders whether the gods' decision to intervene *indirectly* indicates a "divine withdrawal from direct action," and if so, whether this might indicate a degree of literary development (*Narrative*, 97).

85. Batto, "Covenant"; Fritz, "Solange"; Greene, *Messenger*; Moore, *Reconciliation*, 94–96.

86. Moore, *Faith*, 164–71.

87. Ibid., 251–52 (*pace* Batto, "Covenant," 193). Vulpe ("Irony," 279) thinks that "Shamash is less a god who dispenses justice impartially to all than a god who seeks particular justice for his protégé, Gilgamesh."

88. Akk *rigmu . . . ḫubūru*. Pettinato identifies *rigmu* as a referent for moral depravity ("Bestrafung," 165–200), but Moran sees only "evil" connoted by this term, not "sin" ("Flood," 59; see *CAD* R:333–34).

89. Melchior-Bonnet asks, "What is the nature of that which can be learned from a mirror? It can be used in divination, metaphor, analogy, or mimicry. In the West, meditation on the mirror image originates with Plato. Before him, the reflected image was seen as a living animate form, the double that attracted Narcissus from beneath the surface of the water" ("Mirrors," 6063).

90. SB *Gilgamesh* highlights the importance of this question by re-framing the OB tradition as a *narû* stele ("public inscription," *GE* 1:10–28), thereby transforming the *Gilgamesh* tradition into "the key of wisdom" (Moran, "Document," 19). While many argue for varying definitions of "wisdom" (Annus and Lenzi, *Ludlul*, xxxiv–vi), George speaks of wisdom *modes* ("Genre," 53–54).

Several contrasts help set up this all-important question. Where Gilgamesh is "two-thirds divine and one-third human,"[91] Enkidu is the result of a "gazelle" mating with a "wild donkey."[92] Where Gilgamesh's appearance is "dazzling,"[93] Enkidu's is "savage" and "murderous."[94] Where Gilgamesh tyrannizes the citizens of Uruk,[95] Enkidu challenges anyone or anything (perceived to be) exploiting the innocence of the wilderness. The genius of this great text lies not in the way it polarizes its main characters, but in the way it manipulates this polarity to critique the Babylonian economy.[96]

Psychologically the Gilgamesh-vs.-Enkidu rivalry looks like many other rivalries in the great literature—Apollo-vs.-Dionysus,[97] Achilles-vs.-Patroclus,[98] Hesiod-vs.-Perses,[99] Cain-vs.-Abel[100]—the common denominator being the *shadow archetype*,[101] a literary device designed

91. *GE* 1:48. Gilgamesh's father is the human king Lugalbanda and his mother is the cow-goddess Ninsun (*GE* 1:35–36). In *GE* 5:86 the monster Humbaba refers to him as *lillu*, an obscure term meaning something like "fool" or "daimon" (Dalley, *Myths*, 40, 71). George pluralizes the term to capture the thrust of the Gt cohortative of *malāku* ("to advise") to remove the label of "fool" from Gilgamesh's character (*Babylonian*, 607).

92. These are the metaphorical "parents" cited in *GE* 8:3–4, but this characterization is quite different from the earlier claim that Enkidu is the product of an "idea" (*zikru*) implanted within the womb of the goddess Aruru (*GE* 1:100).

93. *GE* 1:35 (*gít-ma-lu*).

94. *GE* 1:178–9 (*lul-la-a* ᵇᵘ*etla šag-ga-šá-a*).

95. Klein, "Oppression," 190–92.

96. Davenport argues that *Gilgamesh* is designed to generate "political criticism, however covert ... in certain political circles" ("Anti-Imperialist," 18).

97. Reacting to the simplistic polarities championed by older anthropologists (e.g., Benedict, *Patterns*), Detienne reads the Apollo-Dionysus polarity as an "ensemble of manipulations and ... approaches" designed to help readers understand the "complex texture" of the culture responsible for producing it ("Delphi," 158).

98. MacCary, *Achilles*.

99. Beye, "Hesiod," 37–39.

100. See below.

101. Philo epitomizes "archetype" as the *imago dei* residing in and molding persons into the likeness of the deity (*Opif.* 1:69), while Irenaeus accuses gnostic Christians of abusing the term in order to create a fantasy world of their own making—the πλήρωμα (*Haer.* 2:7). Eliade refers to it as the condensed sacred reality at the beginning of creation which later evolves institutionally through myth and ritual (*Myth*, 1–47). Jung (*Memories*, 26–98) imagines it to be a reservoir of "mystagogical" memories (see Morris, *Anthropological*, 174) buried within humankind's "collective unconscious" (see von Franz, *Projection*; Meyer, "Utilizing," 521).

to help conflicted readers, like conflicted heroes, learn how to face their fears.[102] Only myth has the power to do this because only myth has the power to project the darkest human conflicts into the Unseen World, where they can be handled more "safely."[103] Thus ancient Near Eastern poets of all stripes gravitate to the *shadow archetype* in order to help vulnerable "little brothers" learn how to survive the aggressions of angry "older brothers."[104]

By "matching up" these characters this way Sîn-lēqi-unnini not only forces this hero to engage his "other self," he invites readers to do the same.[105] Thus, when Gilgamesh succeeds in taming his bestial self, this encourages readers and hearers to hope that the "wisdom" available to him might also be available to them.[106] Homer exploits this archetypal conflict in the *Iliad*[107] and Virgil reproduces it in the *Aeneid*.[108] Anglo-Saxon poets revive it in *Beowulf*[109] and Shakespeare uses it to create fascinatingly complex characters to which contemporary audiences *still* relate.[110] The Hebrew Bible uses *its* sibling rivalry stories, however, in

102. Lévi-Strauss, *Totemism*, 77–102; Lemche, "Sovereign," 109; Launderville, *Piety*, 40; Komoróczy, "Work," 37.

103. From Ricoeur's viewpoint, only myth has the power to "relate our own time to this other time, whether this be in the form of participation, imitation, decadence, or abandonment" ("Myth," 6372).

104. Shulman, "Cain"; Barré, "Wandering," 179–80. Nilson ("Gilgamesh," 92–297) reads *Gilgamesh* through a lens comprised of an amalgam of Freudian, Jungian, and post-Jungian thought, relying heavily on the work of Klein (*Psycho-Analysis*).

105. In *GE* 7:95 Enkidu complains of the "mismatch" (*la ú-šam-ṣa-an-nu*) between himself and Gilgamesh. Von Hendy makes application to contemporary mismatches (*Modern*, 112–33).

106. Van Nortwick sees this dynamic in the literature about three mythical heroes— Gilgamesh, Achilles, and Aeneas (*Somewhere*, 4–6), and Lasine traces it to several Hebrew heroes (*Knowing*, 128–41).

107. Achilles addresses Patroclus like a parent addresses a frightened child (Homer, *Il.*16:7–11), leading MacCary to suggest that what Achilles really sees in Patroclus is a "diminished, effeminized . . . image of himself" (*Achilles*, 150).

108. Weber sees Vergil's description of Apollo (*Aen.* 4:139–49) as "exhibiting more than a trace of the foppishness that is a hallmark of Dionysus" ("Dionysus," 332).

109. Halverson sees this dynamic quite clearly: "In the first part of *Beowulf*, Heorot is the center of the world. Almost all movement is focused on it. Grendel seeks it out for destructive purposes; Beowulf comes to cleanse it" ("Beowulf," 593).

110. Belsey, for example, sees in *Hamlet* a "sibling rivalry" between the despairing ghost (Hamlet Sr.) and the vengeance-driven son (Hamlet Jr.), going so far as to designate it the primary action-generator of the story (*Shakespeare*, 173).

two ways: (a) to preserve a memory of the oldest socioeconomic tensions in Hebrew history,[111] and (b) to build upon this history a Yahwistic theology of election (Abel over Cain, Abraham over Pharaoh, Isaac over Ishmael, Jacob over Esau, Joseph over Reuben, etc.).[112]

Not all rivalry-stories serve the same function, of course. Some focus on concerns more religious than psychological; others on concerns more economic than political.[113] One Middle Assyrian version of the *Creation Myth*, for example, juxtaposes the "king-as-thinking-man" against the "king-as-primal-man" in order to help Assyrian audiences gauge the depth of the Grand Canyon segregating "wisdom" from "wildness" in *their* economy.[114] Just as the Canaanite deity El creates a daemon named Shatiqat to rescue Kirta, so the Babylonian deity Aruru creates a daemon named Enkidu to rescue Gilgamesh.[115] Just as Enki creates a double of Ishtar to help heaven's most restless goddess negotiate *her* journey,[116] so Enki creates a double of Gilgamesh to help Uruk's most restless king negotiate *his* journey.[117] Just as Gilgamesh's decision to neutralize Enkidu helps prepare him for his showdown with Ishtar, so David's decision to neutralize the aggressor in Nathan's parable forces him to deal with the conflict in *his* life.[118] Whatever the applications, the

111. For Gottwald the patriarchal traditions serve "as a kind of socioreligious 'check' or 'damper' on Israelite thought about the authority and power of states" (*Politics,* 172).

112. Recognizing that many readers view "the slaughter of the Canaanites prescribed in the conquest tradition" as "the culmination of the notion of election," Kaminsky argues that the Hebrew concept of *election* presupposes not two (*elect* and *anti-elect*) but three groups (*elect, anti-elect,* and *non-elect*). The anti-elect are enemies of the elect and must be annihilated, but the non-elect are benign, and Israel is obligated to find a way to engage them (*Jacob,* 108–9; see Goldingay, *Theology* 2:192–94, 199–203).

113. Kaminsky, *Jacob,* 15–78.

114. N.B. the *maliku//lullû* parallel (Mayer, "Mythos," 55–68).

115. *CAT* 1.16:5:39–6:14 (see Knoppers, "Dissonance," 580).

116. Foster, *Muses,* 96–106. The name given to Ishtar's double is "Ṣaltu" (Akk "discord"; see Groneberg, *Lob,* 55–93; Foster, "Ea," 79–84).

117. This dynamic resonates well into the Hellenistic period (Marglin, "Hierodouleia," 3968) as well as Second Temple Jewish texts (Arbel, *Secrets,* 71).

118. See 2 Sam 12:1–7; 14:4–21. As Eissfeldt points out (*Maschal,* 45–71), parables operate on the principle of *analogy,* so that when the hearer attempts to resolve the conflict within the parable, the action taken to resolve the imaginary situation often suggests a solution for the real situation (see Pyper, "Enticement," 153–66).

shadow archetype helps explain "the coexistence of the mutually exclusive" in several ancient texts.[119]

Psychologically *Gilgamesh* preserves a complex match-up between
two rivals, a text carefully designed to help conflicted readers learn how
to "meet *their* match."[120] Socioeconomically, however, this match-up
symbolizes the "wilderness"-vs.-"civilization" conflict threatening to
crack open the Babylonian economy into isolated fragments.[121] Where
"Enkidu dominates the wilderness, Gilgamesh dominates the city."[122]
Where Gilgamesh symbolizes the "exponent of civilization," Enkidu
symbolizes the quintessential "child of nature."[123] Where Enkidu symbolizes every foreign invader who ever tries to penetrate the walls of
Sheepfolded Uruk, Gilgamesh symbolizes every "civilized" defender who
tries to keep them out,[124] and Enkidu's transformation from "wild man"
to "radically civilized persona"[125] doubtless connotes the "confluence in
urban life" generated by the perennial cycle of "conquest and civilization" characterizing the earliest stages of Babylonian history.[126]

119. Iser, "Staging," 878.

120. See discussion below on *GE* 7:95–96 (Enkidu's curses). As Vulpe sees it ("Irony,"
280), this hero has to be "matched up" with a counterpart before he "can become conscious of his humanity"; i.e., "recognize his impotence before the ultimate destiny of all
men—death." Near the end of the poem Gilgamesh reverts back to an Enkidu-like role
as a "roamer (*rapādu*) of the wilderness (*sēru*)." This phrase, repeated some ten times on
tablet 10, mechanically reprises the prostitute's words in *GE* 1:208.

121. Hendel makes this observation in his dissertation (*Patriarch*, 116–21), and contemporary reflection on this polarity occurs in Turner, *Geography*; Dürr, *Dreamtime*;
Kowalewski, *Power*.

122. Gardner et al., *Gilgamesh*, 69. Hendel puts it like this: "Gilgamesh is . . . a man of
culture while Enkidu is a man of nature" (*Patriarch*, 118).

123. Ungnad and Gressman, *Gilgamesh*, 93. Turner argues that what drives this socioeconomic polarity is the "desire" among "all men . . . to control the natural world," and
that the myths of the ancient Near East represent humanity's first attempt "to enact the
dream of mastering the natural world" (*Geography*, 20–21).

124. Douglas argues that "the priestly doctrine of purity was designed as an antidote
to popular theories of defilement aimed against immigrant labourers or foreigners"
(*Wilderness*, 26), and van der Toorn argues that the literature preserving "Mesopotamia's
history" resonates with the mythological literature because both preserve "a strong current of contempt for the nomads living on the fringes of the cities" (*Sanction*, 3). Stein
attempts to document this archaeologically (*Rethinking*).

125. Barron, "Separation," 383.

126. Tilly ("Gilgamesh," 391) reads *Gilgamesh* as a literary reflection on the history of urbanism, and Sallaberger distinguishes between the *city* as the center of
Mesopotamian culture vs. the *steppe* as a place of danger (*Gilgamesch*, 23–30).

Not all epic literature operates the same way, of course.[127] Each charts its own course and follows its own style. The Egyptians, for example, portray their socioeconomic history as a cold war between Horus, the "god of the arable land," vs. his "wild man" brother Seth.[128] The Hittites imagine their history as an ongoing battle between the storm-god Telepinu and his dragon-nemesis Illuyanka,[129] while the Canaanites portray theirs as a toxic rivalry between the storm-god Baal ("husband/protector") and two of his siblings, Yam ("Sea/Chaos") and Mot ("Death/Wilderness").[130] The *Erra Epic* boils these tensions down to a single pregnant question: "Warrior Erra! Why do you neglect the field for the city?"[131]

Gilgamesh distinguishes itself from these other "great texts" by the way it uses secondary polarities to sharpen and extend its primary polarity. Alongside the primary polarity between Gilgamesh and Enkidu, for example, a prostitute named Shamhat (doubtless a devotee of Ishtar)[132] involves herself with Enkidu, while a goddess named Ninsun (the queen mother) goes out of her way to protect her son, Gilgamesh.[133] Each lady tries to domesticate the male warrior "in her charge," so to speak,[134] and Shamhat accomplishes this by (a) engaging Enkidu in sexual intercourse, (b) leading him to the threshold of "human reason,"[135] and (c) challenging

127. While appreciative of the work of Gelb ("Alleged," 137–54) and Diakonoff ("Despotic," 173–203), Yoffee refuses to ignore the profound way in which racial/ethnic conflict affects this literature, particularly during the interregnum periods between the great empires of Sargon, Shulgi, and Hammurabi ("Political," 300).

128. In one of the pyramid texts, for example, "Horus orders action for his father (Osiris), the master of the tempest (by) neutralizing the spittle of Seth" (Sethe, *Pyramidtexte*, 261; see Allen, *Pyramid*, 19, 42, 110; te Velde, *Seth*, 39, 148–49; Hendel, *Patriarch*, 122–25; Hollis, *Brothers*).

129. Hoffner, *Myths*, 11–14; Beckman, "Religion," 104–5; Goetze, *Kulturgeschichte*, 139–40.

130. Mot is Baal's enemy in *CAT* 1.4–6; Yam is Baal's enemy in *CAT* 1.2–3 (see Smith, *Baal*, 9–17; Clifford, *Creation*, 117–33; Otto, *Krieg*, 13–75; Kloos, *Combat*, 213–14).

131. *Erra* 1:76.

132. Harris, "Images," 219–30.

133. Foster, "Sex," 25.

134. Eldredge argues that "adventure, with all its requisite danger and wildness, is a deeply spiritual longing" for most men (*Wild*, 5).

135. *GE* 1:202 (*tēmu*). This term denotes the main distinction between "humans" and "clay" in *Atr* 1:223–28: "We-ila, who had the capacity to 'think' (*tēmu*) they slaughtered in their assembly . . . From the flesh of the god there was a 'spirit' (*etēmmu*)." N.B. the morphological word-play on *tēmu* // *etēmmu*.

him to submit to human (royal) authority.[136] Ninsun's efforts, however, are not nearly so successful. Instead, she worries (a) that Gilgamesh may indeed be responsible for "stirring up" the menfolk of Uruk,[137] (b) that his judge-advocate (the sun-god Šamaš) will abandon his case,[138] and (c) that his desire to "slay evil,"[139] though well-intentioned, camouflages another desire buried deep in his heart—the desire to invade the Cedar Forest and steal its treasures.

   She has good reason to worry. Having welcomed Enkidu into the family as an "equal,"[140] her heart recoils when she learns that Gilgamesh has, in fact, decided to invade the sacred Cedar Forest.[141] Rather than speculate on his motives, though,[142] she begs Šamaš to redeem him.[143] This does nothing to change Gilgamesh's plans, of course—the lure of

136. "Come, I will lead you to Sheepfolded Uruk ... where Gilgamesh is perfect in strength, ruling over (gašāru) the menfolk (eṭlūti) like a wild bull" (GE 1:209–12)

137. GE 1:67 (ú-ta-ad-da-ri).

138. Imagining Šamaš to be the source of her son's "restlessness," Ninsun asks, "Why have you assigned him a restless spirit?" (GE 3:46, lib-bi la ṣa-li-la te-mid-su; lit., a "heart which does not sleep"). Arneth emphasizes the power of Šamaš to heal as well as judge (Sonne, 2).

139. GE 3:54 (mim-ma lem-nu). Dating this motif is difficult (but see Schaffer, "Cedar," 307–13).

140. GE 1:258, 266, 285, 290 (maḫāru). After Gilgamesh introduces Enkidu to Ninsun, she "summons Enkidu and says, 'O Mighty Enkidu, you are not the offspring of my womb, but now your brood will be with the oblates of Gilgamesh ... The priestesses will take in the foundling and the divine daughters will bring up the foster-child. I hereby adopt Enkidu, whom I shall love as a son'" (GE 3:120–7). Note the close connection between the literary characters and the cults over which they preside, not just here, but throughout the poem (esp. Ishtar vis-à-vis the Ishtar cult [tablet 6]).

141. Harrison finds it perplexing "that human beings never cease reenacting the gesture of Gilgamesh" (Forests, 17–18), but Shipp sees in Gilgamesh someone who "claims for himself the right and prerogatives of godhood" when, "in supreme arrogance and presumption, he enters the forest, cuts down its trees, and slays its guardian" (Dead, 114).

142. Reflecting on Ninsun's hysterical suggestion that Šamaš is responsible for "assigning" (šakānu), "inflicting" (mâdu), and "touching" (lapātu) Gilgamesh with the idea of "invasion" (GE 3:46–47), Dalley suggests that what drives Gilgamesh is rather a hunger for fame (Myths, 46); i.e., that he feels driven to do something "spectacularly heroic" before the end of his "numbered days" (GE 2:234). George suggests, however, on the basis of more recently discovered evidence, that Gilgamesh invades the Cedar Forest "to distract Enkidu from the misery" of learning about his true origins (Babylonian, 456).

143. In ancient Near Eastern cosmologies the sun-deity usually plays the role of "defense attorney" vs. this or that "prosecutor" on the divine council (Steele, "Mesopotamian," 583–88).

"sacred nature" is simply too strong for him to resist—but it does leave readers wondering whether Gilgamesh either (a) arrogantly dismisses or (b) wisely ignores his mother's prayers, companion's pleas, and Uruk's elders' warnings.[144]

Gilgamesh Invades the Cedar Forest to Plunder its Treasure and Slaughter Its Guardian (Humbaba)

Just as the Hebrews imagine a "dome" separating the heavens from the earth,[145] the Babylonians imagine a "fence" protecting the Cedar Forest from "defilement."[146] The deity responsible for maintaining this boundary is Enlil,[147] lord of the netherworld and "counselor to the gods."[148] For some unstated reason, though, he delegates this job to a vizier-assistant named Humbaba,[149] a monster-guardian whose role eerily echoes that of another monster-guardian, the gorgon Medusa in Greek myth.[150] At first glance, his job looks easy: keep the forest "safe."[151] As subsequent events unfold, however, he fails to do his job for several reasons: (a) Gilgamesh is too shrewd for him;[152] (b) Enlil underestimates the hero's determina-

144. Eliade discusses these options more thoroughly (*Sacred*, 152–53).

145. Gen 1:6 (רקיע); Seely, "Firmament," 227–40.

146. *GE* 3:55 (*itû*). Just as a "guardian" protects the Garden of Eden (Gen 3:24) so a "guardian" protects the Cedar Forest (*GE* 3:52–62). Shipp sees in the Cedar Forest not "normal woodland," but a "dwelling place of gods" (*Dead*, 113), though George suggests a geographical location in Lebanon or Amanus (*Babylonian*, 456). Literarily, Tolkien reprises the "sacred forest" mytheme in Fanghorn Forest, the dwelling place of Treebeard (*Towers*, 59), and the "Lebanon Forest" next to the Jerusalem temple might be cited as another parallel (1 Kgs 7:2; 10:17, 21).

147. Some question Enlil's Sumerian origins (Michalowski, "Unbearable," 237–47; Steinkeller, "Rulers," 103–37), but as Sigrist points out, Enlil's temple in Nippur is famous for housing one of the earliest known scribal schools ("Nippur," 363–74).

148. Enlil receives his office by lot (*Atr* 1:7–18), but eventually loses it to a younger deity, Marduk (Sommerfeld, *Aufstieg*).

149. Vizier-assistants appear in Mesopotamia as early as the Ur III period (Wilcke, *Law*, 18–19; Wiggermann, "Synonym," 225–40).

150. See *GE* 2:221–29 and Apollodorus, *The Gods* 2:4. Napier portrays Humbaba as a "deity lacking omniscience" (*Masks*, 223), a characteristic confirmed by Jason's observation that while Gilgamesh can travel in and out of the Cedar Forest, Humbaba cannot (*Ethnopoetry*, 198). Hopkins believes the character of Medusa to be based on the Mesopotamian monster Humbaba ("Assyrian," 346).

151. Akk *šulmu*. The SB poem repeats this word four times, twice by Enkidu (*GE* 2:218, 227), and twice by Ninsun (*GE* 2:284, 298).

152. Schaffer emphasizes Gilgamesh's ability to outwit Huwawa in the Sumerian tradition ("Cedar," 308–9).

tion; (c) Gilgamesh and Enkidu have already achieved demigod status;[153] and (d) everyone underestimates Ninsun's desire to protect her son.[154]

To avoid oversimplifying the dynamics of this encounter it is important to recognize that Gilgamesh's conflict with Humbaba has as much to do with hubris as it does heroism.[155] Sîn-lēqi-unnini highlights this ambivalent posture by (a) moving the Gilgamesh-Humbaba conflict to the poem's chiastic center, (b) portraying Humbaba's death as the assassination of Enlil's vizier,[156] (c) highlighting the passive-aggressive nature of the divine response generally, and (d) paralleling the Gilgamesh-Humbaba encounter with the Gilgamesh-Ishtar encounter. Like other heroes, Gilgamesh destroys a formidable opponent at a climactic point in an epic poem. The gods' reaction to it, however, is quite different from, say, their reaction to Marduk's slaughter of the dragon Tiamat.[157] Where the *Creation Epic* portrays the gods celebrating Tiamat's death, *Gilgamesh* shows them grumbling at Humbaba's.[158] Where the *Creation Epic* shows the gods rewarding Marduk for creating order out of chaos, *Gilgamesh* shows them punishing Gilgamesh for "violating the sacred."[159] Similarly, where the Hebrew Bible shows God punishing Eve for "invad-

153. SB *Gilgamesh* habitually prefixes the *dingir*-sign to the names of Gilgamesh and Enkidu, thereby identifying them as deities of some kind. In one Hittite fragment Gilgamesh is a seventeen-foot giant and Enkidu is Ninurta, god of war (Heidel, *Gilgamesh*, 17).

154. While Ninsun fails to dissuade Gilgamesh from entering the Cedar Forest, she does not fail to persuade Šamaš from pleading his case (*GE* 3:43–119; 5:137–41).

155. In *GE* 3:2 the elders of Uruk warn Gilgamesh not to invade the Forest by relying on his own *gimru*, a term usually translated "strength," but which in some contexts can mean "financial resources" (see *CAD* G:77–8).

156. Mullen argues that Enlil does little to help Humbaba because "the power of decree or of life ... belongs only to the high god" (*Council*, 284, 279), but George and al-Rawi reject this explanation ("Sippar," 172).

157. In both *Gilgamesh* (*GE* 5:137–41) and the *Creation Epic* (*Ee* 4:41–48) dragon-slayers harness the wind to protect the cosmos (Foster, *Muses*, 459–68; Dalley, *Myths*, 252–55), a process paralleled in Gen 1:2 when creation begins with darkness "covering the face of תהום" ("the deep") before being dispelled by "the רוח אלהים" ("mighty wind"/"spirit of God"). Most interpreters agree with Frymer-Kensky and Pettinato ("Enuma Elish," 2811) that תהום is "the Hebrew cognate of Tiamat" and that the process in Gen 1:2 "bears some similarity to the winds of Anu that roil Tiamat."

158. Gilgamesh and Enkidu kill Humbaba in order "to annihilate the Evil Thing from the land" (*GE* 3:54, *mimma lemnu ša tazeru úḫallaq ina māti*). "Evil Thing" (*mimma lemnu*) is Akk shorthand for "demonic activity" (*CAD* L:121).

159. That is, for destroying the "spirit of the Forest" (Jarman, "Gilgamesh," 331); see Greenspahn, "Proverb," 36–37; Clifford, *Creation*, 7–8.

ing" a sacred *tree* (Gen 3:6), *Gilgamesh* shows the Babylonian pantheon punishing Gilgamesh for invading the sacred *forest*. Why so hostile the response? Because "the line between the human and the divine may not be breached."[160]

More to the socioeconomic point, Humbaba's speech to Gilgamesh exposes the tip of a huge iceberg: "O Gilgamesh! A dead man cannot [serve his master]! [Only a slave] left alive can [serve] his lord! Release me, O Gilgamesh![161] You be the master and I'll be your slave. Let me grow for you cedar, cypress, and juniper,[162] The tallest trees, 'fit'[163] for a palace."[164] Even in its fragmentary state it is easy to see what Humbaba wants to do. He wants to *bribe* Gilgamesh—and with the very same treasure he's been assigned to protect.[165] To make sure readers catch the significance of this point Sîn-lēqi-unnini parallels *this* bribery-speech with another one from yet another divine "tempter." That is, he *inserts into the chiastic center of Babylon's greatest epic poem not one, but two divine bribery-speeches, saturating each with socioeconomic conflict motifs.*

Similar motifs appear in the Sumerian *Gilgamesh* tradition, only there the king is the "tempter" and the guardian is the "target."[166] Why

---

160. Greenspahn, "Proverb," 38 (see Stern, "Knowledge," 405–18; Parpola, "Tree," 161–208). In Gen 3:24 Yahweh delegates the protection of Eden to mysterious creatures called כרובים ("cherubim") and להט החרב המתהפכת ("flame of the whirling sword"; see Hendel, "Flame," 671–74).

161. According to George (*Babylonian*, 256), an LB fragment from Warka has Humbaba say, "Spare my life!" (*e-tir napištī*).

162. Like George, Brinkman sees the Cedar Forest as a real forest located somewhere in Lebanon or northern Syria ("Gilgamesh," 222).

163. Later Gilgamesh uses this term to ask Ishtar whether she plans to give him food "fit" (*simtu*) for a god (GE 6:27–28).

164. GE 5:149–55 (based on presently known OB, LB, and Hittite fragments). The Akkadian text upon which the Hittite fragment relies, translated by Friedrich and accepted by both Speiser (*ANET*, 83) and Heidel (*Gilgamesh*, 49) is attested on LB fragments from Warka and OB fragments from Tell Harmal (George, *Babylonian*, 256, 608). Beckman's translation differs only slightly from Friedrich's (Foster et al., *Gilgamesh*, 161).

165. Sum kadra can mean either "gift" or "bribe," but N.B. that litigation against bribery appears very early (Wilcke, *Law*, 37–41; *CAD* K:33). Noonan and Kahan define "bribery" as "the act or practice of benefiting a person in order to betray a trust or to perform a duty meant to be performed freely," locating its roots, "like many American legal concepts . . . in the ancient Near East" ("Bribery," 1:105–6).

166. One Sumerian text embellishes the bribery motif by having Gilgamesh offer his sisters as "payment" for access to the Cedar Forest (Foster et al., *Gilgamesh*, 110–11; Schaffer, "Cedar," 308).

these roles reverse in SB is never overtly explained,[167] but doubtless it has something to do with Sîn-lēqi-unnini's intention to help his audience think about what *they* would do, if confronted by a similar temptation.[168] Would they lunge at the "cedarwood"[169] and "temples"[170] dangled before *their* eyes, or would they, like Gilgamesh, have the wisdom to walk away?[171]

    Intertextual analysis of SB *Gilgamesh* alongside the OB and Sum versions, when laid alongside intratextual analysis of SB tablets 5 and 6, generates two questions: (a) Why does SB *Gilgamesh* preserve two bribery-speeches to OB's one? and (b) Why does Sîn-lēqi-unnini so intentionally place these speeches in chiastic parallel at the center of his poem?[172] If Karl Polanyi is correct (*myths focus on the "big problems" of the economies responsible for producing them*),[173] then the answer cannot be that he doubts his audience's ability to understand what bribery can do to the economy. More likely he inserts Ishtar's bribery-speech where

167. In *Atr* 1:382 Enki uses Akk *katrû* ("bribe") to describe behavior similar to Humbaba's (Moran, "Flood," 53–54), but the Hittite tradition focuses more intensely on the bribery motif in order to project the notion of "exoneration." That is, if Humbaba can be depicted as trying to corrupt Gilgamesh (instead of *vice versa*), then his death can be made to look like an "execution" instead of a "murder" (Güterbock, "Hittite," 111).

168. Goldman marginalizes this "big problem" in his analysis of international corporations (*Imperial*).

169. *GE* 5:7 (*erēnu*). Because the poem repeatedly mentions this keyword in its divine bribery-speeches, it seems best to translate it consistently as "cedar" (*pace* Dalley, *Myths*, 126).

170. "House" in this context probably means "temple" (see בית in 2 Sam 7:1–16 and *bît* in *CAT* 1.4:5:36, 51, 53, 61; 6:5). To dwell in a "house/temple" is the desire of all Near Eastern deities (and their priesthoods). The Canaanite deity Baal, e.g., is outraged by the fact that his nemesis Yam has a "house" while he does not (*CAT* 1.2–4), a jealousy David tries (unsuccessfully) to project onto Yahweh (2 Sam 7:1–16).

171. Humbaba's attempt to involve Enkidu in his bribery attempt draws even more attention to this "big problem" (*GE* 5:175–80). Güterbock thinks the fascination with Humbaba in the Hittite tradition stems from the fact that he lives "in a region in which the Hittites are more interested—Lebanon" ("Hittite," 110–11).

172. From an intertextual study of anti-bribery passages in Mesopotamian and Syro-Palestinian texts, Weinfeld concludes that "the very notion of social justice" has its deepest roots in ancient Near Eastern texts like *Gilgamesh* ("Patterns," 193–95).

173. Polanyi, *Livelihood*, xli. Neusner believes that "even though Polanyi's basic theses have now gone their way, it is clear that he raised the fructifying questions and directed the field of economic history, and the history of economic theory, from his day forward" (*Economics*, xvi).

he does—right after Humbaba's bribery-speech—because he wants his readers to reflect on what might be truly responsible for the gargantuan bigness of their "big problem."

Moreover, if Dale Launderville is right (*myths are the safest place to criticize tyranny*), then it is no accident that these speeches are chiastically designed to hit Babylonian audiences like a "one-two punch" using the "minor-deity-major-deity" sequence.[174] As one observer puts it, this kind of intensification is not uncommon in the literature of "intense money cultures," especially when pragmatic economic concerns are perceived to be threatening traditional spiritual concerns.[175]

Contemporary Westerners may not realize it, but cedarwood is a coveted status symbol,[176] as desirable to pre-modern Babylonians as "Rolls Royce" or "Rolex" is to postmodern Europeans. The Hebrew prophet Nathan references this substance when, speaking for Yahweh, he asks King David, "When have I ever said, 'Why have you not built for me a house of cedar?'"[177] Nathan asks this question not to humiliate David, but to make him reflect more deeply on why he wants to build Yahweh a "house."[178] Evidently it falls on deaf ears, however, for as soon as David dies, several tons of Lebanese cedar mysteriously show up on the walls of the Temple.[179]

Other prophets refer to cedar (and what it symbolizes) with even greater suspicion. Isaiah, for example, goes out of his way to ridicule any Babylonian who would carve humanoid gods out of cedar, then burn the leftover shavings as fuel.[180] Jeremiah castigates the Judahite king

174. Launderville, *Piety*, 40.

175. Hull, "Bargaining," 241–49. Bolle emphasizes that "in the study of politics, power is a necessary concept. It is, of course, an abstraction. Wielders of power are not sterile laboratory tubes filled with that element. Religion and hence mythological elements play a great part in the exertion of political control over others" ("Myth," 6361).

176. Akk *erēnu*; Heb ארז; Gk κέδρος; Arab ارز (see Mikesell, "Deforestation," 1; Weippert, "Libanon," 644–45; George, *Babylonian*, 93–94; Shipp, *Dead*, 112).

177. 2 Sam 7:7. This text critically parodies the Canaanite tradition about Baal's desire for a "house" (*CAT* 1.4:5:36, 51, 53, 61; 6:5; see Frolov and Orel, "House," 254–57).

178. Janthial reads *Isaiah* as a scroll focused on Yahweh's desire to build David up into a strong "house" (*L'oracle*, 307–21).

179. See 1 Kgs 6:9—7:12, and N.B. that cedar plays a major role in the construction of the *second* Temple (Ezra 3:7).

180. Isa 44:15. Isaiah's intention is to show how the same substance serves such radically different purposes—heating fuel, cooking stove, and object of worship—yet people still cry out to it, "Save me, for you are my god (אל)."

Jehoiakim for paneling his summer palace with expensive cedar, pointedly asking him, "Do you think you are a king because you compete in cedar?"[181] Bemused by the behavior of the Assyrian king Sennacherib,[182] Isaiah uses first-person speech to attack his socioeconomic value-system:[183] "I [Sennacherib] have ascended the heights of the mountains, the utmost heights of Lebanon.[184] I have 'cut down' its tallest cedars,[185] its premium pines. I have scaled its remotest heights, plowed through its thickest forests."[186] Then, suddenly, Yahweh interrupts:

> Have you not heard? I predetermined this a long time ago. Long ago I planned it out, and now I bring it to pass. *I* am the one who allows you to turn "impregnable cities" into piles of stone.[187] Even as my people are drained of power, dismayed and depressed, like plantings in a field,[188] like tender seedlings, like grass sprouting on the roof, scorched before it can take root.[189]

Question: Why does Isaiah so harshly criticize Sennacherib's socioeconomic value-system? *Answer:* Because he believes it to be based on faith

181. Jer 22:15. The contrast cannot be any plainer. Where Josiah's kingship is defined by "justice" (משפט) and "righteousness" (צדקה), Jehoiakim's kingship is defined by how ridiculously he tries to "compete" in cedar (מתחרה; Vg *confero*). Jeremiah aligns the metaphor to the corruption fueled by Jehoiakim's dishonest "plunder" (22:17, בצע), and the author of the *Habbakuk Commentary* found in Qumran Cave 1 similarly accuses the Jehoiakims of *his* day of "accumulating riches and 'plunder'" (בצע, 1QpHab 9:5).

182. Isa 37:24–27 (see Weinfeld, "Patterns," 193–95).

183. Botha reads this oracle through an honor-shame lens ("Sennacherib," 269–82), but Otto reads it through an intertextual lens (*Krieg*, 121–51).

184. Isa 37:24. As already noted, George suggests a close linkage between the mythical Cedar Forest and Lebanon's cedar forests (*Babylonian*, 456)

185. Isa 37:24 (כרת). This term reappears in Isaiah's taunt of Nebuchadnezzar in Isa 14:8: "Even the pines and cedars say, 'Now that you have been laid low, the lumberjack (lit., "the cutter," הכרת) no longer rises against us.'"

186. Isa 37:24 (see Moore, *Faith*, 254–59).

187. Isa 37:26 (ערים בצרות). The term here translated "impregnable" contains the root of the place-name "Bosra" (בצר), a Transjordanian stronghold south of Damascus (see Graf, "Hegra," 113–14, and N.B. Uruk's "impregnability," *GE* 1:63).

188. Isa 37:27. N.B. the contrast between Sennacherib's *destructive* behavior vs. Yhwh's *constructive* behavior.

189. By drawing a metaphorical parallel between the destruction of Judah's cities and the destruction of its people ("tender seedlings"), Isaiah admits the formidability of Sennacherib's power, yet without affirming his Gilgamesh-like claim to semi-divine status (Frymer-Kensky and Mander, "Ashur," 548–49).

in a powerless "guardian."[190] That is why Isaiah satirizes this Assyrian king as a pretentious gadabout naively imagining himself to be invulnerable to the divine will.[191] Sennacherib's invasion of Lebanon's cedar forests may *look* "heroic"—at least to terrified villagers and sycophantic lieutenants—but to Isaiah it looks ridiculous.[192] Why? Because from his perspective Yahweh alone has the power to "strip forests bare," and then merely by the sound of his voice.[193] Sennacherib may *pretend* to be Gilgamesh *redivivus*, but Isaiah refuses to take him seriously.[194]

Like the poet Isaiah, Sîn-lēqi-unnini understands the power of parody. The difference between the two is primarily methodological. Where Hebrew prophecy tends to be straightforward and blunt, Mesopotamian parody tends to be covert and indirect. Like Dostoevsky's *Brothers Karamazov*, Shakespeare's *Hamlet*, and the Hebrew book of *Job*, *Gilgamesh* is a *polyphonic* text.[195] Sometimes it *seems* to be univocal, but more often than not opposing voices are given full freedom to speak their minds. Here in the Humbaba episode, for example, those who desire unlimited access to the Forest (Gilgamesh and Enkidu) speak in direct opposition to those who demand that this access be restricted (Enlil and Humbaba).[196]

Of course, Babylonian poets hold no monopoly on polyphony or satire, nor are they the first to press these tools into the service of socioeconomic critique. One Egyptian writer, for example, relates the story of a "wild" god (Seth) who kills his "wise" brother (Osiris) by locking

190. George, *Babylonian*, 456, 94. Rowton warns against over-interpreting these texts into idealistic portrayals of the timber industry, whether as *threatening* or as *encouraging* urban expansion ("Woodlands," 261–77).

191. The cedar forests of Lebanon represent to many Babylonians the "dwelling place of gods" (Shipp, *Dead*, 113).

192. Whedbee emphasizes how much the Hebrews love to satirize their enemies (*Comic*, 62, 66), as does Jemielity (*Satire*, 148–95).

193. Ps 29:5–9.

194. Moore, *Faith*, 49–50.

195. Bakhtin characterizes as "polyphonic" any text in which he sees a "plurality of consciousnesses" (*Dostoevsky*, 6), sometimes using the term "carnivalesque" to illustrate what he means; i.e., that just as a carnival has several tents, so polyphonic texts have several "voices" (ibid., 122–24). Latin orators use the word *partitio* to denote "the orderly enumeration of our positions, those of our opponent, or both" (Quintilian, *Inst.* 4.5.1).

196. In Davenport's view, "the implications of this episode for imperialist powers are clear: expansion should not be approached with a view to dominating others with unnecessary force" ("Anti-Imperialist," 14).

him up into a box and throwing it into the Nile.[197] Meandering into the Mediterranean, this box floats up the Phoenician coast until it's pulled into a lagoon near the port-city of Byblos and absorbed into a protective tree.[198] When Isis (Osiris' sister) learns that a carpenter has carved this tree into a pillar, she flies to Byblos to negotiate its purchase. Exchanging Egyptian linen for Phoenician lumber, she—and this is the pivotal socioeconomic point—redeems her brother by "sacralizing the transformation of linen into lumber through international trade."[199] Socioreligiously this story validates the power and prestige of the Osiris cult.[200] Socioeconomically, however, it promotes the value of international trade.[201]

Similar motifs promote similar ideas in the *Gilgamesh Epic*. Both of these myths—Egyptian and Mesopotamian—address very similar questions: "If Seth cannot stop Osiris, then how can Humbaba stop Gilgamesh?" "If Osiris triumphs over Seth, then what are Gilgamesh's options *vis-à-vis* Humbaba?" "If the gods punish Seth, then what are they most likely to do with Enkidu?" Each question focuses on a different concern echoing through the halls of the "Great Powers Club,"[202] thus proving that great literature is "great" not simply because of the way it incorporates complex characters and adventurous plotlines, but because of the way it helps businessmen read the socioeconomic DNA of their clients.[203]

---

197. Plutarch, *Mor.* 5:13–16.

198. Saghieh delineates Byblos' long history of socioeconomic cooperation with the pharaohs (*Byblos*).

199. Silver, *Mythology,* 202.

200. Griffiths, *Osiris,* 185–215; Orlin, "Politics."

201. Moore, "Dreams," 205–21.

202. Liverani coins this phrase to distinguish the superpowers Egypt, Mitanni, Hatti, and Babylon from the city-states of Amurru, Byblos, and Jerusalem ("Powers," 15–27), and Zaccagnini observes that "a basic feature of the Near Eastern scenery c. 1600–1200 BCE is a wide-ranging web of political, cultural, commercial, and military transactions encompassing the entire Fertile Crescent" ("Interdependence," 141).

203. Hooke, *Myth*; Fontenrose, *Ritual*; Lambert, "Myth"; Oden, "Contendings."

Exiting the Cedar Forest, at any rate, Gilgamesh and Enkidu give two gifts back to Humbaba's boss, Enlil:[204] a giant cedar door,[205] and Humbaba's head in a sack.[206] Whatever these gifts might symbolize,[207] Sîn-lēqi-uninni mentions them here to create a literary bridge between two divine bribery-speeches set in chiastic parallel. Intertextually this transitional episode resembles another story about another hero (Perseus) who cuts off the head of another guardian (Medusa) in order to deliver it to another divine benefactor (Athena).[208] Where the Greek story forges a connection between "the Mycenaean palace goddess" and "the Minoan snake goddess,"[209] however, the Babylonian story sutures two bribery-speeches together through the standardized "minor-deity-major-deity" sequence.[210]

Ishtar "Invades" Gilgamesh's Life to Plunder his "Fruit/Treasure" and Slaughter Him with Her Weapon (the "Bull of Heaven")

Rather than follow OB *Gilgamesh* and jump straight to the showdown between Gilgamesh and the gods,[211] SB *Gilgamesh* inserts a whole new

204. They send these gifts down the river to Enlil's temple in Nippur (south of Babylon, north of Uruk). Later Nippur becomes famous as the headquarters of one of Babylonia's wealthiest dynasties, the Murashu family (Jòannes, "Commerce," 1480–85).

205. Gilgamesh does not overtly state the rationale for this gift, but his intention may be to refurbish Enlil's temple in Nippur and restore it to its former glory. Lines 10–14 of the "Tummal Chronicle" reinforce this opinion: "For the second time, the Tummal fell into ruin. Gilgamesh built the Dunumunbura, Enlil's dais. Ur-lugal, the son of Gilgamesh, made the Tummal splendid and introduced Ninlil there" (Glassner and Foster, *Chronicles,* 156–59).

206. GE 5:302; a fuller description of this decapitation appears in the Sum myth of *Gilgamesh and Huwawa* (Foster et al., *Gilgamesh,* 114).

207. Silver speculates that Humbaba's decapitation is (a) a metaphor for the taking of profits "from a commercial venture," and (b) a literary foreshadowing of Ishtar's extravagant promises to Gilgamesh (*Taking,* 47). Davenport, however, argues that Humbaba's plea for "vassalage clearly indicates to the reader that Gilgamesh's journey to the Cedar Forest should be viewed in an imperial context of expansion through submission since in the Sumerian tale Gilgamesh needs no offer of tribute in order for mercy to be considered as a course of action" ("Anti-Imperialist," 13).

208. Pausanias, *Descr.* 2:21.

209. Downing, "Athena," 586.

210. Launderville, *Piety,* 40. Harrison argues that Gilgamesh's "resolve to kill the forest demon" and "deforest the Cedar Mountain" depicts the desires of *all* conquerors to control "the quintessence of that which lies beyond the walls of the city" (*Forests,* 17).

211. As Yacoub puts it, "man is not an absolute being, nor the center of the universe, but charged with serving the gods" ("Dignity," 22).

episode into the tradition, one in which a more powerful "tempter" dangles before the protagonist a more dazzling array of "gifts."[212]

> Come to me, Gilgamesh, and be my "lover."[213] Give me the gift of your "fruit/treasure."[214] Come be my husband, and I will be your wife.[215] Let me harness for you a chariot of lapis lazuli and gold, with wheels of gold and horns of amber.[216] Let storm-demons be hitched to it like great mules! Let us enter our cedar-paneled home![217] Let the beauty of the threshold kiss your feet! Let kings, nobles, and princes bow down before you![218] Let them bring you "tribute" from the abundance of mountain and field![219] Let your goats give birth to triplets, your ewes to twins![220] Let your loaded donkey outwork the mule! Let your horses proudly pull the chariot! Let your ox be unrivaled at the yoke![221]

212. Abusch labels the Ishtar episode "secondary" and "superfluous" ("Proposal," 180), but Walls designates this speech a "bribery speech" (*Desire*, 40).

213. *GE* 6:6 (ḫa'iru). Because this term can mean either "spouse" or "lover" (*CAD* Ḫ:31), Frymer-Kensky designates Ishtar (a) a goddess "marginal to the family structure and power hierarchy of the gods," as well as (b) a "bridge" between heaven and earth (*Goddesses*, 58–69).

214. *GE* 6:7 (inbu). This term appears later in the poem to describe a garden of gemstones summarily described as *[meš]-re-u u la-le[e]*, "riches and wealth" (*SAA Gilg* 9:192). Abusch defines *inbu* as the "vigor of the living" ("Proposal," 153), but Veenker reads it as a sexual metaphor ("Forbidden," 57–73). The female lover in the most famous Hebrew lovesong relishes the "sweetness" (מתוק) of her man's "fruit" (פרי, Song 2:3).

215. Greengus, "Contract," 514–20.

216. *GE* 6:10 (elmēšu). Bodi ponders whether this term refers to a metal alloy ("electrum") or an organically produced substance ("amber"), opting for the latter (*Ezekiel*, 88–94).

217. *GE* 6:12 (erēnu). Just as the characters in the *Song of Songs* revel in the fact that "the beams of our house are cedar" (Song 1:16), so this precious wood stands at the center of the divine bribery speeches in *Gilgamesh*.

218. Observing the verbatim repetition of this line in an incantation to Gilgamesh-as-deity (*TuL* 127:15), Abusch ("Proposal," 148–51) argues that Ishtar recites it here to invite Gilgamesh into the "sacred marriage" ritual (the ἱερὸς γάμος). Gilgamesh's refusal, however (in Abusch's view), reflects his abhorrence at the prospect of being transformed into a dying-rising deity (on which, see Mettinger, *Resurrection*).

219. *GE* 6:17 (biltu). This term has a relatively wide semantic range ("yield, produce, burden, tax, tribute"; see *CAD* B:229–36).

220. Sum *Ewe and Wheat* describes humanity's primitive state by means of a similarly worded couplet: "Ewe did not drop her twin lambs // Goat did not drop her triplet kids" (Kramer, *Mythology*, 39), but this hardly implies that an entire creation myth lies underneath the surface of Ishtar's speech (*contra* Abusch, "Proposal").

221. *GE* 6:6–21.

In this speech Ishtar offers Gilgamesh a cedar-paneled home, a lapis-gold chariot, some tribute/cash, some domesticated animals, some storm-demons, and, of course, herself. Why? What does she expect in return from this mortal human? A political partner?[222] A trading partner?[223] A sexual partner?[224] All of the above?[225]

The tradition-history behind this Babylonian text is rich and deep. The Sumerian story of *Gilgamesh and the Bull of Heaven*, for example, narrates a very different version of this divine-human encounter, one in which Gilgamesh plays the role of "tempter" and Inanna plays the role of "target" (another example of role-reversal).[226] Pursuing her with "spike in hand,"[227] the king uses erotic language to woo his "target," but as with the Huwawa-Humbaba trajectory, reversing the roles enables the SB poem to (a) exonerate the hero of corruption, (b) generate support for him among Babylonian audiences, and (c) make the SB "tempter" pay the freight.

Although the "tempters" in each tradition woo their respective "targets" with erotic epithets, each version focuses on the *money* as the "cause or consequence of social change,"[228] as the "sacramental" peak towering over a "mountain of social arrangements," as the persistent symbol of

222. Vanstiphout emphasizes Ishtar's "unabating struggle for domination" ("Controversy," 233).

223. Perhaps she expects something like the Egyptian-Phoenician trade-partnership symbolized by the Isis-Osiris myth (Silver, *Economy*, 202).

224. Reflecting an earlier scholarly era, Albright supposes that Gilgamesh reacts violently to Ishtar because he is a solar/vegetation deity associated "with the sprouting and vigorous instead of the fading and dying; with the virile male rather than the ewe and the lamb." Gilgamesh thus stands, in Albright's view, "in conscious opposition to Tammuz, the darling of women, who comes to grief through the wiles of Ishtar" ("Fecundity," 318).

225. Abusch sees Gilgamesh as a potential netherworld consort ("Development," 621), but Barron posits deep connections between (a) the destruction of wild nature (Humbaba and the Cedar Forest), (b) the dismemberment of the sacred animal (Bull of Heaven), (c) the death of animal-bonded humanity (Enkidu), and (d) the "divorce" of god and goddess ("Wild," 392).

226. Foster, et al., *Gilgamesh*, 120–29. George sees the Ishtar episode as something "not yet extant in the OB period" (*Babylonian*, 18), but Jacobsen disagrees (*Treasures*, 214).

227. Foster sees the Sum word for "spike" in line 24 as a phallic pun (*Gilgamesh*, 122).

228. Kim, "Archaic," 7.

what James Buchan calls "frozen desire."[229] The Sumerian tradition illustrates this via the following exchange between "tempter" and "target":

> My bull, my man, I shall not let you go![230] Lord Gilgamesh, my bull, my man, I shall not let you go! I shall not let you go to dispense justice in my Eanna temple.[231] I shall not let you go to pronounce verdicts in the sacred lordly palace. I shall not let you go to decide legal cases in the Eanna temple beloved by Anu. O Gilgamesh, you be its lord! I'll be its lady!

Suspicious of her motives, Ninsun warns her son to be wary of Inanna's "gifts": "Gifts of Inanna must not enter your lordly palace. The goddess Ninegal must not smother your heroic might.[232] The goddess Inanna must not block your way."[233] And Gilgamesh listens to his mother's advice: "I will let no gifts of Inanna enter my lordly palace. The goddess Ninegal must not smother my heroic might. O goddess Inanna, you must not block my way! I will call the cattle of foreign lands and bring them into pens. I will call the sheep of foreign lands and bring them into folds. I will make silver and carnelian abundant. I will fill [the storehouse] with them."[234]

These last few lines—with their overt mention of silver and livestock and precious stones—allude to a few of the hard assets situated behind the metaphorical surface of the poem as Gilgamesh tries to decide what to do with Inanna's "gifts." He makes this decision, however, not from a perspective driven by the lure of "erotic romance," but out of anxiety over the possibility of losing his estate to an unstable business partner.[235] No

229. "There was something sacramental about ... my wages ... incorporating me into the mainstream of men and things ... taking what was special in me, my most secure and precious sense of myself, and making it general and banal. In short, I was to be civilized" (Buchan, *Frozen*, 8).

230. *Gilgamesh and the Bull of Heaven* (Foster et al., *Gilgamesh*, 122).

231. Eanna ("temple of heaven"), the main temple at Uruk, is the cultic headquarters of Anu (Chiodi, "An," 303).

232. Ninegal ("lady of the palace") is an epithet for Inanna.

233. Foster et al., *Gilgamesh*, 123.

234. Foster et al., *Gilgamesh*, 123.

235. As Davenport sees it, "such a union would cause him to suffer a form of entrapment" ("Anti-Imperialist," 15). Beaulieu discusses the mundane activities associated with the temple of Eanna in Uruk from as early as the fourth millennium (*Pantheon*, 103–78).

one wants to become a "gifted slave."[236] Refusing Inanna's gifts therefore enables him to avoid surrendering (a) his wealth, and/or (b) his freedom. Gift-giving, as Marcel Mauss has pointed out, is a rather complex social activity involving not two, but three elements: *giving, receiving,* and *reciprocation.*[237] All three elements contribute to the socioeconomic shape of the *Gilgamesh* tradition.[238]

Sîn-lēqi-unnini does not dwell on the erotic dimension of this encounter because he does not want his audience to fixate on "male tempts female" or "female tempts male." Instead he wants to impress upon them the axiom that "*tempters tempt targets.*" The primary woman in Gilgamesh's life, the one to whom he defers at every level of the tradition, is Ninsun—not Ishtar. Like Jacob's mother, Rebekah, Gilgamesh's mother, Ninsun, symbolizes wisdom and survival in the face of temptation and trial.[239] Like Lady Wisdom in *Proverbs*, she wants to *train* Gilgamesh, not *tempt* him, and the fact that Gilgamesh so firmly rejects Ishtar's bribery-proposal testifies to the effectiveness of her training.[240] This king listens to his mother's warning not to go "beyond the limits held ultimate by (his) predecessors."[241]

That two of Inanna's "gifts" (animal husbandry and precious metals) carry over from the Sumerian to the Babylonian tradition, moreover, (a) highlights the socioeconomic elements in Humbaba's speech, (b) adorns them with erotized epithets, and (c) constructs from them a

236. Matthews ("Unwanted," 91) relies on the pioneering insights of Mauss (*Gift*). Frymer-Kensky views Inanna as the symbol of "the nondomesticated woman, exemplifying all the fear and attraction that such a woman elicits" (*Goddesses*, 25).

237. Mauss (*Gift*). Riches cautions readers not to isolate these elements ("Obligation," 209–31), and Godelier adds a fourth element, viz., that some objects are too sacred to be exchanged, and must therefore be inherited (*Enigma*, 29–55).

238. Boaz makes a similar offer to Mr. So-and-So (Ruth 4:3–5) which, like the offer here, meets with immediate rejection (Moore, "Ruth," 361–66). Brown speculates that "gold" and "goddess" often go together in ancient texts because gold "can be associated with the pleasures and benefits of sexual gratification." Why? Because it "embodies the power of seduction . . . in the tangible form of jewelry . . . perceived as a process whereby male weakness falls victim to elaborate female deceit" ("Aphrodite," 46).

239. Willi-Plein appears to grasp this without attending directly to the Mesopotamian tradition ("Rebekkageschichte," 315–34).

240. Reflecting on Prov. 8:18, Sandoval notes how consistently Lady Wisdom describes her wealth not merely as "precious wealth" (הון נקר) upon which robbers prey, but as "enduring wealth" (הון עתק) upon which they cannot (*Discourse*, 112; see Moore, "Wise Woman").

241. Buchan, *Frozen*, 268.

bribery-speech more fit for the lips of a goddess than a gargoyle.[242] More elegant than Humbaba's crude back-street bribe, Ishtar's bribery speech dangles before the king "the richest fantasies imaginable,"[243] after which Sîn-lēqi-uninni reframes the poem into a public monument[244] designed to move readers away from purely socioeconomic concerns.[245]

Gilgamesh responds to Ishtar's bribery-speech, at any rate, by sarcastically "complaining" to her about his "inability" to support her in the lifestyle to which she's grown accustomed. "If I were to marry you," he teases, "would you *really* abandon the 'good life' to do housewifely chores for me like 'sew clothing' and 'cook bread?'"[246] Before she can say a word in response, however, he starts reciting to her a list of her "accomplishments," calling her

- "a cooking fire which goes out in the cold,
- a door which keeps out neither rain nor storm,
- a palace which crushes the brave who defend it,[247]
- an elephant (chafing at) its harness,[248]
- a dab of pitch defiling the one carrying it,
- a waterskin soaking the one lifting it,
- a limestone crumbling within a stone wall,
- a battering ram shattering the land of the enemy,
- a shoe biting into its owner's foot."[249]

242. Sandoval focuses great attention on "the rhetoric of riches" (*Discourse*, 112).

243. Kluger, *Archetypal*, 112.

244. *GE* 1:8 (*narû*). Slanski lists several of the public functions of *narû*-monuments ("Classification," 95–114).

245. One of these concerns focuses on the growing tension between *nēmequ*-"wisdom" vs. *kadāru*-"arrogance" in Babylonian culture. Citing Lambert ("Catalogue"), van der Toorn shows how *Gilgamesh* eventually takes its place in the "canonical" wisdom literature ("Wisdom," 21–32; see George, "Thoughts," 53–54).

246. *GE* 6:25–26; Gordon and Rendsburg think Gilgamesh to be acting rather arrogantly (*Bible*, 46).

247. N.B. the repetition of "door" and "palace" in Humbaba's bribery-speech.

248. Since all the other images in these lines come "from the realm of everyday life," perhaps the "elephant" mentioned in *GE* 6:36 (*pi-i-ru*) is a literary preview of the animals mentioned later (*GE* 6:47–63; see George, *Babylonian*, 832).

249. *GE* 6:33–39. Abusch reads this paragraph as the second of three stanzas cursing the netherworld into which Ishtar wants Gilgamesh thrown ("Proposal," 145), and

Where the images in Ishtar's bribery-speech focus on "big-ticket" items like transportation, housing, and taxes, the images in Gilgamesh's rebuttal-speech focus on concerns much closer to "ground-level."[250] Perhaps Sîn-lēqi-unninni puts this list in the king's mouth because it so effectively satirizes what theorists used to call "trickle-down economics"; i.e., the notion that everything at the top of the socioeconomic pyramid automatically "trickles down" to those at the bottom.[251]

Whatever the possibilities, this rebuttal-speech features a "target" sarcastically "praising" a "tempter" for her many "accomplishments."[252] To illustrate these "accomplishments" he then reminds her of the fates she's inflicted on several *previous* "targets"—one from the divine realm (Dumuzi),[253] three from the animal realm (the *allallu*-bird, the lion, the horse), and two from the human realm (the "Shepherd" and the "Gardener").[254] Literarily these vignettes build a bridge between the Seen World and the Unseen World.[255] Socioeconomically, however, they depict an economy so corrupt it takes no less than six vignettes to illustrate it.[256]

The first four vignettes focus on several important, yet (for our purposes) marginal concerns.[257] The fifth one, however, describes Ishtar's encounter with a very popular character in Mesopotamian literature

---

Goetze reflects on the proverbial significance of the "biting shoe" metaphor ("Historical," 2).

250. Just as the socioeconomic approach "more closely" explains why Seth abuses Osiris than the "conventional, strictly funerary interpretation," this approach "more closely" explains why Gilgamesh decides to reject Ishtar's "gifts" (Silver, *Taking*, 209).

251. In the 1970s Todaro proposes "trickle-down" economics as a viable economic theory (*Development*), but today refrains from promoting it at all (Todaro and Smith, *Development*, 15; see Arndt, "Trickle-Down," 1–10).

252. Tigay, *Gilgamesh*, 32–33, 93–94, 112–14.

253. Sefati, *Songs*, 209–17.

254. Parpola interprets these rebuttals as covert critiques of the Ishtar cult (*Prophecies*, xxvi–xxxvi).

255. Jacobsen (*Treasures*, 218) and Abusch ("Proposal," 162–64) point out how the sequencing of these vignettes literarily links the divine world (Dumuzi, 1st vignette) to the human world (Ishullanu, 6th vignette).

256. Walls sees "homoerotic desire" as the driving force behind this rebuttal-speech (*Desire*, 47), but Jacobsen sees only "panic" (*Treasures*, 201).

257. Of particular interest here is the characterization of Dumuzi (*GE* 6:45–47) as *šá bu-di-im-ma*, "the sheep-sacrificer," not to mention the subtle parallel between "wages" (*idū*) and "weeping" (*bi-tak-ka-a*). Like the Shepherd in the fifth vignette, pain is the "payment" Ishtar offers Dumuzi for sacrificing sheep on her behalf.

known simply as "the Shepherd":[258] "You loved the 'protector,' the 'herds-man,' the 'shepherd,'[259] who constantly 'piled up' for you [bread baked in] embers,[260] who constantly 'slaughtered' for you young goats.[261] You wounded him and turned him into a wolf—so that even his own shep-herd boys drove him away, the dogs nipping at his thighs."[262] Structured as a series of alliterative parallels, the message in this vignette coagu-lates around three word-pairs: (a) "slaughter"//"wound"; (b) "change"// "drive"; and (c) "goat"//"wolf."[263] Each targets a specific aspect of Ishtar's ruthlessness. When the Shepherd tries to give her bread, for example, her response is to "wound" him. When he gives her goat-meat from the flock, she turns him into a wolf (the goat's worst enemy). Emboldened by her cruelty, even some of the Shepherd's employees start to follow her example.[264]

Bad as her treatment of the "Shepherd" is, though, her treatment of the "Gardener" is even worse:[265] "You loved Ishullanu, your father's gardener who regularly brought you baskets of dates, daily making your table 'gleam.'[266] You 'raised an eye' to him,[267] saying, 'O my Ishullanu, let

258. Whether this character is based on the story of an actual shepherd is highly debated (Jacobsen, "Dumuzi," 41–45; Sefati, *Love*, 17–29).

259. *GE* 6:58 (*rēʾû, nāqidu, utullu*). Vancil discusses these terms in his unpublished dissertation ("Symbolism"), and Laniak reacts to them in the "background" chapter of his published dissertation (*Shepherds*).

260. *GE* 6:59 (*šapāku*). This term often refers to the "piling up" of investments and assets in administrative texts (*CAD* Š/1:413–16), and Enkidu sarcastically expresses the desire that Shamhat find a "nobleman" (*eṭlu*) whose storage bins are "piled high" (*šapāku, GE* 7:159).

261. Sîn-lēqi-unnini may here be satirizing the obsession with sacrifice in certain priestly circles *à la* Lucian of Samosata (*Sacr.*).

262. *GE* 6:58–63. Pausanias describes a similar incident where the goddess Artemis turns the shepherd Acteion into a wolf (*Descr.* 9:2).

263. In order, *ta-ra-mi // tu-um-ri; ṭa-ba-ḫâ-ki // tam-ḫa-ṣi-šu*; and *tû-te-ri-šu // tâ-ra-du-šu* (see Avishur, *Word-Pairs*, 634–730).

264. Just as Ishtar abuses a shepherd, so Cain abuses a shepherd (Gen 4:1–16). Just as this SB vignette in *Gilgamesh* focuses on the motif of shepherd-as-protector (*rēʾû*), so *Cain-and-Abel* focuses on the motif of "protection" (שמר, Gen 4:9).

265. Keiser publishes another ancient text about another slave-gardener in trouble with *his* master: "Ur-Šara, a gardener, returned from running away" (*Documents*, 190).

266. *GE* 6:66 (*namāru*). Like the fire causing Marduk's crown to "gleam" (*namāru, Erra* 1:142) so Ishullanu makes Ishtar's table "gleam."

267. The idiom *inu našû* ("raise an eye") appears in *GE* 6:6, 67; the Sum equivalent in *Inanna and Šukaletuda* is igi im-kar₂-kar₂ (lit., "blow the eye," line 240).

us taste your strength![268] Put out your hand and stroke our date-palm!'"[269] Ishullanu answered, "What do you want from me? Doesn't my mother bake the bread I devour? Shall I now devour the bread of curses and insults?[270] Shall I make bullrushes my covering against the cold?[271] You listened to his response, Yet you struck him down anyway, turning him into a frog![272] You sat him down in the midst of his labor [so that] 'the pole no longer goes up; the bucket no longer goes down.'"[273] Intertextual analysis of this vignette alongside the Sumerian myth of *Inanna and Šukalletuda*[274] suggests that Ishtar's anger may be rooted in a desire to retaliate against the Gardener for touching her in her sleep (sexually).[275] Whatever the possibilities, Sîn-lēqi-uninni introduces the gardener-goddess relationship via the "speech-within-a-speech,"[276] a well-known literary device, highlighting the parallels between the Ishtar-Ishullanu and the Ishtar-Gilgamesh encounters. Thus, in each encounter

268. *GE* 6:68 (*akālu*). "Taste your strength" and "devour your power" are both possible translations.

269. *GE* 6:67 (*ḫurdat[an]u*). Paul points out that Akk *qātu* ("hand") sometimes euphemistically denotes "penis" ("Ecstasy," 593), and that this euphemism occurs in Canaanite (e.g., *CAT* 1.23:33) as well as Hebrew texts (Isa 57:8; Song 5:4, 1QS 7:13). In light of the other "fruit" metaphors on tablet 6, the translation "date-palm" therefore seems appropriate.

270. *GE* 6:68, 72, 73 (*akālu*).

271. N.B. that Amos indicts those who "lay themselves down beside every altar on garments taken in pledge" (Amos 2:8; see Exod 22:26; Deut 24:17).

272. As in the previous vignette Ishtar "wounds" and "transforms" (*tam-ḫa-ṣi-šu* // *tû-te-ri-šu*) one of her "targets" into something non-human, but *contra* George (*Babylonian*, 623), *dallilu* more likely means "frog" than "dwarf" (*CAD* D:51).

273. *GE* 6:64–79. This line resonates with a line in the biblical Balaam oracles: "He pours out water from his buckets, his seed over many waters" (Num 24:7; see Moore, "Foreigners," 208).

274. In *Inanna and Šukalletuda* the gardener Šukalletuda touches Inanna sexually in her sleep. Waking up, she immediately recognizes what's happened and demands justice from Enki: "Father Enki, I should be compensated! Someone should pay for what's happened to me!" The Sum term for "compensate" in line 247 (he_2-en-ga-mu-e-aj_2) literally means "to weigh out" (Volk, *Inanna*, 28).

275. Note the parallels between Ishtar's abuse of "the shepherd" and Diana's abuse of "the hunter" (Ovid, *Metam.* 3:138). Both myths focus on the motif of "the hunter-becomes-the-hunted" (Dalley, *Myths*, 129).

276. Abusch, "Proposal," 166. Other examples include the "play-within-a-play" in *Hamlet* (Act 3, Scene 2) and the "film-within-the-film" in the films of Jean-Luc Godard (Cohen, "Godard/Lang/Godard," 115–29).

- the tempter "raises an eye" at the target (i.e., "gazes lustfully");[277]

- the tempter verbalizes a desire to "devour" the target;[278]

- the target responds sarcastically to the tempter's proposal;[279]

- the target verbalizes a desire to be protected from the tempter's power.[280]

The final line of this vignette uses euphemistic wordplay to allude to another dimension of this encounter: "You [Ishtar] sat him down in the midst of his 'labor';[281] 'The pole [?] no longer goes up; the bucket no longer goes down.'"[282]

This couplet may immediately refer to the Gardener's reliance on *shaduf* irrigation,[283] but it's difficult to imagine that this is the only kind of "labor" to which it refers. Doubtless it refers as much to Ishtar's labor as it does to Ishullanu's "labor";[284] i.e., that just as "poles" and "buckets" go "up and down" in *shaduf* irrigation, so also do "poles" (male) and "buckets" (female) in Ishtar's daily (sexual) routine. In support of this proposal it's fruitful to observe that *double entendre* language like this routinely colors many ancient Near Eastern songs, not to mention texts about "fertility" generally.[285] One incantation series, for example, homeopathically parallels Sumuqan's ability to impregnate cattle with the Water-Wheel's

277. The idiom *inu našû* ("raise an eye") applies to both Gilgamesh (*GE* 6:6) and Ishullanu (*GE* 6:67).

278. With Gilgamesh she desires his "fruit" (*inbu*, *GE* 6:8); with Ishullanu she desires to "devour" (*akālu*) his "power" (*GE* 6:68). Winckler calls Ishtar a "devouring goddess" (*Constraints*, 202–6).

279. Gilgamesh (*GE* 6:24–32); Ishullanu (*GE* 6:72–73).

280. Gilgamesh (*GE* 6:33–41); Ishullanu (*GE* 6:74).

281. *GE* 6:78 (*mānaḫtu*). This term occurs frequently in administrative texts (*CAD* M/1:204–6).

282. Hurowitz lists numerous examples of wordplay in *Gilgamesh* ("Words," 67–78), as does Kilmer ("Wordplay," 89–101).

283. Volk, *Inanna*, 57; Dalley, *Myths*, 129. The *shaduf* (شايوف) is one of the oldest known irrigation devices.

284. Satirical tit-for-tat is not uncommon in "great texts." Foster cites an example in which Enki commands the filling of a goat's ear with dung because, since the goat insists on filling Enki's ear with noise, it's only appropriate to have its ears filled with dung (*Muses*, 198).

285. Rubio ("Inanna," 271) chides both Sefati (*Songs*) and Jacobsen ("Dialogues," 57–63) for choosing "tame and delicate" renderings in their translations, thereby draining these texts of their "erotic flavor."

ability to impregnate the earth.[286] Another text relies on *double entendre* wordplay in its description of the "tavern business."[287] "Ishtar of the lands, heroic goddess, This is your priestly residence. Exult and rejoice! Come, enter our house! Let your sweet bedfellow enter with you, Your lover, your cult-actor.[288] 'Let my lips be honey, my hands charm![289] Let the lips of my vulva be lips dripping honey![290] Just as birds twitter over a snake slithering out of its hole,[291] Let these gentlemen continue fighting over me!'"[292]

In other words, Gilgamesh's rebuttal-speech criticizes one of Babylon's most volatile deities not only for the way she abuses her lovers, but for the way she corrupts the character and promise of love itself.[293] Sîn-lēqi-uninni inserts this episode into the *Gilgamesh* tradition not only to expose the "willfulness" and "contentiousness" of the world's wiliest whore,[294] but to "challenge . . . the assumptions and associations" of

286. *Maq* 7:23–30. Sumuqan is the cattle-god posted to Queen Ereshkigal's court in the netherworld.

287. Caplice, *Namburbi* §14:43–52. Often placed over the exterior doors of taverns, *namburbi* are prophylactic ritual texts designed to protect houses from potential invasion by evil forces. Tavern-keeping is a traditionally female profession because "the goddess of love reigns there" (Stol, "Private," 493).

288. Harris thinks transvestism is central to the rituals acted out in the Ishtar cult ("Inanna-Ishtar," 270), but Sjöberg thinks male actors merely play female roles ("Hymn," 225).

289. The language here shifts to first person so that the prostitute might speak directly to her client in the "voice" of the goddess.

290. Rubio cites several explicit parallels from well-known love songs ("Inanna," 271), and Bahrani contrasts Oriental openness to talking about genitalia with Hellenistic aversion ("Hellenization," 3–16).

291. "Snake" and "hole" in this *namburbi* parallel the "pole" and "bucket" in *GE* 6:78.

292. Caplice notes that many *namburbi* texts focus on economic as well as erotic concerns, thereby demonstrating a "relationship between tavernkeeping and prostitution" (*Namburbi*, 24).

293. Cole observes that anti-mythical satire takes figures and events from myth, then puts them into contexts "which distort whatever values they may have traditionally embodied, revealing instead a far more cynical network of base or deluded behavior" ("Myth," 76–77). This aptly describes how Sîn-lēqi-uninni interprets the character of Ishtar.

294. Abusch, "Ishtar," 452–56. *Gilgamesh* is not the only ancient text to satirize the behavior of a strong female. The Jehu cycle in 2 Kgs 9–10 satirizes Queen Jezebel in language reminiscent of the Ugaritic Anat myth (Moore, "Coronation").

the hedonistic culture she represents.[295] It's no accident that these lines occur here in one of the most sexually explicit of all the "great texts" (*Exhibit A:* the torrid encounter between Shamhat and Enkidu on Tablet 1)[296]—yet the question, again, is *why*. Why portray Ishtar as a tempter attempting to bribe this hero, only to have him rebuke her so harshly? Why insert an episode like this into so well known a tradition?

If *Gilgamesh* is composed, as many believe, "by men for men,"[297] then it would be appropriate to interpret this poem as so much androcentric propaganda generated by a traditionalist male poet criticizing strong, independent women standing outside "the normative feminine categories of mother, wife, and/or dependent daughter."[298] Yet such approaches often fail to recognize the fact that "goddesses are not solely male projections about the nature of women, [but] the cultural projections of the whole society [as it] reflects what the culture believes that women are and should be."[299] Interpretation degenerates into labeling this episode the fearful musings of a "knee-jerk misogynist"[300] whenever readers ignore (a) the history of the Ishtar-Gilgamesh encounter within the Mesopotamian literary tradition, (b) the chiastic literary structure of SB *Gilgamesh*, and (c) the fact that the only motifs common to the speeches of Humbaba, Ishtar, and Gilgamesh are *socioeconomic* in character, *not* erotic.[301]

295. Cole, "Myth," 78. Pollard observes how easily "the values of a whole society can be castigated by a well-placed parenthesis" (*Satire*, 24).

296. *GE* 1:188–94. Bailey ("Initiation," 139) articulates the ethos of an older scholarly era with the argument that the Mesopotamians place a "high value on sexuality" because "fertility religion asserts that the earth, and sexuality, are the sphere of the power of the gods."

297. Harris, *Gender*, 120.

298. Walls, *Anat,* 158, 217; see Frymer-Kensky, *Goddesses*, 66; Moore, "Bathsheba," 336–46.

299. Frymer-Kensky, *Goddesses*, 14.

300. This is Abusch's description, not his position ("Proposal," 148). Lipton warns that "factors other than race, sex and social status determine the audibility of a textual voice" (Review of *Power*, 423).

301. See Ackerman, *Heroes*, 87. This is not to suggest that unattached female goddesses like Ishtar and Anat are asexual (*contra* Day, "Anat," 37), nor does it affirm that "conflicted sexual attitudes towards sexual activity in Western civilization" are to blame for "the whole tradition of considering ancient pagan religion sexy" (Frymer-Kensky, *Goddesses*, 202). Jacobsen rejects such views as disingenuous (*Harps*, 168), but Townsend argues that such approaches sometimes reflect the efforts of repressed peoples to revitalize themselves ("Revitalization," 179–203).

More likely Sîn-lēqi-unnini criticizes Ishtar for the same reasons other poets manipulate other liminal characters like Anat,[302] Inanna,[303] and Isis[304] (not to mention Zipporah, Jael, and Miriam).[305] Poets use liminal characters to focus audience attention on the legitimate dangers threatening "civilization" at its borders.[306] Regardless of gender,[307] such characters can help readers identify those toxic ideologies which, left unchecked, can puncture and perforate these boundaries, thereby causing those behind them to be "devoured" like . . . , well, like innocent shepherds and gardeners at the mercy of abusive employers. "Tempters" in these scenarios often cruise these boundaries to find unsuspecting "targets" in order to corral them into prisons of "desire and temporary satisfaction [where] sexual love has paramount authority; for where men have no beliefs or traditions or curiosity or power, money and pleasure alone seem real."[308]

Shamhat's speech to Enkidu clearly illustrates this intention: "O come, Enkidu, into Sheepfolded Uruk, where young men wear bright sashes,[309] where every day is a feast day, where the drums rumble,[310] where

302. See Walls (*Anat,* 217–24), and note Dennis Pardee's assessment: "Walls' presentation is superior to those who would see in certain Ugaritic stories a rather advanced form of feminism in that he accepts the androcentric nature of the society which produced this literature and hence accepts that Anat was being depicted as inimical to androcentric norms. She would belong, therefore, to that very important stratum of mythological literature in which a given phenomenon is deified, not because it is viewed positively, but because it corresponds to a reality of life" (Review of *Anat,* 506).

303. Jacobsen, *Harps,* 3–84; Frymer-Kensky, *Goddesses,* 58–69.

304. Assmann, "Isis," 456–58; Takács, "Isis," 4557–60.

305. Ackerman engages the theories of van Gennep and Turner in her attempt to figure out the roles enacted by these Hebrew heroines ("Miriam," 47–80).

306. Van Gennep, *Rites;* Turner, *Ritual Process,* 94–130. Walls depicts Anat's "liminal identity" as "a source of discord and strife within the pantheon" (*Anat,* 217).

307. Henninger documents the gender shift in Venus deities in pre-Islamic Arab texts ("Venussterngottheit," 129–68), and Chan documents it within texts about the Chinese deity Hsi-ho ("Chinese," 9–81).

308. Buchan, *Frozen,* 124.

309. Like Adam and Eve before *their* "fall," Enkidu first enters the world unclothed and unbound.

310. That *alû* ("drums") sounds so much like *ālu* ("city") is no coincidence.

the whores[311] [are fair] of form, where imbued with 'sexual charm'[312] and joy, they keep the Great Ones (awake) in their beds at night![313] O Enkidu, this is the good life!"[314] From Shamhat's perspective the "good life" has nothing to do with "wisdom," nor does it reflect the kind of *imago dei* sexuality championed by Hebrew writers.[315] Sex in Shamhat's world does not even reflect the *imago dei* of Enki, the Mesopotamian god of wisdom.[316] No, sex in Shamhat's world is the ultimate weapon "beautiful people" use to punish anyone who dares resist their "charms."[317]

Thus, when Ishtar realizes that her bribery-speech has failed, the mask comes off and readers finally get to see her for who she really is—a self-centered teenager "perpetually suspended in the liminality of adolescence."[318] Demanding from her father (Anu) the "Bull of Heaven"

311. Edzard ("Gilgameš," 46–55) suggests a philological connection with *šamḫiš* ("proudly, pompously"), but the term for "whore" (*šamḫatu*) doubles as the name of the prostitute delivering this speech (*GE* 6:163; 7:143; Hurowitz, "New Life," 68–69). Postgate recognizes the Ishtar cult to be a place in which countless young women are forced into slavery (*Mesopotamia*, 106).

312. *GE* 1:231 (*kuzbu*). That this term has explicit sexual connotations is clear from Shamhat's earlier reliance on *kuzbu* to domesticate Enkidu (*GE* 1:181; see Walls, *Desire*, 17–18, 22–24).

313. As Foster points out, the motif of the Great Ones retiring for the night is a well-known metaphor for the "silence and loneliness of deep night" ("Sex," 29). Shamhat mentions the inability of the Great Ones to sleep in order to impress Enkidu with her colleagues' sexual prowess.

314. *GE* 1:226–33 (*hadû balaṭa*). Moses offers a different definition of the "good life" (Deut 10:13), and Aristotle notwithstanding (*Eth. nic.* 1095a), the more appropriate Greek equivalent is ἡδονή ("hedonism"), not εὐδαεμονία ("pleasure").

315. The *imago dei* ideology laid out in Gen 1:27 looks very different from the ideology here (*GE* 1:226–33). According to an OB fragment discovered at Sippar, a female tavernkeeper named Siduri converses with Gilgamesh in language very similar to that used by Shamhat (see Dalley, *Myths*, 150; George, *Gilgamesh*, 279).

316. Ironically, where "Shamhat transforms the animalistic Enkidu into a civilized human . . . Ishtar would reduce her human lovers to actual animals," and though it might be inappropriate to denigrate Shamhat as an individual, it's more than appropriate to identify her as a "highly cultured representative of her indulgent civilization" (Walls, *Desire*, 36, 32). In terms of Edwards' model, Shamhat's hedonism looks more "quantitative" than "qualitative" (*Pleasures*, 109).

317. *GE* 1:231 (*kuzbu*). Davenport sees "corruption in Ishtar's actions" ("Anti-Imperialist," 16), but Harris sees in her a symbol of the "cultural perspective of woman's power as disorder threatening to disrupt the social order" (Review of *Anat*, 718).

318. This is Day's description of Anat ("Mistress," 183). Wright finds a parallel in the Hebrew character of Abigail ("Dumuzi," 54–63), but the stronger parallels are Anpu's wife (*ANET* 23–25) and Potiphar's wife (Gen 39:1–20).

(the ancient equivalent of an ICBM),[319] she threatens to break down the gates of the netherworld and "bring up the dead to consume the living."[320] Such is her determination to destroy the man she "loves."

Veteran Bible readers will recognize in this episode a "tempter" much like the one who targets the patriarch Joseph.[321] Just as Anu's daughter browbeats her father into punishing Gilgamesh, so Potiphar's wife browbeats her husband into punishing Joseph.[322] Just as Potiphar's wife sends Joseph to prison, so Ishtar tries to have Gilgamesh imprisoned. Most importantly, just as Potiphar's wife fails in her attempt to corrupt Joseph, so Ishtar fails in her attempt to corrupt Gilgamesh. William Congreve famously calls this the motif of the "woman scorned."[323]

Question: Why does Sîn-lēqi-unnini insert the "woman scorned" motif into this revered tradition? *Answer:* Because, like the "three traps of Belial" in the *Damascus Document* (*wealth-fornication-defilement*),[324] and the *sight-money-wealth* triad in Thucydides' *Peloponnesian Wars*,[325] the *sex-wealth-power* triad here challenges audiences to engage that which would in any other circumstance look to be an obvious question: Why is the king so famous for deflowering the wives of his subjects *not* having sex with the very Goddess of Sex?[326] Nowhere does the poet *directly* address this question, of course, he simply (a) doubles Humbaba's

319. Akk *alû* simply means "bull," but in the "great texts" it often personifies monstrous creatures like Humbaba. Where Humbaba's home is on earth, however, Alu's home is in the heavens, causing Jacobsen to speculate that *alû* is "an older form of the god (Anu) himself" (*Treasures*, 96). Brinkman surmises that the Bull of Heaven symbolizes "seven years of drought" in Mesopotamian tradition ("Gilgamesh," 222).

320. *GE* 6:97–100. Anat similarly threatens El in the Baal cycle (*CAT* 1.3:5:22–25), and Hackett imagines a parallel in Anat's treatment of the hero Aqhat ("Hagar," 12–27; see *CAT* 1.17–19).

321. The Egyptian tale with which Gen 39 most deeply resonates, *The Story of Two Brothers* (*ANET* 23–25), resonates with the "woman scorned" motif as well, but Hecht ("Gilgamesh") sees further parallels between *Gilgamesh* and Euripides' *Hippolytus* in that (a) both texts show a hero refusing a desperate woman's attentions, and (b) both focus on the satisfying of her vengeance via a sacred bull.

322. Goldman (*Wiles*) discusses this motif at greater length.

323. "Hell hath no fury like a woman scorned" (Congreve, *Mourning*, act 3, scene 2).

324. *CD* 4:13—6:9. See below.

325. Thucydides, *Hist.* 1:13; 6:31, 46 (Kallet, *Money*, 21–23). N.B. the dominance of the *sex-wealth-occult* triad in postcolonial Africa (Geschiere, *Witchcraft*; Niehaus, "Perversion," 269–99).

326. Other authors recognize similar triads in other "great texts" (Roth, "Dowries," 19–37; Tickamyer, "Wealth," 463–81; Rohrlich, "State," 76–102; Harris, "Inanna," 266).

bribery-speech with Ishtar's bribery-speech, then (b) relocates these bribery-speeches to the chiastic center of the SB poem, thereby trumping *ploutos* over *eros*.[327]

Interpretation: Sîn-lēqi-unnini uses the *Gilgamesh* tradition to address a "big problem" threatening the Babylonian economy. In the name of "love," he suggests, the Ishtars of the world pander to the powerful in order to prey on the vulnerable. In the name of "love" they devise schemes to seduce the vulnerable into socioeconomic tarpits from which escape is difficult, if not impossible.[328] In the name of "love" they offer "gifts" to other "beautiful people" because no one else quite measures up to their artificial standards.[329] In the name of "love" they give "gifts" to their "lovers" not to bless their lives, but to drag them into bottomless pits of debt and despair.[330] By rejecting Ishtar, therefore, the hero of this epic rejects the hedonistic worldview she represents. Why? Because he refuses to end up like the "Shepherd" and the "Gardener."

Where Humbaba symbolizes those corrupt officials who fleece the economy for personal gain, Ishtar personifies every "young, independent, and willful" Babylonian who chooses to champion "hedonism" over "wisdom."[331] Where the Humbaba episode criticizes the "big problem" of governmental corruption, the Ishtar episode criticizes the hedonistic lifestyle nourishing and protecting it.[332] By having Gilgamesh stand up to both Humbaba *and* Ishtar, Sîn-lēqi-uninni thus makes a powerful statement about (a) the corruption threatening the Babylonian economy, (b)

---

327. Vernant (*Myth*, 180) tries to explain how πλοῦτος ("wealth") relates to ἔρος ("sexual love") in ancient literature: "The belly of the woman, which man must plough if he wishes to have children (and hence support in his old age) is like the belly of the earth, which man must plough if he wishes to have wheat."

328. Citing a Hebrew parallel, Rand notes how Jezebel corrupts a whole village in her desire to destroy Naboth ("David," 90–97).

329. Harris, "Inanna," 264.

330. A contemporary parallel would be tobacco company Brown and Williamson's decision to force all its employees to sign "intellectual property" agreements prohibiting them from telling anyone outside the company about the addictive properties of tobacco. Filmmaker Michael Mann documents how this contemporary "Ishtar" persecutes one of its employees (*The Insider,* Touchstone Pictures, 1999).

331. On the *kuzbu* vs. *nēmequ* polarity ("hedonism" vs. "wisdom") see Abusch, "Ishtar," 453.

332. Without mentioning satire *per se* Foster comes to a similar conclusion, calling Gilgamesh's rejection of Ishtar "the personification of unproductive attraction to the opposite sex" ("Sex," 22).

the possibility of reform in spite of it, and (c) the power of "wisdom" to orchestrate this reform.[333]

The Gods Un-Create Gilgamesh's "Double"

Gilgamesh's response to Ishtar is not to destroy her (as if he could), only dismiss her. Doubtless his friendship with Enkidu, whom Shamhat *successfully* "targets," helps temper his response as Sîn-lēqi-uninni sets before the "Enkidus" of his world an alternative to the "good life" she so enticingly represents.[334] Several intratextual cues help bring this point into clearer focus. Just as Enlil's "Humbaba" strategy fails, so also does Ishtar's "Bull of Heaven" strategy. Where Gilgamesh slaughters Humbaba within the secluded confines of the Cedar Forest, however, Enkidu slaughters the Bull of Heaven in full view of Ishtar and her colleagues. Not only does this humilate her, it forces her colleagues to face up to the growing power of this "dynamic duo."[335] Like befuddled referees they huddle together to try to figure out how to respond to this power, eventually deciding not to destroy the duo *in toto*, only uncreate Enkidu, the "mirror" originally created to neutralize the king's "bestial spirit."[336] Not only does this neutralize the power of the "dynamic duo," however, it boldly deconstructs Gilgamesh's character into that which used to control him—the "wild man."

Warned about this decision in a dream,[337] Enkidu responds to the gods in a rebuttal-speech considerably more bitter than Gilgamesh's

333. Vulpe argues that, as in the Prometheus myth, "the conflict of rights in *Gilgamesh* finds its resolution with the education of the king and his transformation into a just ruler" ("Irony," 280). Forest focuses on how the poem focuses on the need for kings to maintain some sense of "equilibrium" between "wisdom" and "force" ("L'Épopée," 26).

334. Böhl, "Gilgamesch," 248; Bailey, "Initiation," 142.

335. Hurowitz uses this colloquialism to describe the Gilgamesh-and-Enkidu duo ("Words," 73).

336. Lincoln sees a parallel in the *Homeric Hymn to Hermes* where Hermes, though still a child, steals cattle from his brother Apollo and is forced to face the consequences. Why? Because "the unrightful slaughter of cattle is always a most serious crime among cattle-herding peoples" ("Cattle," 1465–66).

337. Stefanini thinks Šamaš spins the gods' decision "positively" because they want to save face by giving the "princes of the earth" a chance to "kiss (Enkidu's) feet" ("Enkidu," 40–47), but Davenport more convincingly argues that "the anti-heroic sentiment ... openly disapproving of (Gilgamesh's) actions ... is concealed in the form of dreams that relate the true nature of Humbaba to the audience," and this because the poet's intention is to "portray *Gilgamesh* as anti-heroic without openly condemning the hero."

rebuttal-speech to Ishtar.[338] Cursing the hunter/trapper (Shangashu), he cries out, "O Šamaš, on behalf of my 'precious' life,[339] May the hunter—the trapper-man,[340] the one who did not let me "match up" as much as my friend,[341] May the hunter/trapper not 'match up' as much as his friend![342] May his profits disappear![343] May his wages be cut!"[344] Cursing Shamhat, he cries out, "May you never have a wealthy/desirable house ... !"[345] May you never have a house with nice furniture!"[346] Continuing his curse as a satirical "blessing,"[347] he adds, "May you [Shamhat] receive obsidian, lapis-lazuli, and gold![348] Multiple earrings as your gift ... ! May Ishtar send you to a nobleman whose house is secure, whose storage bins are 'piled high!'"[349]

In this way "Gilgamesh escapes all blame for the crimes committed against the gods, and Enkidu becomes the scapegoat" ("Anti-Imperialist," 12).

338. Where Job's farewell speech portrays Job as a kingly builder, sage and protector (Job 29–31), Enkidu's farewell speech parodies these roles (see Moore, "Terror," 674–75).

339. *GE* 7:93 (*aqrātu*). Akk *aqrātu* means "scarce, expensive, costly, precious, valuable, in short supply" (*CAD* A/2:207). Knudtzon discusses the roles attributed to Šamaš in neo-Assyrian prayer texts (*Gebete*); see also Taylor, "Solar"; Smith, "Solar"; Arneth, *Sonne*, 201–9.

340. Some ignore the fact that Enkidu curses not only the prostitute, but the hunter/trapper as well (e.g., Walls, *Desire*, 9–92; Foster, "Sex," 36).

341. *GE* 7:95 (*maṣū*). Presumably the "friend" to whom Enkidu refers is Gilgamesh (*GE* 4:96, 99).

342. *GE* 7:96. Note the deliberate repetition of *maṣū*, "to match up."

343. *GE* 7:97 (*nēmelu*). This term often appears in administrative texts to denote the "surplus profit" of various business ventures (*CAD* N/2:159).

344. *GE* 7:97 (*idū*). This term means "hire, wages, rent" (*GE* 6:45; *CAD* I–J:16–20).

345. *GE* 7:102 (*bīt lalû*). This phrase can mean either "house of desire" or "house of wealth" (*CAD* L:49–51).

346. *GE* 7:131 (*rašû*). This term can mean "to acquire goods, assets, real estate, wealth" (*CAD* R:196).

347. *Pace* Walls (*Desire*, 33) and Hendel (*Patriarch*, 121), the satire here seems just as pointed as that which colors Gilgamesh's rebuttal-speech. Since Akk *marṣātu* portrays Enkidu as "deranged" (*GE* 7:162), this implies that the "blessing" here is a blessing-*parody*, much like Balaam's "blessing" of Israel (Num 22–24), or the "blessing" of Job's children (Job 1:5).

348. Payment via precious metals occurs early in Mesopotamia (Wilcke, *Law*, 77–78).

349. *GE* 7:162 (*šapāku*). In *GE* 6:59 Gilgamesh rebukes Ishtar for abusing the Shepherd, even though he "piles the bread high" for her (*šapāku*).

Like all curses, these lines pour white-hot liquid into an ice-cold frame.[350] Where Gilgamesh's rebuttal-speech responds to the conflict motifs in Ishtar's bribery-speech (partially re-treaded from motifs pulled out of Humbaba's bribery-speech),[351] the first curse in Enkidu's rebuttal-speech focuses on a single word—"match."[352] Because Shangashu has cheated him out of *his* "match" (Gilgamesh), he demands that Šamaš "un-match" Shangashu from the things *he* loves—especially his "profits" and "wages." Because Shangashu has destroyed *his* business, Enkidu asks Šamaš to destroy *Shangashu's* business. Sîn-lēqi-unninni puts these curses in Enkidu's mouth, apparently, because he wants his audience to understand how difficult it is for naïve "wild men" to become "civilized" whenever the "good life" championed by their "civilized" neighbors becomes dominated by thinly-masked savages only pretending to be wise.[353]

The curse against Shamhat follows the same basic pattern. Retreading several socioeconomic motifs from *her* speech,[354] Enkidu chides Shamhat for even *thinking* she can domesticate a "wild man" like himself. Much like the monster in Mary Shelley's *Frankenstein*,[355] he laments the persecution heaped on him by "civilized" practitioners of the "good life," bewailing Shamhat's understanding of the "good life" as something applying only to the "beautiful people." Big, ugly "wild men" need not apply.[356] Thus Enkidu asks Šamaš to destroy *Shamhat's* "good life," especially her "nice things" and her "nice house."

Apart from some understanding of the poet's socioeconomic intentions these curses make little sense. After all, why have Enkidu curse the livelihoods of two human beings when the *gods* are the ones responsible

---

350. Steymans, *Deuteronomium*, 1–17; Schottroff, *Fluchspruch*, 97–104.

351. Humbaba's speech appears in *GE* 1:153–60, Ishtar's in *GE* 6:6–21. The *Erra Epic* uses this retreading technique even more extensively (Dalley, *Myths*, 285–312; Cagni, *Poem*, 26–61).

352. Akk *maṣû*.

353. This theme runs throughout many "great texts." The gang-of-seven demons in *Erra*, for example cannot understand why anyone would prefer a pampered life in the city to an adventurous life "in the field" (*Erra* 1:76). Similarly, Esau cannot understand why Jacob would trick him out of his birthright (Gen 25:33).

354. That is, her speech to Enkidu in *GE* 1:226–33.

355. Shelley, *Frankenstein*.

356. Bentley argues that *Frankenstein* "endorses political communities whose social relations and standards of justice are forged through choice and impartial standards of justice rather than by sentiment or genealogy" ("Family," 326).

for decreeing his doom? Why use such overtly economic language to curse *anyone at all*? Interpreted in context, however, Sîn-lēqi-unnini has Enkidu curse what these two individuals represent because in Enkidu's voice he finds a vehicle to criticize the Babylonian economy, an economy so corrupt, the only way it knows how to deal with truth-telling whistle-blowers is to denigrate them as "wild men."[357]

Further, because the gods condemn Enkidu instead of Gilgamesh,[358] the poem here serves yet another function. That is, where Humbaba and Ishtar *dangle* their "gifts" before *their* "targets," Enkidu's life *becomes* a "gift"—a substitutionary gift ransoming another potential "target" from disaster. Not only does this redeeming gift rescue the hero of *this* poem, it opens doors for other poets to develop this motif, something most famously accomplished in the fourth Servant Song of *Isaiah*.[359] In short, Enkidu is the prototypical "Abel" to Gilgamesh's "Cain,"[360] the prototypical "Jonathan" to Gilgamesh's "David,"[361] the prototypical "Patroclus" to Gilgamesh's "Achilles,"[362] even the prototypical "Laertes" to Gilgamesh's "Hamlet."[363]

Gilgamesh Abuses Himself

Enkidu's death impacts Gilgamesh so deeply, some readers try to make it the pivotal hinge of the poem.[364] Structurally this is impossible, of course, because to go in this direction is to ignore the chiastic parallel between Gilgamesh's abuse of his *subjects* as well as his corresponding abuse of *himself*.[365] Such approaches also fail to explain why this once-mighty

357. Mobley, "Wild," 233; Glazer, *Whistleblowers*; Alford, *Whistleblowers*. The film *Michael Clayton* depicts the story's whistleblower as a manic-depressive lawyer who refuses to take his medication (Warner Brothers, 2007).

358. Bailey parallels Enkidu's curse of Shamhat with Adam's blaming of Eve, but this marginalizes Shamhat's connection to the Ishtar cult ("Initiation," 149).

359. Isa 52:13—53:12. Following the suggestion of Gray ("Atonement"), Schloen identifies a mytheme in the Canaanite myths he calls "the exile of disinherited kin," then compares it to the "exile-of-Enkidu" mytheme he sees in *Gilgamesh* ("Exile," 209–20), and Walton applies these parallels directly to *Isaiah* ("Imagery," 734–43).

360. Barré, "'Wandering,'" 177–87; Shulman, "Myth," 215–38.

361. Dietrich, "Synchronie," 9–14.

362. Homer, *Il.*16:7–11; MacCary, *Achilles*, 150.

363. Veith, "Wait," 70–83. This is not an exhaustive list.

364. See, e.g., Wolff, "Gilgamesh," 392.

365. That is, it fails to explain why Gilgamesh, after Enkidu's death, "roams like a wild man" (Abusch, "Proposal," 181).

warrior no longer prepares for battle but roams the wilderness grieving his "unfinished life."[366] Having rammed his head repeatedly against the entangled wall of hero-vs.-hubris,[367] he finally begins to realize, like the titan Prometheus, how *many* walls separate the "wise" from the "wild."[368] "Smitten by limitations in his quest for immortality,"[369] the warrior who once so easily conquered others now finds *himself* conquered. The tyrant who once abused others now abuses *himself.* This realization pokes its nose out into the open at Enkidu's funeral, when the king says, "I shall make the people of Uruk weep for you; I shall make them mourn for you.[370] On a people so 'prosperous'[371] I shall impose 'hard work.'[372] And me? Now that you're gone I'll take up the matted-hair of mourning.[373] I'll put on the lion's skin and 'wander'[374] the wilderness,[375] so that when I die, shall I not become like Enkidu?"

Pedagogically, of course, the death of Enkidu sets up an important "teaching moment."[376] Where the poem's beginning shows the king's behavior to be so oppressive the gods have to create a humanoid "double" to challenge and contain it, all that remains now is a battered "wild man"

---

366. Abusch, "Development," 619. Lasse Hallström's film, *An Unfinished Life,* focuses on another battered "hero" struggling to deal with the problem of death (Miramax, 2005).

367. Abusch, "Development," 621.

368. Ibid., 616.

369. Yacoub, "Dignity," 23.

370. *GE* 9:1–2 (*bakû // damāmu*). This couplet finds an echo in David's lament over his son Absalom (אבל // בכה, 2Sam 19:3).

371. *GE* 9:3 (*šamḫatu*). The choice of adjective here hardly seems coincidental since *šamḫatu* ("prosperous") is the name of the prostitute (Shamhat) whose "prosperity" Enkidu has just cursed (*GE* 7:102–31, 155–62). Both nominalized forms derive from the verb *šamāḫu*, "to flourish, prosper" (*CAD* Š/1:288–90, 311–12).

372. *GE* 9:3 (*dullu*). This term denotes "hard work" in *Atr* 1:2.

373. *GE* 9:4 (*malû*). By putting on "matted hair" Gilgamesh returns to the disheveled look he achieves after the slaughter of Humbaba (*GE* 6:1). Enkidu's initial appearance in the poem is that of a wild man "matted with hair" (*GE* 1:105).

374. *GE* 9:4 (*rapādu*). This verb often connotes the freedom "wild men" enjoy in the wilderness before they succumb, Enkidu-like, to the seductive promises of "prosperity" (*šamḫatu*; see *CAD* R:148).

375. N.B. the intratextual parallel between Shamash's prediction (*GE* 7:144–47) and Gilgamesh's lament (*GE* 8:88–91), as well as the intertextual parallel to "Nebuchadnezzar's" exile (Dan 4:28–33; *ANET* 305–7; 308–15; 562–63).

376. Wolff, "Gilgamesh," 393.

aimlessly roaming the "wilderness."[377] Moving the tradition from the world of "court entertainment" (OB version) to "practical wisdom" (SB version),[378] Sîn-lēqi-unnini boldly raises a number of new questions[379] as the king's experience, now publicly posted on a *narû*-stele, begins the process of "canonization."[380]

A similar process occurs in the "wild man"-vs.-"wise man" stories of the Hebrew Bible (Cain-vs.-Abel, Ishmael-vs.-Isaac, Esau-vs.-Jacob, Joseph-vs.-his brothers, Saul-vs.-David),[381] yet this is not the only point of contact between the two traditions.[382] Just as the Mesopotamian king Gilgamesh tries to stop the bestial politics of poverty-bankruptcy-unemployment-bribery-lust-corruption from consuming his country,[383] so Ruth the Moabite tries to stop the bestial politics of famine-depression-childlessness-prejudice-patriarchal-death from consuming her adopted country.[384] Just as *Gilgamesh* responds to the political-moral-economic

377. Reading *Gilgamesh* alongside the *Odyssey*, Gresseth argues that "the hero's original intention is to seek life (i.e., true life, immortality) and not simply to make a name for himself" ("Gilgamesh," 11).

378. George, *Babylonian*, 34–35. Several other episodes in *Gilgamesh* allude to economic matters, though not in explicit contexts of economic conflict. For example: (a) Gilgamesh compares the weight of the horns of the Bull of Heaven to various measures of lapis lazuli and gold (*SAA Gilg* 6:164–68); (b) he unlocks the treasury to pay for Enkidu's statue (*SAA Gilg* 8:90–111); and (c) Utnapishtim loads up his boat with vast amounts of silver and gold in his preparation for the catastrophic flood (*SAA Gilg* 11:80–83).

379. George, *Babylonian*, 32.

380. *GE* 1:10 (*narû*). This term means "stele" (*CAD* N/1:364–67) and refers to a genre of literature "written on stone tablets for the benefit of future generations," often characterized by "a didactic, moralizing tone" (George, *Babylonian*, 32).

381. See below. Jasper notes that "the authors of the Hebrew Bible borrow freely from earlier literatures of the ancient Near East, shaping and adapting texts for their own theological purposes" (*Hermeneutics*, 28), and Ingraffia questions why contemporary thinkers simply ignore the accomplishments of these authors (*Postmodern*, 92).

382. It is impossible to list every biblical passage influenced by *Gilgamesh* or every study exploring its influence. The classic study is Heidel (*Gilgamesh*), but the most thorough is George (*Babylonian*).

383. For similar conclusions (albeit through different methods) see Foster, "Sex"; Leick, *Sex*.

384. Moore, "Ruth," 203–17.

chaos threatening Babylon,[385] so *Ruth* responds to the political-moral-economic chaos threatening Israel.[386]

ATRAHASIS

Like *Gilgamesh*, the *Atrahasis Epic* uses a number of heroic characters, role-reversals, plot-twists, and socioeconomic conflict motifs to critique a "big problem" in the Babylonian economy.[387] Formulated as a creation myth, each version of the poem follows the same bicameral format:

- The Igigi Myth;

- The Flood Myth.[388]

The Igigi Myth

Like the *Creation Epic* (*enūma elish*), the Igigi Myth narrates (a) a conflict in the heavens between opposing groups of gods, (b) the sacrifice of a ringleader rebel-god to appease the wrath of the "greater gods" (Annunaki) against the "lesser gods" (the Igigi),[389] (c) the belief that the blood of this ringleader can bring magically inseminated clay to life, and (d) the belief that the clay-creatures created by the "great gods" can free the "lesser gods" from "hard labor."[390]

Like these two texts, The Sumerian poem of *Enki and Ninmah* manipulates several cosmological motifs to show that "the lesser gods carry the basket" while "the great gods supervise the work."[391] Where

---

385. The neo-Assyrian "Catalogue of Texts and Authors" lists Gilgamesh as part of the "wisdom curriculum" alongside *Etana, Series of the Fox, Sidu,* and *Series of the Poplar* (Lambert, "Catalogue," 59–77).

386. Zakovitch, *Rut,* 32; Moore, "King," 27–41.

387. Lambert and Millard publish an OB version collated with NA fragments (*Atra-Hasis*); George and al-Rawi publish fragments of an SB version ("Sippar," 147–90); and Frymer-Kensky outlines the literary-historical context ("Atrahasis," 147–55).

388. Moran emphasizes the symmetrical intentionality of this bicameral structure ("Considerations," 245–46).

389. "The gods are subdivided into two categories, the Anunnaki and the Igigi, who are respectively the greater and lesser gods" (Pettinato, "Overview," 5965).

390. *Atr* 1:1–243. *Enūma elish* 6:31–34 reads, "They bound and held him [i.e, Kingu, Tiamat's "counselor"] before Enki / They imposed the punishment on him and shed his blood / From his blood he made "humankind" (*a-me-lu-tú*)/ He imposed the "hard labor" (*dul-li*) of the gods and exempted them" (Talon, *Creation,* 63).

391. Jacobsen, *Harps,* 154; Komoróczy, "Work," 9–12.

the Sumerian *Ninurta Myth of Lugal-e* portrays this "hard labor" as the gods' "assignment,"[392] one Middle Assyrian scribe argues that "The gods' 'assignment' shall be theirs forever. Forever shall they dig the canal … The hoe and the basket in their hands."[393] Influenced by this history of tradition, *Atrahasis* sets out to explain how this traditional "assignment" lands on the backs of clay-based "human beings,"[394] beginning with the following famous lines: "When the gods, like men,[395] bore the work and suffered the toil,[396] The toil of the gods was great, the work was heavy, the stress was great. The seven great Annunaki[397] made the Igigi suffer hard labor."[398] Just as *Gilgamesh* begins with a businessman complaining to the authorities about a "wild man" challenging *his* labor, *Atrahasis* begins with the lesser gods complaining to the greater gods about *their* "hard labor." It's difficult to know whether the Igigi complaint stems from having to do the worst *kind* of labor, or from having to do any labor at all,[399] yet every ancient reader knows what's going on here. River-digging and

392. Jacobsen, *Harps*, 251–52; Komoróczy, "Work," 13.

393. The term here translated "assignment" is *iškaru* (see *CAD* I–J:245; Pettinato, *Menschenbild*, 75).

394. Wiethoff shows how this dichotomous terminology shapes the proslavery rhetoric of antebellum judges in the Old South (*Humanism*).

395. *Atr* 1:1 (*i-nu-ma i-lu a-wi-lum*). Translators render this opening line several ways: (a) "When the gods like men" (Lambert and Millard, *Atra-Hasis*, 43); (b) "When the gods were (still) men" (von Soden, "Götter," 417); (c) "When the god (Enlil) was boss" (Jacobsen, "Inuma," 113–17); (d) "When [some] gods were mankind" (Moran, "Flood," 59); (e) "When the gods were men" (George and Al-Rawi, "Sippar," 147). The translation here takes *awīlum* as inclusive of both genders and presumes, on the basis of poetic parallelism, that the "gods" specified in line 1 must be the Igigi. Alster's pun-theory ("*Ilu awilum*," 35–40) needs reconsidering in light of the SB version from Sippar where the sacrificed deity is *Alla*, not *We-e* (George and al-Rawi, "Sippar," 149).

396. *Atr* 1:2. The SB version reads *i-lu ni-ra ib-nu-ú tu-up-ši-ik-[ku]*, "the gods fashioned the yoke, the soil-basket." N.B. the parallel דור/סבל ("labor"//"basket") in Ps 81:7. The fact that SB repeats *ilū* ("gods") in line 2 underlines the Igigi's outrage at having to do *any* kind of labor.

397. *Atr* 1:5 (see *CAD* A/2:171–73). Lambert discusses the likely *dramatis personae* of the Annunaki ("Hurrian," 129–34), and Kilmer parallels the "seven Annunaki" with the seven antediluvian sages—the *apkallū* ("Nephilim," 29–43).

398. *Atr* 1:1–6. Note the same dichotomy in *Ee* 6:10 (Komoróczy, "Work," 19). In spite of one apparent exception (OB *Atr* 1:172 // SB *Atr* 2:44), *Atrahasis* always designates the "upper gods" as "Annunaki" and the "lower gods" as "Igigi." Foster refers to this polarity as "supernal" vs. "infernal" (*Muses*, 469).

399. Sterba publishes several helpful flow-charts ("Organization," 21).

channel-clearing are jobs for *slaves*, not *citizens*; menial tasks for "human beings," not "gods."[400]

Prior to these opening lines *Atrahasis* presumes the taking of a "divine lottery" in which Anu draws the lot for the sky, Enlil the lot for the earth, and Enki the lot for the sea.[401] Preoccupied with their respective domains, the "great gods,"[402] like executives everywhere, delegate the daily operations of their fiefdoms to vizier-assistants.[403] These assistants, summarily called "those of the heavens" (Annunaki), then delegate the *really* "hard labor" to "those of the earth" (Igigi).[404] However, unlike the "lesser gods" in *Enki and Ninmah*,[405] the Igigi do more than just complain about their situation. They rebel against it. Inspired by one of their own, the ringleader PI-*e*,[406] they even go so far as to declare war against it, psyching themselves up for battle with slogans like "let's confront the

---

400. A good place to see how "citizens" and "slaves" are *supposed* to interact is the Code of Hammurabi (*ANET* 164–77). The Sumerian myth *Gilgamesh, Enkidu, and the Netherworld* imagines the internecine political conflicts between Amorites, Akkadians and Sumerians continuing on into the netherworld (Foster et al., *Gilgamesh*, 142), a motif which finds reflection in the Hebrew prophets Isaiah (Isa 14:1–21) and Ezekiel (Ezek 32:17–32). Sum dumu.gi⁷.r usually refers to a free-born citizen but, as Westbrook points out, occasionally it refers to *any* redeemed person ("Freedman," 333–40).

401. *Atr* 1:13–18. Hallo describes the technique of lot-casting in the ancient world ("Purim," 20–21).

402. The texts cited in *CAD* R:34–35 elaborate the privileges enjoyed by the *ilū rabūtu* ("great gods").

403. The Hebrew tradition closely parallels this when the deity delegates to the first man the task of "working" (עבד) and "protecting" (שמר) the primeval garden (Gen 2:15, 19–20). It is irrelevant to this study whether Adams (centralized government *precedes* the building of the great irrigation canals; "Civilization," 280), or Wittfogel is correct (the great city-states directly *result* from the building of the great canals; *Despotism*, 18). In either case the canals are essential to Babylon's socioeconomic health.

404. SB *Atr* 1:19–20 contrasts these two divine classes as "heavenly" vs. "earthly" (Lambert and Millard, *Atra-Hasis*, 42–43). The logic of this portrayal is simple: since there are slaves on earth, there must also be slaves in heaven. Mani shows how this mythopoeic logic still defines the structure of Indian society, where in spite of the implementation of constitutional law, "brahmanical pseudo-religion" still dominates the Indian economy (*Debrahmanising*, 45–46).

405. Jacobsen, *Harps*, 151–66.

406. *Atr* 1:223 (Akk *We-ila*); SB *Atr* 1:42 reads NAGAR (*Alla*). George and Al-Rawi discuss the etymological possibilities ("Sippar," 149–50).

steward,"[407] "let's break the yoke," and "let's fetch him from his dwelling."[408] Rhetoric quickly turns to reality, however, when they decide to burn their shovels and march on Enlil's palace, generating enough "noise" to wake up the cosmic neighborhood.[409]

Curiously, however, none of this noise awakens Enlil. He just sleeps right through it, oblivious to the revolt taking place on his doorstep.[410] Only after his vizier (Nusku) shakes him from his slumber does he start barking out commands like "Bar the gate!" "Take up your weapons!" and "Stand before me!"[411] Alarmed by the violence of his response, though, Nusku cries out, "My lord! Your sons are your inheritance! Why do you fear your own sons?"[412] Good question. Why *does* Enlil fear his own "sons?"[413] Why *does* the lord of the earth wish for the destruction of his own "inheritance?"[414] Does Nusku raise this question (a) because he finds the Igigi revolt objectionable, (b) because he finds Enlil's response to it objectionable, (c) because he wants to restrain his master from do-

---

407. SB *Atr* 1:41 (*guzzalâ*, lit., "chair-bearer," *CAD* G:146). N.B. how SB intensifies OB *maḫārum* ("confront") to *nêru* ("kill"). This "steward," of course, is Enlil.

408. With George and al-Rawi ("Sippar," 172) the present study rejects Lambert and Millard's (*Atra-Hasis*) suggestion that *šašû* be translated as "disturb."

409. *Atr* 1:67 (*rigmu*). In *Atr* 1:358 Enlil complains about the *rigmu*-noise of the clay creatures replacing the Igigi (i.e., the *amēlūtū*). Apsu and Tiamat also complain about the problem of divine "noise" (*Ee* 1:25), and Gilgamesh warns Enkidu not to make *rigmu*-noise on his netherworld descent (*GE* 12:22).

410. This section of *Atrahasis* may be influenced by the Sumerian (Eridu) tradition where Enki does not wake up until aroused by the mother goddess. Later on in the Flood Myth Enlil becomes such a light sleeper, he develops a four-stage program for dealing with the noisy *amēlūtū* (first drought, then famine, then plague, then flood).

411. *Atr* 1:87–88. Sum *Curse of Agade* (line 1) shows Enlil destroying whole cities simply by "frowning" on them (saj-ki gid₂-da ᵈen-lil₂-la₂-ke₄; lit., "Enlil made his forehead long" (see Cooper, *Agade*, 50). Nusku is the deity to whom the bewitched and demon-possessed pray for deliverance (Foster, *Muses*, 717–20).

412. *Atr* 1:93–6 (*be-li bi-nu bu-nu-ka / ma-ru ra-ma-ni-ka mi-in-su ta-du-ur*). The problematic word in Nusku's speech, as Lambert and Millard point out, is *bu-nu* (*Atra-Hasis*, 150). Komoróczy translates it "offspring" ("Work," 20), but the better choice is "inheritance" (see *CAD* B:319, *bunnu*).

413. Akk *māru* (Sum dumu) can mean "citizen" as well as "son." One OB letter defines the term via the following couplet: "He is not a son/citizen of the city (Sum dumu uru) // he is not a 'freeborn man'" (Akk *mar awilim*; lit., "son of a human being"; see *CAD* M/1:315).

414. Moses asks a similar question about Yahweh's "inheritance" (נחלה, Deut 9:26, 29).

ing something inappropriate,[415] or (d) because he envisions a cosmos in which the Grand Canyon between "debt-slavery" and "freedom" becomes, in his mind, cross-able?[416]

The text is silent, of course, yet another vizier-speech in another Babylonian epic sheds intertextual light on this one. In the *Epic of Erra* another vizier deity (Ishum) asks another angry master (Erra) another pointed question in the midst of another cosmic crisis: "Lord Erra![417] Why do you 'plot' against the gods?[418] Why do you plot to devastate and destroy the lands? Are you not plotting against your own future?"[419] The similarities between these encounters are striking:

- Both masters are chthonic deities (Enlil//Erra);[420]

- Both questioners are vizier-deities (Nusku//Ishum);

- Both viziers plead on behalf of "the (lesser) gods";

- Both viziers plead to stop a potential catastrophe.

Just as Nusku pleads with his master (Enlil) to weigh the consequences of *his* actions, so Ishum pleads with his master (Erra) to weigh the consequences of *his* actions. Where Ishum successfully restrains *his* master's behavior, Nusku restrains *his* master's behavior. Where *Atrahasis* only alludes to what's bothering Enlil, however, *Erra* openly states what's gnawing at Erra: "All the gods are afraid to do battle [with me, but] the black-headed people treat me with "contempt."[421]

---

415. This assumes, of course, that Enlil is capable of "beneficence" (Marcus and Pettinato, "Enlil," 2800).

416. As Bachvarova makes clear, the Hittite *Song of Release* also critiques the "big problem" of debt-slavery ("Relations," 55).

417. *Erra* 1:102 (Cagni, *L'Epopea*, 68).

418. *Erra* 1:102 (*kapādu*). The phrase *kapādu lemuttu* ("plot evil") appears in its entirety in *Erra* 3C:36, where Ishum asks Erra why he "plots evil" against both "gods and men" (*ili u amēli*).

419. *Erra* 1:102–3. Cagni translates "without drawing back from your purpose," (*Erra*, 30), but this discounts the alliterative sequence animating the string of 2nd person verb forms (*takpud . . . takpudma . . . tatur*).

420. A "chthonic" deity (Gk χθών) is a permanent inhabitant or regular visitor to the netherworld. "Chthonic divinities are spirits that wreak vengeance" (Klinger, "Revenge," 7782).

421. *Erra* 1:119–20 (*šitutum*). Cagni (*L'Epopea*, 248) argues that the "sin" in *Erra* 5:6 (*ḫitu*) refers to the "contempt" (*šitutum*) shown Erra in *Erra* 1:120. *Atrahasis* operates within the same semantic field, but avoids the word *ḫitu* ("sin"). The "black-headed people" are the Babylonians.

The "big problem" in *Erra*, in other words, is *contempt*,[422] and though this term does not appear in *Atrahasis*, each of these vizier-speeches serves the same basic function.[423] Further, because *contempt* increases dramatically in honor-shame cultures during times of socio-economic unrest (invasion, war, famine),[424] the texts produced by these cultures often depict the "wilderness" as a place populated by chthonic demonic powers more inclined to revenge than redemption.[425] Since the Babylonian wisdom tradition frequently alludes to this cosmology,[426] it's no accident that *Erra* and *Atrahasis* preserve parallel traditions in which a cautious vizier restrains an angry master from giving in to his destructive desires. Behind these vizier-characters, of course, stand whole banks of Babylonian mid-level managers sandwiched between "Annunaki"-bosses on the one hand (governors and high priests) and "Igigi"-workers on the other (corvée and other slave-laborers).[427] Indeed, many a war has

422. Frankena views "contempt . . . as the *Leitmotif* of the *Erra* epic" ("Irra-Epos," 5), but Bodi downplays its importance (*Ezekiel*, 69–81). Sommerfeld (*Aufstieg*, 27) plausibly suggests that the historical referent for *Erra's* "contempt" is Marduk's usurpation of Enlil's/Erra's/Nergal's throne at the Chaldean conquest of Babylon. N.B. that *šitutum* adorns a popular proverb: "Do not show contempt (*šitutum*) on the downtrodden . . . / Do not sneer at them autocratically" (*BWL* 100:57–60).

423. Another parallel appears at the beginning of *Esther* when the vizier Memucan warns King Ahasuerus that Queen Vashti's "wickedness," if left unaddressed, may encourage *all* Persian women to treat their husbands with "contempt" (בזה; Esth 1:16–17). A more sinister parallel is the ongoing practice of "honor-killing," a barbaric custom still practiced in many parts of the world (Jafri, *Honour*; Khan, *Honour*).

424. Homer-Dixon insightfully writes about "how and where environmental stress— or what I have come to call 'environmental scarcity'—contributes to social breakdown and violence" (*Environment*, 4).

425. Klinger, "Revenge," 7779–84. Jastrow suggests that the "mediatorship" demonstrated in the Enlil-Nusku // Enki-Marduk relationships reflects the presence of underlying social institutions largely shaped by tribal, familial priorities (Review of *Vater*, 473).

426. The terms *adāru* ("fear") and *māru* ("son") come together again in the Assyrian version of *Atrahasis* (Lambert and Millard, *Atra-Hasis*, 124:21–22), suggesting to Lambert and Millard that Nusku's question may allude to a "proverb" (*Atra-Hasis*, 151). One of these terms, e.g., (with accompanying socioeconomic connotations) occurs in the following contrast: "There is a man who supports a wife, and there is a man who supports a 'son' (*māru*); the king is a man who does not 'support' (*ramanu*) himself" (*BWL* 255:11–14).

427. Von Rad argues that a primary purpose of the wisdom literature is to train effective managers ("Josephsgeschichte," 122), and Sterba points out that two of these mid-level managers are the *sangu* priest and the *nubanda* steward ("Organization," 21).

erupted in this part of the world over the mere "threat" of *contempt*, "no matter how slight."[428]

Anu tries to stay out of this fight, of course,[429] but when this strategy fails he allows himself to become a reluctant mediator only half-heartedly committed to its resolution. Enlil, however, responds to Anu's half-heartedness with a blistering tirade against his rebellious "sons"—to the point of denigrating them as worthless "pirate-scum."[430] Anu tries to shield them from this attack, but this only provokes Enlil into demanding that the following questions be put to the Igigi: "Who is the god responsible for this conflict? Who is the god responsible for this combat?[431] Who is responsible for stirring up this war, bringing the battle to Enlil's gate?"[432]

Question: Why does Enlil voice these questions? *Answer:* Probably because he wants to deflect attention away from his vizier's questions— "Why do you fear your own sons?" "Why do they rebel against your leadership?" "What can be done to stop their persistent "noise?" While it is true that the older gods desire sleep above everything else,[433] sleep deprivation *per se* does not fully account for the complexity of Enlil's behavior.[434]

Interestingly, not only do his "sons" anticipate this behavior, they formulate a response strategy. Ignoring the blustery dramatics of their

428. Scheff, "Shame," 97 (see Alberts, "Shame"; Gould, "Collective").

429. Like most old deities, Anu does not want to be bothered with the day-to-day problems of the cosmos (Cross, "Olden Gods," 73–83). N.B. that some Sumerian texts depict Enlil as Anu's "son" (Chiodi, "An," 302).

430. SB *Atr* 2:32, 44 (ḫupšū). In the Amarna letters this term refers to marginalized folk often scapegoated by the mayors of Syro-Palestinian townships (*EA* 117:90; 118:23; 125:27; *CAD* P:37–49). The term λῃστής has similar connotations in Nazarene literature (Luke 10:30).

431. SB *Atr* 2:15–16; lit., "Who is the 'lord of the conflict' god? Who is the 'lord of the battle' god?" (*i-lu be-el qá-ab-lim* // *i-lu be-el ta-ḫa-zi*).

432. SB *Atr* 2:15–18 (OB 1:140–43). Where earlier the Igigi shout, "Let's 'stir' (*balālu*) hostility into battle" (1:62), Enlil now demands the life of the ringleader responsible for "stirring up" trouble (*balālu*). Enki's "stirring" of blood and clay into human protoplasm plays off this same term (*balālu*, OB *Atr* 1:231).

433. Cross, "Olden," 73–83.

434. Whatever the possibilities, Enlil's anger historically reflects the anger of the Enlil priesthood over their displacement at the hands of the Marduk priesthood (Foster, *Muses*, 881; Sommerfeld, *Aufstieg*). Cross reflects on the viciousness of Israelite priestly conflict ("Priestly Houses," 195–215).

"father," they argue before the divine council that although Enlil's anger is understandable, it obviously makes no sense. Unlike Erra, the chthonic deity who *relentlessly* covets power,[435] the Igigi insist on claiming no desire to oust Enlil from his chthonic throne.[436] All they want from him is their "freedom."[437] Freedom is what drives this rebellion, they argue, not greed or lust or filial "contempt." Freedom is what brings "every single one of us gods" to the divine council for help. Repeating the phrase "every single one of us gods" over and over,[438] the Igigi hope to win over the council to the justice of their cause.

Enlil's response, meanwhile, catches everyone off guard. He *weeps*.[439] Whether from compassion or indignation is not clear, but with tears in his eyes he cries to Anu: "O noble one, carry your authority away with you to the heavens—the pow[er of] your 'objection.'[440] When the Annunaki are present before you summon one god and have him put to death."[441] Not only does he weep, in fact, he *compromises* (something very unusual for Enlil).[442] Instead of destroying *all* "his sons," he suggests, why not assassinate only one of them—the ringleader PI-*e*?

Stunned by this compromise proposal, the gods fall silent. Before anyone can react, however, Enki jumps in with another one.[443] Rather

435. *Erra* 1:124–91; 2:1–10.

436. *Atr* 1:144–52.

437. *Atr* 1:148 (*andurārum*). This term refers primarily to the "freedom" which results from the cancellation of debts and manumission of slaves (*CAD* A/2:11–17), not the idealistic state suggested by afficionados of the "Greek miracle" (Snell, *Flight*, 137–56).

438. *Atr* 1:146, 151, 159, 164.

439. Weeping is something lamenting goddesses do—not the lord of the netherworld (Kramer, "Weeping," 69–80; Dobbs-Alsopp, *Lamentations*, 6–12).

440. *Atr* 1:171 (*idu*). Moran observes several extended meanings for this term: "reason/excuse/objection"; in some cases "wages/rent" (*CAD* I–J:16). Inclusion of the term *qatu* in SB *Atr* 2:58 ("hand/power"), however, supports a sociopolitical connotation, which further suggests that the parallel term (*parṣu*) more likely denotes "power" than "rites" (*pace* Lambert and Millard, *Atra-Hasis*, 109).

441. *Atr* 1:170–73//SB *Atr* 2:57–60. Whether the term in SB *Atr* 2:58 (*parṣu*) changes the last word in OB *Atr* 1:173 (*tamtum*, "death") in order to create (or restore) an inclusio with *parṣu* in OB *Atr* 1:171 is a tantalizing possibility, but whatever the possibilities, OB *Atrahasis* makes Enlil the first one to suggest deicide, not Enki (SB *Atr* 2:91).

442. Falkenstein documents Enlil's unbridled rage in the *Curse of Agade* ("Fluch," 43–124; see *ANET* 646–51).

443. *Atr* 1:208–17. As Kramer and Maier point out, Enki is the quintessential opportunist (*Myths*, 176).

than waste the blood of PI-*e*, he asks, why not mix it together with spe-
cially inseminated clay to create a new race of creatures able to assume
the "hard labor" of the cosmos?[444] Should the divine council approve *this*
compromise, Enki suggests, then everyone can go home happy. Enlil can
go back to sleep; Enki can find an outlet for his creative gifts; the Igigi can
win their freedom; and the clay-based humans, like newly-arrived immigrants, can receive "gainful employment."[445] From the divine council's
perspective this looks like an ideal solution. From a human perspective,
though, this looks like a rigged game of musical chairs. Everyone knows
who's going to be left standing when the music stops.[446]

The Flood Myth

The Flood Myth in the second half of *Atrahasis* raises these tensions
to a whole new level. Where the Igigi Myth addresses the problems
Babylonian managers have to face by proposing the creation of a new
labor force, the Flood Myth fast-forwards to a time when this labor force
starts "multiplying" uncontrollably,[447] to the point that the "great gods"
start feeling more than a little "oppressed."[448] Instead of genocide or assassination, however, Enlil now proposes to the council that they thin
out the human "herd" by attacking them in stages (first drought, then
famine, then plague, then flood).[449]

To this more nuanced proposal Enki at first says nothing.[450] Soon
afterwards, however, he proposes to the clay-based creatures a carefully

444. Clifford emphasizes Enki's role as "inseminator of the earth" (*Creation*,
32–49).

445. That older immigrants tend to force newer immigrants into the most menial
jobs is a fact recognized by sources as diverse as novelists (Puzo, *Godfather*) and social
scientists (see sources cited in Moore, "America").

446. McCoy illustrates the time-honored practice of "passing the buck" ("Parable,"
103–8).

447. *Atr* 1:353 (Akk *mâdu*; *CAD* M/1:24–27). The book of *Exodus* replicates the
same motif of "slave-multiplication": "Now a new king arose over Egypt who did not
know Joseph. He said to his people, 'Look, the Israelites are more numerous and powerful than we, so let us deal shrewdly with them. Otherwise they will multiply and, in the
event of war, join our enemies and fight against us'" (Exod 1:8–10).

448. *Atr* 1:355 (*adāru*; see *CAD* A/1:105–7). N.B. the "oppressive" behavior of
Gilgamesh toward the citizens of Uruk (*GE* 1:65, same word, *adāru*).

449. *Atr* 1:352–end (Lambert and Millard, *Atra-Hasis*, 67–105). Later writers per-
sonify these "natural disasters" into chthonic spirits (Moore, *Balaam*, 20–65).

450. See *Atr* 1:360.

thought-out, *Realpolitik* response to this "thin-the-herd" strategy. Like Ishtar in *Gilgamesh* he even proposes the selection of a (new) "target": "Command the heralds to make 'noise' in the land,[451] proclaiming, 'Do not worship your gods! Do not pray to your goddesses![452] Seek instead the gate of Namtaru,[453] and put a baked loaf in front of it.' The sweet offering of flour may so please him that, after storing the 'bribe'[454] in a 'safe place,'[455] he may lift the 'plague.'"[456]

Enki's role in the Flood Myth deeply resonates with the role he enacts earlier in the Igigi Myth—"wily mediator" to Enlil's "angry prosecutor"—only the *Atrahasis* poet seasons his personality with a dash of Ishtar and a pinch of Humbaba. Enki advises his human clients to avoid direct confrontation with Enlil, encouraging them instead to re-route their daily offerings away from their "personal gods"[457] and send them over to the house of Enlil's vizier-assistant Namtaru. When Namtaru—the secondary "target"—receives these "gifts," Enki hopes they will be enough to motivate him to help. Put simply, "if the front door is locked, try the side door." *Translation:* If the "manager" is unapproachable (Enlil), try the "assistant manager" (Namtaru).[458]

---

451. *Atr* 1:376–77 (*rigmu*; N.B. the alliterative parallel *nagiru*//*rigmu*). Moran thinks Enki wants the *amēlūtū* (humans) to *stop* making noise, but this unnecessarily presumes the presence of antithetical parallelism ("Flood," 53–54).

452. *Atr* 1:379 (lit., "do not pray to 'your Ishtars,'" *iš-ta-ar-ku-un*).

453. The chthonic deity Namtaru tends to be associated with plague and pestilence (Foster, *Muses*, 506–24; Lewis, "First-Born," 333), but the fact that SB *Atrahasis* consistently replaces him with Adad (e.g., SB *Atr* 5:11 // OB *Atr* 2:2:11) implies later adaptation to the expectations of a northwest semitic audience (Lipiński, "Adad," 27–29).

454. *Atr* 1:383 (*katrû*). Moran emphasizes that what Enki proposes is a "bribe," not a "gift" ("Flood," 53–4). For the socioeconomic connotations see the texts cited in *CAD* K:33.

455. *Atr* 1:383 (*bašû*). *Contra* most translations it makes little sense to translate *bašû* as "shame" when the more contextually appropriate *bašû* means "put into storage" (*CAD* B:145–46). OB mentions this term no less than five times (*Atr* 1:383, 398, 410; 2:2:14, 28), but SB consistently omits it, perhaps to avoid misinterpretation.

456. *Atr* 1:383 (*qātu*, lit. "hand"). Roberts notes that "hand" is a metaphor for "plague" in several semitic texts ("Hand," 244–51).

457. To make sense of their bewilderingly diffuse pantheon most Mesopotamians tend to revere only one deity as their "patron deity" (Bottéro, *Religion*, 39–40).

458. A similar dynamic occurs in the Baal Cycle when Baal offers "gifts" to El's consort Athirat (*CAT* 1.4:1:25–35) in the hope that she might turn her powers of persuasion on her husband, who might then remove the stain of contempt (unjustly) laid upon Baal (*CAT* 1.4:2–3). Athirat complies and El agrees to build Baal his own palace (*CAT* i.4:4–5; see Smith and Pitard, *Baal*, 451–527).

Babylonian managers know that bribery is a crime: "If the citizens of Nippur are brought to the king for judgment and he accepts a bribe, [then Enlil is justified in] bringing a foreign army against him."[459] Yet "big problems" often require creative solutions, as anyone who's ever worked in a corporate office can readily attest. Put under pressure, "Enlil"-type executives can often become unreasonable, petty, even vengeful,[460] and mid-level managers who fail to deal with them "appropriately" usually don't keep their jobs very long. Generally it's foolish to confront them directly—i.e., show "contempt" by, say, "blowing the whistle" on their favorite projects ("plague, drought, famine, flood"). Usually it's wiser to find a "side door," particularly when the job on one's desk comes directly from "corporate headquarters" (the divine council).[461]

Far from being a lawcode or a lamentation, *Atrahasis* is an epic poem designed to address a "big problem" threatening the welfare of the Babylonian economy. Like most myths it projects its "solution" to this problem into the Unseen World, where difficult problems like "bribery" and "slavery" can be more safely "handled."[462] Unable to resolve the "freedom-slavery" conflict in the Seen World, no human hero ever shows up, like Moses, to "free the slaves."[463] No Lincoln-esque orator ever delivers an "emancipation proclamation,"[464] no Douglass-esque legislator ever makes a case for "constitutional equality,"[465] and no Jeffersonian statesman ever declares anyone "equal" to anyone else.[466]

---

459. *BWL* 112:11 (*katrû*). The legislative context in which this statute appears goes on to warn that "if he takes the silver of the citizens of Babylon and adds it to his own coffers," then Marduk will "give his property and wealth to his enemy" (*BWL* 112:15; see Prov 31:1–9).

460. Fleming imagines Enlil to be an "arbitrary and merciless character" ("Ur," 17).

461. Sarachek identifies three leadership styles in the *Iliad* ("Leadership," 39–48), each based on a Mesopotamian model: (a) "authoritarian judgment" (Agamemnon/Enlil); (b) "wisdom/craftiness" (Nestor/Enki); and (c) "valor/action" (Achilles/Gilgamesh).

462. Launderville, *Piety*, 40.

463. N.B. that PI-*e*'s rebellion does not succeed (at least not for PI-*e*!).

464. Dirck, *Lincoln*.

465. Blight, *Douglass*.

466. Yet N.B. that Thomas Jefferson "passes the buck" on slavery in an infamous letter to a French correspondent: "We must await with patience the working of an overruling providence, and hope that it is preparing the deliverance of our suffering brethren. When the measure of their tears shall be full, when their groans shall have involved heaven itself in darkness, doubtless a god of justice will awaken to their distress" (O'Brien, *Affair*, 254).

Granted, Anu *does* object to Enlil's original proposal: "What accusation can we bring against the Igigi? The work is too hard, the suffering too much. Every day the earth closes in ... The work is too hard."[467] But to Enki's modification he raises no objections: "When the mothergoddess Belet-ili comes,[468] let her create a 'human being'[469] to carry the soil-basket of the gods. Let her create humankind to carry the yoke, the task imposed by rulership. Let them carry the yoke, the task imposed by Enlil."[470] Paralleling the "task imposed by Enlil" with the "task imposed by rulership," Anu tries to clarify the ambiguity in Enki's modifying proposal,[471] but like bureaucrats everywhere he refuses to take responsibility for actually *resolving* anything. Thus the divine council does nothing until the "noise" of the clay-based creatures grows so loud, it can no longer be ignored. Only when the clay-based creatures start "bellowing like bulls" do the gods re-engage the labor-management dispute they fail to engage earlier in the Igigi Myth.[472]

Interpretation: Atrahasis identifies several problems associated with the "big problem" of slavery, but never does it suggest a practical strategy for dealing with them. Although the Igigi Myth climaxes with Mami's proclamation—"I have destroyed the yoke! I have established *freedom!*"[473]—the "freedom" to which she refers has little in common with the Hebrew law of Jubilee,[474] or the Rousseauian individualism inspiring

467. SB *Atr* 2:63–66, restoring *[id-du-uk]-na-a-at* in line 65 on the basis of the parallels in SB *Atr* 2:35–36.

468. *Belet-ili* ("mistress of the gods) is Mami's title in *Atr* 1:246–47.

469. *Atr* 1:69 (*lullû*). This term signifies the first primeval human (// *amēlu* in *GE* 1:95).

470. SB *Atr* 2:63–74.

471. *Pace* Jacobsen, "Democracy," 167.

472. *Atr* 1:354; 2:3.

473. *Atr* 1:243 (*andurārum*; see *CAD* A/2:115–17). Postgate argues that *andurārum* derives from Sum amar.gi, a term which originally "refers to the liberation of members of a family enslaved for debt" (*Mesopotamia*, 195), but Snell defines *andurārum* from a perspective informed by both administrative and literary texts (*Flight*, 23–9). Kraus thinks that the phrase *andurāram šakānum* ("establish freedom") often simply refers to the creation of mechanisms needed to protect the socioeconomic assets of a given community (*Königliche*, 99–126).

474. Lev 25:10–54 (Lowery, *Sabbath*, 37–56). Lemche doubts whether the Jubilee laws ever find actual historical application ("Manumission," 38–59), but Ollenburger challenges this cynicism (*Jubilee*, 208–34).

the American *Declaration of Independence*.[475] True, the Igigi protest their enslavement, as do the "human beings" who replace them,[476] and true, Mami's proclamation does echo the sentiments embedded in emancipation texts like the Edict of Ammiṣaduqa[477] and the Rosetta Stone.[478] Yet the patrician class of citizens symbolized by the Annunaki is not abolitionist, nor is the *Atrahasis Epic* a forerunner to *The Emancipation Proclamation*.[479] Slavery is simply too embedded in Babylonian culture, and in too many forms:

- persons made slaves by foreign invaders;

- persons captured via piracy and sold as slaves;

- persons born into slavery (i.e., into a slave "class");[480]

- persons made slaves by a loss of livelihood (temporary or permanent);

- persons (usually foreign) made into slaves as prisoners of war.[481]

475. Gourevitch, *Social Contract*. Appleby imagines a "Jeffersonian ideal" in early American thought (*Inheriting*, 1–6), but Hammond thinks Jefferson's definition of "freedom" applies only to other patricians ("Unlimited," 353–54).

476. See *Atr* 1:174–81 (Igigi) and *Atr* 1:376–83 (*amēlūtū*).

477. In the seventeenth century BCE the Babylonian king Ammiṣaduqa issues a *mīšarum*-decree designed to release his subjects from several kinds of tax-induced debt (*CAD* M/2:116–17; *ANET* 526–28; *TDOT* 6:1–7). Hallo illuminates the socioeconomic context of this decree ("Sharecropping," 205–16), and Kraus documents over one hundred examples of manumission decrees from Babylonia, Mari, Assyria, Hana, Elam, Kanesh, and Eshnunna (*Königliche*, 1–126). Otto analyzes the problem of debt-slavery from an ideological perspective ("Soziale," 125–60), but Lemche rejects any and all parallels between *andurārum* (*Atr* 1:243) and דרור (Lev 25:10; "*Andurārum*," 11–22).

478. Ptolemy V's decree on this *narû*-stele repeals several kinds of taxes (Solé and Valbelle, *Rosetta*).

479. Lincoln, *Emancipation*.

480. Starr denies the existence of "solid evidence for the common view that industry and commerce . . . rested on the backs of slaves" ("Overdose," 21), but Chirichigno (*Debt-Slavery*) divides ancient Mesopotamian society into three classes: (a) free citizens, (b) semi-free citizens, and (c) chattel slaves (see Gelb, "Serfdom," 195–207; Dandamaev, *Slavery*). Patterson defines "slavery" as a socioeconomic institution in which "slaveholders" use "slaves" to gain "the very direct satisfaction of power over another." Thus, a "slave" is a person who is "degraded and reduced to a state of liminality" (*Slavery*, 337).

481. Gelb, "Freedom," 84–85. Gelb insists that "the evidence concerning the foreign derivation of POWs, both in early Mesopotamia and elsewhere in ancient times, is so overwhelming as to allow the conclusion that the ethnic factor . . . must have operated with the same force in respect to the permanent enslavement of native POWs" ("Prisoners," 95).

Atrahasis is one bureaucrat's attempt to address what economist Karl Polanyi calls "the great problems of the human race—freedom and centralization, initiative and planning."[482] Granted, it focuses on "anthropology and social forms ... (more) than any other Babylonian epic,"[483] but never does it champion the kind of autonomous freedom to which (post)modern Westerners often feel entitled.[484] Why? Because "nowhere in the vast literature of the Sumero-Akkadian world is a protest raised against the institution of slavery, nor is there anywhere an expression of the mildest sympathy for the victims of this system. Slavery is simply taken for granted."[485]

Historically speaking, the conflicts symbolized in this "great text" go back to the Ur III period,[486] including (but not limited to) the well-documented skirmishes between "resident Sumerians" and "immigrant Akkadians."[487] Like all myths it uses mythopoeic metaphors to symbolize these conflicts,[488] but even though an earlier academic age oversimplifies them ("bourgeoisie vs. proletariat";[489] "Sumerian vs. Semite"[490]) there's

482. Polanyi, *Livelihood*, xli.

483. Lambert and Millard, *Atra-Hasis*, 21.

484. Many historians think, by the way, that "the precise nature of the internal constraint on freedom is not terribly clear in the works of Rousseau, Jefferson, or de Tocqueville," and that this imprecision affirms the thesis "that Jefferson's praise of the farmer reflects his own position as landed gentry" (Schmitt, *Alienation*, 120).

485. Mendelsohn, *Slavery*, 123. Like Chirichigno (*Debt Slavery*), Dandamaev distinguishes between three socioeconomic classes in the ancient world: (a) property owners not engaged in productive labor; (b) property owners engaged in productive labor, but not exploiting the labor of others; and (c) non-property-owning compulsory laborers (*Slavery*, 1–23). Postgate calls for a more nuanced understanding of ancient Near Eastern sociology (*Mesopotamia*, 108).

486. Centralizing power through the creation of the first "bureaucratic state," Ur-Nammu establishes the third Dynasty of Ur (2060–1950 BCE; see Moran, "Mesopotamia," 528).

487. Von Soden ("Götter," 429) comes to this conclusion from a study of the primary texts collected and transcribed by Edzard (*Zwischenzeit*, 30–49). Still, while it's true that early release-decrees like the Edict of Ammisaduqa clearly distinguish between "Akkadians" and "Amorites" (*ANET* 526–28), Jacobsen plays down the racial/ethnic factors in a study published at the height of the Nazi regime ("Assumed," 485–95).

488. Komoróczy, "Work," 35–37.

489. Jaruzelska, for example, still clings to polarized Marxist categories (*Amos*, 20–21).

490. Cooper warns that "Akkadian participation in the production of the earliest known Sumerian literary texts should make scholars wary about talking in terms of 'Sumerian' vs. 'Akkadian'" (Review of *Menschenbild*, 583).

no denying the historical kernel blossoming at the center.[491] In short, this epic poem (a) attends to the managerial requirements necessary for sustaining the health of Babylon's riverine economy, (b) reflects on the complex ways in which this economy depends on slave labor, and (c) vocalizes a desire for labor-management harmony in view of this dependency.[492]

Herodotus describes Babylon as "the most powerful city of the known world,"[493] praising its canal-networks as an engineering feat no less remarkable than the pyramids of Egypt.[494] Yet, to summarize this discussion via a sorites,[495] Babylon (a) cannot maintain its standard of living without cities; (b) cannot sustain these cities without food; (c) cannot grow this food without irrigation; (d) cannot provide this irrigation without canals; (e) cannot maintain these canals without "hard labor"; and (f) cannot provide this "hard labor" without slaves. Supported by both public[496] and private funds,[497] Babylonian citizen-managers therefore need to learn how to deal with "Igigi-rebellions" of all shapes and sizes, and the *Atrahasis Epic* contributes to their education by showing them how to recognize and distinguish two very different management styles: "Enki" vs. "Enlil."[498]

491. Bottéro, "Désordre," 113–67; van Dyck, "Insurrection," 1–25.

492. Yoffee, "Political," 290; Snell, *Flight*, 63–98; Edzard, *Zwischenzeit*, 30–49; Diakonoff, "Socio-Economic Classes," 41–52; Eyre, "Agricultural Cycle," 176.

493. Herodotus, *Hist.* 1:178.

494. Yoffee downplays ("Political," 282), but Butzer highlights the salinization problems constantly challenging this riverine economy ("Environmental," 144–45).

495. A sorites is "a series of propositions in which the predicate of each is the subject of the next, the conclusion being formed of the first subject and the last predicate" (*OED*, s.v. "sorites"; from σωρεύω, "heap one thing on another," *LSJ* 1750).

496. As Sterba puts it, "the common laborer is forced by economic circumstances to concentrate upon fulfilling personal and family survival and security needs. To such a person the opportunity to farm a plot of the temple's land and to share in the fringe benefits which temple employment provides must surely be most welcome" ("Organization," 24).

497. Most of the extant primary evidence attests the power of private family-owned businesses in the neo-Babylonian period (see Stolper, *Entrepreneurs*), but Archi documents centralized businesses operating as early as the 3rd millennium ("Debt," 95–108).

498. Wiggerman's assessment is harsh, but accurate: the figure of Enlil symbolizes a managerial class which "cares little for what happens to human beings and is prepared to destroy them, even for minor offenses" ("Theologies," 1861).

Intertextually, of course, it's difficult to examine Enki's bribery-strategy in *Atrahasis* apart from Ishtar's bribery-strategy in *Gilgamesh*. Where Ishtar tries to bribe Gilgamesh into abandoning "wisdom," however, Enki proposes bribery only as a last-resort for dealing with the "Enlils" of the world.[499] Where *Gilgamesh* describes bribery as an indicator of hedonistic corruption, *Atrahasis* delicately affirms it, under limited conditions, as a necessary evil.[500] Less polyphonic than *Gilgamesh*,[501] it nevertheless engages this "big problem" from two angles. Like the Hebrew Bible it recognizes that *contempt* constantly threatens the health of labor-management relations,[502] but also like the Hebrew Bible it recognizes that rebellion is sometimes the only way to respond to the "Enlils" of the world.[503]

In short, *Atrahasis* uses "common human language to express unwelcome contradictions."[504] Attending to the "bigness" of the labor-management problem always threatening the Babylonian economy, it tries to explain not just *why* things are the way they are, but why things ought to *stay* that way. Working with definitions of "freedom" centuries removed from Rousseau, it focuses on the practical needs of citizen-managers in charge of maintaining the canal networks connecting the city-states of Nippur, Uruk, Umma, Kish, Susianna, Lagash, and the Dialaya Basin.[505]

---

499. This strategy looks very different from, say, the *responsibility-risk-reason* strategy conveyed by the Abigail story (1 Sam 25; Moore, *Reconciliation*, 23–34).

500. Parallel examples appear in Gen 38, Josh 2, Esth 5–7. Howard explains Rahab's deception of her neighbors as a last resort (*Joshua*, 106–12), much the same way that Bonhoeffer explains his reasons for deciding to assassinate Hitler (Bethge, *Bonhoeffer*, 358; Adler, "Lying," 435–52.

501. Bakhtin, *Dostoevsky*, 1–7; Newsom, *Job*, 20–22.

502. In 1 Kgs 9:10–28, e.g., the narrator asserts that Solomon never imposes "forced labor" (מס) on native-born Israelites, but many see this as special pleading (Moore, *Faith*, 200).

503. See Exod 1–15 and Burkert, *Structure*, 16–22. Collins points out that for all the Bible's diversity, "no biblical author reads the Exodus story from the perspective of Pharaoh" ("Exodus," 261).

504. Welbourn, Review of *Totemism*, 233.

505. Komoróczy, "Work," 35–37. The letters of Paul in the GNT walk a similar tightrope in that they simultaneously (a) condemn slavery (Gal 3:29) and (b) encourage slaves to be submissive (Col 3:22). Snell concludes from this tension that "Paul is supportive of kind treatment of runaway slaves, but certainly does not see the freedom of slaves as a value" (*Flight*, 145).

Celebrating the "rational liberty" embedded in the *idea* of freedom,[506] it nevertheless concedes slavery to be a socioeconomic institution necessary for survival.

Like all "great literature," *Atrahasis* addresses issues in "the human world, and within it the peculiar reflection of given social relations."[507] What this means socioeconomically is that its greatest impact lies not in the way the *gods* treat each other, but in the way the poem's heavenly relationships intentionally mirror earthly relationships.[508] Where *Gilgamesh* criticizes the problem of corruption in these relationships, *Atrahasis* affirms the "balance" in the "present order of things."[509] Like *Gilgamesh* it uses role reversal and shadow archetype to illustrate this "balance," but never does it challenge it. Instead, where the lesser gods in the Sumerian myth of *Enki and Ninmah* blame Enki for their slavery, the Igigi in the Babylonian myth of *Atrahasis* shift the blame to another, more convenient "target"—the Sumerian chthonic deity Enlil.[510] In this way *Atrahasis* (a) preserves many of the cosmogonic motifs already operating within the Mesopotamian literary tradition,[511] (b) re-applies them to socioeconomic conflicts plaguing second-millenium Babylonia, and (c) makes Marduk's rival pay the freight.[512]

THE EPIC OF ERRA

Less polyphonic than *Gilgamesh,* yet more verbose than *Atrahasis,* the *Epic of Erra* rivals both poems in its use of mythopoeic metaphor.[513] One

---

506. Cuthbertson uses this epithet to describe the universal longing animating both "democratic" and "totalitarian" mythologies (*Political,* 211).

507. Komoróczy, "Work," 37.

508. Walton, *Ancient,* 43.

509. Moran, "Flood," 57. Balentine understands *Atrahasis* to be a scribal construal of "the way the world works, and . . . how human beings may understand and order their lives in this world" ("Reason," 352–53).

510. Kramer and Maier, *Enki,* 13–14, 31–37, 124, 132–33, 176.

511. Batto, *Dragon,* 1–14; Greengus, "Legal," 469–72.

512. Sommerfeld, *Aufstieg,* 167–72; Jacobsen, *Harps,* 154; Komoróczy, "Work," 18–27. Following the lead of van Dyck ("Motif," 1–59), Clifford explains these literary shifts as the result of irresolvable conflicts between the scribes in Eridu (home of Enki's temple) and the scribes in Nippur (home of Enlil's temple (*Creation,* 15–16).

513. Dalley, *Myths,* 285–312; Foster, *Muses,* 881–911. Cagni publishes a transliterated Akkadian text (*L'Epopea*), and newer fragments of tablet 2 are published by al-Rawi and Black ("Erra," 111–22).

of the most popular of the Akkadian epics,[514] its most complete version comes from the hand of a "composer"[515] named Kabti-ilāni-marduk, a scribe who claims to have received it miraculously through a nocturnal vision.[516] Like Ares in Greece and Durgā in India,[517] the Babylonian deity named Erra symbolizes the deification of violence in a world where "hostile forces are active and must be kept at bay."[518] Geopolitically isolated Westerners often misconstrue this world, but "many religions contain rituals, stories, and representations that are directly violent. The pantheon of a polytheistic religion usually contains one or more violent divinities ... often connected with the irrational violence of warfare, such as Ares in Greece or Erra in Mesopotamia ... These divinities define a world in which war is a bitter necessity."[519] *Erra* not only addresses the needs of a world threatened by "wars, floods, famines"[520] and "the instigating spirit of riot and rebellion,"[521] it also tries to engage the needs of a fragile Babylonian economy struggling to survive the depredations of a "dying social order" deeply disturbed by "evil and confusion."[522]

While its historical context cannot be pinpointed with precision, internal evidence leads many to associate the conflicts in this poem with the conflicts perpetrated by Aramean invaders attacking the northern borders of the Babylonian empire.[523] Others link it to a plague afflicting the city of Uruk,[524] but since tablets 4 and 5 overtly mention a group of

---

514. Machinist, "Erra," 221. Postgate notes the widespread use of *Erra* on amulets and other paraphernalia (Review of *Ezekiel*, 137).

515. *Erra* 5:42 (*kāṣir*). Bodi translates this term as "composer" (*Ezekiel*, 57).

516. *Erra* 5:43. N.B. the Hebrew parallels in Exod 25:9; Num 8:4; 1 Chron 28:19. Oppenheim believes that documents like *Erra* often claim an "authenticity faithfully reflecting a prototype in heaven" (*Dreams*, 193, 225).

517. Higgins, "Double-Dealing," 24–35; Santiko, "Durgā," 209–26.

518. Graf, "Violence," 9598.

519. Ibid., 9597.

520. Bailkey, "Babylonian," 108.

521. Roberts, "Erra," 15. The protagonist of this poem has two names: "Erra" (*Erra* 1:4) and "Nergal" (5:38). Nergal rules the netherworld in myths like *Nergal and Ereshkigal* (Dalley, *Myths*, 165–81; Foster, *Muses*, 509–23; Hutter, *Unterwelt*), and possesses a "Janus-like" ability to create as well as destroy (Bailkey, "Babylonian," 129).

522. Bailkey, "Babylonian," 111.

523. Cagni, *Poem*, 57; Hallo, "Gutium," 717.

524. Von Soden, "Etemenanki," 256.

Aramean invaders known as the "Suteans"[525]—liminal groups of tribes-men known to be hostile to Babylonian rule during the reign of Nabû-apal-iddina (d. 855 BCE)[526]—most interpreters view it as "a theological myth describing the divine machinery behind the Sutean invasions into Babylonia."[527]

Whatever the possibilities, *Erra* narrates the story of an angry warrior-god determined to address a national crisis via a management style quite different from the one promoted in *Atrahasis*.[528] That is, where *Atrahasis* attempts to alert Babylonian citizen-managers to the advantages of choosing "Enki" over "Enlil," *Erra* pits Erra against the "black-headed people" and their national god Marduk, the deity who eventually replaces Enlil as the center of Babylonian life and culture.[529] More to the socioeconomic point, just as *Gilgamesh* structures itself upon a "civilization-vs.-wilderness" polarity, so *Erra* structures itself upon a "city-dweller-vs.-field-dweller" polarity,[530] a polarity introduced by the opening speech of the Sibitti:[531]

> Why are you lounging in the city like a feeble old man? Why are you resting in the house like a helpless little baby? Shall we eat women's food like those who refuse to go into the field? Shall we tremble and quake like those who know nothing of battle?[532] The youth marching in the field is like a man going up to a feast. The prince who stays in the city never has enough food, [but instead turns to] vomit[533] in the mouth of his people, his head

525. *Erra* 4:54, 69, 133; 5:27. Artzi documents the activity of these tribal groups in the Amarna correspondence ("Unrecognized," 163–71).

526. Lambert, Review of *Erra*, 400.

527. Brinkman, *Political History*, 322.

528. Cagni, *L'Epopea*, 58–129; *Poem*, 26–61; Dalley, *Myths*, 285–312; Machinist, "Rest," 221–26.

529. Sommerfeld, *Aufstieg*; Frymer-Kensky, "Marduk."

530. *Erra* 1:55–56 contrasts *ša ašib āli* ("he that dwells in the city") with *ša akil šēri* ("he that goes into the field").

531. Sibitti (Akk "seven") refers to the gang-of-seven demons in Erra's entourage, a chthonic motif with traceable echoes in Hebrew texts (Ps 78:42–49; Job 5:19–23; see Moore, "Terror," 662–75).

532. The Sibitti contrast "having tea with the ladies" with military unpreparedness, *not* misogyny (see *CAD* S:289; Bergmann, "Warriors," 651–72).

533. *Erra* 1:53 (*šumsuk*). Von Soden (*AHw* 2:752) plausibly argues that *šumsuk* derives from the š-form of *nasāku* ("to repel, throw out"), and given the parallel with *qalālu* here, "vomit" seems the best English equivalent.

"despised."[534] How can such a person do battle against a "field-dweller?"[535] Though the strength of the "city-dweller" be great,[536] how can he prevail against the "field-dweller?" City food, however fancy, cannot compare to food cooked over the campfire. Aged beer, however sweet, cannot compare to pure water from the canteen, nor can terraced palace compare to the shepherd's tent. Warrior Erra! Go into the field![537]

Obviously written from a "field-dweller" perspective, this speech lays out several antitheses. City-dwellers eat; field-dwellers fight. City-dwellers lounge; field-dwellers march. City-dwellers age; field-dwellers rejuvenate. City-dwellers grow feeble; field-dwellers grow powerful. City-dwellers act like women; field-dwellers act like men.[538] *Conclusion:* Life in the city, with its fancy imported beer and dainty food, is profoundly inferior to life "in the field"—at least to "field-dwellers."

From here it is but a short step to the conclusion that "field-dwellers" are inherently *superior* to "city-dwellers." Where *Gilgamesh* begins with a hunter/trapper complaining to the king about a "wild man,"[539] *Erra* begins with a whole *gang* of "wild men" (the Sibitti) complaining to *their* king (Erra). Where *Atrahasis* begins with a gang of Igigi-gods marching on Enlil's palace,[540] *Erra* begins with a gang of Sibitti-demons determined to bathe themselves in the blood of anyone they even *imagine* treating them with "contempt":

Warrior Erra! Why do you leave the "field" to settle down in the "city?"[541] Šakkan's herds and the wild beasts hold us in "contempt!"[542] Warrior Erra! We must tell you something, though our speech may upset you. You should listen to our words before the

534. *Erra* 1:53 (*qalālu*, lit., "to make light of"). Just as the Sibitti lament the "despising" of Erra, so Esau laments the "despising" of his birthright (בזה, Gen 25:34).

535. *Erra* 1:54 (*alik ṣēri*). This epithet occurs in *Erra* 1:49, 51, 54, 56.

536. *Erra* 1:55 (*ašib āli*). This epithet occurs in *Erra* 1:47, 48, 52, 55.

537. *Erra* 1:47–60.

538. Bergmann, "Warriors," 651–72.

539. *GE* 1:157–60.

540. *Atr* 1:41.

541. *Erra* 1:76 (*ṣēru . . . ālu*).

542. *Erra* 1:77 (*šiṭutum*; Šakkan is the god of herds and flocks). N.B. how the wild beasts hold Enkidu in "contempt" after becoming "civilized" by human contact (*GE* 1:196–98).

land turns against us forever![543] Pay homage to the Annunaki [who love deathly silence]! Sleep abandons the Annunaki because of the "noise of men."[544] Beasts wander onto the threshing-floors, the very life of the land! The farmer weeps bitterly ... The lion and the wolf attack his livestock.[545]

The Sibitti fear what all warriors fear; viz., that the war will be over before they can get into it.[546] More than this, they fear that Erra's toleration of the "city-dwellers" may lead to *all* "field-dwellers" being treated with "contempt."

Apparently the speech works because immediately after hearing it Erra jumps out of bed, agitated and angry and ready for a fight. The violence of his response, however, so alarms his vizier-assistant Ishum, he immediately voices the following questions: "Lord Erra! Why do you plot against the gods? Why do you plot to devastate the lands and destroy (the people)? Are you not plotting against your own future?"[547] Like the vizier of Enlil in *Atrahasis* (Nusku), Ishum enacts several roles within the "cautious adviser" role-set—roles like "respectful critic," "lonely whistle-blower," and "moral conscience." Kabti-ilāni-marduk allots more lines to Ishum than the poet of *Atrahasis* allots to Nusku, but this may be due simply to the wordiness of his style.[548]

At any rate, Erra responds to Ishum's questions with a compelling case for war, championing it as an appropriate, legitimate, last-response to the "big problem" of "contempt."[549] For Erra and the Sibitti (and the military hawks they symbolize) field-dwellers can put up with a lot of things, but not "contempt." Why? Because contempt can turn friendly al-

543. *Erra* 1:79–80. Just as "chaotic noise" threatens to come "over you" (*ḫu-bur-ši-na . . . eli-ka*) in *Erra* 1:41, so the land threatens to grow "over us" (*ir-bu-ú eli-ni*) in *Erra* 1:79–80. Both lines refer to the persistent fear that the *amēlūtu* are too powerful to control (the same fear expressed in *Atr* 1:355 and Exod 1:9).

544. *Erra* 1:82 (*ḫubur nišī*; see *Erra* 1:41 and *CAD* Ḥ:220–21).

545. *Erra* 1:76–85. "Predator" metaphors occur twice in *Erra* (1:85 and 3:15).

546. Keeley explores several "warrior tales" from an anthropological perspective (*War*), and Resic explores their mythological roots (*Warriors*).

547. *Erra* 1:102. Compare Nusku's parallel warning to Enlil (*Atr* 1:102, discussed above).

548. Roberts explores the roles enacted by ancient Near Eastern deities generally (*Pantheon*, 12–56). On the usefulness of role theory for understanding ancient Near Eastern characters and behavior see Moore, *Balaam*, 1–19.

549. See *Erra* 1:119–20 (*šitutum*) and Bodi, *Ezekiel*, 69–81. Scheff emphasizes the "extreme sensitivity" many feel toward "the amount of deference they are accorded," and how "even slight discrepancies generate shame or embarrassment" ("Shame," 97).

lies into restless enemies, loyal friends into subversive conspirators, "new order" progressives into "old order" reactionaries.[550] Therefore, just as the gods punish Gilgamesh for violating the boundaries of the Cedar Forest, so Erra punishes the black-headed people for the "sin" of "contempt."[551]

Ishum is careful not to question Erra's right, as a netherworld ruler, to mete out divine punishment, only whether he has the wisdom to do it appropriately. He fears that Erra's outrage, once released, will do irrevocable harm to an already fragile cosmos (read: "tottering old-order economy"). He specifically wonders whether his master's management style can deliver what the Babylonian economy needs to rebuild a "new order."[552] All this may sound strange to postmodern Western consumers, idyllically privileged to enjoy the "good life" at the top of the global economic pyramid.[553] But this kind of conflict challenges every economy in which *tribal confederacy* proponents ("field-dwellers") institutionally clash and conflict with the proponents of *centralized monarchy* ("city-dwellers").[554]

Eventually Erra approaches Marduk for help, convincing him to evacuate the throne long enough to have his image refurbished.[555] Erra's

550. Bailkey, "Babylonian," 125; Heinz and Feldman, *Representations*.

551. Cagni convincingly shows that the "sin" in *Erra* 5:6 (*ḫiṭu*) directly parallels the "contempt" (*šitutum*) in *Erra* 1:120 (*L'Epopea*, 248).

552. Bailkey, "Babylonian," 125.

553. Gills insists that the present "paradigm of international relations, with its enduring feature of governance by a few great powers based on their ability to use military force" is morally, politically, and economically bankrupt ("Democratizing," 159), yet this remains a dangerous opinion, especially in G8 countries.

554. Flanagan, "Chiefs," 47–73. Euro-American economies are culturally conditioned to think in terms of sin-guilt, yet as Nye points out ("Honor," 103), honor-shame economies operate on the basis of "different sentiments . . . about action (or inaction) in particular instances relating to kin, marriage, wealth, military reputation, and precedence"—actions in which "shame is not so much the opposite of honor as its lack." To illustrate, Zuhur points out that "ancient and modern Arabs . . . adopt ideas of honor that reinforce the ties of an individual to his or her tribal clan or extended family. One type of honor, شريف (*sharif*), applies to men and is attained through maintenance of a family's reputation, hospitality, generosity, chivalry, bravery, piety, and, sometimes, nobility or political power. Another type, عرض (*'ird*), pertains to women, or more specifically, to the sexual use of their bodies, their virginity, or their chaste behavior" ("Honor," 1011). Hosseini illustrates this dynamic in his best-selling novel, *The Kite Runner*.

555. Mesopotamian priesthoods follow very elaborate rituals for refurbishing the statues of deities (Walker and Dick, *Induction* 4–31).

request makes Ishum wonder, however, whether his deeper intention might be to seize back his power. Like Ninsun, who doubts whether Gilgamesh *truly* plans to "slay evil," Ishum doubts whether Erra *truly* plans to help Marduk.[556] Marduk, meanwhile, worries that any plan involving evacuation from the throne—however temporary—might trigger a catastrophe. Erra reassures him otherwise, but this does little to allay his fears:

> Once, long ago, I [Marduk] grew extremely angry—I even left my temple to send down the Flood![557] When I left my temple the "vortex" of heaven and earth collapsed.[558] The collapse of heaven led to the positions of the stars changing; I could not re-align them.[559] The collapse of the earth led to a diminishing of the harvest, making it more difficult to farm the land.[560] The disintegration of heaven and earth led to the underground water receding and the surface water evaporating.[561] The productivity of all living things declined. I could not stop it, even though, like a farmer, I held all the seed in my hand![562]

556. *GE* 3:54. Miller creates a contemporary parallel in *The Crucible*, the play in which the witch-hunts of seventeenth century Massachusetts become a "safe lens" through which to criticize the twentieth century witch-hunts led by Joseph McCarthy and other progenitors of the Big Red Scare (Ackerman, *Hoover*; Blauner, *McCarthyism*).

557. The Chaldeans' rise to power in the late second millenium leads to a transformation of all the old myths as the Marduk priesthood reassigns the leadership roles enacted by Enlil/Erra/Nergal and Enki to Marduk and his advisors (Sommerfeld, *Aufstieg*; Foster, *Muses*, 880–81).

558. *Erra* 1:134 (*šiptu*). This term means "judgment, verdict" in judicial contexts, but like its Heb cognate (שׁפט) it can denote socioeconomic as well as legal/military "judgment." Thus "vortex" seems a better translation than "regulation" (*pace* Foster, *Muses*, 887).

559. In Babylonian thought astronomical bodies exercise great influence over earthly events, and since their constant movement in the night sky makes the yearly floods hard to predict, this generates great uncertainty about the future (Bottéro, *Everyday*, 183–98).

560. Note here the link between astronomical and agrarian reality. Where the reason for the land's infertility in *Genesis* is human sin (Gen 3:17–19), the reason for the land's infertility in *Erra* is the collapse of divine power.

561. Clifford traces most of the Babylonian "water" traditions to Sumerian myths about Enki (*Creation*, 16).

562. *Erra* 1:32–38. Kabti-ilāni-marduk's use of socioeconomic metaphors to describe the Flood goes well beyond the metaphorical descriptions in *Atrahasis* and *Gilgamesh* (not to mention *Genesis*).

Concerned about what his absence might do to the stability of the "universe" (read: "tottering old-order economy"), Marduk worries that "the (waters) will 'rise up' and sweep over the land! Bright day will turn to darkness! Whirlwind will rise and heaven's stars will be [scattered]! Ill winds will blow and the eyes of all living creatures [will dim]! Demons will 'rise up' and seize [their prey]! They will [terrorize] the unarmed who confront them! The Annunaki will 'rise up' and strike down all living creatures! Who will keep them at bay while I put on my weaponry?"[563] To this worst-case scenario, however, Erra reassures Marduk that "while you are gone I will keep the vortex of heaven and earth intact. I will ascend to heaven and instruct the Igigi-gods; I will descend to the depths and manage the Annunaki. I will dispatch the wild demons to the netherworld ... At the house you plan to enter,[564] O noble Marduk, I will station Anu and Enlil to the right and left, like bulls."[565]

However, Ishum's suspicions about Erra, like Ninsun's about Gilgamesh and Nusku's about Enlil, soon prove to be horrifyingly correct. As soon as Marduk evacuates the throne the cosmos starts convulsing, and Erra can do nothing to stop it. Enter Enki. Outflanking Erra the same way he outflanks Enlil,[566] Enki (a) takes command of the situation, (b) puts Marduk back on his throne, and (c) dismisses Erra without so much as a "thank you."[567] Saving the Babylonian economy from catastrophe, he nevertheless does it in a way that humiliates Erra in front of his divine peers. Ashamed and embarrassed, Erra then slinks back down to his netherworld throne, bitter and angry and fully convinced that his divine colleagues now hold him in as much "contempt" as do the black-headed people. Reflecting on all this in a Hamlet-like soliloquy,[568] he

563. *Erra* 1:127–28, 140–62, 171–78. Note the three-fold repetition of the verb *êlu* ("to rise up") as Kabti-ilāni-marduk connects the "rising up" of the floodwaters with the "rising up" of the demonic hordes. Note also Ishtar's threat to unlock the gates of the netherworld so that *its* imprisoned spirits might "rise up" (*GE* 6:97–100).

564. This refers to the workhouse to which priestly craftsmen retire to refurbish the statues of their deities.

565. *Erra* 1:182–89. Erra brags that he has the power to turn "old order" deities like Anu and Enlil into frozen gargoyles like those regularly posted on the heads of city gates. Edzard aptly describes this description of Marduk as "parody" ("Irra," 166–70).

566. *Atr* 1:207–14.

567. This parallels the occasion in Canaanite myth in which Athtar seizes Baal's throne, but because he cannot perform Baal's job (generate rain), he, too, is summarily dismissed (*CAT* 1.6:1:53–67).

568. Reading tablet 2 with al-Rawi and Black ("Second," 119–20).

talks to his "heart," which immediately urges him to seek revenge against his enemies:

> He [Erra] took counsel with himself on this matter, his heart stung, unable to give him an answer for what he asked,[569] [yet responding,] "Lead the way, Begin the campaign . . . He who waxed great in days of plenty, Let them bury on a day of drought!' . . . I will lay waste to cities and turn them into open spaces! . . . I will destroy humankind; I will leave no creature alive! Nor will I retain anyone [to provide] seed for . . . the land . . .[570] I will cut off the clamor of humankind . . . and rob them of happiness . . . I will confiscate [their] households and cut their lives short . . . I will stir up the robber and cut off all travel. People will rifle the possessions of others right in the heart of the city. Lion and wolf will attack the livestock . . . I will banish the work-song of harvest from the fields. Both shepherd and herdsman will forget their corrals."[571]

Furious with everyone now—gods, humans, beasts, demonic hordes—Erra's wrath explodes so violently, Ishum begs for calm in language practically identical to Nusku's plea:[572] "Why have you plotted evil against god and humanity? Why have you plotted evil against the people of this land?"[573] When Erra responds to these questions he does so via a speech much like Gilgamesh's rebuttal-speech to Ishtar, pointedly warning Ishum not to worry too much about the black-headed people. Why? Because (a) they're too ignorant to understand what's going on, and (b) Marduk has already ceded them over to his control.[574]

Yet Ishum does not back down. Demanding that Erra consider the long-term consequences of his behavior, he massages his master's ego, trying to convince him that he has nothing left to prove:

---

569. Just as Erra's "heart" (*libbu*) provokes him into taking desperate action, so the "heart/inner spirit" (Ug. *ggn*) of Yaṣṣib provokes *him* into taking desperate action (*CAT* 1.16:6:26).

570. It's one thing to destroy crops; it's quite another to destroy all the seed for future crops.

571. *Erra* 2C9/37'–3:19.

572. *Atr* 1:93–96. Abigail's speech similarly attempts to restrain David (1 Sam 25:23–31; Moore, *Reconciliation*, 31–33).

573. *Erra* 3:36–38.

574. *Erra* 3C:45–55; Gilgamesh's rebuttal-speech appears in *GE* 6:33–79.

> Warrior Erra! you hold the "nose-rope" of heaven![575] You are master of all the netherworld, lord of the land ... [though you say to yourself, "They hold me in contempt."] When the troops see you they gird on their weapons. The heart of the governor—the avenger of Babylon—turns to fury. He commands his army to plunder their enemies, [saying] ... "Plunder Babylon's enormous wealth!" When the great lord Marduk saw this he cried "Woe!" and his heart melted, [saying,] "Alas for Babylon, which I filled with seed, like an evergreen, but of whose delights I cannot reap what I've sown! Alas for Babylon, which I tended like a thriving orchard, but whose fruit I cannot taste!"[576]

At first blush Ishum appears to be wasting his time. The "old order" is collapsing and the Sibitti are mopping up the detritus of the remains, destroying every recalcitrant resistor. Why? Because Erra's "heart" thinks it's more important to revenge than redeem; more important to punish than show mercy; more important to look for scapegoats than learn the discipline of self-sacrifice.[577] Yet just as Phineas stops a plague with a spear,[578] so Ishum stops a war with a speech, successfully persuading his master to stop what he is doing and think things through. Finally, as the dust settles, Erra's colleagues begin to listen to his proposals for a new economic order: "Let the people of the country, who have dwindled, become numerous again ... Let the gods of livestock and grain descend to the land. Let the mountain deliver its yield, the sea its produce. Let the ruined fields deliver their harvest ... And let abundance accumulate in the sanctuary of the deity who honors this poem."[579]

575. *Erra* 3D:3 (*ṣeretu*). This term denotes the rope inserted into the camel's nose-ring to make it go where its rider directs.

576. *Erra* 3D3—4:42. N.B. the interesting parallel between Marduk's "fruit-tasting" and Ishtar's "fruit-tasting" (*GE* 6:7).

577. Erra's behavior looks very much like Ishtar's (*GE* 6:97–100).

578. Num 25:8.

579. *Erra* 5:24–60. Bailkey sees in the character of Erra a symbol in which "the true nature and purpose of the destructive work of Erra-Nergal" is bound up with "the fact that change and progress are essential characteristics of human history ... Rejecting the established prelogical belief in the estrangement of the gods as the cause of decline, a view which modern scholars have taken to be the poem's theme, Kabti-ilāni-marduk substitutes the advanced concept of change as the product of the forces of benevolent destruction." For Bailkey, *Erra* intentionally promotes a three-stage socioeconomic program: (a) destruction of the corrupt old order with its "seemingly permanent set of values and institutions"; (b) engagement in a period of uncertainty where "the old order of things collapses, leaving society uprooted and men unbelieving," finally leading up to (c) "a new age of piety and order and renewal of humanity's creative powers" ("Babylonian," 125–29).

SUMMARY

These three "great texts" representatively articulate some of the most deeply embedded socioeconomic conflict motifs in Mesopotamian literature, covertly, yet determinedly addressing what economist Karl Polanyi calls the "big problems of the human race."[580] *Gilgamesh* addresses the "big problem" of corruption using standardized symbolic language designed to indicate that whenever "arrogance" and "hedonism" are allowed too much power, "wisdom" is the best way (if not the only way) to restore the economy back to health.[581] *Atrahasis* suggests that the best way to deal with the "big problem" of management-labor relations is to "fight fire with fire"; i.e., use "bribery" when necessary as a "last resort" to restore the economy back to health. *Erra* intensifies this strategy by focusing on the "big problem" of "contempt" as the single greatest threat to stagnant economies threatened by the failed policies and failed values of intractable "old orders."[582]

Question: What socioeconomic conflict motifs do the Hebrews manipulate in *their* "great texts" in their attempt to address *their* "big problems?"

---

580. Polanyi, *Livelihood*, xli.

581. Denning-Bolle thus correctly points out that "in Mesopotamia, the relationship between dialogue and wisdom is continuously renewed" (*Wisdom*, 188).

582. Like *Erra*, the final chapters of *Genesis* describe an economy characterized by "self-promotion, jealousy, and revenge," but which eventually changes into an economy characterized by "change and reorientation" (Oosthuizen, Review of *Genesis*).

3

Socioeconomic Conflict Motifs in the Hebrew Bible

CONTEMPORARY INTERPRETATION OF THE Hebrew Bible suffers two extremes. On one end of the interpretive spectrum, readers dissect this ancient Near Eastern library into thousands of atomized parts, dismissing the literary framework in which they operate and marginalizing the "great literature" against which they take shape.[1] Some view these "great texts" as little more than political propaganda created by homeless exiles desperate to redefine themselves through a process of selective memory.[2] Others view it as religious propaganda purposefully designed to promote a narrow political ideology.[3]

1. See, for example, the European introductions of Eissfeldt (*Old Testament*); Fohrer (*Old Testament*), and Kratz (*Komposition*). Since the primary influence behind these introductions is Julius Wellhausen—whose impact on contemporary biblical studies cannot be overemphasized—each tends to rely more or less on (a) a rigid preoccupation with origins; (b) a general tendency to ignore critical Jewish scholarship (inherited from the blatant anti-Semitism embedded in nineteenth-century academic circles (Cuffari prefers the term "anti-Judaic," *Judenfeindschaft*, 21–55); and (c) a simplistic tendency toward tripartite periodization—"nature religion » prophetism » Judaism" (Wellhausen, *Prolegomena*, 125–74; Blenkinsopp, *Pentateuch*, 1–12). British and American scholars often dismiss what they perceive to be European obsession with these issues, but sometimes through overreaction (e.g., Alter, *Narrative*, 13).

2. Smith believes the Hebrew Bible to be selective memory, not history (*Memoirs*, 126–64), and Whitelam argues (*Invention*), in the spirit of Said (*Culture*, 15–19), that the Bible's ultimate goal is to "silence" Palestinian history.

3. The ideology in question, of course, is monotheistic Yahwism, regarding which Koch comments: "The worship of the One God developed in the Hebrew Bible and raised to the status of an ethical postulate has in the past few decades run into strong opposition in intellectual circles. The ghost of an immutable 'Old Testament' God has been exorcised; diffident colleagues now speak of an 'intolerant monotheism.' The current international situation, conditioned by constant encounters between individuals

Populist readers gravitate to the other end of the spectrum, imagining the Bible to be a "holy book" written by "holy authors" living inside a "holy bubble."[4] Dismissing its claims to be a revelatory message *resonating* within "clay jars" and "human hearts,"[5] many in this camp overemphasize its transcendence to the virtual exclusion of its immanence,[6] sometimes to the point of reducing this library to little more than gaudy religious wallpaper pasted onto the back of "secret golden tablets."[7] Sustaining *this* approach takes great energy, of course, yet many proponents believe it to be the best (if not the only) way to protect their most cherished religious beliefs from human "defilement."[8] Like other populist approaches (e.g., *The Bible Code*),[9] this one often wraps itself in the flag of "miraculous

---

and cultures from different religious or atheistic or skeptical backgrounds, has aroused a need for a kind of tolerance in which everyone believes and lives 'according to his fashion,' creating his/her own community. What universally binding religious truth would dare challenge this view of the human condition?" ("Monotheismus," 9; see Beck, *Monolatrie*, 28–29).

4. This kind of interpretation becomes "gnostic" when "pagan magic and beliefs from the Babylonian and Greek world as well as from the Jewish" are mixed together (Flusser, "Gnosticism," 650).

5. Both Jeremiah (Jer 31:33) and Paul (2 Cor 4:7) challenge the view that human beings cannot receive or respond to divine revelation (Gardner, "Docetism," 2381; Weippert, "Wort," 336–51).

6. Stone explores the dynamics of the immanence-transcendence polarity (*Minimalist*, 9–40), and Sparks shows how an understanding of the Mesopotamian epics can help pave the way for a better understanding of the Hebrew Bible (*Word*, 57–72).

7. Mauss and Barlow observe that "the position of the Bible within the (Mormon) canon has shifted and modified across time to reflect the changing Mormon relationships with the surrounding culture of North America" ("Church," 397; see Givens, *Mormon*, 35–39), and Glazov criticizes any approach to interpretation which marginalizes "the elements of pain, pathos, wonder and dread" in the Bible (*Bridling*, 32).

8. Lenzi assesses the sociopolitical factors compelling ancient Near Eastern scribes to create and preserve "secret knowledge" (*Secrecy*, 377–80), and Simundson theologically critiques this all-too-human tendency (*Job*, 1–20).

9. Drosnin asserts, for example (*Bible Code*, 108–12), that the assassinations of John Kennedy, Anwar Sadat, and Yitzhak Rabin are "encoded" into the Bible via an encrypted numerological system. Geller responds by outlining the checkered history of populist numerological speculation ("Influence," 52–53).

clairvoyance" in order to defend opinions so bizarre,[10] it's difficult to assess their value within the categories of normal, rational thought.[11]

To buttress this approach some try to reposition the Hebrew Bible behind Potemkin façades designed to exempt it from all the conventional rules of literary analysis.[12] Interpretive methods applied to *those* texts do not apply to *this* text, they argue, because *this* is a "perfect book" governed by "special rules."[13] In this way the attempt is made to shift attention away from *understanding* the Bible to *packaging* it for consumption; i.e., as the quintessential religious handbook on hyper-marketable topics like "How to Develop Seven Habits for Effective Living,"[14] "How to Survive the Coming Holocaust,"[15] and of course, "How to Become Wealthy Beyond Your Wildest Dreams."[16]

10. As the Hebrew prophet Jeremiah points out, populists tend to blur the boundaries between *prophecy* and *clairvoyance*: "Thus says Yahweh, 'Do not listen to the words of the prophets who prophesy to you. They are deluding you. They speak visions of their own minds, not from Yahweh. They keep saying to those who despise the word of Yahweh, "It shall be well with you," and to all who stubbornly follow their own hearts they say, "No calamity shall befall you"'" (Jer 23:16–17).

11. Dodds documents pertinent ancient examples (*Greeks*), and Boyer documents pertinent contemporary examples (*Prophecy*). Kirsch notes that deep-rooted fears about God are "deeply woven into the fabric of Western civilization, both in high culture and in pop culture, starting in distant biblical antiquity and continuing into our own age" (*History*, 2).

12. In 1787 Grigori Potemkin hastily constructs a number of village facades on the shores of the Dnieper river to impress his queen, Catherine II, and though it's difficult to separate fact from fiction in this story, the name "Potemkin" has come to refer to anything "fake" or "phony." *Application:* In spite of the fact that all known biblical texts are copies of copies of copies, populist interpreters tend to (a) ignore the actual history of the text, and (b) replace the worship of God with worship of (their favorite translation of) the Bible. LaSor publishes a thoughtful discussion of these issues (*Survey*, 591–97).

13. Brettler, *Bible*, 1.

14. *Examples*: Covey (*Habits*); Osteen (*Keys*); Luciani (*Self-Coaching*). Sternberg observes that every Bible reader operates—whether they realize it or not—within three constraints: (a) the ideology preserved within the text itself, (b) the poetics of character and history within the text itself, and (c) the desire to reach rhetorical consensus with other readers ("Persuasion," 45–82).

15. *Examples*: LaHaye and Jenkins (*Behind*); Rosenberg (*Days*). See the penetrating critiques of Frykholm (*Rapture*) and Morgan (*Brothers*).

16. *Examples*: Tracy (*Rich*); Lowell (*Rich*). See the critiques of Barron (*Health*); Jones and Woodbridge (*Overshadowed*); Fee (*Disease*).

Whatever else it may be, however, the Bible is not easily "packaged."[17] In fact, this ancient Near Eastern library has a long history of driving all would-be packagers to the "familiar ground of safe practices, blessed ideologies, and liberal crusades."[18] From any rational perspective it therefore seems more than a little ridiculous to read it through a blatantly ahistorical lens, then insist that this lens be canonized as the only "correct" one.[19] Yet this is precisely what many populist "3-step" interpreters do, thereby forcing contemporary Western readers to react, either by (a) rejecting the Bible as a hopelessly prejudiced account of an irrecoverable past, or (b) changing the lens through which they read it.[20] Pursuing the latter strategy need not condemn all readers for failing to achieve sinlessness,[21] nor need it indict the scribes writing the Bible for the "crime" of premodernism.[22] Particularly problematic is the presumption that everything in the Bible must be demythologized before (post)modern readers can understand its message.[23] "The stakes are high. The modern period has

17. As Clements observes, the Bible "poses more questions than answers. Its God remains resolutely hidden. Like the prophet Jeremiah it views its role to be as much that of 'pulling down' as of 'planting' (Jer 1:9–10). The emphasis on the elusiveness of God which it presents continues to challenge the easy faith of popular piety and this remains a hallmark of its legacy" ("Enduring," 42). See Terrien, *Elusive.*

18. Brueggemann, *Memory,* 4.

19. To Rorty's assertion ("Texts," 8–9) that any search for a theory of interpretation is "pointless," Stecker counters that even nihilists presume a "theory of interpretation" ("Pragmatism," 181–91).

20. Gunkel criticizes anyone who would "free himself from an earlier supernaturalism" whenever it leads to failure to "understand that history is the proper domain of revelation" (*Israel,* 62). Lipton cautions the "faith communities from which most biblical scholars and their readers emerge" not to "overlook the Bible's complex compositional history," or to "identify simplicity . . . as the source of the Bible's extraordinary capacity to educate and inspire" (*Longing,* 3).

21. Responding to Hitchens' cynicism (*Poison*), Heinegg believes it "useful to bring unrelenting nay-sayers like . . . Hitchens into the conversation." Why? Because "the bitter-end positions they've staked out serve to demarcate the field . . . and clear the air" (Review of *Poison,* 468).

22. Halpern resists all popular attempts to "lay the blame . . . on the ancient authors," especially when the intentions of these authors can be shown to be "authentically antiquarian" (*Historians,* xvii, 3). Similarly, Grabbe resists the temptation to argue that postmodernism's "impact . . . requires us to abandon the historical task" ("Reflections," 189).

23. Adam observes that "modern scholars advise us that we need to overcome a hermeneutical abyss that divides us from the biblical texts," noting that "this argument frequently is made with cavalier references to what modern people can or cannot be-

seen the gradual breakdown of the Bible story as the defining story of Western culture. What was once regarded as a unified narrative whole ... has come to be seen largely as a collection of larger or smaller fragments, unrelated to each other, and requiring recontextualization by the individual reader if they are to be properly understood."[24]

At any rate, the following chapter does not attempt to lay out every tool needed to grind out the "perfect interpretive lens" (diachronic,[25] synchronic,[26] anthropological,[27] sociological,[28] legal,[29] political,[30] theological)[31]—as if such a lens were possible.[32] What it *does* try to do is identify the major socioeconomic conflict motifs animating the primeval stories of *Torah* and assess from this identification how much they resonate with the socioeconomic conflict motifs animating the "great texts" in their literary-historical context, the goal being to help contemporary Westerners more easily recognize where "secular civilization accords with ancient Israelite perspectives, and where it diverges."[33]

---

lieve. It would be convenient simply to accept this claim on its own terms, saying, 'All right; the people who can't believe this we will call "modern" and those who can believe it are not just "modern people,"' but in so doing we would conceal the extent to which even those who dispute 'can't believe' claims usually do so within the bounds decreed by modern interpretation" (*Faithful,* 21; see Schmithals, "Problem," 166–206; Müller, "Entmythologisierung," 1–27; Firestone, "Prophethood," 331–32).

24. Provan, *Kings,* 5.

25. Noth, *History*; Long, *History.*

26. Frye, *Code*; Alter, *Narrative*; Sternberg, *Poetics.*

27. Kunin, *Incest*; Steinberg, *Kinship.*

28. Gottwald, *Bible*; Esler, *Israel.*

29. Buchholz, "Laws." Amador appreciates it when biblical interpreters (a) try to wrestle authority away from dogma and tradition, (b) contribute to the humanities, (c) hold populist extremists accountable, and (d) hold academic antiquarians accountable (*Constraints,* 280–84).

30. Gerstenberger, *Theologies*; Lilla, *Stillborn.*

31. Brettler, *Bible,* 5; Brueggemann, *Theology*; Goldingay, *Theology*; Koch, *Gott Israels.* This list is not exhaustive. Sandoval is right to insist that "no single study" can "show how the language of poverty and riches functions" in the Bible (*Wealth,* 2).

32. Martin thinks that biblical interpreters ought to "break out of the captivity of Scripture to modernity" and "reclaim the premodern heritage" (*Pedagogy,* 98).

33. Brettler, *Bible,* 5. Hughes and Allen document the histories of several primitivist American sects whose founders summarily reject the discipline of literary-historical investigation (*Illusions,* 22–28). Thiel pleads for a reading strategy committed to interpreting the Hebrew Bible against its "ancient Oriental environment" (*Geschichte,* 1).

CAIN AND ABEL: THE "BIG PROBLEM" OF ACQUISITION
(GEN 4:1–16)

Like the wise-man-vs.-wild-man stories in other "great texts," the wise-man-vs.-wild-man stories in *Torah* engage a number of "big problems."[34] This is not all they do, of course, yet this is one of their greatest (if least celebrated) accomplishments.[35] One of the most famous pits a "servant of the earth" (Cain) against a "herder of sheep" (Abel).[36] Like the Ishtar episode in *Gilgamesh*, this story features a powerful deity engaging two iconic characters who in turn symbolize two iconic vocations: *shepherd* and *farmer*;[37] and, like the Sumerian story of *Dumuzi and Enkimdu*,[38] the *farmer* in this story (Enkimdu//Cain) takes the offensive against the *shepherd* (Dumuzi//Abel).[39]

34. Polanyi, *Livelihood*, xli. Interpreters argue over whether the monotheism in *Genesis* is pre-exilic (Albright, *Yahweh*) or post-exilic (Lang, *Wisdom*; Smith, *History*). Beck finds no evidence for full-blown monotheism in pre-exilic Israel, nor does he find evidence for full-blown polytheism (*Elia*), yet Assmann still posits that "the change from polytheistic to monotheistic religion" is one of history's most important turning-points (*Monotheismus*), and Koch argues that the fundamental message of the Hebrew Bible focuses on "the one God and his singular relationship to humankind" ("Monotheismus," 9).

35. Gunkel sees *Genesis* as a collection of "sagas—not falsified stories, but a particular type of epic poetry" (*Genesis*, ii).

36. Gen 4:2 (עבד אדמה, Cain; רעה צֹן, Abel). Qur'an renames these characters قابيل ("Qabil," from قبل, "to guarantee, put up surety") and هابيل ("Habil," from هبل, "to take advantage") in order to show that the legacies of these characters have become distorted (*Sura* 5:27, 32). Weippert thinks that pre-Mosaic Amorite tribalists practice farming *as well as* sheepherding ("Nomaden," 265–80, 427–33).

37. Heard explores the intratextual dynamics of these polarities (*Dynamics*), and von Rad discusses their history of transformation (*Theology* 1:105–28). Leach argues that *Cain-and-Abel* reflects a binary paradigm much like that structuring the first two creation narratives (*Genesis*), but Carroll finds this approach too "heuristic" ("Leach," 663–77).

38. *Dumuzi and Enkimdu* is a Sumerian myth in which two minor deities woo the hand of Inanna (*ANET* 41–42), and though Inanna finds herself attracted to the farmer (Enkimdu—*not* Enkidu), she mates with the shepherd (Dumuzi). Aware of these parallels, Huffmon nevertheless dismisses any intertextual comparison to *Cain-and-Abel* ("Cain," 110).

39. Underemphasis should be avoided as much as overemphasis. Writing for an audience heavily influenced by the parallelomania associated with the name of James Frazier (*Golden Bough*), Hooke points out several philological parallels (e.g., רבץ // *rābiṣu*, "lurking demon"), but pushes the evidence too far when he tries to equate Cain's flight with "the motif of ritual flight" ("Cain," 61–63). Dissimilarities between these traditions are too pronounced: (a) the shepherd is the aggressor in the Sumerian myth, not the farmer;

The names of these siblings reflect opposite poles on a primitive socioeconomic continuum:[40] "Cain" (*acquisition*)[41] stands over against "Abel" (*weakness*).[42] Comparative intertextual analysis sheds little light on the process by which these names are assigned,[43] yet it's fruitful to note that the Sumerians preserve a similar story in which Enlil creates a demigod (Enten) "to make the ewe give birth to the lamb," after which he creates a sibling (Emesh) to "take charge of the trees and fields."[44] When these siblings quarrel—as siblings often do—Enlil summons them to his temple in Nippur to hammer out a compromise.[45] *Cain-and-Abel* ends on a less positive note, of course, yet just as Gilgamesh focuses on "civilized" vs. "wild" characters, and *Erra* focuses on "field-dwellers"-vs.-"city-dwellers," so this old Hebrew story focuses on how difficult it is for competing vocations to work the same land at the same time.[46] None of this suggests that "the killing of Abel marks the beginning of the as-

---

(b) the Sum shepherd "woos" Inanna to change her mind, but the Hebrew text gives no rationale for Yahweh's preference for the shepherd's sacrifice; and (c) the brothers reconcile in the Sumerian tradition, but not in the Hebrew tradition. Wettengel (*Erzählung*) argues that the *Tale of Two Brothers* (*ANET* 23–25), where the brothers also reconcile, operates from a literary perspective similar to that of *Cain-and-Abel*.

40. Likely this occurs because the priestly writer of Gen 1–11 positions this story alongside three others in order to create an abbreviated "history of sin" (Adam and Eve, Cain and Abel, Flood, Tower of Babel). See Westermann, *Genesis*; Trimpe, *Schöpfung*).

41. Gen 4: 1 (קין, "acquisition," from קנה, "to acquire"). Philo's idiosyncratic etymology ("Cain" = "possession," *Sacr.* 2) is picked up by Josephus (*A.J.* 1:52) and several other interpreters.

42. Gen 4:2 (הבל, "weakness/futility"). In *Qoheleth* this term stands in tension with יתרון ("profit," Qoh 1:3; 2:11, 13; 3:9; 5:15). See Kugel, "Qohelet," 32–49.

43. This is not to delimit *all* socioeconomic discourse to dualistic categories (*contra* Hudson, "Dynamics," 1–26).

44. Kramer discusses the relationship between *Enten and Emesh* (*Sumerian*, 49–54).

45. Sigrist recognizes the sociohistorical tensions symbolized by this quarrel ("Offrandes," 169–83).

46. Matthews, *Nomadism*; Lincoln, *Priests*. This is not the only way to read this story. McNutt interprets *Cain-and-Abel* through lenses ground by studies of the role-sets enacted by artisans and smiths in traditional African and Middle Eastern societies ("Shadow," 45–64). Boyle reads it from a psychotherapeutic perspective, arguing that Cain is responsible *to*, but not *for* his brother ("Brother," 89–99). Soelle sees in the story two male roles ("executioner" and "victim") whose conflict is designed to show the impossibility of שלום ("peace") until the role of "human being" (which she views as inherently female) comes to greater appreciation ("Peace," 83–91). Qur'an has Habil warn Qabil that *any* "older brother" (read: "the Jews") attacking any "younger brother" (read: "the Muslims") must face divine judgment (*Sura* 5:20–36).

sociation of shepherds with peace and innocence and of farmers with violence."[47] But it does suggest that just as *Gilgamesh* uses the "sibling rivalry" polarity to engage a "big problem" in the Babylonian economy, so *Cain-and-Abel* uses it to engage a "big problem" in Israel.[48]

Further, just as Enlil refuses to recognize the labor of the Igigi, so Yahweh refuses to recognize the labor of Farmer Cain;[49] and just as *Gilgamesh* refuses to explain why Gilgamesh's acquisition of cedar is unacceptable, so *Genesis* refuses to explain the unacceptability of Cain's "gifts."[50] Both traditions—Mesopotamian as well as Hebrew—focus on human reaction to divine behavior, *not* the divine behavior itself.[51] Unaware of (or uninterested in) this context, many choose to read *Cain-and-Abel* through lenses refracting different types of anachronistic bias.[52] Some, for example, throw Cain into a rogues gallery populated by several shady characters (Korah, Balaam, Doeg, Ahithophel, Gehazi, Absalom, Adonijah, Uzziah, Haman), cartoonishly depicting him as "Israel's enemy."[53] Others read the story as a text focused on (what else?) the "problem of divine inscrutability."[54] Still others read it as a tract on tithing,[55] a saga distinguishing "gifts" from "sacrifices,"[56] or as a cryptic prediction of the outcome of the Final World Battle (Abel=Yahweh;

47. Stoll, "Agrarian," 6.

48. Gottwald, *Tribes*, 237–343; Smith, *Memoirs*, 126; Goldingay, *Theology* 2:199–203; Galling, *Erwählungstraditionen*; Rowley, *Election*; Silberman, "Chosen," 669–72. Not everyone dates these traditions early; in fact, some date them quite late (see discussion in Heard, *Dynamics*; Moore, "Moabite").

49. Gen 4:5 (שָׁעָה לֹא, "he did not take notice of"); see *Atr* 1:39).

50. According to Hendel, either (a) Cain is irredeemably evil; or (b) the story is allegorical (Cain and Abel represent socio-ethical concepts); or (c) God's will is mysterious; or (d) Yahweh is capricious and arbitrary ("Book," 46–50).

51. Huffmon contrasts Cain's rejection of the *mysterium tremendum* with Abraham's acceptance of it ("Cain," 112–13).

52. Lewis documents several of these approaches ("Offering," 481–96).

53. See *b. Sot* 9b, and compare the rabbinic denigrations of Ruth (*Tg. Ruth* 1:4; *b. Nazir* 23b) and Balaam (*b. Sanh.* 105b).

54. For many this temptation is simply too strong to resist, and not just in *Genesis*. Brown, for example, views the second half of *Qoheleth* as a veritable commentary on "divine inscrutability" ("Ecclesiastes," 195–208).

55. Waltke, "Cain," 363–72.

56. See Philo, *Agr.* 127–28. Gen 4:7 (LXX) takes לפתח as an infinitive, reading ὀρθῶς δὲ μὴ διέλῃς ("but have not properly divided"), suggesting to some that the essence of Cain's sin is his failure to measure out the vegetables in his sacrifice "properly" (see Levine, "Syriac," 72).

Cain=Satan).[57] Even among those who *do* recognize the socioeconomic character of this text, some imagine it showing how "the animal offerings of . . . nomadic religion are superior to the vegetable offerings made to the Canaanite Baals,"[58] or more broadly, how the "pastoral ideal" in Israel eventually comes to overshadow all others.[59]

Latching onto the "therapeutic ethos,"[60] some go so far as to reimagine Cain's deity not as sovereign lord, but as Western psychotherapist.[61] Reading this postmodern vocation into the "falling" of Cain's face, proponents suggest that the "big problem" in Cain's life—the one around which everything else revolves—is the "disease" of depression.[62] No less a writer than Elie Wiesel defends this view, even to the point of castigating Abel for "ignoring his brother's pain."[63] Depression in the ancient Near East, however, has nothing to do with the unquestioned primacy of Individual Need (*individualism*),[64] nor does it presume that the alleviation of individual suffering equates to The Ultimate Good (*victimology*).[65]

More to the point, anachronistic approaches like these fail to recognize the socioeconomic conflict motifs embedded in this ancient Near Eastern text, beginning with Yahweh's description of "sin" as a predator "crouching" at Cain's door.[66] Just as Ishtar targets *her* prey (Gilgamesh),

57. Gen 4:8 (Syr) has Cain say to Abel נֵאזֵל לבקעתא, "let us go down to the valley" (i.e., "the valley of the shadow of death," Psa 23:4).

58. Skinner, *Genesis*, 105–6.

59. Huffmon dismisses all these approaches ("Sufferer," 109–10).

60. See Moskowitz, *Therapy*; Tyler, *Unspeakable*; Nolan, *Therapeutic*.

61. See Gruber, "Tragedy," 89–97; Barré, "Wandering," 179–80; Boyle, "Brother."

62. Gen 4:5 (נפל, "to fall"). See Leventhal and Martell, *Depression*; Katz and Liu, *Codependency*; Klunzinger and Moore, "Codependency."

63. Wiesel, "Brother," 20–21.

64. Van der Toorn emphasizes that for the Babylonians "the inner life has no autonomous reality" (*Family*, 117). Meador and Henson argue that "the psychotherapeutic mindset of the first half of the twentieth century evolves in the afterglow of high modernity and its convictions regarding an autonomous self. Whether the goal is framed as self-actualization, the freeing of one's psychic structure from dependency conflicts, or the deliverance from externally binding contingencies, there is no question but that the supremacy of self-determination and autonomous rationality are ascending to new heights of significance within our therapeutic culture" ("Growing," 185).

65. Burgess et al. begin their textbook with a forensic analysis of Gen 4:1–16 (*Victimology*, 4). Mouton questions the legitimacy of any interpretive approach "which is, in effect, the product of contemporary occidental societies" (*Rêves*, xxiv).

66. Gen 4:7 (רבץ . . . חטאת). Levine ("Syriac," 70–78) argues that when Syr translates Heb נפל ("to fall") with ܚܫܟ ("to darken") the translator's intention is to attribute Cain's behavior to Satan.

so the "Croucher" targets *his* prey (Cain).[67] Just as Ishum stands up to protect the black-headed people from the wrath generated by their "sin,"[68] so Yahweh warns Cain not to be seduced by the Croucher "desiring" to "dominate" him.[69] And just as Gilgamesh violates the *itû*-boundary surrounding the Cedar Forest, so Cain violates the boundary separating legitimate "acquisition" from illegitimate "seizure."[70] In short, *Cain-and-Abel* reflects not so much the contemporary ethos of the postmodern therapeutic culture as the pre-modern ethos epitomized by Humbaba's fearsomeness, Ishtar's ruthlessness, and the shrewdness of the serpent "targeting" Cain's parents.[71]

67. The nominal form of רבץ ("to crouch") often refers to the "bed" of a prostitute, yet whether or not this text intends to convey this nuance cannot be determined from the evidence at hand. Janowski ("Jenseits," 37–59) imagines the פתח ("door") in v. 7 as a portal to the Unseen World, but this is too speculative.

68. See Akk *ḫitu* ("sin") in *Erra* 5:6. Sarna suggests that the dialogue between Yahweh and Cain "expresses clearly the idea that evil is not metaphysical" ("Cain," 340), but this ignores the intertextual context.

69. Gen 4:7 (משל . . . תשוקה). The term תשוקה often refers to the "desire" of a woman for a man (Gen 3:16) or a man for a woman (Song 7:11). The verb משל ("to dominate") occurs in the feminine form (תמשל) because its subject is the feminine noun חטאת ("sin"), but given the intertextual context (particularly Ishtar's seduction of Gilgamesh in *GE* 6:6–21) this may not be coincidental.

70. Rudman argues that what Cain tries to do is retreat behind the boundaries established before "the Fall" by (a) disclaiming knowledge of his brother, and (b) challenging Yahweh to state whether or not he has explicitly commanded him to look after Abel, concluding that "Cain's denial of knowledge . . . and its concomitant curse, becomes his undoing as its appropriation is the undoing of his parents" ("Knowledge," 465).

71. Gen 3:1–6. Gen 4:7 LXX misses (or ignores) the "crouching" metaphor by translating, "but if you do not divide (the sacrifice) properly you sin, as that which you set in motion silently returns to you." For Ricoeur the serpent represents "that aspect of evil which cannot be absorbed into the responsible freedom of man, which is perhaps also the aspect that Greek tragedy tries to purify by spectacle, song, and choral invocation. The Jews themselves, although they are well armed against demonology by their intransigent monotheism, are constrained by truth, as Aristotle would say, to concede something—to concede as much as they can without destroying the monotheistic basis of their faith—to the great dualisms which they are to discover after the Exile. The theme of the serpent represents the first landmark along the road of the Satanic theme which, in the Persian epoch, permits the inclusion of a near-dualism in the faith of Israel. Of course, Satan will never be another god; the Jews will always remember that the serpent is a part of the creation; but at least the symbol of Satan allows them to balance the movement toward the concentration of evil in humanity by a second movement which attributes its origin to a prehuman demonic reality" (*Symbolism*, 258–59).

None of these parallels should be overemphasized, of course, but neither should they be underemphasized.[72] In *Atrahasis*, for example, things begin with a "divine lottery." Not so in *Genesis,* where things begin with a divinely-spoken "word."[73] In *Enki's* vision of creation the great gods manufacture a race of clay-based creatures to free the "lesser gods" from divinely-imposed "slavery." Not so in *Genesis,* where Yahweh promotes a universal imperative designed to balance "protection" *alongside* "acquisition."[74] Cain refers to this imperative in his famous question, "Am I my brother's *protector*?"[75] The meaning of this term may be debated,[76] but intertextually it points to the possibility that the Hebrews have the ability to define Farmer Cain's behavior alongside that of any other *farmer,*[77] not to mention any other *tempter.*[78]

Just as Gilgamesh's problem begins with a bold decision to violate a sacred boundary (the Cedar Forest),[79] so Cain's problem begins with

---

72. Gunkel's 1903 question remains relevant: "What kind of faith would it be that is afraid of facts, that abhors scholarly research?" (*Israel,* 31).

73. Gen 1:3 (אמר); see also 9:13, 16; 15:18; 17:11; 21:27; Exod 34:10; Lev 26:45; Deut 4:23, 31; Pss 78:10; 105:10. Westermann argues that to believe "that God created the world, and that God created human life, does not contradict the scientific explanation of the origin of the world ... This contradiction ... is a fateful misunderstanding of biblical talk about the creator" (*Elements,* 85–86).

74. Gen 4:9 (שמר, "protect"). Yahweh puts humans in the Garden to "work" (עבד) and "protect" (שמר, Gen 2:15), and Farmer Cain fulfills half of this assignment.

75. Gen 4:9 (שמר). The presumption here is that Cain would not use this term were it not central to his understanding of the divine imperative. Breitbart speculates that (a) Cain kills Abel, (b) Yahweh tries to educate him about the consequences of what he's done, and this causes Cain to ask, (c) "Does my brother need a keeper as an animal would?" ("*Cain,*" 122–24)—but this type of approach significantly marginalizes the socioeconomic context.

76. Riemann argues, from a concordial analysis of שמר, that the Hebrew Bible contains no "single instance where a man's keeping another man is an expressed covenant norm or even a recognized social obligation" ("Brother," 483), yet this reading ignores (a) the intertextual context of Gen 4 as well as (b) the prevalence of social institutions (like levirate marriage) designed to protect the weak from "annihilation" (מחה, Deut 25:5–10; see Burkert, *Structure,* 16–22).

77. Like Farmer Ishullanu (*GE* 6:64–79).

78. Like Ishtar. N.B. that (a) Cain refuses to "protect" *his* shepherd just as much as Ishtar refuses to "protect" *her* shepherd (*GE* 6:58–63); and (b) that just as *Gilgamesh* champions the motif of "servant shepherd," so also does the Bible (see Ps 23; Isa 53; Ezek 37). According to the midrashic tradition "the desire of the Tempter is for none but Cain and his associates" (*Gen. Rab.* 20:7).

79. *GE* 3:24–27.

a decision to violate the sacred boundary protecting human life from the invasive power of death.[80] The "big problem" in this story, in other words, is not the desire to acquire, only the desire to acquire *at any cost*. Acquisitiveness *per se* is not the "big problem" because Yahweh himself is the Great Acquirer, Israel being his chief Acquisition.[81] Instead, to borrow the language of *Gilgamesh, Cain-and-Abel* focuses on another clay-based creature's desire to "invade the Forest" and "steal its treasures."[82] Like Ishtar, Cain chooses an unsuspecting "target." Like Enlil, he sheds innocent blood for no justifiable reason.[83] Just as Enlil's problem grows in proportion to the amount of "noise" *his* sons generate (the Igigi), so Yahweh's problem grows in proportion to the amount of "noise" *his* son generates (Cain).[84]

The greatest difference between these traditions is that where Akkadian myth locates this conflict in the heavens, the Hebrew story locates it squarely upon the earth. Not only does Cain decide to kill a weaker "target" (like the assassinations of Enkidu in *Gilgamesh* and PI-*e* in *Atrahasis*), but *Genesis* resists the temptation to project this conflict into the Unseen World where difficult social questions in Babylonia are most often "handled."[85] Certainly Yahweh is capable of enacting the role of "righteous judge" in the Hebrew tradition,[86] but such is not the role he enacts here. Here he looks more like Nusku than Enlil, more like Ishum than Erra. Conspicuously absent is the "frustrated warlord"[87]

---

80. The Canaanites deify this polarity in their worship of Mot ("death/chaos") alongside his brother Baal ("life/fertility," *CAT* 1.5–6; see Handy, *Heaven*; Mettinger, *Riddle*; Berlejung and Janowski, *Tod*; Blenkinsopp, "Judah").

81. Ps 74:2. N.B. the parallelism in this lament between קנה ("acquire") and גאל ("redeem").

82. Schaffer highlights Gilgamesh's aquisitional spirit ("Gilgamesh," 307–13).

83. Interestingly, the "voice" (קול) of Abel's "blood" (דם, Gen 4:20) develops a life of its own in the Hebrew tradition, eventually becoming a sermonic rallying point in later texts (e.g., Matt 23:35; Luke 11:51; Heb 12:24).

84. *Atr* 1:358; *CAD* R:328–34.

85. Brueggemann interprets the biblical narrator's critique of Cain's behavior as partially influenced by the wisdom tradition (*Man*, 57), and Smith points out that, generally speaking, Hebrew writers commit to the "reduction of myth" (*Origins*, 176).

86. N.B. the execution of Uzzah for touching the ark (ארון, 2 Sam 6:7), as well as the executions of Nadab and Abihu for offering "strange fire" (Lev 10:1–2). Mafico's attempt to turn Yahweh into an administrative "deputy (שפט) among the gods" is highly speculative (*Emergence*).

87. Richards and Waterbury document "abundant evidence" in contemporary

or the "contempt-loathing sheikh," now replaced by the divine *protector* determined to redeem a flawed son from potential harm, enacting within this role-set the complementary roles of (a) *watchman* (warning Cain about the power of sin), (b) *savior* (rescuing Cain from the consequences of sin), and (c) *manager* (defusing the cosmic chaos created by Cain's sin).[88]

Few of these observations may seem immediately obvious, but taken together they vigorously challenge all attempts to (re)imagine Yahweh as an Enlil-like clone trapped within a cosmos where, "due to the different characters and responsibilities of deities, a remarkable range of constellations of divine malevolence and benevolence can be traced."[89] Philo of Alexandria, for example, has Yahweh ridicule Cain out of petulant indignation,[90] while the historian Josephus has him interrogate Cain like a fussy Roman lawyer.[91] Contemporary readers label him everything from "clumsy surrogate"[92] to "powerless daemon"[93] to "abusive father,"[94] but interpreters aware of the socioeconomic context put a different set of questions to this text. Could it be, for example, that Yahweh rejects Cain's sacrifice out of concern that divine approval—however tacit—might spark a "rebellion" much like that which eventuates in the Flood a couple of chapters later (*à la* Enlil in *Atrahasis* or the divine council in *Gilgamesh*)?[95] Could it be that Abel's sacrifice is chosen over Cain's because Yahweh wants to protect the created order from "contempt" (*à la* Marduk in *Erra* or Enlil in *Atrahasis*)? Questions like these, however

---

Middle Eastern sources linking "red tape" and "administrative paralysis" to "corruption and patronage" (*Economy*, 179).

88. Merton, "Role-Set"; Petersen, *Roles*, 16–34; Moore, *Balaam,* 12–19.

89. Spieckermann, "Wrath," 3.

90. Philo, *Det.* 69.

91. Josephus, *A.J.* 1:56.

92. Perry, "Cain," 259 (drawing heavily from Greenspahn, *Brothers*).

93. Kushner, *Things*. Augustine focuses not on the deity, but on the Christ-killing Jews he thinks he sees symbolized in Cain (*Faust.* 12:10).

94. Lasine, *Kings*, 239–61.

95. Gen 6:1–4 (see Frymer-Kensky, "Atrahasis," 147–55). The midrashic tradition speculates that Cain's greatest desire is to "turn the earth back to formlessness and emptiness" (*Gen. Rab.* 2:3), but Hendel argues that when "the Yahwist includes Gen 6:1–4 in the Primeval Cycle of Genesis 2–11," he does so to show that "he does not find it objectionable and that it is indeed an authentic Israelite myth" ("Demigods," 14).

strange they might sound to contemporary ears, at least refuse to read arbitrary scenarios into this text driven by "every conceivable vagary."[96]

At any rate, just as *Gilgamesh* concludes with a divinely chastened "wild-man" roaming the wilderness, so *Cain-and-Abel* concludes with a divinely chastened "wild man" roaming the land of the "Wanderers."[97] Opinions vary over the function of his divinely-given "mark,"[98] but that which it provides for Cain is the very thing he has just taken away from Abel—*protection*.[99] Unlike the Igigi, who *win* their freedom through bloodshed, Cain *loses* his freedom through bloodshed,[100] yet because life in the "wilderness" is more dangerous than "city" life, Yahweh steps in to protect him from the possibility of Sibitti-like reprisal.[101] Even as Enki steps in to restore order in *Atrahasis*, so Yahweh steps in to restore order in *Genesis*.[102] Like Nusku, he rescues the life of a "rebellious son."[103] Like Ishum, he redeems the life of a clay-based "inferior."[104]

96. Davies, "Passages," 218. Nebelsick argues that *Genesis'* use of these stories "qualifies and transforms them so that they became quite other than they were in their 'primal contexts'" (Review of *Meaning*, 265).

97. Gen 4:16 (נוד, "to wander," transliterated "Nod" in most English translations). Görg tries to define נוד as an Egyptian loanword meaning "God's land" ("Kain," 5–12), but this is doubtful.

98. Gen 4:15 (אות, "mark"/"sign"). Some imagine Cain's אות to be a hairstyle like those worn by Babylonian slaves (*CAD* A/1:48; Mendelsohn, *Legal,* 31–37). Others take it to be a symbolic wound marking his rite of passage, like Jacob's broken hip (Gen 32:25) or Moses' "disfigurement" (Exod 34:33; see Propp, "Symbolic," 17–24). In Exod 12:13 lamb's blood is the אות which directs the death-angel to "pass over" the house where it's been applied.

99. In Job 31:35 Job hides under a "sign" (אות) like the one inscribed on the foreheads of those grieving over Jerusalem (Ezek 9:4). Mellinkoff lists other interpretive possibilities (*Mark*).

100. In Gen 4:10 Yahweh says the "voice of the bloods (pl.) of your brother cry out to me" (קול דמי אחיך צעקים אלי). Noting that a plural noun matches a plural participle, Mishnah speculates that these "bloods" include "Abel's blood plus the blood of his posterity" (*m. Sanh.* 4:5).

101. *Erra* 1:47–60. The Tekoite woman's parable uses similar "survival" motifs (2 Sam 14:4–7; Moore, "Women," 154).

102. In Gen 1–11 Yahweh restores Creation four times: (a) when Eve is named "mother of all living"; (b) when Cain receives his protective mark; (c) when Noah and his family survive the flood; and (d) when Abraham receives directions to go to Canaan (Guinan, *Pentateuch*, 23–30).

103. *Atr* 1:93–96. That is, he protects Cain against anything which might "devour" him.

104. *Erra* 2:1:31. In *Erra* 1:127–28, 140–62, 171–78, Marduk repeats the verb *ēlu* ("to ascend, rise up") three times to connect the "rising up" of the floodwaters with the

Dissatisfied with the story's ending, one reader reformats it as a wrestling match between rivals,[105] imagining (a) that Cain marries Abel's twin sister (a Hebrew variant of the "doubling" motif?);[106] (b) the marriage falters; and (c) Cain murders Abel to avenge the loss of his sister's dowry. This murder so enrages the creatures of the wilderness, however, that Yahweh has to "mark" Cain with animal horns to protect him from harm, particularly from those wild beasts who want to "target" him for reprisal.[107] Other readers produce similarly refracted readings.[108] Reading into Cain's name several allegorical definitions—none anchored in historical philology—Philo of Alexandria (d. 50 CE) likens him to Alexander of Macedon—a headstrong adolescent too proud to bow before the "source of all possession."[109] Another reader, the pastor of a fledgling church in Asia, denigrates him as "wholly evil,"[110]

"rising up" of cosmic chaos; thus it hardly seems coincidental that whatever its internal focus, the Hebrew flood narrative appears only two chapters later in *Genesis* (see Spina, "Rejection," 319–32).

105. *Gen Rab.* 22.8. Whether this "wrestling match" might reflect the wrestling match between Gilgamesh and Enkidu (*GE* 2:111–15) is a tantalizing possibility. Surveying the Second Temple Hebraic literature, Harkins observes that ancient interpreters of *Cain-and-Abel* tend to focus on two issues: (a) God's "capriciousness" in choosing Abel's sacrifice over Cain's; and (b) the absence of a motive in Cain for killing Abel ("Cain," 62–84).

106. *GE* 1:96 describes the "doubling" of Gilgamesh's "bestial nature" via the creation of Enkidu.

107. *Gen. Rab.* 22.12–13 (see Budge, *Treasures,* 69–70). N.B. the parallels to the contents of Gen 34:12 and Exod 22:16 in Babylonian and Hurrian lawcodes (Paradise, "Marriage," 1–36). *Genesis Rabbah* practically transforms Cain into another Enkidu.

108. Students of this text's afterlife identify two major streams of interpretation—one Augustinian, the other Romantic. The Augustinian stream, represented by Melville (and others), puts Abel in the "city of God" and Cain in the "city of man." The Romantic stream, represented by Byron, Coleridge, Gessner (and others), replaces "the whole set of ancient theological questions . . . with modern psychological issues" in order to transform Cain from "tormented sinner" into "heroic criminal" (see Kelly, "Melville," 24–40).

109. Philo, *Cher.* 63–65. Elsewhere Philo retreats to the "holy bubble" when he asserts that "God, . . . having added the good doctrine (that is, Abel) to the soul, took away from it evil doctrine (that is, Cain)" (*Sacr.* 5).

110. 1 John 3:12 (πόνηρος, "evil"; see Brown, *Epistles,* 102). John Byron hypothesizes a Second Temple tradition which uses "a number of Jewish and Christian works . . . to portray Cain as the representative of wicked individuals who oppress the poor" ("Shadow," 262).

a one-dimensional depiction closely echoed by Josephus (d. 100 CE).[111] Abandoning history altogether, John Chrysostom (d. 407 CE) speculates that the "mark" of Cain is a muscle disease like that mentioned in the *Gospel of Matthew*.[112]

The English poet Lord Byron rejects this line of interpretation as so much syrupy sentimentalism, suggesting instead that Cain (re)acts the way he does because of the justifiable anger he feels over "the inadequacy of his estate."[113] American novelist Herman Melville, the author of *Moby Dick*, takes a similar tack, describing Cain as a "citified man" whose story reveals more than a few "ironic counterpoints to naïve notions about brotherhood."[114] Hannah Arendt agrees, to the point of suggesting that *all* notions of brotherhood ultimately trace their origins to fratricidal conflicts pulsating at the core of other sibling rivalry stories: "Cain slew Abel and Romulus slew Remus; violence was the beginning and by the same token, no beginning could be made without violence. The tale speaks clearly: whatever brotherhood human beings may be capable of grows out of fratricide, whatever political organization men may achieve has its origin in crime."[115] Each of these approaches, however, says more about interpreter than text—so much so, in fact, that the more contemporary the interpreter, the greater the emphasis on *horizontal* ("sibling rivalry") vs. *vertical* angles of interpretation ("divine inscrutability").[116]

111. *A.J.* 1:53 refers to Cain as πονηρότατος ("very wicked").

112. Matt 9:2; see Mark 2:1–12; Luke 5:17–26; Chrysostom, *Paralyt.* 5. Propp suggests that Cain's mark, Adam's rib, and Jacob's hip-ailment all exemplify "initiatory wounds" which heroes suffer at the beginning of "heroic journeys" ("Symbolic," 20).

113. Cited in Prothero, *Works*, 5:470.

114. Cited in Kelly, "Melville," 25–26. In another Melville novel a misanthropic "wild man" asks, "How came your fellow-creature, Cain, after the first murder, to go and build the first city?" (*Confidence*, 193).

115. Arendt, *Revolution*, 10. Lisca (*Steinbeck*, 84–85) traces this tension into the interaction between "George" (Cain) and "Lenny" (Abel) in Steinbeck's *Of Mice and Men*. Butting suggests ("Abel"), however, that even though *Cain-and-Abel* challenges Yahweh's vision of a peaceful cosmos, the birth of Seth as Abel's "replacement" drains the fratricide motif of all its power.

116. Shakespeare is one of the more notable examples because, in Foakes' words, the bard "finds a power in this tale" which goads him into making "references to Cain and Abel" in the "frames (of) his early history plays" where "the rivalry of brothers is a recurrent theme . . . most notably in the fratricide that triggers the action of Hamlet" (*Shakespeare*, 27). In Shulman's opinion, few interpreters since Shakespeare ask questions about "divine inscrutability" anymore ("Myth," 215–38).

Socioeconomic interpretation of the *Cain-and-Abel* story has a history of its own. Ambrose of Milan, for example (d. 397 CE), raises several questions about Cain's "acquisitiveness" in order to assess the character of the boundaries distinguishing "public property" from "private property" in the minds of his Italian constituents.[117] Agreeing with the Roman stoic Cicero (d. 43 BCE) that socioeconomic "justice" necessitates the treatment of "public property as public, and private property as private,"[118] he nevertheless criticizes him for clinging too closely to a worldview he finds patently unable to explain the facts of "nature." Why? Because "nature has discharged all things for all men for common use. God has ordered all things to be produced, so that there should be food in common for all, and the earth a common possession for all. What nature generates as a 'common right' (*ius commune*), greed turns into a 'private right' (*ius privatum*)."[119]

One of Ambrose's students, Augustine of Hippo (d. 430 CE), reformulates these reflections into a dualistic view of creation by means of the now famous metaphor of "two cities" (earthly vs. heavenly),[120] and Martin Luther (d. 1546 CE)—an Augustinian monk to the day of his death—concretizes this transformation into a full-blown theology of "two kingdoms" ("sacred" vs. "secular").[121]

In short, since so few contemporary interpreters read the story of *Cain-and-Abel* against its original context, few can see (a) that just as Gilgamesh's acquisitional spirit leads him to violate the sacred boundary protecting the Cedar Forest, so Cain's acquisitional spirit leads him to violate the sacred boundary protecting Abel's "life-breath"; and (b) that just as Erra's suspicion of "contempt" provokes him into attacking *his*

117. Ambrose, *Cain*; Augustine, *Civ.* (cited in Quiñones, *Changes*, 123). Stoll pursues this tack too far when he asserts that "Cain gives rise to the division of labor and to the agrarian economy that eventually takes over the world" ("Agrarian," 7).

118. Ambrose, *Off.* 1:28:131–32.

119. Cited in Swift, "Iustitia," 177.

120. *City of God* is a response to (a) the sacking of Rome by Alaric the Visigoth in 410 (CE), as well as (b) the accusation that Christian abandonment of the Roman pantheon is at least partially responsible for the success of the Visigoths (Quiñones, *Changes*, 26–27). Van Oort argues (*Jerusalem*, 43–52) that Augustine draws less from a specific source (like Ambrose) than on Christian tradition generally (like *Did.* and Herm. *Vis.*) filtered through a North African lens.

121. Pelican, *Works* 1:246–59. Luther puts interpretation into practice by challenging his students "to resist the institution of primogeniture whenever it "impedes the consolidation of German princely power" (Fichtner, *Protestantism*, 24).

enemy, so Cain's suspicion of "contempt" provokes him into attacking *his* "enemy."[122] Perhaps this also explains why it's so difficult "to come to terms with Cain because we are his children, and with his city because we live in it."[123]

ABRAHAM AND THE "BIG PROBLEM" OF "CIVILIZATION" (GEN 11:27—14:16)

Where the "civilization-vs.-wilderness" polarity animating many of the "great texts" of Mesopotamia finds a close parallel in *Cain-and-Abel*, two vignettes about Abraham re-engage it via highly-polished stories about a transplanted Mesopotamian interfacing with (a) the prejudices and peccadilloes of Egyptian "civilization," as well as (b) the "good life" promoted in the Canaanite "cities of the plain."[124] However indirectly or covertly, these two vignettes engage a "civilization-vs.-wilderness" polarity patterned after that which is found in other "great texts."[125]

---

122. *GE* 3:43–53; *Erra* 1:120; 5:6.

123. Shulman, "Myth," 236.

124. Gen 13:12 (ערי הככר). Heb ככר only secondarily means "steppe/plain." Primarily it means "round loaf" or "round disk"; e.g., a "round disk" of gold, silver, or lead (*HAL* 451; *CAD* K:49–50; *UT* §19:1229). Some question the historicity of Abraham, but this is heavily debated (see Smith, *Memoirs*; Hendel, *Abraham*).

125. Trigger, *Understanding*; Baines, "Egyptian," 81–105; Fall, "Seeds," 107–25; Kemp, "Unification," 679–90; Bard, "Egyptian," 265–88. Wander tries to parallel the patrilineality of Abraham's culture—what little we know of it—with the patrilineality of Arab bedouin culture ("Structure," 75–99), but Benjamin argues (*Deuteronomy*) that the repeated appearance of עיר ("city") in *Torah* (Deut 4:41—26:19) challenges all attempts to turn pre-exilic Israel into a rural backwater. See Branigan, *Urbanism*; Chesson and Philip, "Urbanism," 3–16; Cowgill, "Origins," 525–49; Herzog, *Archaeology*.

The first begins when Yahweh calls Abraham out of urban Mesopotamia[126] into rural Canaan.[127] Accompanied by his wife Sarah,[128] his
nephew-heir Lot,[129] and "their possessions which they possess"[130] (including "the souls 'acquired' in Haran"),[131] Abraham hikes the socioeconomic Grand Canyon separating "city-dwellers" from "field-dwellers" in
the ancient Near East.[132] In spite of his wealth, he soon finds himself
forced by the infamous Palestinian famine-cycle to haul his family down
into Egypt for the basics of food and water.[133] Preparing Sarah for the
journey, he warns her that the Egyptians may "target" her for abduction
into Pharaoh's harem, assassinating him to "acquire" her.[134]

Most interpretations of this vignette focus on Abraham's survival
in Egypt, highlighting his acquisitional victories and downplaying his
behavioral improprieties.[135] Because so few read it from a perspective

126. The origin of "Ur" is not clear (Gen 11:28). Some argue that אור derives from
Sum uru ("town"). Others point to the homonym אור ("light"), translating "the place
of the dawn" (Gen 1:3). Abraham's hometown "Ur of the Chaldeans" (אור כסדים) may
reflect to some degree the fact that Chaldeans occupy Israel when the Abraham tradition starts hardening into written form (Moorey and Wooley, *Ur*).

127. Not all of Canaan is rural, as the Amarna texts indicate (Moran, *Amarna*, xxvi–
xxxiii). The name כנען ("Canaan") may be derived from the Hurrian word *kinaḫḫu*
("reddish purple") since Φοῖνιξ means "reddish purple" and Φοινίκη ("Phoenicia") is
the traditional locus of reddish-purple dye production. Eventually כנען comes to mean
"middle-man"/"merchant" as Canaan develops its socioeconomic identity (Oded and
Gibson, "Canaan," 391–93).

128. This story occurs before Abram and Sarai become Abraham and Sarah, but for
the sake of consistency only the later spelling is used here.

129. Helyer, "Separation," 77–88.

130. Gen 12:4–5 (רכשם ... רכשו). The word "possessions" pluralizes the noun רכוש,
which in turn derives from the verb רכש ("to acquire," *HAL* 1152–55).

131. Gen 12:5 (הנפש אשר עשו בחרן); NKJV, NIV, and NRSV all translate the common verb עשה ("to make/ do") as "to acquire."

132. Qur'an preserves this polarity in its understanding of Lot's "cities" (*Sura*
15.78–79), a polarity which, according to *Tafsir al-Jalalayn*, encompasses "the cities of
the people of Lot and those of his 'companions in the woods'" (اصحب لايكه).

133. Deut 11:10–12 (Rabinowitz, "Famine," 707–8; Moore, *Faith*, 139–53). The Nile
delta, to quote Tarn's memorable description, is the "breadbasket" of the Mediterranean
(*Hellenistic*, 14).

134. Firestone, "Difficulties," 196–214.

135. As Firestone sees it, "Abraham seems to be caught in a moral double bind: quite
simply, the patriarch appears either as a liar or as involved in a relationship of incest"
("Prophethood," 336). Fretheim examines these options (*Abraham*, 46–65), but Kunin
(*Incest*, 65–93), following Lévi-Strauss (*Anthropology*), argues that the wife/sister texts

informed by the "wilderness-vs.-civilization" polarity, the following questions tend to be marginalized and ignored: (a) Why does Abraham *presume* Sarah's abduction by the Egyptians? and (b) How does this description of Egyptian behavior resonate with other descriptions? Questions like these would be easier to engage, however, were not so many of the story's earliest interpreters so blatantly racist. One commentator, for example, denigrates Egypt as a land filled with "black and ugly" people,[136] while another goes out of his way to smear the pharaonic court as a cesspool of immorality.[137] Still another goes so far as to suggest that even after Pharaoh learns of Sarah's marital status he tries to seduce her anyway, though this flatly contradicts the words ascribed to him in *Genesis*: "What is this you have done to me? Why did you not tell me that she was your wife? Why did you say, 'She is my sister,' so that I took her as my wife?"[138]

Genesis complicates these tensions considerably by intratextually paralleling the wife/sister incident in chapter 12 with two more wife/sister incidents in chapters 20 and 26, causing some readers to wonder whether these incidents might not originate from different "sources."[139] Some imagine all three incidents coming from the same "source,"[140] but others view the episodes in chapters 20 and 26 as free-flowing reflections on a partially preserved folktale lying underneath the surface of chapter 12, sometimes to the point of hypothesizing the later episodes as "solutions" to the "problems" generated by the earlier one.[141] No hard evidence exists, however, to prove the existence of such "sources," nor do

---

in Genesis are there to help Israel resolve its ambivalence over the choice of endogamy vs. exogamy in the aftermath of foreign invasion.

136. *Gen. Rab.* 40:4.

137. *Sifra* 7:11; Josephus, *A.J.* 1:162. Shapiro presumes (without a shred of evidence) that "it was common practice for Egyptians to abduct the wives of strangers for sexual purposes" ("Moses," 494).

138. Gen 12:18-19 (*contra Gen. Rab.* 41:2).

139. In chapters 20 and 26, e.g., Abraham receives no financial compensation "on her behalf" (as in Gen 12:16, בעבורה). See Dillmann (*Genesis*, 226, 278-79, 322-23); König (*Genesis*, 56-57, 67); Skinner (*Genesis*, 242-43, 315, 363); Speiser (*Genesis*, 91); von Rad (*Erste*, 193, 235).

140. Koch, *Formgeschichte*, 121-48.

141. Van Seters, *Abraham*, 167-91; Westermann, *Genesis 12-36*, 187-88, 389-90, 516-17. Attempting a connection between "woman's body" and "social body," Frick argues that "the sexually endangered matriarch represents the vulnerability of the Israelite community amidst more powerful nations" ("Political," 203).

chapters 20 and 26 consciously set out to fix any "problems" "caused" by such hypothetical sources.[142] Source critics have a long history of ignoring intertextual matters.[143]

Following a suggestion from pioneer critic Umberto Cassuto,[144] on the other hand, Moshe Weinfeld suggests that the Egyptian decision to exchange "gifts" for Sarah probably reflects the ethos of a legal statute mandating that any man who "journeys" with another man's wife must compensate him by (a) taking an oath, and (b) giving him a "gift."[145] Presumably the purpose of this oath is to validate the oath-taker's ignorance of her marital status, while the purpose of the "gift" is to compensate the offended husband for the "contempt" he has been forced to endure.[146] Nevertheless, many ignore this interpretive possibility and insist that Pharaoh never touches Sarah,[147] often conflating the stories in chapters 12 and 20 to "protect her purity."[148] This approach, however, fails to identify, much less address the "big problem" facing this Mesopotamian immigrant.

Intertextual analysis shows this vignette to be an accurate reflection of the horrid realities of a world in which women are little more than a "primordial means of social exchange."[149] In this world Egyptians take their neighbors' daughters in marriage without reciprocating their own,[150] a startling one-sidedness which may or may not reflect the possibility that Egyptians regard *their* women as inherently superior,[151] but also the

142. Firestone suggests that "the latter rendition of the story appears to have served, at least in part, as exegesis on the Genesis 12 rendition" ("Abraham," 335; see Alexander, "Wife," 145–53).

143. Wenham deftly weighs the pros and cons of the source critical approach before concluding, wisely, that all "critical theories are based on the weighing of probabilities" ("Method," 108).

144. Abrahams and Roth, "Cassuto," 510–11.

145. Weinfeld, "Sarah," 431–36. English translation in *ANET* 181 (§A22).

146. In cases like these it's wise to question, with Wells, which laws reflect actual practice vs. which do not ("Law," 223–43).

147. See, e.g., Philo, *Abr.* 98; Josephus, *B.J.* 5:381

148. The *Genesis Apocryphon* from Cave 1 reads Gen 12 through the "eyes" of Gen 20 (Wise, *Scrolls*, 99–102).

149. Avruch, "Reciprocity," 163.

150. Kunin cites several examples (*Incest*, 164).

151. Aeschylus illustrates this attitude in a story about fifty daughters of an Egyptian king (Danaus), who refuse to be manipulated by his court into political marriages designed to "seal" international treaties (*Suppl.*1–18). Spier argues that their resistance has less to do with the fear of "loveless marriage" than "marriage in general" ("Motive,"

possibility that women are considered more in terms of "tribute" than "gifts," a process designed to create the legal fiction that women are "exchangeable property."[152] Another possibility is that Egyptian inheritance customs are so fragile, political marriage evolves into little more than a microcosmic version of "foreign invasion."[153]

Whatever the possibilities, the point here is that Sarah is not the first foreign woman to suffer socioeconomic prejudice at the hands of the Egyptians.[154] Within Egypt's "great literature," in fact, one document illustrates this prejudice more clearly than others—the *Tale of Sinuhe*.[155] One of the "accomplished pieces of Middle Kingdom prose,"[156] *Sinuhe* tells the story of a government official in the court of Pharaoh Amenemhat I (d. 1962 BCE)[157] who, at his master's death, flees the country to escape the draconian repercussions so often attending such transitions.[158] Making his way to Byblos, a Phoenician port-city which just happens to

---

315).

152. Liverani, *International*, 6.

153. Bryan, "Egyptian," 82.

154. *Example:* Mitannian king Tushratta sends a cuneiform letter to Egyptian pharaoh Amenhotep IV listing several challenges to their "brotherhood," the most obvious being the pharaoh's failure to reciprocate the "gift" of his daughter Tadu-Ḫeba (*EA* 29:28–54; Moore, "Dreams," 205–21).

155. Parkinson calls *Sinuhe* a "funerary autobiography" designed to "encourage reflection on the nature of Egyptian life" (*Sinuhe*, 21), but Spalinger reads it, "in contrast to a standard Egyptian autobiography," as a "totally artificial presentation" ("Orientations," 324). English translations appear in *ANET* 18–22 and Lichtheim, *Literature* 1:222–35.

156. Lichtheim, *Literature* 1:222. Baines questions the existence of an "historical Sinuhe" ("Sinuhe," 31–44), but van Seters observes that "in view of the paucity of royal inscriptions . . . biographies often constitute the most important historical resource" (*History*, 182). Goedicke calls *Sinuhe* the "kingpin" of Middle Kingdom literature (Review of *Erzählung*, 236).

157. Internal evidence suggests that Sinuhe works in the service of Princess Nefru before she becomes queen (Grajetzki, *Egypt*, 28–35), and Gardiner calls him a "henchman . . . of the Royal *harim*" (*Sinuhe*, 168).

158. Lichtheim argues that "Sinuhe was specifically in the service of Princess Nefru, the wife of Sesotris I, the latter being co-regent at the time of his father's death" (*Literature*, 233), and Hollis ("Otherworld," 320–37) argues that since the Egyptians view themselves as living at the center of the cosmos, their literature often portrays other countries as places of punishment and exile (a motif dominating not only *Sinuhe*, but also the *Story of Two Brothers* and the *Prince and His Fates*. Each of these stories involves (a) the notion that "Asia" (Syria–Palestine) is a place of exile, death, and transformation; and (b) a hero forced to undergo trial in a foreign land before triumphantly returning home.

be Egypt's major trading partner,[159] he experiences a dramatic change in socioeconomic status (i.e., he becomes "rich").[160] Of greater interest to the present study, however, is the way in which this tale emphasizes Egypt's superiority over all her neighbors, especially those the Egyptians pejoratively call *retenu*.[161]

When Sesostris I comes to power (Amenemhat's successor)[162] he sends a message to the still-exiled Sinuhe, urging him to

> come back to Egypt! See the residence in which you lived! Kiss the ground at the great portals, mingle with the courtiers . . . ! A night is made for you with ointments and wrappings from the hand of Tayet.[163] A funeral procession will occur for you on the day of your burial; the mummy case is of gold, its head of lapis lazuli, the sky above you as you lie in the hearse, oxen drawing you, musicians playing before you. The dance of the funerary dancers will be performed at the door of your tomb; the offering-list read to you as sacrifice is made before your offering-stone. Your tomb-pillars, made of white stone, will be among those of the royal children. You shall not die abroad! No *retenu* shall inter you. You shall not be wrapped in the skin of a ram as your coffin.[164]

Responding positively to this message, Sinuhe returns to Egypt, even though the ordeal of "re-entry" soon throws him into a state of anxiety.[165] This anxiety comes to a head when Queen Nefru, hearing Sinuhe introduced at court as *retenu*, screams "a loud scream, triggering even louder screams from the royal daughters."[166] Blurting out, "Is it re-

---

159. Byblos is the Syro-Palestinian city most closely associated with the Egyptian economy (Wright and Pardee, "Sources," 143–61).

160. "Egyptian society at all levels is plural and cosmopolitan . . . from the second millennium onward" (Leahy, "Diversity," 232).

161. This Egyptian term refers to "Asiatics/Palestinians" (Murnane, "Egypt," 700). Baines similarly identifies the *retenu*, but not from an explicitly socioeconomic perspective ("Sinuhe").

162. King suggests that Sesostris I is Joseph's pharaoh, but this cannot be determined with certainty ("Joseph," 577–94).

163. Tayet is the Egyptian goddess of spinning and weaving (el-Saady, "Tayet," 213).

164. *ANET* 20–21. As Fitzenreiter points out, Egyptian funerary ritual extravagantly underlines Egypt's most deeply embedded values ("Grabdekoration," 67–140).

165. Kim, "Intercultural," 452–59.

166. *ANET* 22.

ally him, my lord?" she hears Pharaoh reply, "Yes, it is."[167] Then, realizing
the precariousness of her former servant's situation,[168] she takes off her
jewelry and gives it to Pharaoh, publicly asking him to "reward" her with
Sinuhe as a "gift."[169] Not only does this demonstrate her concern for a val-
ued servant, it shows her determination to "redeem" a vulnerable "little
brother." Like the Ishtar episode in *Gilgamesh*, it shows a strong female
leader using *economic* (not *erotic*) language to address a "big problem"
before which she might otherwise appear helpless.[170]

At any rate, when Pharaoh accepts the queen's redemption-propos-
al, this elicits the following response from Sinuhe:

> I left the audience-hall, the royal daughters extending their hands
> to me. We went through the great portals and I was put in the
> house of a prince, a house with a bathroom and mirrors. In it
> were riches from the treasury; clothes of royal linen, myrrh, and
> the choice perfume of the king and his favorite courtiers wafting
> through every room. Every servant was busy doing his job. They
> removed years from my body, shaving me and combing my hair.
> Thus was my squalor returned to the foreign land, my clothes to
> the Sand-people.[171] They clothed me in fine linen, anointing me
> with fine oil. I slept on a bed.[172]

In short, the *Tale of Sinuhe* illustrates the prejudices of "city-dwelling" Egyptians toward their "field-dwelling" *retenu*-servants, the under-

---

167. *ANET* 22.

168. Sinuhe is still charged with abandoning his post years earlier—a very serious
crime (Snell, *Flight*, 106–8). As Baines observes, "flight from Egypt and Egyptian values
is difficult to accomplish and intensely painful. An Egyptian may well succeed in another type of life abroad, but his success is hollow because the greatest triumph there is
nothing compared to a position of modest esteem in Egypt. Egyptian values supplant
all others" ("Sinuhe," 37).

169. Wilson translates "Give us our 'goodly gift'" (Eg *ḥn-t, ANET* 22), and Gardiner
comments: "the royal children clearly demand ... the freedom of Sinuhe as a 'reward'
(Eg *mnt*) for their song and dancing" (*Sinuhe*, 106).

170. *GE* 6:6–79; Ackerman, "Queen Mother," 396–97.

171. "Sand-people" is pejorative nickname for *retenu*.

172. *ANET* 22. Rendsburg interprets this paragraph as a typical "homecoming" text
in which returnees always receive new clothes ("Notes," 363).

class upon whom they depend to build their cities and manage their estates.[173] Abraham's warning reflects the depth of these prejudices.[174]

In the next socioeconomically significant vignette Abraham encounters the Canaanite "cities of the plain."[175] A man of "great wealth,"[176] he soon finds himself forced, more-or-less, to divide up his wealth with his nephew Lot. Why? Because "the land cannot support both of them living together. Their possessions are so great they cannot live together[177] as strife breaks out between the herdsmen of Abraham and Lot."[178] Like Shangashu with Enkidu and Cain with Abel, Abraham and Lot find it difficult to manage divergent economies determined to work the same land at the same time.[179]

Intertextually, of course, the Abraham cycle resonates with several other "great texts" in which (a) sonless patriarchs (b) appeal to a deity who (c) responds by giving them male heirs.[180] Not only does this type-scene anchor many stories in *Genesis*,[181] it also anchors a couple of stories in the Canaanite corpus,[182] thereby provoking two more questions: (a) How deeply does the Abraham-Lot rift resonate with other patriarchal rifts in

173. Like Eg *retenu*, Akk *ḫupšu* is another pejorative term ("pirate-scum"; see *EA* 117:90; 118:23; 125:27; *CAD* P:37–49). See also ληστής ("brigand/terrorist," Xenophon, *Cyr.* 2:4.23; Luke 10:30). According to Gen 46:34, shepherding is assigned to the *retenu* because Egyptians find it to be a "detestable" profession (תועבה, *HAL* 1568–70).

174. Gen 12:12–13.

175. Abela, "Genesis 13," 53–80; Cohn, "Negotiating," 147–66; Jeansonne, "Characterization," 123–29.

176. Gen 13:2 (כבד מאד). The adjective כבד primarily means "heavy, glorious," but here (as in Num 22:17, 37; 24:11) it denotes "wealth."

177. Gen 13:6 (N.B. the repetition of יחדו, "together"). Qumran sectarians nominalize this adverb (יחד) to designate their notion of "community" (1QS 1:1; 1QpHab 12:4; 1QH 6:18). The socioeconomic conflict between the tribesmen of Abraham and Lot threatens their "togetherness" (יחד).

178. Gen 13:6–7. Ruppert reads this text as a post-exilic narrative highlighting the differences between unequal "brothers" ("Abram," 235–50).

179. *GE* 1:157–60; Gen 4:1–7. Edens addresses this tension from a geopolitical perspective ("Dynamics," 118–39).

180. McAfee, "Patriarch."

181. Alter defines a "type-scene" as "a series of recurrent narrative episodes ... dependent on the manipulation of a fixed constellation of predetermined motifs" (*Narrative*, 51).

182. See especially *CAT* 1.14–16 (*Kirta*) and 1.17–18 (*Aqhat*). Hendel examines these texts alongside the patriarchal stories of *Genesis* (*Patriarch*, 37–59).

other "great texts?" and (b) How deeply does this conflict resonate with the "wilderness-vs.-civilization" polarity in the socioeconomic context?

The *Epic of Kirta,* for example, tells the story of another tribal heir challenging the authority of another sonless patriarch.[183] Having lost his family to disaster (famine? illness? war?), the patriarch Kirta recruits an army of warriors to pressure his neighbor Pabil into handing over his daughter in marriage.[184] Through this union he then rebuilds a new family in the face of several more challenges, including (a) a mysterious illness,[185] and (b) a rebellion instigated by his son Yaṣṣib.[186] Motifs like these animate several Syro-Palestinian texts because "threats (involving) the lack of an heir, of sickness, and of usurpation are common concerns of ancient monarchs . . . all three appearing in the accounts of the kings of Israel and Judah."[187] Socioeconomically, however, this Canaanite text generates two questions: (a) What causes Kirta and Yaṣṣib to have such a falling out? and (b) To what degree is this conflict driven by socioeconomic concerns?

Near the outset of *Kirta* a stricken patriarch prays to his patron-deity El, who responds by offering "diverse tokens of wealth and privilege."[188] Significantly, however, Kirta rejects these gifts, using language similar to that found in other rejection-speeches (e.g., Gilgamesh's rejection of Ishtar's "gifts"):[189] "What to me is silver, or even yellow gold alongside land and slaves forever mine? Or a triad of chariot-horses from the

---

183. Dietrich et al. publish a transliterated Ugaritic text (*CAT* 1.14–16), and Parker provides an English translation (*UNP* 12–48). Wyatt justifiably calls *Kirta* an "epic" ("Epic," 246–54).

184. Roche cites several lines of evidence to show that "marriages among differing Syrian dynasties in the 14th–13th centuries assure important ties between the different courts," so that "the queen of the land of Ugarit is able to play not only a political or legal role in the internal affairs of the kingdom, but also a vital economic role" ("Lady," 214).

185. *CAT* 1.16:5:42—6:2; Herrmann, "El," 274–80.

186. *CAT* 1.16:6:41–53. The name *Yaṣṣib* probably means "one who takes a stand" (cognate of נצב, *HAL* 408).

187. Parker, "Ugaritic," 230. Knoppers argues that Kirta's illness "becomes an intrinsic part of Yaṣṣib's claim that his father should abdicate" ("Dissonance," 577).

188. Greenstein, "Kirta," 13.

189. *GE* 6:22–79. Seow points out that both Solomon and Kirta reject offers of wealth in their dream-encounters with the Unseen World ("Syro-Palestinian," 149), and the book of *Esther* emphasizes that the Jews, though given royal permission to take "spoil" (בזה), nevertheless decline (Esth 9:10, 15, 16).

stable of a slavewoman's son?"[190] Afterwards Kirta repeats this rejection several more times to several more offers from other potential donors. Conversing with his soon-to-be father-in-law Pabil, for example, he hears an offer much like the one extended earlier by El: "Take silver and yellow gold alongside land and slaves forever. Take a triad of chariot-horses from the stable of a slavewoman's son. Take offerings, O Kirta, offerings of peace!"[191] But again he rejects it: "What to me is silver, or even yellow gold alongside land and slaves forever mine? Or a triad of chariot-horses from the stable of a slavewoman's son?"[192] Where Gilgamesh rejects Ishtar's "gifts" to avoid a dangerous business partnership, however,[193] Kirta rejects the "gifts" offered to him because his eye is fixed on another prize altogether: "What is not in my house you must give me. You must give me Lady Huraya,[194] the Fair One, your firstborn child, who's as fair as the goddess Anat, who's as comely as Astarte, whose eyes are lapis lazuli,[195] whose eyelids are gleaming alabaster,[196] whom El has given me in my dream, the Father of Man in my vision, who will bear a child for Kirta, a lad for the servant of El."[197] In short, Kirta's desire for progeny, itself a socioeconomic desire, helps him resist any desire he might have to "acquire" *at any cost*, thus preserving his "incorruptibility."[198]

Kirta's second challenge occurs when a mysterious "genie" goads Yaṣṣib into challenging his father's authority.[199] Just as Erra's "heart" provokes Erra into action,[200] so Yaṣṣib's "genie" provokes him: "Hear now, 'no-

---

190. *CAT* 1.14:1:51—2:3 (restoring on the basis of the better-preserved lines in 3:33–34 and 6:17–18).

191. *CAT* 1.14:6:4–8.

192. *CAT* 1.14:6:17–18.

193. *GE* 6:33–79.

194. Roche argues that Kirta's primary motivation for marrying Huraya is *economic* ("Lady," 213).

195. N.B. Ishtar's words to Gilgamesh: "let me harness for you a chariot of lapis lazuli and gold" (*GE* 6:9)

196. N.B. Ishullanu's desire to make Ishtar's table "gleam" (*GE* 6:66, *namāru*).

197. *CAT* 1.14:6:22–35.

198. Aitken thinks that Kirta's desire to acquire Huraya resonates with "the wider ideological context of the need for progeny to demonstrate his fitness to rule as king" ("Rebekah," 12).

199. *CAT* 1.16:6:26 (Ug *ggn*). See Akk *gngn* in *CAT* 1.4:7:48–49 (// *npš*) and the Arabic cognate جن ("jinn/daemon," Wehr and Cowan, 138).

200. *Erra* 2:C10/38′ (Akk *libbu*; al-Rawi and Black, "Ishum," 119).

ble' Kirta![201] Listen! Bend your ear! When bandits pillage, you [settle for] governing and ruling from [outposts in] the mountains.[202] You let your hand touch any base thing.[203] You do not pursue the widow's case; you do not take up the claim of the wretched. You do not expel the oppressor of the poor; you do not feed the orphan before you, nor the widow behind you[204] ... Step down! Let me become king!"[205] Here Prince Yaṣṣib, like Prince Absalom in Judah,[206] threatens his father's authority by trumping up charges against him—charges covertly tied to the "big problem" of *corruption*.[207] Yet where Absalom rebels against David for reasons rooted in the primogenitural politics of *monarchy*, Yaṣṣib challenges Kirta for reasons rooted in the *tribal* politics of primogeniture.[208]

201. *CAT* 1.16:6:41 (*t*'). This term (here translated "noble") can mean "gifted" in other Ugaritic texts (see *UT* §19:2715).

202. While Ug *dbr* can be translated "turn your back" (*CML* 102), intensive forms of دبر can mean "to govern" (*UT* §19:641), thus providing a parallel to Ug *twy* ("to rule," *UT* §19:2662).

203. Gordon translates "thou hast let thy hand(s) fall into inactivity" (*UT* §19:1965), but Parker translates "You've let your hand fall to vice" (*UNP* 41). The psalmist parallels with "I will not set before my eyes any 'base thing'" (דבר בליעל; lit. "thing of Belial," Ps 101:3).

204. As noted above, several poets critique the problem of corruption as a "big problem," so Yaṣṣib's complaints doubtless "amount to more than a reproach of Kirta for having become bed-ridden" (Knoppers, "Dissonance," 580).

205. *CAT* 1.16:6:41–53. Again, why *Kirta* focuses on these *particular* socioeconomic motifs is not immediately obvious, though the poet's word choices may have as much to do with liturgical rhythm as ideological critique.

206. In 2 Sam 15:1–6 Absalom rebels against David's leadership. Further comparisons appear in the *Combabos* myth in Lucian (*Syr. d.* 17–27; see Grotanelli, "Combabos," 19–27).

207. Parker interprets this as evidence that *Kirta* intentionally sets out to criticize "a society in which total faith in the king as an extension of the divine sphere has been lost" ("Composition," 173). Knoppers, however, argues that "the king's dependence upon the gods and his heirs evinces both royal power and royal vulnerability," and that *Kirta* simply "reaffirms the institution it complicates" ("Dissonance," 572; see Tadmor, "People," 46–68; Parker, *Pre-Biblical*, 152–65; Moore, *Reconciliation*, 49–60, and *Faith*, 59–64).

208. It's wise to avoid drawing too rigid a distinction, but Gray wonders whether "the legal duties of the king are in process of devolution" in Israel's case, "or whether there is here rather a vestige of tribal conditions where all business is discussed and settled at the open *mejlis* ... the chief sheikh being but *primus inter pares*" ("Canaanite," 210). Coote thinks that the oldest Hebrew politics take shape through tense interfaces between tribal clan and monarchical court ("Tribalism," 35–49; see Heard, *Dynamics*, 38–47; Moore, *Faith*, 301–42).

Question: Why does Lot reject Abraham's leadership? *Answer:* Probably not because he believes his uncle to be "corrupt," but rather because he doubtless feels a desire to free himself from the socioeconomic restrictions ingrained into all tribal cultures, hoping instead to network himself more lucratively into the "breadbasket of the Jordan."[209] Borrowing from the language of *Gilgamesh,* what Lot seems to want is an unimpeded shot at the "good life"—not as defined by Moses, but as defined by Shamhat.[210] In short, where "Abraham desires that the land of Canaan should be *partitioned* between himself and Lot, what actually happens is that 'Abraham lives in the land of Canaan, while Lot lives *among the cities of the plain*'" (Gen 13:12).[211]

Archaeologically the "cities of the plain" have never been found, not definitely. Some believe them to lie beneath the Lisan peninsula of the Dead Sea,[212] while others link the city names in *Genesis* with names discovered on third millennium tablets from Tell Mardikh (ancient Ebla).[213] The latter hypothesis has never found anything approaching universal acceptance,[214] however, and many now doubt whether these cities ever existed at all.[215] Nonetheless, *Genesis* does describe Lot's character—his dealings with *Abraham,* his response to the divine messengers, his treat-

209. Gen 13:10 (כבר ירדן). As noted above, the primary meaning of כבר is "round loaf" or "disk"—as in "round disk"/"talent" of gold or silver (*HAL* 451; *CAD* K:49–50; *UT* §19:1229).

210. Contrast Deut 6:18–24 with *GE* 1:233 (Ipsen, *Sex*, 23–45). Vaughn argues that the structure of the Abraham cycle focuses on the movement from incomplete obedience to complete obedience, beginning with the patriarch's failure to obey Yahweh's command to leave all blood-relatives in Haran (Gen 12:4), and ending with his decision to sacrifice Isaac ("Disobedience," 111–23).

211. Helyer, "Separation," 79.

212. The Lisan peninsula (لسان, "tongue") extends into the Dead Sea from its southeastern shore (van Hattem, "Sodom," 87–92). A few still argue, however, that these cities lie buried beneath the southernmost section of the Dead Sea (Albright, "Archaeological," 2–12).

213. Freedman, "Ebla," 143–64.

214. Pettinato, "Ebla," 203–16; Archi, "Ebla," 151–52.

215. Van Seters is characteristically blunt: "The special effort to fit the war between Abraham and the kings of the east into the history of the second millennium by trying to identify the various kings and nations involved has failed to yield plausible proposals. The four eastern kingdoms, Elam, Babylonia, Assyria, and that of the Hittites, referred to cryptically in this text, never form an alliance, nor do they ever control Palestine either collectively or individually during the second millennium BCE. The whole account is historically impossible" ("Abraham," 13).

ment of his daughters—as something which evolves within a cycle of vignettes pointedly designed to contrast the patriarchal leadership of Uncle Abraham with the "rebellious spirit" of Nephew Lot,[216] and one of the ways *Genesis* highlights this tension is to segregate "the five cities of the plain" from the "land of Canaan."[217] Thus, where *Kirta* focuses on Yaṣṣib's rebellion against his father Kirta, *Genesis* "draws attention to the crisis of faith which Lot precipitates by his choice of pasturage outside the land of Canaan. At stake is nothing less than Lot's elimination as heir to the covenant promise. Furthermore, this crisis provides its intended meaning within the entire Abraham cycle when it is seen as one of eight such crises threatening the fulfillment of one aspect of the tripartite promise of Gen 12:1–3, 'I will make you into a great nation' (v. 2). Thus the overall concern of the cycle is, 'Who will be Abraham's heir?'"[218]

In other words, this Hebrew episode interfaces not only with the Canaanite story of Yaṣṣib's rebellion, but with the "wilderness-civilization" polarity undergirding the Mesopotamian epics of *Gilgamesh*, *Atrahasis*, and *Erra*—even though the Hebrew tradition quickly moves away from Abraham's socioeconomic life to his roles as "priestly intercessor" (Gen 18:22–33), "tested servant" (22:1–19; Ps 105:6), "seer/dreamer" (1QapGen 19:14), "prayer warrior" (20:10–29; *b. Ber.* 26b), "exorcist" (1QapGen 20:28-29; CD 16.6), "wise man" (Philo, *Cher.* 7; *Somn.* 1.70), "philosopher" (*Gig.* 62), "forefather" (Josephus, *B.J.* 5:380; *A.J.* 1:214, 239–41), and "eschatological sage" (Luke 16:22–30).[219]

JACOB AND THE "BIG PROBLEM" OF PRIMOGENITURE (GEN 25:19–34)

Like the *Erra Epic,* the Jacob-Esau cycle gingerly straddles the "Grand Canyon" separating "city-dwellers" from "field-dwellers" through several vignettes about a "wild man" from the "field"[220] staunchly opposing his

216. Jeansonne, "Characterization," 123–29.

217. Helyer highlights this point ("Separation," 80; "*Abraham,*" 20–27).

218. Helyer, "Separation," 85. Towner points out that as early as the eighth century CE several interpreters begin reflecting on how this crisis in Abraham's life links up with other crises in his life (*Rabbinic*).

219. Moore, "Abraham" 2–3.

220. Gen 25:27 (שׂדה). Like Enkidu, Esau is a "man familiar with wild game" (אישׁ ידע ציד).

"civilized" brother who lives in tents.[221] Like Enkidu, a "mantle of hair" covers the "wild man's" body,[222] and like Gilgamesh, the "civilized man's" public heroism has a dark side.[223] This section of *Genesis* manipulates the sibling rivalry metaphor to symbolize "conflict between two ways of life, one of a member of what has become ... the civilized society, and the other of a member of the sphere of lawlessness."[224]

Predictably the names of these siblings are (again) symbolic. "Jacob" means "trickster/deceiver,"[225] while "Esau" means "doer/actor."[226] Like Ishmael, Elijah, and Samson, Esau spends so much time in the wild his father identifies him by his "gamey smell."[227] Like the Sibitti he questions the values and motives of "city-dwellers." Like Erra he "despises" anyone who might be conniving against him with "contempt."[228] Like the "wild man" Enkidu, moreover, he makes an easy "target."[229] "Exhibit A" is the famous socioeconomic transaction between the "smooth man" and the "hairy man."[230] Just as Odysseus tricks a "wild man" (Polyphemus) into

221. Gen 25:27 (תם). Fundamentally this word means "complete" or "whole."

222. Gen 25:25, אדרת שׂער; see *GE* 1:105, šuʿur šartu ("hairy with hair").

223. Mobley, *Heroic*, 19–74; Moore, *Reconciliation*, 73–85. Niditch tracks the following sequence in many ancient "brother-stories": (a) unusual birth; (b) conflict over status; (c) journey/adventures; (d) successes in new environment; (e) resolution of rivalry (*Prelude*, 72).

224. Malul, "Heel," 206.

225. The name יעקוב derives from the verb יקב, "to trick" (*HAL* 825). Niditch describes Jacob and Joseph as "underdogs, youngest sons who inherit, exiles who outwit their masters, marginal people who end their tales with financial and social success" (*Prelude*, 70).

226. The name עשׂו probably derives from the verb עשׂה, "to do, make" (*HAL* 845). Philo abandons the canons of historical philology altogether when he tries to make the argument that, "as the head is the chief of all the aforementioned parts of an animal, so is Esau the chief of this race, whose name is interpreted 'an oak' or 'a thing made.' It is interpreted 'an oak' in reference to his being unbending, and implacable, and obstinate, and stiff-necked by nature ... It is interpreted 'a thing made' inasmuch as a life according to folly is an invention and a fable, full of tragic pomp and vain boasting" (*Congr.* 61).

227. Gen 27:27 (כריח שׂדה, lit., "like the smell of a field").

228. Just as the Sibitti worry that Erra is "despised" (qalālu (*Erra* 1:53), so Esau "despises" his birthright (בזה, Gen 25:34).

229. Mobley sees Jacob as the "Shamhat" to Esau's "Enkidu" ("Wild Man," 231–33.).

230. Gen 25:19–34. Ahroni delimits this transaction to "any merchandise subject to purchase through an agreement between the parties concerned" ("Esau," 324). Bernheimer argues that the most distinctive trait of "wild men" is their "hairiness" (*Wild*, 1).

doing what *he* wants,[231] so Jacob tricks Esau into doing what *he* wants—
even to the point of finagling from him his primogenitural "birthright."[232]
Esau's response to *his* "tempter" parallels Enkidu's response to *his*
"tempter"—naiveté, betrayal, anger, and (eventual) reconciliation.[233] Like
Ishtar with Gilgamesh,[234] the "tempter" here dangles another "gift" before
another "target" in order to highlight (a) the "target's" vulnerability as
well as (b) the "tempter's" shrewdness.[235]

Like *Atrahasis,* the Esau-Jacob cycle features a "weaker" entity
(Jacob/Igigi) relying on his wits to overcome a "stronger" one (Esau/
Enlil). Joel Kaminsky extrapolates from this that *Genesis* uses this story
to highlight "the problems which arise when someone is mysteriously
singled out as God's special elect."[236] Robert Alter agrees, suggesting that
firstborn sons often become "losers in *Genesis* by the condition of their
birth."[237] Fred Greenspahn also agrees, commenting that "the prevalence
of seniority-based imagery in the Bible and its repeated efforts to justify
deviations from this norm make it impossible to accept it as simply the
result of Israelite law or custom."[238] David Marcus, however, marvels at
the way this story resonates with so many other Hebrew stories in which
"the younger son eventually supplants the older, both in cases where
property is concerned (e.g., Ishmael < Isaac; Esau < Jacob; Reuben <

231. Homer, *Od.* 9:281–82, 507–12 (the "Cyclops" episode). Page observes that, "no single detail . . . receives so much attention in the *Iliad* and the *Odyssey* as gift-giving" (*Odyssey,* 5).

232. Gen 25:31 (בכרה). Frymer-Kensky discusses the rights accorded firstborn sons in tribal cultures generally ("Patriarchal," 209–14), and Marcus focuses on their anthropological/legal implications ("Law," 4734–37).

233. *GE* 1:201–33.

234. *GE* 1:226–33; 6:6–21. As Mobley points out, when Delilah challenges the "wild man" Samson, this shows that both Samson and Enkidu "become captive to culture through the agency of a woman" (Mobley, "Wild," 231).

235. Later interpreters, uninterested in the socioeconomic context, denigrate Esau as "immoral" (πόρνος) and "profane" (βέβηλος; Heb 12:16; see *Jub.* 15:30; 35:13; *4 Ezra* 3:16; Philo *Leg.* 3:88–89, 191–93; *Sacr.* 17–18, 81, 120, 135; *Ebr.* 9–10; *Det.* 45–46; *Migr.* 208; *Congr.* 61, 129; *Fug.* 24, 39, 43; *Virt.* 209–10; *Praem.* 62; *Sobr.* 26–27; b. *Šabb.* 145b–47; b. *B. Bat.* 16b; b. *Sanh.* 12a; *1 Clem.* 4:8; *Ps-Clem.*16:6; *Acts Thom.* 84). Greene thinks that the denigration of Balaam follows a similar devolutionary pattern (*Balaam,* 162–69; see Moore, "Prophet," 17–21).

236. Kaminsky, "Reclaiming," 135.

237. Alter, *Narrative,* 6.

238. Greenspahn, *Brothers,* 30.

Joseph; and Manasseh < Ephraim) and in cases of dynastic succession (e.g., Eliab < David; Adonijah < Solomon)."[239]

One thing is clear. Hebrew writers never portray primogeniture, for all its power and persistency, as something divinely *created*, only something divinely *allowed* (like kingship, war, or divorce).[240] Birth-order may shape the fate of individual heroes "in important ways ... so fundamental as to be invisible,"[241] yet the Bible never canonizes it as something upon which Yahweh must rely to manage his own creation.[242] In fact, just the opposite is the case, as story after biblical story challenges the traditionalist boundaries of this hoary institution. Jacob's character may *look* "flat,"[243] but underneath the surface "Jacob" symbolizes *every* vulnerable little brother who's ever had to rely upon the *Yahwistic* imperative:

CREATION = ACQUISITION *plus* PROTECTION.[244]

Just as *Atrahasis* avoids outright condemnation of the socioeconomic institution of slavery, so *Genesis* avoids outright condemnation of the socioeconomic institution of primogeniture.[245] When Jacob tricks Esau out of his birthright this affords the narrator an opportunity to describe much more than a shrewd little brother outwitting a privileged older brother. It creates an opportunity to criticize the institution of primogeniture itself.

As is well known, tribal cultures tend to elevate firstborn males to the top of the socioeconomic pyramid.[246] So precious are they, in fact, the priests in these cultures sometimes demand the shedding of first-

239. Marcus, "Israelite," 4734.

240. According to Mal 2:16, e.g., Yahweh "hates" divorce, even though the deuteronomistic tradition allows "bills of divorcement" (ספר כריתת, Deut 24:1). Similar ambivalence characterizes biblical statements about kingship (contrast Deut 17:14–20 with Ps 110) and war (contrast Deut 20:1–20 with Josh 6:17).

241. Longino, Review of *Birth*, 967.

242. Schneidau, *Discontent*, 1–12, 243.

243. Forster discusses "flat" vs. "round" characters (*Aspects*, 72–73).

244. Levine, "Firstborn," 45–46; Coote, "Tribalism," 40–49; Whiteley, "Indians," 6720–30.

245. Kaiser tries to reconcile the tension between "child-sacrifice" and firstborn-redemption (Exod 13:13; 22:28; 34:20) by suggesting that in Gen 22 God exercises sovereignty over the life of Isaac, yet foregoes this legal tradition in response to Abraham's faith ("Bindung," 199–224).

246. Agarwal (*Field*) points out how persistently male primogeniture still shapes the structural dynamics of contemporary developing economies.

born male blood in order to placate this or that "angry deity."[247] The
Moabite king Mesha, for example, sacrifices his firstborn son in the hope
of securing the help of his patron deity Chemosh against the threat of
foreign invasion.[248] Ancient law codes testify to similar anxieties felt by
other parents in similarly stressful situations.[249]

Question: Why, then, do so many economies—pre-modern and (post)
modern—rely so strongly on the institution of primogeniture?[250]
Answer: In the words of economist Adam Smith, it's because of the way
the institution has consistently proven itself over time.[251] "City-dwelling"
Westerners often fail to understand this because they so often fail to
understand (a) how tribal economies actually function, and (b) what a
serious economic crisis can do.[252] Thus they also fail to understand that a
patriarch's greatest desire is simply to see "every daughter well-married"
and "every son supporting his own family"—both fundamentally *socioeconomic* concerns.[253] Granted, tribal patriarchs can and do sometimes
degenerate into Enlil-like abusers, and granted, this can and does invite
the Jacobs of the world to look for ways to "demand their freedom."[254] Yet
the fact remains that primogeniture "succeeds" because it has the ability to *protect* children while *perpetuating* their family identity[255]—two

247. Some question whether human sacrifice ever occurs among the Hebrews (e.g.,
Weinfeld, "Molech," 133–54; Koch, "Molek," 32), but Levenson insists that ritual sacrifice
of the "beloved son" (though not necessarily the firstborn) stands at the center of Judeo-
Christian tradition (*Death*, x).

248. 2 Kings 32:27; see *KAI* 181; Moore, *Faith*, 306–12.

249. Taggar-Cohen, "Law," 74–94; Rowe, "Egyptians," 335–43; Wilcke, *Law*, 55–58.

250. From a Nazarene point of view the "firstborn" trope describes big ideas like
"firstborn of all creation" (πρωτότοκος πάσης κτίσεως, Col 1:15), but as Marx notes,
"gift" and "giving" do not always connect to the notion of "sacrifice" (*Systems*, 50–51, 76;
see Moore, "Sacrifice," 533–36).

251. Smith, *Inquiry*, 361–62.

252. Moore, "Ruth," 359–60.

253. Cole and Wolf, *Frontier*, 176.

254. *Atr* 1:148; Chu, "Primogeniture," 78. Several Hebrew texts document this "big
problem" (the Jacob-Esau cycle; the Joseph novella; the Gehazai-Naaman cycle; the
Ahab-Naboth cycle), and Goodkin shows how primogenitural motifs operate in sev-
enteenth-century French plays designed to help "heritocratic" feudal audiences move
closer to "meritocratic" capitalism (*Birth*, 9–28).

255. Chu, "Primogeniture," 80; Nakane, *Kinship*, 10–11.

accomplishments few other economic systems, pre-modern or (post) modern, have been able to replicate.[256]

Interpreters unaware of (or uninterested in) the intertextual parallels tend to read this text from a variety of angles; e.g., (a) Esau sells his birthright because he wants Jacob to offer it back to God in ritual sacrifice;[257] or (b) Esau acts the way he does because he has "strayed away" from "the prayers of his father Isaac";[258] or (c) Esau sells his birthright to Jacob because Isaac is too poor to pass on *any* inheritance;[259] or (d) the story's *raison d'être* is to champion the "rights" of second-born sons denied the privilege of officiating at public religious ceremonies.[260] The book of *Jubilees* adopts this kind of reading strategy when it has "Isaac" refuse to make "Esau" stop bullying "Jacob," thereby forcing "Rebekah" to conclude that "Esau's" bullying arises from an "evil inclination" in his "soul."[261] Why does *Jubilees* re-tell the story like this? Because its goal is not to *explain* the text from a literary-historical perspective, only *re-package* it for popular consumption (sound familiar?). In fact, *Jubilees* highlights "Rebekah's" decision to rescue "Jacob" from "Esau" because its goal is to denigrate all things Edomite.[262] When poet-laureate John Dryden (a second-born son) similarly re-packages the Jacob-Esau cycle,[263] James Joyce challenges it, choosing to commend *each* of these brothers

256. Pryor, "Simulation," 54.

257. *Num. Rab.* 6:2.

258. Josephus, *A.J.* 1:295.

259. Ibn Ezra makes this argument even though the biblical text affirms Isaac to be a wealthy man (Gen 25:3; 26:12–14; see Ahroni, "Birthright," 323–31).

260. *Gen. Rab.* 63:13; see Biddle, "Ancestral," 617–38.

261. *Jub* 35:9–17. *Jubilees* reimagines the revelation to Moses on Sinai from an angelic perspective (Wintermute, "Jubilees," 35–142). Like other Second Temple texts it dualistically distinguishes between יצר הטוב ("good inclination") and יצר הרעה ("bad inclination"), a dualism which leads Hengel to propose that the only kind of Judaism after Alexander's invasion is hellenized Judaism (*Judaism,* 1:1–5; see Marcus, "Evil," 606–21).

262. Wahl recognizes that *Jubilees* "carries over the logical sequence of events (birth, Isaac, Laban, Esau, Joseph, death, burial) and the names of persons treated in the text. It even cites several biblical passages *verbatim.* But it reinterprets individual events by freely facilitating transitions and recombining tradition-blocks with midrashic exposition" ("Jakobserzählung," 525). Preuss critiques other, similar "election" ideologies (*Theology* 1:27–38), as does Galling (*Erwählungstraditionen*).

263. Cotterill, "Rebekah," 212.

for striving to "win the blessing of God" by any means available (no matter how "unbrotherly").[264]

Intertextually, however, this text looks like other "great texts" in which a restless hero bangs his head against a traditional boundary in order to recover his "freedom." Just as Gilgamesh bangs his head against the *itû*-fence protecting the Cedar Forest, so Jacob bangs his head against the "sacred boundary" protecting the socioeconomic institution of *primogeniture*.

REBEKAH AND THE "BIG PROBLEM" OF PROTECTION (GEN 27:1–26)

Contemporary Westerners may not realize it, but the "blessing-curse" polarity embedded in the 27th chapter of *Genesis* resonates with other, similar polarities in other "great texts."[265] Defining the dynamics of this polarity can be challenging, however, because "blessing" encompasses much more than "the expression of a vow or wish in favor of a particular person."[266] It rather possesses "two fundamental meanings. In its first meaning it's a form of prayer—humanity's adoration and praise of God. In its second meaning it's a divine gift which descends upon humanity, nature, or things, a material or spiritual benefit which results from divine favor . . . the transfer of a sacred and beneficent power emanating from the supernatural world."[267] Just as Ninsun defends Gilgamesh,[268] so Rebekah's desire to defend Jacob raises profound questions about the degree to which the blessing-curse polarity embedded in this text resonates with the blessing-curse polarity of its broader context, not to mention the tribal economy out of which it finds its original shape.[269] For

264. Morse, "Jacob," 123.

265. Moore, "Foreigners," 203–17.

266. Ries, "Blessing," 247.

267. Ibid., 247. In Scharbert's view the ברוך ("blessing") formula "can be used as an announcement of recompense for a praiseworthy behavior" ("ברך," 287), but for Mitchell blessing "results from God's dramatic intervention in the course of history" (*Bless,* 52). Ross refers to it as an "endowment" designed to enrich "physically, materially, emotionally, and of course spiritually" (*Holiness,* 224), and Grüneberg describes it "not simply as a commendation, or an acknowledgement of relationship," but as something designed to "make a material difference in the world" (*Abraham,* 99). See Leuenberger, *Segenstheologien.*

268. *GE* 3:46–47; Steinberg, "Gender," 175–88.

269. Alt investigates the tension in *Genesis* between the promise of many descen-

example, when Jacob deceives his blind father in order to steal Esau's blessing, the intention of the Hebrew writer *appears* to be economic,[270] yet this is not what most readers see. Instead, most readers see "two major traditional Jewish responses . . . one holding that the deception (of Isaac) is not justified, the other holding that it is. Those acknowledging that the deception is wrong offer a moral interpretation or attempt to shift the blame from Jacob to Rebekah or even to Isaac himself. Those who celebrate the deception justify it in various ways by means of legal niceties or theological explanations."[271]

Among those aware of the intratextual context, however, many compare the deception motif in this text to the deception motifs embedded in other Hebrew texts.[272] When Laban, for example, tells Jacob that his culture allows no exceptions with regard to the marital primacy of older daughters (Gen 29:26), many argue that this protest intends to show that Jacob *does* allow exceptions—otherwise Laban would feel no need to "state the obvious."[273] Others describe this encounter as the product of a zero-sum game in which change occurs *only* in response to role deprivation,[274] or that Isaac is not *really* deceived, only plays along with Jacob's ruse until finally deciding to surrender to the divine will.[275]

---

dants vs. the promise of a homeland ("Fathers," 1–77), concluding that the promise of descendants is older. Zimmerli agrees that the promise of land does have a significant function in the original patriarchal promises, yet firmly disagrees with his late dating of it ("Promise," 89–122). Hoftijzer, reading Genesis 15 as a literary unit, assigns both promises to the same plane, viewing them as sequential—the promise of land being Abraham's immediate reward for trusting in the promise of many descendants (*Verheissungen*). Wolff, however, sees a fundamental sociohistorical difference between the two promises: (a) the promise of land is confirmed via an oath, while (b) the promise of descendants is rooted in divine *blessing* ("Kerygma," 41–66). Therefore the divine blessing driving Yahweh's desire to reclaim his creation (Gen 12:1–4a) is in no way dependent upon his covenantal promises to Abraham, Isaac, and Jacob. Each promise, in other words, arises out of a different *Sitz im Leben*.

270. Westermann, *Elements*, 85–117.

271. Marcus, "Traditional," 295. Pleins sees a parallel between two Hebrew mothers, Rebekah and Bathsheba, each using deception to protect a vulnerable little brother ("Murderous," 121–36).

272. Williams observes, e.g., that Jacob does not kill, only deceives his brother, thereby exemplifying more "civilized" behavior than Cain (*Deception*, 37; see Heard, *Dynamics*, 97–138).

273. Marcus, "Traditional," 296.

274. Steinberg, "Gender," 186–88.

275. Goodnick, "Rebekah," 221–28 (this is "Isaac's" attitude in *Jub.* 35:13–17).

This is not the first time a determined woman "targets" a man in an ancient Near Eastern text. Alongside several texts from Mesopotamia and Egypt, this story resonates with several other Hebrew texts; e.g., Jael targets Sisera,[276] Tamar targets Judah,[277] Rahab targets her neighbors,[278] and Bathsheba targets David.[279] What makes the Rebekah Cycle unique, however, is the way in which the "bribery" motif animating the Mesopotamian literature of Rebekah's ancestors is manipulated here in order to spotlight a *particular* socioeconomic conflict motif.[280] Camouflaging Jacob in clothing designed to duplicate Esau's smell and feel, the "wise woman" in this story goes so far as to create an Enkidu-like "double" in order to protect a vulnerable little brother from potential harm.[281] Moreover, just as Ishtar's bribery-speech adjoins and embellishes the bribery-speech of a less powerful "tempter" (Humbaba), so Rebekah's bribery-speech adjoins and embellishes the bribery-speech of a less powerful "tempter" (Jacob).[282] Just as nothing deters Ninsun from "protecting" her son, so nothing deters Rebekah from "protecting" *her* son.[283]

JOSEPH'S TWO FAMILIES (GEN 37:1—47:26)

The final cycle of stories in *Genesis* is fascinating for many reasons, not least because it contains no miraculous or supernatural elements.[284] A

---

276. Judg 4:17–22; see Reis, "Uncovering," 24–47.

277. Gen 38:1–26; see Sharon, "Results," 289–318.

278. Josh 2:1–21; see Williams, *Deception*, 115.

279. 1 Kgs 1:1–27; see Moore, "Bathsheba," 336–46.

280. Rebekah comes from ארם נהרים ("Aram-Naharaim," Gen 24:10) in northwest Mesopotamia (Pitard, "Aram-Naharaim," 341; Sasson, "Servant," 241–65).

281. This intertextual explanation is preferable to Ibn Ezra's speculation that Esau sells his birthright to Jacob because he knows that Isaac is too poor to give him much of an inheritance (Ahroni, "Birthright," 323–31). Alter suggests that Rebekah's "affection is not dependent on a merely material convenience that the son might provide her," but on "a more justly grounded preference" ("Sacred," 159)—yet offers no suggestion as to what this "more justly grounded preference" might be.

282. *GE* 6:6–21; Gen 27:5–29. Doubtless it's no coincidence that the more powerful "tempter" in each tradition is a determined female.

283. Spero points out that Rebekah's behavior not only saves Jacob from death, but prevents Esau from becoming a fratricidal murderer like Cain ("Jacob," 245–50).

284. Sarna, *Genesis*, 211. Perlitt creates a detailed reconstruction of Gen 37–50 only marginally relevant to the present study ("Aporie," 31–48).

fitting conclusion to *Genesis*, the carefully structured Joseph *novella*[285] contains "no divine revelations, no altars, no cultic associations," nor does the deity ever "intervene directly in Joseph's life as he does with Abraham, Isaac, and Jacob."[286] Nevertheless "all the ancestral narratives of *Genesis* [come] to completion"[287] in this story about an alienated refugee's decision to reconcile the two families among whom he tries to live his life, one "field-dwelling" and rural, the other "city-dwelling" and "civilized."[288]

The plotline begins with a seventeen-year-old boy trying to share with his "field-dwelling" family a symbolic dream in which several sheaves of grain "encircle"[289] another, single sheaf in an open "field."[290] Responding angrily, his half-brothers imagine that his reason for sharing this dream arises out of a Gilgamesh-like desire on his part to exercise "dominion" and "kingship."[291] Listening in on the conversation, one reader imagines Joseph "longing to see his brothers bow down to him," yet deciding only "to dream about it."[292] Others view this dream as the

285. Opinions diverge, but Humphreys argues convincingly that this is the only example of a *novella* (short story) in *Genesis* ("Novella," 82–96).

286. Sarna, *Genesis*, 211.

287. Williams, "Symbolism," 86. Von Rad is the first modern interpreter to point out the more sophisticated character of the material in Gen 37–50, at least when compared to the sagas in 12–36 ("Josephsgeschichte," 120–27).

288. Levin interprets this text as a much later attempt to explain a much later situation; i.e., how the *tribe* of Judah successfully sets out to annex a section of the *tribe* of Benjamin ("Joseph," 223–41).

289. Gen 37:7 (סבב). N.B. that exorcists often prepare boundaried "circuits" to protect their clients from demonic attack (Moore, *Balaam*, 20–65). Noegel shows how wordplay plays a significant role in "enigmatic" dreams (*Nocturnal*, 83–85). Oppenheim calls this type of dream "symbolic" (*Dreams*, 206).

290. Gen 37:7 (שׂדה). Qur'an does not mention this dream, only its astronomical parallel in Gen 37:9 (Sura 12:4; see Mouton, *Rêves*, 38). Kass argues that Joseph assimilates so far into Egyptian culture, he necessarily develops "an Egyptian soul that dreams Egyptian dreams" (Review of *Assimilation*, 60–61). Others, following von Rad (*Wisdom*, 46–47), read the Joseph novella as wisdom literature on a par with, say, Qohelet, though Fox finds this to be problematic ("Wisdom," 26–41).

291. Gen 37:8 (מלך ... משׁל). Schorn argues that the biblical traditions about Reuben should be dated relatively late because they reflect, in her opinion, the loss of Transjordanian territory to the Assyrians in the eighth century (*Ruben*, 282–87). Cross, however, rejects all attempts to date these traditions late ("Reuben," 46–65).

292. Bar, *Letter*, 47; see Butler, *Mesopotamian*; Husser, *Dreams*; Szpakowska, *Dreams*.

subconscious projection of a lonely teenager's "search" for acceptance from a dysfunctional blended family.[293]

Intratextually, of course, Joseph's brothers' suspicions cannot be taken for granted because the previous sagas in *Genesis* strongly emphasize the dangers associated with the "big problem" of *primogeniture*,[294] particularly since so many use it to *persecute* instead of *protect* the vulnerable.[295] What the Joseph novella does is project these socioeconomic concerns onto an international stage. That is, instead of simply contrasting the primogenitural tensions segregating Rachel's firstborn (Joseph) from Leah's firstborn (Reuben), the Joseph cycle reexamines these tensions from a much wider angle. Where previous stories in *Genesis* focus on the socioeconomic conflicts between *brothers*, this story focuses on the socioeconomic conflicts between vastly different *families*.

Most interpreters miss this, even when they try to read the text from a socioeconomic perspective. One reader, for example, views this part of *Torah* as a comparison between Joseph's "assimilative" leadership vs. the "liberational" leadership of his successor Moses,[296] myopically suggesting that Joseph himself is "the cause of Israel's bondage. Two hundred years before the exodus, is it not Joseph who cunningly brings up and monopolizes much of the land on behalf of the Pharaoh during the seven years of famine?"[297] Leaving aside the relative (de)merits of this suggestion, it's nevertheless important to recognize (a) that Joseph "wanders" in search of his brothers, and (b) that *Genesis* describes this "wandering" via a word with a Mesopotamian cognate sometimes used to describe a particular

---

293. See Guyette ("Joseph," 181–88), and the note on בקשׁ ("to search") in Moore (*Reconciliation*, 169).

294. The Joseph novella, in other words, explores the same primogenitural dynamic as that explicated by the Abraham and Jacob cycles; thus, if Sarah's son Isaac is preferable to Hagar's son Ishmael, then it comes as no surprise that Rachel's son Joseph is preferable to Leah's son Reuben.

295. Qur'an has Joseph's brothers repeatedly ask their father to release him into their care as his نصحون ("counselors," *Sura* 12:11) and حفظون ("protectors," 12:12).

296. Wildavsky argues that Joseph and Moses are "different in every conceivable dimension," but that "their significant characteristics and actions are mirror images. Moses, born in Egypt, becomes Hebraicized; Joseph, who grows up a Hebrew, becomes Egyptianized" (*Assimilation*, 1).

297. Wildavsky, *Assimilation*, 2 (see Shapiro, "Moses," 497). Lipton argues that *Exodus* is about the Hebrews "fearing loss of identity more than annihilation at enemy hands" (*Longing*, 7).

kind of socioeconomic "wandering" (i.e., "bribery").[298] Intratextually this episode describes Joseph's behavior toward *his* shepherd-brothers in language closely resembling that used to describe Farmer Cain's behavior toward *his* shepherd-brother.[299] Intertextually, though, just as *Atrahasis* highlights Enki's "trickery,"[300] so Joseph's brothers sarcastically nickname him the "*ba'al* ('master') of dream-trickery," a pejorative epithet which comes back to haunt them later.[301]

Yet the deepest and most significant intertextual parallel occurs in the "two-stage" attack-strategy which Leah's children execute against Rachel's firstborn. Failing to enact "plan A" (*murder*), immediately they switch to a more palatable "plan B." Where "plan A" involves the killing of a hated "target"—*coupled with a decision to do something symbolic with the blood*[302]—"plan B" focuses on the selling of this "target" into *slavery*. *Genesis* thoroughly monotheizes this sequence, yet still it looks remarkably similar to the "two-stage" attack-strategy laid out in *Atrahasis*.[303] Further, when Joseph's brothers lie to their father Jacob, blaming their brother's "death" on a "wild beast," the term used to denote this beast

298. Gen 37:15 (תעה, *HAL* 1626; see Akk *tātu*, *AHw* 1382; Ug *tġy*, *CAT* 1.4 iv:33; طغا, Wehr-Cowan 561).

299. Not to mention Ishtar's treatment of *her* Shepherd (*GE* 6:58–63). These comparisons find further support in the appearance of the polysemantic verb נקל ("to trick") in Gen 37:18 (LXX reads πονηρεύω, "to plot with evil intention"), and Akk *nakālu* can also connote "trickery" (see *Ee* 1:62; 6:9).

300. *Atr* 1:376–83.

301. Gen 37:19 (בעל החלמות). Green argues (a) that Joseph's dreams dominate and direct the action of Gen 37–50; and (b) that the interpretation of these dreams by each conflicted character is crucial to the reuniting of Jacob's family (*Profit*, 1–23). Lanckau argues that Gen 37–50 portrays Joseph as a "dream-lord" gifted not only with the ability to interpret others' dreams, but also to understand his own dreams as messages designed to help his "field-dwelling" family (*Träume*, 1–16).

302. Gen 37:31 // *Atr* 1:208–17.

303. Within *Atrahasis* itself N.B. the development from Enlil's two-stage attack-strategy in the Igigi Myth ("kill them all," *Atr* 1:87–88) with his compromise in the Flood Myth ("kill the ringleader," 1:170–73).

more commonly denotes the notion of "evil,"[304] thereby echoing, however subtly, the "devouring predator" motif embedded in other "great texts."[305]

But that's not all. Reuben's objection to his brothers' "plan A" looks very much like Anu's objection to Enlil's "plan A."[306] That is, just as Anu tries to make Enlil re-think the consequences of *his* assassination proposal, so Reuben tries to make his brothers re-think the consequences of *their* assassination proposal.[307] Later, when the decision is made to shift to "plan B" (*slavery*), Reuben voices Anu-like concern as his mediatorial efforts begin to unravel. Unsurprisingly, the shepherd-brother most supportive of "plan B"—Judah—looks much like Enki, the primary defender of the oppressed in Mesopotamian tradition. That is, just as Enki helps save the Igigi and their clay-based replacements in *Atrahasis*, so Judah helps save Joseph and Benjamin in *Genesis*.[308]

At this point in the story two things happen: (a) the setting abruptly shifts from Canaan to Egypt, and (b) the socioeconomic conflict motifs become a bit more intense. Successfully "acquiring" Joseph from the Ishmaelites,[309] for example, one Egyptian (a middle manager named Potiphar) starts to experience "Yahweh's blessing,"[310] even as his Ishtar-like wife starts "targeting" him for "consumption."[311] Her efforts fail,

304. Gen 37:33 (חיה רעה). The fact that *Genesis* uses רעה (instead of, say, פרא (Job 6:5; 11:12; 24:5; 39:5; *HAL* 905) may be due to the fact that רעה ("evil") has a homonym in רעה ("shepherd"). Kilmer documents similar polysemanticisms in the Akkadian literature ("Wordplay," 89–101) and Greenstein documents examples within the Bible ("Wordplay," 968–71).

305. See, e.g., *GE* 6:68, 72, 73 (*akālu*). Qur'an highlights Jacob's fear that Leah's children may allow Joseph to be "devoured" (اكل, *Sura* 12:13).

306. *Atr* 1:140–43; SB *Atr* 2:15–18.

307. Gen 37:25–32 // SB *Atr* 2:63–74.

308. Gen 37:26; 44:18–34. The term בצע ("profits") in 37:26 resonates deeply with the language in *Atr* 1:208–17. Note also (a) that the "contempt" of Leah's children resonates with the "contempt" of Erra (*Erra* 1:119–20), and further, (b) that the "contempt" trajectory in *torah* climaxes in the plagues narrative (Exod 7:14—12:32). Qur'an emphasizes the antipathy of Leah's children toward *both* of Rachel's children (*Sura* 12:8).

309. Gen 39:1. קנה ("to acquire") is the root from which "Cain" derives (קין, Gen 4:1).

310. Gen 39:5, 23 (ברכת יהוה). Levinson questions why so many Second Temple texts eroticize this encounter ("Woman," 269–301), but Pirson overemphasizes Joseph's "flaws" to the point that his rejection of Potiphar's wife is his only positive accomplishment (*Dreams*, 8–22).

311. Ignoring the Ishtar episode in *Gilgamesh*, Goldman (*Wiles*, 31–56) nevertheless gives intertextual attention to the "spurned wife" motif in the *Story of Two Brothers*

of course, but not because Joseph is superhumanly immune to sexual temptation.[312] Her efforts fail because just as *Gilgamesh* uses the "woman scorned" motif to highlight the incorruptibility of the hero Gilgamesh, so *Genesis* uses the "woman scorned" motif to highlight the incorruptibility of the hero Joseph.

Joseph's first conversation with Pharaoh engages two parallel metaphors: "lean-cows"-vs.-"fat-cows" and "full-ears-of-grain"-vs.-"empty-ears-of-grain."[313] Each portrays the "big problem" of "famine,"[314] a perennial poetic symbol of creaky "old orders" facing uncertain futures.[315] Just as *Erra* depicts the breakdown of Babylon's "old order" via agrarian metaphors,[316] so *Genesis* depicts Egypt's economic crisis via agrarian metaphors, here embedded within an oneiromantic cluster of royal dreams.[317] Like Erra, moreover, Pharaoh goes "outside the system" to resolve his "big problem."[318] Just as Erra appoints a "foreigner" (himself) to guide Babylon through *its* socioeconomic crisis, so Pharaoh appoints a "foreigner" (the *retenu*-slave Joseph) to guide Egypt through *its* so-

---

(*ANET* 23–25), the *Iliad* (book 6), Lucian's allusion to "Stratonike and Combabos" (*Syr. d.* 17–27), and Qur'an (*Sura* 12, يوسف, "Yusuf").

312. *Contra* the hagiographical portrayal of Joseph in Talmud (e.g., *b. Mas. Yoma* 35b), see Pirson, "Potiphar," 248–59. According to *Tafsir al-Jalalayn* on *Sura* 12:21, Potiphar's wife's name is Zulaikha (probably derived from زلق, "to make slippery," Wehr-Cowan 380).

313. Gen 41:32. From an oneiromantic perspective this kind of literary "doubling" confirms the truth of revelatory visions, and is not intended to be read as a psychological mirror into which one must look to ascertain the essentials of personal identity (see Moore, *Balaam*, 20–23).

314. Brinkman points out that the "Bull of Heaven" sometimes personifies "seven years of drought" in Babylonian texts ("Gilgamesh," 222).

315. Chavalas and Adamthwaite suggest that the Joseph story reflects conditions in the unstable twelfth dynasty because the story references (a) Pharaoh's aversion to Asiatic pastoral culture as well as (b) the sweeping nature of Joseph's land reform initiatives, likely reflecting early second-millennium policies and practices provoked by the socioeconomics of famine ("Archaeological," 59–96).

316. *Erra* 1:76–85. See Kuhrt, *Ancient* 1:74–78; Pientka, *Spätaltbabylonische*.

317. Mouton compares Pharaoh's seven-fold warning with the seven-fold warning to the Hurrian hunter Kešši (*KUB* 17:1), as well as the five-fold warning to Enkidu (*Rêves*, 37).

318. Coser argues that social violence can serve three functions: (a) as a danger signal, (b) as a catalyst, and/or (c) as a symbol of in-group achievement ("Violence," 8–18).

cioeconomic crisis.[319] Uninterested in hagiographical portrayals which sanitize Zaphenath-paneah[320] into St. Joseph,[321] *Genesis* rather tells the story of an heroic foreigner doing whatever is necessary to redeem his "field-dwelling" family without alienating his "city-dwelling" family.[322]

Genesis thus concludes with a series of comparisons highlighting the differences between two socioeconomic worlds coexisting on opposing sides of the "civilization-wilderness" continuum:

- Jacob commands Leah's children to go to Egypt and buy grain;[323]

- Joseph recognizes his brothers when they arrive, yet refuses to reveal his identity, choosing instead to imprison them on a trumped-up charge of "espionage";[324]

- Three days later he then decides to release everyone in his *retenu-*family except Simeon, who remains under house arrest until Benjamin's arrival;[325]

319. *Erra* 2:1–9; Gen 41:43. N.B. that Pharaoh gives his signet ring not to his "second-in-command," but to his *retenu-*slave Joseph.

320. Gen 41:45 (Joseph's Egyptian name). The closest anyone has come to explaining the meaning of this name is the Egyptian phrase *dje-pa-nate-ef-ankh* ("The god says, 'he will live!'"). *Which* god, of course, is impossible to ascertain, though the fact that Joseph marries the daughter of a priest of Ra is significant (Redford, *Joseph*, 230).

321. Talmud sets this hagiographical trajectory in motion with the following comment: "Rabbi Hiyya ben Abba says in the name of Rabbi Yoḥanan, 'At the moment when Pharaoh says to Joseph, "and without you no man shall lift up his hand," Pharaoh's astrologers exclaim, 'Will you set in power over us a slave bought by his master for twenty pieces of silver?' And Pharaoh replies to them, 'I discern in him royal characteristics'" (*b. Sot.* 36b).

322. Following Meinhold ("Sinuhe"), King reads the Joseph novella intertextually alongside other ancient Near Eastern stories about exile-restoration—stories like the Egyptian *Tale of Sinuhe*, the Syro-Palestinian *Story of Idrimi*, the Anatolian *Apology of Hattušili*, and the Mesopotamian *Nabonidus and his God*—each featuring a "young man exiled from his home because of dynastic struggle later reconciled with his people through divine guidance" ("Joseph," 577).

323. Gen 42:1–5 (Green, *Profit*).

324. Gen 42:9. Such an accusation would fall on sympathetic Egyptian ears among those who perceive the Hebrews to be *ḫabirū* (Greenburg, *Hab/piru*; Lemche, *Israel*, 5–11).

325. Gen 42:18–20. Ben-Reuven reads this part of the story as an inversion of chapter 37. That is, where Gen 37 has Jacob sending his beloved son Joseph to meet his brothers, then receives them all back *except* the "beloved son," Gen 42 has Joseph suggest to his brothers in Egypt that they send one "beloved son" back from Canaan, then sends them *all* back except Simeon ("Measure," 185–90).

- Returning Jacob's "gift" Joseph sends his *retenu*-family back to Canaan, speeding them on their way with extra "provisions";[326]

- Reflecting on their journey, Leah's children begin to wonder whether Simeon's imprisonment might be "guilt-payment" for their earlier crime;[327]

- Reuben says (in so many words), "I told you something like this would happen, but you would not listen to me, and now 'his blood is being sought'";[328]

- Arriving in Canaan, Leah's children (minus Simeon) return Jacob's "gift" to him, reporting Zaphenath-paneah's directives and suggesting to him that obedience to this "Egyptian" might open a door to international "trade";[329]

- This international "trade" does not materialize, however, and the famine deepens, forcing Jacob to send his sons back to Egypt to buy more food;[330]

- Reminding Jacob of Joseph's preconditions, Judah offers himself as a "guarantee,"[331] agreeing to be held "culpable" should anything happen to Benjamin;[332]

- Reuben offers the lives of his two sons as well, but Jacob rejects both offers, lamenting instead the loss of *his* two sons (Joseph and

---

326. Gen 42:25 (צידה). This is the first of several gifts Joseph gives his *retenu*-family, culminating in the large צידה-gift given on the day he reveals his Hebrew identity (Gen 45:21).

327. Gen 42:21 (אשם). The *Habakkuk Commentary* from Cave 1 uses this priestly term to describe the "Wicked Priest" who "seizes public money, thereby adding 'guilt' to his sin" (אשם, 1QpHab 8:12), and the *Rule of the Community* addresses itself to those who walk in the stubbornness of a "guilty heart" (לב אשמה, 1QS 1:6).

328. Gen 42:22 (דמו נדרש). Note the intertextual parallel to the "seeking of blood" as "payment" in *Atr* 1:208–17 (see *Ee* 6:30–34), a parallel only slightly diminished by the Hebrew writer's decision to inflect דרש passively ("to seek").

329. Gen 42:34 (סחר). In Ezek 27 Ezekiel laments the fall of Tyre, even though its economy has a long history of international "trade" (the verb סחר occurs five times in this chapter).

330. Gen 43:1–2.

331. Gen 43:3–9 (ערב). The word ערב does not describe Reuben's offer, only Judah's; Paul uses the transliterated Greek equivalent to depict the Spirit as a "guarantee" (ἀρραβών, Eph 1:14; see Heltzer, "Hostage," 208).

332. Gen 44:32 (חטא).

Simeon);[333]

- Finally Jacob relents, sending twice the amount of silver to Za-phenath-paneah than before, along with balm, honey, gum, resin, pistachios, almonds ... and Benjamin;[334]

- Arriving in Egypt, Joseph's *retenu*-family fears that Zaphenath-paneah will condemn them for the crime of "thievery" (i.e., until the palace steward tells them to stop worrying: "I have received your silver");[335]

- Still, they make sure to deliver Jacob's "gift,"[336] attempting to recip-rocate something they fear had been earlier "lost";[337]

- Seeing Benjamin, however, overwhelms Joseph emotionally, caus-ing him (like Enlil in *Atrahasis*) to weep.

- Returning to table, however, he refrains from sitting down with his *retenu* "field-dwelling" family because Egyptian custom finds it an "abhorrent" practice;[338]

- When everyone finally does sit down to eat, however, "the firstborn according to his birthright," Joseph challenges the primogenitural hierarchy to which his "field-dwelling" family pays adherence, in-creasing Benjamin's "gift" to five times that of every other "gift";[339]

333. Gen 42:37–38.

334. Gen 43:11–14. Wildavsky thinks that Jacob "experiences the fear of recognition that something already latent in the context of his family life is about to happen, though without knowing that his sons have special reason to feel guilty ... How much of this grief is for what the brothers have done to one another and how much for what their fa-ther has half-knowingly done to them, Jacob does not say, for it was he who sent Joseph to brothers full of hatred (and) Benjamin is a second Joseph" (*Assimilation*, 99).

335. Gen 43:18–23. Joseph's tricksterism is much less ruthless than Jacob's or Enki's because unlike Cain, he simultaneously *protects* his "targets."

336. Gen 43:26 (מנחה). Levin thinks this section emphasizes the "competition" be-tween Joseph and Judah over Benjamin's "protection," arguing that the more relevant context is the much later struggle between Israel and Judah over what to do with the *tribe* of Benjamin ("Joseph," 223–41).

337. Godelier (*Enigma*, 205–7) believes that some things are too "sacred" to be ex-changed or reciprocated, and that Jacob's מנחה ("gift") may fall into this category.

338. Gen 43:32 (תועבה). This priestly term appears twice in the Joseph novella to indicate both (a) *social* distinction ("it is תועבה for Egyptians to eat with Hebrews," Gen 43:32); as well as (b) *socioeconomic* distinction ("all shepherds are תועבה to the Egyptians," Gen 46:34).

339. Gen 43:33–34. These verses clearly contrast the rural expectations of Joseph's *Hebrew* family with the urban expectations of his *Egyptian* family.

- Before his brothers go back to Canaan Joseph hides his silver cup in Benjamin's sack, the one with which he practices "divination,"[340] then uses its "discovery" to indict them for "breaching the sacred,"[341] thereby pulling off his plan to take Benjamin away from them without violence;[342]

- Judah pleads with Joseph to arrest him instead, alerting him to the fact that (a) he stands as a "guarantee" for Benjamin, and (b) that failure to bring him back to his father will seal his (Judah's) "culpability";[343]

- Judah's plea finally triggers Joseph's decision to reveal himself to his *retenu*-family, after which he quickly advises them on how to avoid becoming future "targets": "Five more years of famine are yet to come, but I will provide for you so that and your household (and all that you have) do not have to suffer the pain of 'acquisition'";[344]

- To support his *retenu* vizier, Pharaoh sends to Canaan to retrieve the rest of his "field-dwelling" family, urging them to give "thrifty consideration" to which possessions they can reasonably bring to their new home in Egypt;[345]

- To persuade his father to come down to Egypt, Joseph recipro-cates Jacob's "gift" with one of his own: ten donkeys carrying "the goodness of Egypt," ten she-asses carrying "grain and food," and enough provisions to make the trip comfortable;

340. Gen 44:5 (נחש).

341. Hanson, "Deviance," 11–25.

342. As Godelier puts it, "in order for there to be movement, exchange, some things must be left out" (*Enigma*, 166–67).

343. Gen 44:32 (ערב . . . חטא). Having Judah repeat these terms to Joseph (after earlier pledging them to Jacob) both (a) highlights the danger that Judah's failure has inevitable consequences, and (b) verifies the fact that at least *some* of Leah's children view the boundary around Benjamin as "sacred."

344. Gen 45:11 (ירש). This twice-used term can mean either "possess" (Gen 15:8; Deut 1:8; Isa 14:21) or "dispossess" (Num 21:32; Judg 11:23; Gen 45:11). LXX translates ἐκτρίβω ("to rub out"), but the Gk term most often used to translate it is κληρονομέω ("acquire"; 1 Macc 1:32; 2:10).

345. Gen 45:20 (חוס). Pharaoh uses an interesting word when he says, "Give no 'consideration' (חוס) to your possessions" (see Deut 7:16; 13:9; 19:13; Isa 13:18; Ezek 7:4; 20:17). LXX, however, translates חוס with φείδομαι (primary meaning—"to spare"; secondary meaning—"to live thriftily"; LSJ 1920).

- Before sending his *retenu*-family back to Canaan, however, Joseph counsels them not to become "angry" or "agitated" about what's happened, after which he advises them to list their occupations as "shepherds" upon their return. Why? Because the vocation of shepherd, while "abhorrent" to Egyptians, might easily become a niche profession for his *retenu*-family;[346]

- In this way Joseph provides steady jobs[347] and "landed property"[348] for his "field-dwelling" family.

In spite of its socioeconomic accent, interpreters still read the Joseph novella as (a) a critique of hyper-exclusivistic notions of election;[349] (b) an early illustration of PTSD (post-traumatic stress disorder);[350] (c) an illustration of purely cynical behavior ("he who has himself been sold, then sold others, now sells out his people");[351] (d) a depiction of the kind of scarcity which inherently creates violence among "natural competitors";[352] or (e) a tale depicting how "Jews can serve foreign kings *and* bring . . . salvation to their own people."[353]

346. Gen 43:32 (תועבה; Chavalas and Adamthwaite, "Archaeological," 59–96). Hopkins reflects on the conflict between urbanized Egyptians and *shoshu*-pastoralists ("Pastoralists," 200–11).

347. Gen 47:11; 50:21. See 2 Sam 19:33; 20:3; 1 Kgs 4:7; 17:4, 9.

348. Gen 47:11 (אחזה). N.B. Zelophehad's daughters' request for "landed property" (אחזה, Num 27:4).

349. Heard, *Dynamics*, 171–84; Brett, *Genesis*, 137–46.

350. As Mann puts it, "Joseph recognized them (they did not recognize him), and although it is his forgiveness that is most prominently remembered, he first took the opportunity to exact revenge. He accuses them of spying, jails one of the brothers, and also torments Jacob, his father, by demanding that they bring Benjamin, the surviving son of Rachel, to Egypt" ("Joseph," 336).

351. Caine, "Numbers," 11. Brueggemann (*Memory*, 70) overinterprets when he argues that, "Pharaoh is afraid that there are not enough good things to go around," suggesting this to be the reason why "he must try to have them all. Because he is fearful, he is ruthless. Pharaoh hires Joseph to manage the monopoly. When the crops fail and the peasants run out of food, they come to Joseph. And on behalf of Pharaoh, Joseph asks, 'What's your collateral?' They give up their land for food, and then, the next year, they give up their cattle. By the third year of the famine they have no collateral but themselves. And that is how the children of Israel become slaves—through an economic transaction."

352. Schwartz, *Curse*, 162–66; see Fung, *Victim*, 198–206.

353. Gnuse, "Prison," 31.

From a socioeconomic perspective, however, this novella, like *Genesis* as a whole, reaches a conclusion much brighter than its shadowy beginning. Though many argue that Joseph conceals his identity from his "field-dwelling" family because (a) he wants to avoid unleashing his pent-up wrath against them, Erra-style, or (b) he wants to find out whether Benjamin has survived the "fraternity" responsible for the abuse earlier inflicted on *him*,[354] Joseph remains *incognito* because he wants to "test whether his brothers have changed,"[355] a motif which, when highlighted, depicts Jacob as another fearful father trying to protect another favorite son from "harm"[356]—Benjamin, the last living reminder, he thinks, of his wife Rachel.[357] Similar fears provoke Joseph's decision to imprison Simeon until his brothers bring Benjamin before him.[358] Not only this, but Joseph's decision represents the first time in *Genesis* where someone dares to answer Cain's rhetorical question ("Am I my brother's *protector*?") in the affirmative.

MOSES AND THE "BIG PROBLEM" OF SLAVERY (EXOD 3-20)

Continuing where *Genesis* leaves off, the book of *Exodus* preserves one of the most famous stories ever told—the liberation of the Hebrews from Egyptian slavery.[359] The person most responsible for this liberation is a larger-than-life hero who, like Gilgamesh, knows precisely what he wants to do: "Yahweh your God is bringing you into a good land, a land with flowing streams, with springs and aquifers saturating the hills and valleys; a land of wheat and barley,[360] of vines and fig trees and pome-

354. Guyette argues, e.g., that Joseph's life goes through three stages: (a) self-absorbed adolescence; (b) self-controlled young adulthood; and (c) self-sacrificing adulthood ("Joseph," 181–88).

355. Wilson, *Joseph*, 246.

356. Gen 42:4, 38 (אסן), repeated by Judah to Joseph in 44:29.

357. Mandolfo ("Truth") sees a fundamental tension in this text between "positive order" (represented by the voice of Joseph) and "negative consequence" (represented by the voice of Jacob), but this interpretive approach ignores the socioeconomic context.

358. Heltzer cites a Middle Assyrian parallel from a letter written by an actual hostage: "The Assyrians have taken me hostage; servant work must I do. If you've received the silver, then send the tin. I will give it (to them) and secure my freedom" ("Hostage," 209).

359. Rapoport acerbically describes it as "the first account of a liberation and a founding in Western history, and . . . probably our most influential" ("Moses," 123).

360. As Noegel observes, the plague of hail destroys important cash crops (Exod 9:31–32; "Plague," 532–39), and as Hopkins points out ("Field," 149–72), the work to which Exod 1:14 refers covers a broad spectrum, both agricultural (plowing, sowing,

granates; a land of olive trees and honey, a land where one may eat bread without scarcity and lack nothing; a land whose stones are iron and whose hills produce copper. You shall eat your fill and bless Yahweh your God in the good land he has given you."[361] This vision comes equipped, however, with some clearly-defined boundaries:

> When you have eaten your fill and built fine houses and settled in them, and when your herds and flocks have multiplied, and when your silver and gold and everything you have has multiplied, do not exalt yourself by forgetting Yahweh your God, who brought you out of the land of Egypt, out of the house of slavery, and who led you through the great and terrible wilderness—an arid wasteland filled with snakes and scorpions—who made water flow for you from solid rock, and who fed you in the wilderness with manna[362] ... Do not say, 'My power and the might of my own hand have created this wealth for me.' Remember that Yahweh your God is the one who gives you the ability to 'create wealth.'"[363]

Many date this speech to the time of King Josiah (d. 609 BCE).[364] Others interpret it as a covert critique of all the totalitarian regimes which have ever attempted to enslave the Hebrews.[365] Still others read it as a focused contrast between Moses' leadership style and that of his Babylonian, Assyrian, and Persian neighbors.[366]

Whatever the possibilities, the manifesto encapsulated in this vision finds its deepest taproot in Yahweh's words to Moses "in the wilderness":

---

weeding, harvesting, threshing, winnowing) and arboricultural (planting, terracing, viticulture, olives, figs).

361. Deut 8:7–10. Buchholz argues that the Hebrews rely heavily on "laws regarding economic acts," and that "these laws ... have an overwhelming effect on the rate and degree of economic progress" ("Laws," 390).

362. N.B. that the "wilderness-civilization" polarity pulsates at the core of this farewell-speech.

363. Deut 8:12–18. Because the primary verb in the phrase "to create wealth" (לַעֲשׂוֹת חַיִל, v. 18) means simply "to make" (עָשָׂה), Hardmeier reads this passage alongside others voicing similar economic promises ("Prosperität," 15–24; see 2 Kgs 18:32, Hos 13:4–8, Jer 2:4–8).

364. "After two centuries of critical scholarship, the evidence would seem to indicate that if Deuteronomy is not a record of the actual words of Moses, it is at least a tradition that accurately represents him and faithfully reflects his application of the covenantal laws and statutes of Yahweh to the needs of the Israelites about to enter Canaan" (LaSor et al., *Survey*, 117; see Wright, *Deuteronomy*, 1–20).

365. Liverani, "Powers," 15–27.

366. Otto, *Mose*, 43–83; Liverani, "Powers," 15–27.

"I have observed the misery of my people who are in Egypt; I have heard their cry on account of their taskmasters.[367] I know their sufferings, and I have come down to deliver them from the Egyptians, and bring them out of that land to a good and broad land flowing with 'milk and honey.'"[368] Saturated with agrarian metaphors, this text stands at the beginning of a long trajectory focused around one of the Bible's "most paradigmatic themes."[369] Sometimes it's difficult to know how to apply this theme to other peoples at other times,[370] but where *Atrahasis* portrays slavery as humanity's "natural" state, *Exodus* describes it as something profoundly *un*-natural,[371] a truth communicated via the structure of Moses' birth narrative:

- Prologue (1:1–7);
  - *Slavery* begins (1:8–14, story about men);[372]
    - Midwives (1:15–22, story about women);
      - *Birth of Moses* (2:1–10);
    - Priest's daughters (story about women: 2:16–22);
  - *Slavery* not abolished (story about men: 2:11–15);
- Epilogue (2:23–25).[373]

Intertextually, however, *Exodus* refocuses the "wilderness-vs.-civilization" polarity structuring other "great texts" from a perspective duly informed by the "field-dwellers"-vs.-"city-dwellers" polarity, as well

---

367. Exod 3:7 (נגשׂים, "oppressors"). LXX translates ἐργοδιώκτων (lit., "work-oppressors").

368. Exod 3:7–8. As Stern points out, Yahweh's ability to create a land flowing with "milk and honey" so closely parallels Baal's ability to provide "oil" and "honey" (*šmm* // *nbt*, CAT 1.6:3:6–7), "it is difficult not to imagine that 'a land flowing with milk and honey' has its origin in the rivalry with Baal" ("Origin," 555).

369. Meyers, *Exodus*, 35.

370. Pixley applies the *Exodus* paradigm to all "enslaved peoples," but Levenson restricts it only to the Hebrews (Ogden Bellis and Kaminsky, *Scriptures,* 231–40).

371. Weimar, "Freiheit."

372. Exod 1:1—2:25. In many ways oppressed Israel's situation parallels the situation of the oppressed *amēlūtū* (Atr 1:355).

373. This is Siebert-Hommes' chiastic analysis ("Geburtsgeschichte," 398). Boadt's chiastic analysis deemphasizes the slavery-freedom polarity ("Wonders," 48–49).

as the "wild man"-vs.-"wise man" polarity. Moses' first conversation with Pharaoh (after his Midianite "exile") inductively fleshes this out:

> Moses and Aaron went to Pharaoh and said, "Thus says Yahweh, God of Israel, 'Send my people into the wilderness[374] where they can celebrate a *haj* to me.'"[375] But Pharaoh said, "Who is Yahweh? Why should I listen to him and send Israel away? I do not know this Yahweh, nor will I send Israel away."[376] They answered, "The God of the Hebrews has met with us, so let us take a three-day walk in the wilderness to sacrifice to Yahweh our God; otherwise he may strike us with pestilence or the sword."[377] But the king of Egypt said to Moses and Aaron, "Why are you trying to compensate these people for their labor?"[378]

Many things stand out in this conversation, but of greatest importance here is the fact that one of the most famous conflicts in the Bible occurs between a "city-dweller" (Pharaoh) and a "field-dweller" (Moses). Unsurprisingly, then, Moses does not demand a jubilee release-decree,[379] nor does he try to negotiate a new covenant-treaty with his urban counterpart.[380] Instead, he asks him to release some of his *retenu*-slaves into "the *wilderness*," thereby triggering the counter-demand that they first

374. Exod 5:1. Most English translations abstractly translate "let my people go," but the text uses the transitive verb שלח ("to send") to specify *where* they are to go (i.e., במדבר, "into the wilderness").

375. Transliterating חגג to maximize the influence of the cognate verb حج (*hajja*; see *HAL* 278; Wehr-Cowan 156). Several times Yahweh commands his people to "celebrate a festival" (חגג; see Exod 23:14; Num 29:12; Deut 16:15), but this is the very first.

376. Egyptian religion makes little room for *retenu* deities like Baal, Anat, and Shaushka, and those which do usually assimilate them into the deity Seth, lord of the "wilderness/desert." Thus, even though Pharaoh probably does recognize Yahweh, he doubtless assimilates him to the "dark side" of his native pantheon (te Velde, "Theology," 1736–40).

377. This passage (Exod 5:1–4) echoes the preceding passage (Exod 4:24–26) where, in Robinson's words, "Moses shows himself far from enthusiastic about confronting the Pharaoh and threatening him with the death of his son." Even though Yahweh "shows Moses that he is safe from other men (Exod 4:19), he faces a much greater danger in the wrath of the God whom he is so reluctant to serve (4:14). Like Jacob before him, Moses must undergo a night struggle with this mysterious deity before he can become Yahweh's worthy instrument" ("Zipporah," 459–60).

378. Exod 5:4 (פרע). LXX translates this verb with διαστρέφω ("to turn away, pervert"; see Vg *sollicitatis*, "disturb, incite"), but פרע can also mean "to compensate" (*HAL* 912–13).

379. Akk *mišarum* ("release-decree"). See *CAD* M/2:116–17; Kraus, *Verfügungen*.

380. Crook, "Reciprocity," 78–91; Moore, "Dreams," 205–21.

finish building Pharaoh's treasury *cities*.[381] In this way this text (a) echoes Moses' earlier wilderness encounter with Yahweh at the "burning bush," and (b) highlights the intensity of Pharaoh's "contempt" for the *retenu* and their gods,[382] an attitude ultimately rooted in the conviction that "slavery is an economic convention a society maintains for as long as there is economic superiority of slave labor over free labor."[383]

Unlike Enlil, Pharaoh never goes to "sleep." He rather proactively quells the dissidence fomenting within his workforce before it can break out into open rebellion.[384] Realizing that the Hebrews are more numerous than other *retenu*-populations in his workforce, he makes a fateful decision to rely on the "stick" instead of the "carrot" in his treatment of them: "Pharaoh commanded the taskmasters of the people and their supervisors:[385] 'Stop giving the Hebrews straw to make bricks. Let them go out and gather straw for themselves, yet still require from them the same quota of bricks.[386] Do not lessen it one bit, for these people are lazy.[387] That's why they demand, "Let us go and sacrifice to our God!" The more work we lay on them, the less they'll listen to such deceitful talk.'"[388] Just as Enlil punishes the Igigi for their rebellion, so Pharaoh

381. Exod 1:11; see Uphill, "Pithom," 291–316.

382. In Pharaoh's opinion Moses, like Sinuhe, is simply another disaffected Egyptian who foolishly abandons his homeland for the "uncivilized" world of the *retenu*—behavior which automatically disqualifies him from future citizenship (Hollis, "Otherworld," 334–37).

383. Glass, "Land," 27–28.

384. The decision to ignore such dissidence is what encourages the Thracian gladiator Spartacus to rebel against Roman authority (Plutarch, *Crass.* 8:1–2; Appian, *Bell.civ.* 1:116; Livy, *Per.* 95:2; Florus, *Epit.* 2:8).

385. Exod 5:6 (שוטריו). Like the Babylonian economy (Sterba, "Organization," 21), the Ramesside economy of Egypt has multiple layers. Thus שוטר ("supervisor") likely parallels Akk *šatāru*, "to write, record, supervise" (*HAL* 1337–8; *AHW* 1203; *CAD* Š/2:225).

386. Like the Mesopotamians, the Hebrews make it clear in their "great literature" that "slavery" is a very "big problem" (Parish, *Slavery*, 1–4).

387. Exod 5:8 (נרפים). The verb from which this passive participle derives is probably רפה ("to be lax"), though רפא is not impossible ("to be weak"; see *HAL* 1190–91; 1186–88).

388. Notice that the Hebrews never call for vengeance against Pharaoh, quite unlike the Igigi ("Let's confront the steward"; "Let's break the yoke"; "Let's fetch him from his dwelling," *Atr* 1:41). Instead they simply request from Pharaoh the privilege of going on חג ("pilgrimage") into the wilderness to worship the deity of their new leader.

punishes the Hebrews for *their* "rebellion."[389] Just as Enlil resists the demand to give away his "property," so Pharaoh resists the demand to give away *his* "property."[390] Even the graduated nature of Pharaoh's response (i.e., the gradual "raising of the stakes" via straw, then no straw) echoes Enlil's graduated response to the rebellion among *his* workers (drought, famine, plague, *then* flood).[391]

From Yahweh's perspective, however, the only appropriate response to this or any other socioeconomic situation is the Yahwistic imperative:[392]

> God spoke to Moses and said, "I am Yahweh. I appeared to
> Abraham, Isaac, and Jacob as El Shaddai,[393] but by my name
> Yahweh I did not make myself known to them. Yet I established
> my 'covenant'[394] with them to give them the land of Canaan,
> the land in which they once sojourned as aliens.[395] I have heard
> the groaning of the Israelites enslaved by the Egyptians and I
> remember my covenant promise. Say therefore to the Israelites,
> 'I am Yahweh. I will lead you out[396] from under the burdens of
> the Egyptians and deliver you from their enslavements.[397] I will
> redeem you with an outstretched arm and mighty acts of judg-

389. *Atr* 1:170–73. Assuming Ramses II to be the pharaoh to whom *Exodus* refers, it's possible that what drives this negative response is the fear of another monotheistic uprising like the one led by Amenhotep IV (Redford, *Akhenaten*, 169–78).

390. *Atr* 1:166–73. Commenting on the problem of American slavery, Earle argues that "recent critics misapply the economic model, erroneously concluding that slavery is the most efficient agrarian labor system in North America, incorrectly inferring that the North rejects slavery for ideological-moral reasons rather than economic ones" ("Slavery," 51).

391. *Atr* 1:352–54.

392. Westermann, *Promises*; Carmichael, *Origins*; Dumbrell, *Covenant*.

393. "Shaddai" (שדי) is usually translated "Almighty," but Koch thinks it has no less than eight possible meanings ("Šaddaj," 308–9).

394. Exod 6:4 (ברית). Crook ("Reciprocity") defines this term within sociological categories laid out by Sahlins (*Economics*).

395. N.B. that by repeating the root גור ("to sojourn") in the phrase ארץ מגריהם אשר גרו בה (lit., "the land of their sojourn where they sojourned in it," GKC §113w) the text emphasizes the radical temporality of Israel's attachment to things Canaanite.

396. Just as שלח is best taken as a transitive verb in Exod 5:1 ("to send"), so also is the causative verb הוציא and its participle (מוציא) best translated transitively in 6:6–7 (i.e., "the one who causes to go out"). The narrator's decision to parallel causative הוציא with causative הציל confirms this reading.

397. By specifying the actual "burdens" (סבלות) of the Egyptians and "their enslavements" (מעבדתם) the narrator resists the temptation to interpret slavery as something ahistorical.

ment. I will take you as my people and I will be your God. You shall know that I am your God, Yahweh, who leads you out from under the burdens of the Egyptians. I will bring you into the land I swore to give to Abraham, Isaac, and Jacob. I will give it to you as an inheritance.[398] I am Yahweh.'"

Many read this speech as a recapitulation of the earlier one in Exod 3,[399] but some attend more intentionally to its chiastic structure:

- I am Yahweh;[400]
  - Covenant established;[401]
    - Giving of land;[402]
      - Burdens of Egypt;[403]
        - *Redemption*;[404]
      - Burdens of Egypt;
    - Giving of land;
  - Covenant remembered;[405]
- I am Yahweh.

398. Exod 6:8 (מורשה). Ezekiel uses this noun several times to emphasize that Judah's right to have "possessions" hinges on whether or not it will choose to live "righteously" (Ezek 11:15; 25:4, 10; 33:24; 36:2, 5; 33:8; see *HAL* 421).

399. That is, many read the speech in chapter 3 as "J" and the speech in chapter 6 as "P" (e.g., Westermann, *Genesis 12–36*, 258; Brueggemann, "Kerygma," 405; Whybray, *Pentateuch*, 63–72; Childs, *Exodus*, 108–20).

400. Exod 6:2 (אני יהוה). This speech begins and ends with the declaration "I am Yahweh," even as it stakes everything on Yahweh's ability to redeem, deliver, and endow—attributes carefully examined by Zimmerli in his classic study (*Yahweh*).

401. Exod 6:4 (קום ברית). The word ברית is one of many used to describe Yahweh's relationship with Israel, and though opinions remain divided over whether it refers to a pre-exilic idea *rooted* in Israel's past or a post-exilic idea *reformulating* Israel's past, the occurrence in the Amarna letters of Akk *kittu* ("treaty"), *raḥâmu* ("love"), *aḫḫûtu* ("brotherhood"), *māmītu* ("oath-treaty"), and *epēšu šulmu* ("make peace") shows the existence of a "covenant-making" semantic field preceding the Hebrew Bible by several centuries (Moore, "Dreams," 219–21).

402. Exod 6:4, 8 (נתן . . . ארץ).

403. Exod 6:6, 7 (סבלות מצרים).

404. Exod 6:6 (גאל). Several terms occur in the ancient Near Eastern languages to denote the idea of "redemption," but "the root גאל seems to be almost exclusively Hebrew" (Ringgren, "גאל," 350; see Moore, "*Haggōʾēl*," 27–35).

405. Exod 6:8. Garr thinks that the ברית negotiated by El Shaddai is qualitatively different from the one negotiated by Yahweh ("Grammar," 398–401).

Though each layer of this speech is significant, pulsating at its core stands one of the most profoundly socioeconomic motifs of the Hebrew Bible: *redemption*. The significance of this cannot be overstated.[406] One of the Bible's most persistent, most distinctive, and most important "paradigmatic themes" is not theological or philosophical, but *economic* in nature.[407]

Like Cain, Yahweh desires to *acquire*, but unlike Cain he never abandons his coordinate desire to *protect*. Like Enki, he desires to *protect*, but unlike Enki he never approves of bribery to pay for it.[408] Instead he "redeems" and "buys back,"[409] exchanging "gifts" with *his* "business partners" which look very different from those doled out by other divine benefactors. The gift of *land*, for example, looks like nothing else ever transacted through a "reciprocating covenantal exchange."[410]

At any rate, the motif of *redemption* pops up repeatedly in *Exodus*; e.g., in the fourth plague narrative:[411] "On that day I will set apart the land of Goshen, where my people live. No flies shall swarm there, so that you may know that I, Yahweh, am here in this land. Thus will I put *redemption* between my people and your [Pharaoh's] people."[412] It's difficult to know

406. Smith situates the redemption motif at the center of *Exodus* because its literary structure consists of two main sections centered around a victory poem praising Yahweh for "redeeming (גאל) his people" (*Pilgrimage*, 205–26).

407. See Fischer, "Exodus," 25–44.

408. Contrast Exod 6:2–9 with *Atr* 1:376–83. Scherer investigates three proverbs (Prov 17:8; 18:16; 21:14) which appear to portray bribery as a "wise" practice, but concludes that the context in which they appear bridges a "tightrope" profoundly threatened by "the danger of abuse" ("Bribery," 66).

409. Moore, "*Haggōʾēl*," 27–8. Ohrenstein and Gordon argue that "God does not go to the trouble of redeeming the nation so that, in its turn, it could set up a social order as harsh and inhumane as the one from which it is delivered" (*Economic*, 27).

410. Crook, "Reciprocity," 78–91. Brueggemann emphasizes that, "land is never simply physical dirt, but sacral space "freighted with social meanings derived from historical experience" (*Land*, 2).

411. Hendel ponders the historicity of the plagues narrative ("Exodus," 601–22), but no one (to my knowledge) has attempted to document the degree to which the socioeconomic conflict motifs in this "great text" resonate with those in other "great texts."

412. Exod 8:22–23 (MT 8:18–19). The noun פדות, from the verb פדה, clearly means "redemption" in Isa 50:2; Pss 111:9, 130:7, but because LXX here translates διαστολή ("distinction"; Vg *divisio*), most English versions translate "distinction" or the like (e.g., NIV, NRSV). Yet, as MacIntosh observes, "the Masoretic pointing and the subsequent rabbinic understanding of פדת in Exod 8:19 reflects a semantic development attested in Aramaic rather than in Hebrew," and this bestows on "the Jewish tradition a particular understanding of redemption" ("Exodus," 555).

what kind of "redemption" to which this text exactly refers, but whatever it is these lines refer to a sacred space enclosed by a sacred boundary protecting a sacred "treasure."[413] Further, this redemptive gift foreshadows a much greater "gift" yet to be given—the promised "land."[414]

Redemption pops up again in the narrative about the seventh plague, when Yahweh commands his people to hide behind another "sacred boundary": "Tomorrow at this time I will cause the heaviest hail to fall which has ever fallen in Egypt since the day it was founded. Secure your livestock and all which you have in the field, for every human or animal sent out into the field and not gathered under a shelter will die when the hail hits them."[415] Expanding his protection over non-Hebrews, Yahweh promises that "the hail will strike down everything in the open field throughout all the land of Egypt, both animal and human. It will strike down all the plants of the field and shatter every tree. Only in the land of Goshen, where the Israelites live, shall no hail fall."[416]

In the following paragraph, however, *Exodus* disjunctively separates the foregoing nine plagues from the plague against the firstborn,[417] revisiting the "big problem" of primogeniture.[418] Moses said, "Thus says

413. In *GE* 3:45–55 a divine council similarly attempts to protect *its* "sacred treasure."

414. Tucker argues that Ps 105:26–36 reformulates the plagues narrative in order to make "the idea of land central to interpreting the plague tradition" ("Plagues," 401), yet Grosby argues that the emergence of Israel as a "nation" is a much lengthier process involving the combining of many sacred sites into one territory (*Nationality*, 69–91).

415. Exod 9:18–19. Noegel argues that the plague of hail and thunderstorms, like the "wounding" of the firstborn, possesses special significance. Why? Because, like other "top-ten" lists, the placement of this plague stands in the all-important seventh position ("Significance," 532–39).

416. Exod 9:25–26. Rainey argues, from a study of Papyrus Anastasi (*ANET* 259), a thirteenth century Egyptian document alluding to Shosu bedouin in Wadi Tumilat (*Goshen*), that the Egyptians consider the Israelites to be a subset of the Shosu ("Unruly," 481–96).

417. Lemmelijn argues (a) that the first nine plagues are an independent tradition; (b) that the death-of-the-firstborn text originates from a combination of passover and unleavened bread traditions; and (c) that only later does it evolve into a "tenth plague" ("Setting," 443–60).

418. Many ancient cultures divinize dead leaders (e.g., Julius Caesar; Weinstock, *Julius*), but it's no coincidence that the "deification" of Alexander takes place in *Egypt* (Griffiths, "Hellenistic," 3900–3901). Primogenitural divinization is so pronounced in Egypt, Brueggemann concludes, Yahweh's triumph over Pharaoh symbolizes a desire to reorder the country's entire economy, even though the pharaohs of the world always resist the belief that divine governance transcends human power ("Pharaoh," 27–51).

Yahweh: About midnight I will go out through Egypt and every first-born in Egypt will die, from the firstborn of Pharaoh who sits on his throne to the firstborn of the female slave who works at the mill, even the firstborn of the livestock—though not a dog shall growl at the Israelites or their livestock—so that you may know that Yahweh 'distinguishes' between Egypt and Israel."[419] Just as *Genesis* critiques the tribal abuse of primogeniture, so *Exodus* condemns its urbanized divinization.[420] Where the first nine "plagues" target the traditional deities of Egyptian myth,[421] the tenth "wounding"[422] targets one of the most blatantly arrogant, radically narcissistic, and patently corrupt forms of primogeniture ever conceived.[423]

Question: How do the Hebrews escape this final disaster? Behind what sacred boundary do they now huddle for "protection?" *Answer:* Those heeding Moses' warning (Hebrews and non-Hebrews alike) hide behind something as powerfully symbolic as it is mysteriously sacred—the ritual of Passover.[424] Few interpretations of this ritual read it through a socioeconomic lens, but in point of fact Passover, like Jubilee, is a socioeconomic firewall behind which the vulnerable *still* huddle for

419. Exod 11:4–7 (פלה). Just as Yahweh "distinguishes" (פלה) between Israelite and Egyptian livestock (Exod 9:4), so also he "distinguishes" (פלה) between Israel and Egypt.

420. The name "Ra-meses" means "born of (the god) Ra," and "Tut-mose" means "born of (the god) Tut" (Grumach, "Ramses," 89). The re-telling of this event in Ps 105:36 associates Egypt's "firstborn" (בכור) with the "best of all their labor" (ראשית לכל אונם).

421. Exod 9:14 (מגפת). According to Num 33:3–4, the Israelites "set out from the city of Pi-Rameses on the fifteenth day of the first month; on the day after passover they went out boldly in the sight of all the Egyptians, while the Egyptians were burying all their firstborn whom Yahweh struck down, thus executing judgments against their gods." N.B. that the "Cannibal Hymn" in the Pyramid Texts speaks of a king "being judged . . . on the day of the slaying of the firstborn" (Lichtheim, *Literature* 1:36–37; see Gilula, "Smiting," 94).

422. Exod 11:1. *Exodus* uses a different word to distinguish the tenth plague (נגג, "wound") from the previous nine (מגפות, "plagues").

423. Greenstein rejects the idea that Yahweh strikes Egypt's *firstborn* in retribution for their persecution of the Hebrews, proposing instead that the tenth plague has its own cultic identity and history ("Firstborn," 555–68).

424. Exod 12:11 (פסח; see *HAL* 892–4; Bokser, "Unleavened"; Jacobs, "Passover," 7003).

"protection."[425] Where Jubilee interrupts the "poverty cycle,"[426] Passover interrupts the "contempt cycle."[427] Where publically-displayed blood creates prophylactic boundaries within the religions of Israel's neighbors, publically-displayed blood provides purification as well as prophylaxis in the Hebrew Bible.[428] In short, Passover addresses one of Israel's "big problems" because it (a) protects foreign slaves (*retenu*) victimized by "contempt,"[429] while (b) condemning the divinization of primogeniture practiced by their "city-dwelling" taskmasters.[430]

"PROVISION" VS. "DEPRIVATION" IN THE WILDERNESS (NUM 10:11—36:13)

After their redemption from Egypt, the Hebrews encounter another "big problem" in the wilderness: food and water.[431] Characteristically, Yahweh responds to this crisis in stages, posting a "sacred boundary" at each stage: "I will rain down bread from heaven for you. Each day the people will go out and gather enough food for that day, and in this way I will test them to see whether they will follow my instructions.[432] On the sixth day, when they prepare what they gather, it will include twice as

425. Redford suggests that one of the festivals observed by Egyptian pharaohs (the *heb-sed*) socioeconomically parallels the Hebrew Jubilee (*Akhenaten*, 51–52; see Reeder, "*Heb-Sed*," 60–71).

426. Greenberg observes how many of the legal texts depict (a) "resistance in principle to the alienation of patrimonial lands," as well as (b) "periodic royal releases from certain kinds of debt and obligation" ("Jubilee," 625–26; see Kraus, *Verfügungen*; Payne, *Poverty*).

427. Spieckermann, "*Dies*," 194–208; "Wrath and Mercy," 3–16.

428. McCarthy, "Symbolism," 166–76.

429. Braulik, "Impact," 338. Attending to the Hebrew critique of Egypt, Assyria, Babylonia, and Persia, Brueggemann reflects on the practical divinization of technocracy, capitalism, consumerism, and militarism in contemporary Western culture, arguing that Passover still liberates victims of slavery (*Words*, 73–87).

430. Levine and de Tarragon read *CAT* 1.161 as a funerary ritual divinizing Niqmaddu III ("Rephaim," 649–59), but Lewis (*Cults*, 32) and Smith (*Monotheism*, 268) disagree.

431. The title of the fourth book of the Bible is במדבר, *In the Wilderness*.

432. "Testing" occurs frequently in the Bible. Yahweh tests (a) to see what kind of "healing" people want (Exod 15:25–26), (b) to see who will follow his instructions (16:4), (c) to instill healthy respect for the Unseen World (20:20), (d) to distinguish Israel from other nations (Deut 4:34), (e) to humble and examine human hearts (8:2), (f) to discover the genuineness of his people's "love" (13:3), and (g) to prepare his people for the "good life" (8:16).

much as what they gather on other days."[433] When several refugees ask questions about this food, Yahweh gives them clear instructions on how to gather, ingest, and store it. "Gather as much of it as you need, one omer per person, each providing for those in his own tent."[434] It doesn't take, long, however, for people to start testing these boundaries, (a) when they try to gather more than one omer of food per day; (b) when they try to store this food on forbidden nights of the week; and (b) when they try to gather food on the Sabbath day.[435]

With the violation of each boundary another test is failed[436]—the first when some try to gather more than a day's allotment; the second when some try to store this "heavenly food" on a forbidden night of the week; the third when some try to gather food ("work") on the day divinely reserved as a day of "rest."[437] Not only do these tests gradually institutionalize the concept of "Sabbath,"[438] but the decision to administer them at this critical point in Israel's history painfully weans them away from the "old order" thinking hammered into their minds over centuries of slavery; i.e., the "deprivation myth."[439] This ideology, so deeply ingrained into their minds, only stubbornly gives way to a "new order" of thinking in which an "organized covenant community" can be "centered around" the concept of "unfailing generosity."[440]

Of course, this is not the only "heavenly food" tradition embedded in the "great literature."[441] The Babylonian myth of *Adapa*, for example,[442] features a situation in which Anu offers the mortal Adapa "heavenly food"

---

433. Exod 16:4–5; Beuken, "Exodus."

434. Exod 16:16. An omer is one-tenth of an ephah (about five pints).

435. Exod 16:23 (שבת); Jacobs, "Shabbat"; Hasel, "Sabbath."

436. On the pedagogical significance of "testing," see Moore, "Searching," 35–37.

437. Some speculate that the giving of "heavenly food" is one of the ways in which the Sabbath is "hallowed" (*Gen. Rab.* 11:2); or that its taste varies according to the one tasting it (*Exod. Rab.* 5:9); or that in addition to the "heavenly food" Yahweh also rains down precious stones and pearls (*Exod. Rab.* 33:8).

438. Geller observes that שבת in Exod 16:23 is the first appearance of the term ("Manna," 7).

439. Brueggemann, *Memory*, 69–76.

440. Olson, "Power," 323.

441. Wong cites several other examples ("Manna").

442. In Babylonian myth Adapa is a "steward of Enki" (Jacobsen, "Religions," 5953). Critical editions of *Adapa* are published by Picchioni (*Adapa*) and Izre'el (*Adapa*). English translations appear in Dalley (*Myths*, 182–88) and Foster (*Muses*, 525–29).

in order to keep him from returning back to earth (Enki's realm).[443] Anu makes this offer because, like all other hosts, he finds himself bound "to treat Adapa as a guest."[444] From a socioeconomic perspective, however, Adapa carefully refuses this *bribe*,[445] not because the food Anu offers is not desirable, but because he believes (thanks to Enki) that it is poisonous.[446] In Israelite tradition Moses participates in a heavenly banquet on Mt. Sinai for Israel's tribal elders,[447] even though the *kind* of "heavenly food" is never specified.[448]

These examples show "heavenly food" to be an established mytheme,[449] and although each has its own focus, each of these texts intertextually shows (a) that heavenly food is a "gift" from the Unseen World; (b) that it comes with a strict set of rules for ingestion; and (c) that its *raison d'être* is temporal, not eternal. What the mytheme here suggests is not only that Yahweh's "heavenly food" helps the Hebrews survive a difficult time in their history,[450] but that Yahweh's imperative remains preferable to the "deprivation myth." As Brueggemann puts it, "when the children of Israel are in the wilderness, beyond the reach of Egypt, they still look back and ask, 'Should we really go?' . . . Then something extraordinary happens. God's love comes trickling down in the form of bread . . . They had never before received bread as a free gift which they could not control, predict,

443. Izre'el, *Adapa*; Jacobsen, "Investiture," 201.

444. Jacobsen, "Investiture," 202.

445. Anu's offer to Adapa, in other words, looks very much like Ishtar's offer to Gilgamesh (*GE* 6:6–21).

446. *Adapa* B:77–78 (cited in Foster, *Muses*, 529). Dalley points out an example of wordplay when, after Anu offers Adapa something *šamūti* ("heavenly"), Enki suggests that what he's actually been offered is *ša mūti* (lit., "that which is of death"; *Myths*, 188).

447. Exod 24:1–11; Wong, "Manna," 55–153.

448. Wong views the "mythological connection of manna" as something which occurs when "the descriptions of manna in the Bible are related to primeval time/suspension of profane time, cosmic mountain, archetypical acts of God/gods and Israel's forefathers, and a ritual" ("Manna," 56).

449. Lévi-Strauss defines a "mytheme" as a unit within a primeval story which focuses not on content or structure, but on the dynamic between *function* and *subject* (*Anthropology*, 211).

450. According to Exod 16:35, "the Israelites eat manna forty years until they come to a habitable land (ארץ נושבת; lit., a "land for dwelling") . . . to the border of the land of Canaan." After this, however, it's no longer provided.

plan for, or own … It's a wonder, it's a miracle, it's an embarrassment, it's irrational, but God's abundance transcends the market economy."[451]

In spite of Yahweh's persistence, however, it still takes the Hebrews an entire generation (forty years) to wean themselves away from the "deprivation myth,"[452] and then only after the Sinai generation perishes in the wilderness through a series of incidents.[453] The first occurs when several refugees (the text calls them "rabble")[454] begin complaining to Moses: "The rabble gave in to their addictions by weeping and complaining,[455] 'If only we had meat to eat! We remember the fish we used to eat in Egypt for free,[456] not to mention the cucumbers, the melons, the leeks, the onions, and the garlic. Now our soul[457] dries up because we have nothing to eat here but this manna!'"[458] Yahweh responds to this complaint by giving them so much meat to eat, they start gagging on it: "Then a wind went out from Yahweh, drawing in quail from the sea and dropping them around the camp about a day's journey on one side and a day's journey on the other, about two cubits deep on the ground.[459] The people worked day and night gathering up the quail—the least anyone gathered was ten omers—but while the meat was still in their teeth Yahweh's anger burned against them, striking them down with a great plague. Thus the name of that place is called *Graves of Addiction*."[460]

451. Brueggemann, *Memory,* 71. This Yahwistic imperative recurs throughout *torah*: in the redistribution of silver and gold from "civilized" Egyptians to "uncivilized" Hebrews (Exod 3:21–22; 11:2; 12:35–36); in the ratification of laws designed to protect widows, orphans, aliens, and all others "lacking the social leverage (necessary) to secure resources" (Deut 12–26); and in the "heavenly food" texts championing a new "model of alternative management" (Brueggemann, *Theology,* 736–37).

452. Num 32:13.

453. Moore, "Numbers" 186.

454. Num 11:4 (הָאסַפְסֻף). If this noun derives from the root אסף ("to gather"; see *HAL* 73), then it's more than a little ironic that those who complain about the "gathered food" are "the gatherers."

455. Num 11:4. The phrase הִתְאַוּוּ תַאֲוָה (lit., "they repeatedly desired [their] desire") combines the reflexive form of the verb אוה with its nominal form to create a syntactic construction designed to convey emphasis (GKC §117p-r).

456. Num 11:5 (חִנָּם). LXX δωρέα ("gift").

457. Num 11:6 (נֶפֶשׁ); LXX ψυχή; Vg *anima.*

458. Num 11:4–6; Moore, "Numbers," 190–91.

459. McRae observes that the quail in Exod 16:13 merely *appear* alongside the manna, while the quail in Num 11:31 are *consumed* alongside it ("Bread," 217–29).

460. Num 11:34 (קִבְרוֹת הַתַּאֲוָה).

The rabble's problem has nothing to do with the quality of the "heavenly food" they have received, nor does it have anything to do with their failure to appreciate the principles of good nutrition.[461] Their "big problem" is that they want to define the "good life" according to a lifestyle alien to the Yahwistic imperative; i.e., one more attuned to the words of Ishtar than the words of Yahweh.[462] The keyword in this text, here amplified into its reflexive form, denotes a *continuous* "craving"[463]— what contemporary observers now call "addiction."[464] Thus, when the "rabble" meet their doom, the place where this occurs comes to be known as "Graves of Addiction."[465] This punishment occurs because, like Gilgamesh, these "rabble" willfully decide to violate a "sacred boundary." Heschel comments: "Whoever would enter the holiness of the Sabbath day must first lay down the profanity of clattering commerce, of being yoked to toil. He must go away from the screech of dissonant days, from the nervousness and fury of acquisitiveness."[466]

The next incident occurs between Moses and several "tribal leaders"[467] when he instructs them to "leave the Negeb and go up into the hill country, and find out whether the people who live there are strong or weak, whether they are many or few, whether the land they inhabit is good or bad, whether their cities are walled or unwalled,[468] whether their land is rich or poor."[469] What stands out in these instructions is not simply their polarized format, but their socioeconomic intentionality.[470] Two focus

461. Berkman, "Consumption," 174–90; Davidson, "Vegetarian," 114–30.

462. Contrast *GE* 1:226–33 with Deut 6:24 (see Marcovich, "Ishtar," 43–59).

463. Num 11:34; התאוה is the reflexive form of אוה, "to crave" (GKC §54e).

464. Asenjo defines "addiction" as "a dependence on a behavior or substance that a person is powerless to stop" ("Addiction," 50; see Adams, *Fragmented*; Alexander, *Addiction*; Boellstorff, *Human*, 176–78; Erchak, *Anthropology*, 151).

465. Num 11:34–35 (קברות התאוה, *Qivrot Hit'awah*).

466. Heschel, *Sabbath*, 13. From a Hebrew perspective "addiction" finds its taproot in disobedience, not intrapsychic conflict or chemical imbalance (Gold and Herkov, "Addiction," 62–68; Massey, "Addiction," 9–80).

467. Num 13:2 (נשיא). This term appears sixty-two times in *Numbers*.

468. Num 13:19; lit., whether they live in "tented camps" (מחנים) or behind "fortifications" (מבצרים).

469. Num 13:17–20.

470. Interpretations hypothesizing the agricultural lay of the land tend to obscure this (e.g., Philo, *Mos.* 1: 221–31), as do those which read incriminating etymologies into the name of each tribal leader (e.g., *b. Soṭah* 34b).

on the Canaanite people; two more on the Canaanite *economy*, particularly (a) the relative strength of its cities (walled vs. unwalled)[471] vs. (b) its overall health (i.e., "rich" vs. "poor").[472]

Of greatest interest here, however, is the *attitude* these tribal leaders develop after their scouting trip into Canaan, particularly when they describe it afterwards as a land which "devours its inhabitants"[473] disparagingly referring to themselves as "grasshoppers."[474] Not only does this intertextually resonate with other texts about "devouring,"[475] it highlights this resonance though wordplay,[476] coyly manipulating the "devouring predator" metaphor in yet another attempt to address another "big problem."

The next wilderness conflict occurs between Moses and Korah, a disgruntled refugee aided and abetted by two others, Dathan and Abiram.[477] Frustrated by the Aaronid hold on priestly power, Korah instigates a rebellion against Moses which finds itself rooted just as much in priestly politics as tribal economics.[478] To be specific, Dathan and Abiram are Reubenites, a factor which immediately implies that their reason for joining up with Korah against Moses has ultimately to do

---

471. That is, "field-dwellers" vs. "city-dwellers" (Burke, *Fortification*).

472. Moran notes how the leaders' descriptions of these cities parallel the socioeconomic descriptions of the Canaanites (*Amarna*, 177).

473. Num 13:32 (אכל ארץ; lit., "land which devours").

474. Num 13:33 (חגב). This term can refer to the devouring "locust" as well as the harmless "grasshopper," a polyphony encouraging Lerner to posit a "tremendous semantic tension" within "the grasshopper/locust trope" ("Grasshoppers," 547).

475. Because Ishtar craves the taste of Gilgamesh's "fruit" (*inbu*, *GE* 6:8) and begs to "devour" (*akālu*) Ishullanu's "power" (6:68), Winckler justifiably calls her a "devouring goddess" (*Constraints*, 202–6).

476. In Lerner's opinion, "the grasshopper simile is shot through with ironic tension, for while the individual insect may fairly represent weakness and timidity, grasshoppers massed together become perhaps the most terrible destructive force … the locust swarm" ("Grasshoppers," 546).

477. Goodnick, "Korah," 177–81.

478. Num 16:1–50. Some see Num 16 as a combination "of at least two stories: an Epic tradition (JE) concerning the civil/political conflict between Dathan and Abiram, in which they charge Moses with "making himself a prince" over the people; and a priestly tradition concerning the cultic/religious conflict between the Korahites and Aaron over the exclusive claims of Aaron to the priesthood (Hutton, "Korah," 101). Mirguet suggests that spatial considerations should also be taken into consideration when interpreting this text ("Spatial," 311–30).

with the socioeconomic problem of *primogeniture*.[479] It would be mono-dimensional to insist that this is the *only* reason for their involvement—i.e., to formulate an attempt to seize back their Reubenite "birthright" from Moses and Aaron[480]—yet it's important to realize (a) that Korah's name does not appear in Moses' re-telling of the incident,[481] and (b) that *Numbers* goes out of its way to emphasize the *economic* dimension of this conflict: "Moses sent for Dathan and Abiram, but they said, 'We will not come! Is it too little that you have brought us up out of a land flowing with milk and honey to kill us in the wilderness, that you would also lord it over us? Clearly you have not brought us into a land flowing with milk and honey,[482] nor have you given us any 'inheritance' of fields or vineyards."[483] Moses' response underscores this socioeconomic dimension. Reporting to Yahweh, he says, "Pay no attention to their 'gift.' I have not taken one donkey from them, nor have I harmed any of them."[484] Like Samuel before *his* critics, Moses denies the charge of "corruption" leveled against him by men determined to treat him with the greatest "contempt."[485]

479. Citing Gen 49:4, Sicherman and Gevaryahu point out that Reuben loses his primogenitural status because of his sexual affair with his father's concubine ("Foremost," 17–25). Whatever the reasons, the text encapsulating this memory stands at the beginning of a trajectory in which (a) Ephraim, Joseph's younger son, takes Reuben's place (Gen 48:14; 49:22); then (b) Korah tries to revive the old Reubenite tradition (Num 16); then (c) the Ephraimite Samuel responds negatively to Israel's demand for a king (1 Sam 8); then (d) the Jerusalem cult invalidates Ephraim's claim (2 Sam 6); then (e) Jeroboam's Ephraimite descent qualifies him for kingship in the eyes of northern Israelites (1 Kgs 12). Cross argues, however, that the association of Moses with Reuben represents an unsuccessful attempt to validate Reubenite power claims ("Priestly," 195–215).

480. Cross, "Reuben," 46–65.

481. Deut 11:6. Weinfeld observes (*Deuteronomy*, 432) that 4Q128, 4Q138, and Sam insert the following line to this verse, ואת כל האדם אשר לקרח ("and all the men who belonged to Korah," Num 16:32).

482. Twice these Reubenites use the "milk-and-honey" metaphor to underline their complaint, once to describe *Egypt* as a land of "milk-and-honey," another to describe Canaan as a land *without* "milk-and-honey."

483. Num 16:12–14 (נחלה). The Reubenites' complaint that they never received a נחלה ("ancestral inheritance") is sharpened by the fact that no "tribe of Reuben" appears on any map of Israel (though this has not stopped historians from speculating where it *might* have been (e.g., Cross, "Reuben," 56–63).

484. Num 16:15 (מנחה, "gift").

485. In 1 Sam 12:3 Samuel demands, "Here I am; testify against me before Yahweh and before his anointed. Whose ox have I taken? Whose donkey have I taken? Whom have I defrauded? Whom have I oppressed? From whose hand have I taken a 'bribe?'" (כפר, lit., "ransom payment").

In short, this episode focuses on an embattled leader (Moses) forced to defend himself against angry refugees less interested in the Yahwistic imperative than the traditionalist securities perceived to be bound up with the socioeconomic institution of primogeniture. This interpretation contrasts sharply with others depicting the incident as (a) a "cultic/religious conflict between Aaron and the Korahites over the exclusive claims of Aaron to the priesthood";[486] or as (b) a dispute driven by the "great riches" of Moses' detractors;[487] or as (c) a political conflict between "rival priestly families";[488] or as (d) a disgruntled employee's desire to "set his eye on that which is improper."[489]

The final socioeconomic conflict in the *wilderness* begins with a conversation between Moses and five female refugees over (what else?) primogeniture.[490] One of Joseph's descendants through the tribe of Manasseh, a man named Zelophehad, dies in the wilderness before the second census is taken.[491] This creates a crisis which, as his daughters take great pains to point out,[492] threatens the extinction of his very name.[493] Why? Because there is no male heir left to ensure that Zelophehad's family will inherit Zelophehad's "property."[494] Unlike Korah and his con-

---

486. Hutton, "Korah," 101.

487. Josephus, *A.J.* 4:14.

488. Cross, "Reuben," 70.

489. *b. Sotah* 9b (see Litke, "Korah," 118).

490. Num 27:1–11. This is not the only problem addressed by this text. Sakenfeld reads it as an episode focused on "the preservation of the father's name by the proper distribution of his inheritance" ("Zelophehad," 46). Derby tries to read it as a story about the Bible's "first feminists" ("Zelophehad," 169). Shemesh, however, observes that even though the story involves "a legal breakthrough benefiting women," this text focuses on an "androcentric" concern ("Gender," 83).

491. Num 26:33. The first census occurs at the beginning of *Numbers*, the second after the Sinai generation dies in the wilderness (Olson, *Death*, 175).

492. Zelophehad's daughters are Mahlah, Noah, Hoglah, Milcah, and Tirzah. Ahituv notes that two of these names are place names (*Handbook*, 192).

493. That is, Zelophehad "was not among the company of those who gathered themselves together against Yahweh in the Korah congregation" (Num 27:3). Levine points out that Zelophehad, had he participated in the Korah rebellion, might have seen his name "legitimately withdrawn from the register of his tribe, and his lands expropriated" in accordance with the ancient "law of the *herem*, by which those condemned to death by the judicial process lost title to their estates" (*Numbers*, 345).

494. Num 27:4 (אחזה). In Gen 47:11 this term describes Joseph's determination to grant his *retenu* family "landed property" in Egypt (אחזה; see Levine, "Semantics," 134–40).

gregation, the daughters of Zelophehad approach Moses *privately*—not to challenge his leadership, but to find a way to escape the institutional impoverishment sure to befall them should their father's "name"[495] be "deleted" from the census-rolls.[496]

Moses' response to this dilemma leads to one of the most remarkable socioeconomic pronouncements in the Bible, one which (a) grants women the right to inherit land;[497] (b) institutionalizes a chain of command which, though later modified by priestly tradition,[498] accounts for the Transjordanian settlement of the tribe of Manasseh;[499] (c) explains "the context of the settlement of Canaan put forward by members of the priestly school";[500] and (d) challenges all traditionalist attempts to prioritize primogeniture over the Yahwistic imperative.[501]

Sidestepping the socioeconomic implications, Mishnah's commentary shifts attention away from primogeniture *per se* to sycophantic questions about the *size* of Zelophehad's "inheritance."[502] Talmud continues this in its attempt to anticipate every possible legal response to the proposals laid out in Mishnah,[503] yet later critics shift the focus back to the original meaning of the text, albeit via a rather spotty "argument": (a) the keyword in Jacob's blessing should be translated literally, not figu-

495. Num 27:4. As in most Semitic languages, שֵׁם (Ug *šm*; Arab اسم) denotes "legal authority," not just "identity" (*HAL* 1432–35).

496. Num 27:4 (גרע). Levine argues that this term is "part of the ancient mathematical vocabulary" and means "to subtract, withdraw an amount or item" (*Numbers*, 345).

497. According to Westenholz, the Enlilemaba archive suggests that inheritance rights can and do pass to women as "property of the mother" (*Sumerian*), and Wilcke notes that even the oldest legal texts treat female inheritance as an innovative idea (*Law*, 71–72).

498. In Num 36:1–12 leaders of the Manasseh tribe convince Moses to qualify his pronouncement by prohibiting Zelophehad's daughters from marrying outside the tribe. Josephus comments: "If they marry into their own tribe, they shall carry their estate along with them, but if they dispose of themselves in marriage to men of another tribe they shall leave their inheritance in their father's tribe" (*A.J.* 4:175; see Turner and Frese, "Marriage," 5725–26).

499. Snaith, "Daughters," 126.

500. Levine, *Numbers*, 344.

501. The book of *Ruth* addresses a similar situation in which another patriarchal "name" falls into danger because of another socioeconomic crisis (see Moore, "Ruth," 309–11).

502. *m. B. Bat.* 8:3 (נחלה).

503. *b. B. Bat.* 116b–22b.

ratively (i.e., as "daughters," not "branches"),[504] so (b) these "daughters" most likely refer to the daughters of Zelophehad.[505]

SUMMARY

The Hebrew Bible addresses many of the same "big problems" covertly engaged by other "great texts" from the ancient Near East, creatively manipulating the motifs of *acquisition, protection, slavery,* and *deprivation.* By addressing these problems within categories influenced and shaped by the "civilization-wilderness" polarities structuring the Mesopotamian epics, the writers of *torah* include, adapt, and in some cases transform these socioeconomic conflict motifs to fit the parameters of a Yahwistic (vs. Ishtaristic or Enlilistic or Baalistic) imperative.

We turn next to consider how Alexander the Great's invasion affects these parameters.

504. Gen 49:22 (בנות).

505. That is, that these "branches" are born into the tribe of Manasseh, Joseph's son (*Gen. Rab.* 98:18; *Num. Rab.* 14:7).

4

Socioeconomic Conflict Motifs
in Early Jewish Texts

WHEN ALEXANDER OF MACEDON invades Syria-Palestine in the fourth century BCE he brings with his armies a socioeconomic culture that changes the region forever,[1] though historians continue to argue over exactly how much.[2] Most of the Aramaic-speaking[3] cultures indigenous to the Fertile Crescent quickly assimilate to the "Greek invasion,"[4] but some do not,[5] and others try to stake out delicate median

1. Alexander's campaigns are "not only wars of liberation of Greek colonies in Asia Minor but also revenge for Persian depredations in Greece in years past. Within eleven years Alexander's empire stretches from the Balkans to the Himalayas, and includes most of the eastern Mediterranean countries, Mesopotamia, and Persia. He dies in Babylon contemplating the conquest of Carthage and perhaps Rome. His legacy is a fragmented empire, but he also inspires a new Hellenistic age of cosmopolitan culture" ("Alexander," 137–38).

2. Rostovtzeff (*Social*) argues for greater influence of internal vs. external factors, *contra* Gibbon (*History*), yet his reliance on Marxist theory renders his conclusions problematic in many circles (e.g., Heichelheim, Review of *Social*, 59–61).

3. As Griffiths observes, "Greek bears the official stamp of the ruling powers," but "within Alexander's empire other languages continue to flourish, including Aramaic, Hebrew, Egyptian, Babylonian, and Latin" ("Hellenistic," 3900–901).

4. Droysen (*Geschichte*) draws upon the dialectical presumptions of Winckelmann (Potts, *Winckelmann*) and Hegel (Gadamer, *Hegel*) to define "Hellenism" as an historical movement of "inevitable Greek progress." Some Hegelians imagine it as the "thesis" against which Judaism's "antithesis" collides, thereby producing the "synthesis" of Christianity. Others think this analysis too simplistic (e.g., Shavit, *Athens*; Rajak, "Jews," 535–57).

5. 2 Macc 4:13–15 remains one of the clearest "resistance texts": "There is 'such extreme Hellenism' (ἀκμή τις ἑλληνισμοῦ) and 'emphasis on foreign ways' (πρόσβασις ἀλλοφυλισμοῦ) . . . that the priests no longer perform their service at the altar. Despising the sanctuary and neglecting the sacrifices, they participate instead in the unlawful proceedings of the wrestling arena, . . . disdaining the honors prized by their ancestors and

positions between "total assimilation" and "total resistance."[6] Identifying
these responses can be difficult given (a) the "paucity of our evidence,"[7]
(b) the "yawning gaps" in the "biased testimony" of the evidence,[8] and (c)
the contemporary biases influencing the thinking of the (predominantly
Western) specialists most familiar with it.[9]

Some distinguish between "Hellenism" as a "cultural milieu" vs.
"Hellenization" as the "process of adoption and adaptation . . . on a local
level,"[10] defining the latter as the "penetration of . . . Greek civilization
into territories which, though subject to Graeco-Macedonian rule for a
period of time, carefully preserve their national culture."[11] Others deny
the existence of *any* syncretism between "Judaism" and "Hellenism,"[12]
presuming instead the existence of an "essentialist Judaism" based on
a so-called "Nehemiah model."[13] Still others segregate "diaspora" from
"Palestinian" Judaism as if these two adjectives denote completely different religions.[14]

---

investing greater value in Greek notions." As Davies points out, this text clearly shows
the "invasion" of "Hellenistic terminology" into Second Temple Judaism (*Christian*,
141).

6. Following Droysen, Hengel defines "Hellenism" as a fusion of Greek and Oriental
cultures created by Alexander's conquests long before the Maccabean revolt (*Judaism*,
310–14).

7. Hopkins, Review of *Institutions*, 106.

8. Weitzman, "Antiochus," 220. See Brutti, *Priesthood*, 29–116; Gafni, "Josephus,"
116–31.

9. Relying on the Marxist presumptions of Rostovtzeff, Hengel argues that Qoheleth
"encounters not the school opinions of the philosophers, but the popular views of the
Greek 'bourgeoisie'" (*Judaism*, 125), yet many do not accept his presumptions (see
Moore, Review of *Amos*, 758–60).

10. Levine, *Judaism*, 16–17.

11. Momigliano, "Hellenism," 784.

12. Gruen, *Heritage*, 3–4; Levine, *Judaism*, 3–32. Feldman argues that some Jewish re-
actions to Hellenism in this era are best described as "counterattack" (*Jew*, 44). In Colpe's
opinion the Greek word "syncretism" (συγκρητίσμος; Plutarch, *Mor.* 490a) denotes
any substantive connection "between languages, cultures, or religions" ("Syncretism,"
8926).

13. Nodet, *Search*, 90. Blenkinsopp argues that, "since great antiquity implies great
authenticity, Jewish authors are anxious to compete with the claims advanced for their
more powerful neighbors, the Egyptians, Babylonians, and Greeks" (*Judaism*, 16).

14. See, e.g., Moore, *Judaism*. Isaac observes that some interpreters "divide Jewish
literature into a Palestinian and Hellenistic group on the assumption that Jewish literature in Palestine is invariably written in Hebrew or Aramaic and by Pharisees, while
literature from the Diaspora would normally be Hellenistic in outlook and written in

Most historians believe, however, that the various "Judaisms"[15] of the Second Temple period each exhibit *some* measure of Greek influence,[16] and further, that Jewish socioeconomic activity in this period focuses more on the "realization of stability" than the "modern pursuit of expansion."[17] Most agree with Martin Hengel's assessment that "something fundamentally new arises in Hellenism—through the encounter of Greece with the Orient—which differs from the time of classical Greece, just as Judaism undergoes a gradual but deep-rooted change in the Hellenistic period through its encounter and conflict with the social, political, and spiritual forces of this epoch, on the basis of which it differs in essential points from its earlier forms in the Old Testament."[18] Interacting with this assessment, the following pages reflect on a few Jewish texts from the Second Temple period in order to ascertain how they incorporate, modify, and/or transform the socioeconomic conflict motifs animating the "great texts" before them. Aiming for balance and perspective, these reflections focus on two *types* of texts:

Greek. It is now clear, however, that Greek is also written in Syria-Palestine and that Semitic languages are used in many parts of the diaspora" (Review of *History*, 244). Jacobs adds that "Jewish thinkers who hold that an essence of Judaism can be perceived tend to speak of 'normative Judaism' with the implication that at the heart of the Jewish faith there is a hard, imperishable core, to be externally preserved, together with numerous peripheral ideas, and expressed, to be sure, by great Jewish thinkers in different ages, but not really essential to the faith, which could be dismissed if necessary as deviations. Unfortunately for this line of thinking, no criteria are available for distinguishing the essential from the ephemeral, so that a strong element of subjectivity is present in this whole approach" ("Judaism," 513).

15. Interpreters who prefer to speak of *Judaisms* (pl.) include Scholem, Baron and Neusner (Swartz, "Judaism," 4969); interpreters who resist this tendency include Boccaccini (*Beyond*), Nickelsburg (*Judaism*), and a few others. Porton analyzes the pros-and-cons of each position ("Diversity," 57–80).

16. Hengel notes that this influence begins much earlier than Alexander (*Judaism*, 310–14), and Neusner thinks that even a document so Jewish as Mishnah "treats subjects . . . bearing upon issues of economics . . . within the economic theory of Aristotle" (*Economics*, x).

17. Samuel, *Athens*, 61; see Tcherikover, *Civilization*, 186–203.

18. Hengel, *Judaism*, 2–3. Hengel reaffirms his position later ("Revisited," 6–37), and Momigliano suggests that "if one looks at Greece as a political organization, Rome is the next step: Hellenism is just a transition between Greece and Rome" ("Rostovtzeff," 117).

- Texts written from a Hasmonean historical perspective;[19] and

- Texts written from a dystopian sectarian perspective.[20]

HASMONEAN HISTORICAL TEXTS

The histories known as *1* and *2 Maccabees* focus on characters and events in the second century BCE from a perspective at least Hasmonean,[21] and perhaps also Sadducean.[22] The longer of the two, *1 Maccabees,* breaks down into four parts: a short prelude followed by three sections narrating the lives of three siblings in the Hasmonean clan—Judas, Jonathan, and Simon.[23] The shorter of the two, *2 Maccabees,* focuses on the most famous of these siblings, Judas (nicknamed *Maccabaeus,* "the Hammer").[24]

19. *1–2 Maccabees* is not included in the Hebrew Bible, only the LXX translation adopted by the Nazarenes as the "Old" Testament (Nodet, "Dédicace," 321–75), following Tcherikover ("Palestine," 48–51). Schwartz suggests that the events narrated in *1–2 Maccabees* reverberate not so much with the Pharisaic rabbinic tradition as the tradition defended by "village strongmen/landowners living in areas relatively remote from centers of government authority" ("Hasmonean," 306).

20. Preeminent in this category stand the sectarian texts from Wâdi Qumran and nearby sites on the western shore of the Dead Sea, most thoroughly analyzed from a socioeconomic perspective by Catherine Murphy (*Wealth*), whose analysis, as Elgvin notes, "convincingly demonstrates how (the) theological views (of the) *Yahad*" show it to be "a society of its own with a material and juridical system, providing an alternative to the Temple-centered system of Hasmonean and Herodian Judaea" (Review of *Wealth*, 351). A third category would take into consideration the undatable texts from Pharisaic/rabbinic perspectives in Mishnah, Talmud, Tosefta, and the midrashim (Kuyt and Necker, *Orient*; Neusner, *Economics*; Ohrenstein and Gordon, *Economic*; Stern, *Parables*). Some put Josephus' writings in this category, too, but as Baumgarten points out, Josephus, even though he "claims to have been . . . a Pharisee . . . shows little indication of Pharisaic belief or practice in his life or writings" ("Pharisaic," 63).

21. According to Josephus, the name Ἀσαμωναῖος (from which comes the transliterated term "Hasmonean") is the name of Mattathias' great-grandfather (*A.J.* 12:265; see 1 Macc 2:1), and may derive from an old place name (perhaps חשמון, "Heshmon," Josh 15:27). Though it does not appear in *1–2 Maccabees*, it does appear in Josephus, Mishnah (*m. Mid.* 1:6), and Talmud (*b. Šabb.* 21b; *b. Taan.* 18b; *b. Sot.* 49b; *b. Bab. Kama* 82b). See Goldstein, *Maccabees*, 17–21; Grintz, "Maccabees," 316–17; Fischer, "Maccabees," 439–50.

22. Fischer, *Seleukiden*, 56.

23. Attridge, "Historiography," 172–76; Schwartz, "Hasmonean," 305–9.

24. Josephus identifies Judas as Μακκαβαῖος (*A.J.* 12:285), doubtless a transliteration of מקבי (from נקב, "to strike"; מקבת means "hammer" in Judg 4:12). Feldman points out several similarities between *1–2 Maccabees* and Josephus: (a) accentuation of the status of individual leaders (*vis-à-vis* their supporters); (b) emphasis on the struggle for religious (as well as political) independence; (c) avoidance *of* Davidic/messianic allusion; and (d) de-emphasis on the deity's activity ("Josephus," 41–68).

Prefaced by introductory letters to Alexandrian Jews, it breaks down into two parts, each concluding with the death of a prominent Gentile opponent.[25]

Much has been written about these apocryphal scrolls[26]—their historical reliability,[27] their literary structure,[28] their ideological intentionality[29]—yet very little has been written about the socioeconomic conflict motifs embedded within them or the various ways in which these motifs resonate with other socioeconomic motifs in other "great texts."[30] This is unfortunate because the motifs in *1-2 Maccabees* resonate rather loudly with socioeconomic conflict motifs which earlier appear on this trajectory, particularly those which engage the "big problems" of *acquisition, corruption, bribery,* and *slavery*.[31]

Alexander's invasion accomplishes many things, not least the imposition of an imperial culture of *acquisition* over the region much like that earlier imposed by Assyrian, Babylonian, and Persian dictators.[32] Critical

25. Doran, *Temple*, 110–14; Ellis, "Maccabees," 5–9; Fischer, "Maccabees," 442–50. Weitzman argues that the depiction of Seleucid rule in *2 Maccabees* "absorbs (several) elements of Babylonian literary tradition … using a fictionalized Nabonidus (d. 539 BCE) as a model for Antiochus IV" ("Persecution," 230).

26. The term "apocrypha" (ἀπόκρυφα, "hidden") refers to the sixteen books absent from the Hebrew Bible, but preserved in the Greek codices of Vaticanus, Sinaiticus, and Alexandrinus (Grintz, "Apocrypha," 258–61).

27. According to Goldstein, "propagandists can and do lie, but propagandistic historians lie only where it is to their advantage and only where there is small danger of being exposed" (*Maccabees*, 4). Thus, in Ellis' words, "there is no reason to doubt the substantial historicity" of *1-2 Maccabees* ("Maccabees," 7; see Abel, *Maccabees*, 1–64; Xeravits and Zsengellér, *Maccabees*). Bar-Kochva argues the minority position against historical reliability (*Maccabaeus, 403–11*).

28. Martola, *Capture*; Williams, *Maccabees*; Doran, *Temple*, 47–109.

29. Aguilar sifts the text of *1 Maccabees* through several anthropological filters ("initiation" model, "generational" model, "regimental" model) in an attempt to explain the origin and character of its war ideology ("Maccabees," 240–53), and Doran shows how *2 Maccabees* emphasizes the "deuteronomic theme that the invincible God of the Jews protects his temple and his people" (*Temple*, 110).

30. *1-2 Maccabees* alludes to and directly quotes from the Hebrew Bible (Goldstein, *Maccabees*) as well as several of the "great texts" from Greece (Fohl, *Herodot*) and Babylonia (Weitzman, "Antiochus"), but few investigate how *1-2 Maccabees* manipulates the socioeconomic conflict motifs permeating its environment.

31. This trajectory continues on into *3-4 Maccabees* when, e.g., Ptolemy IV (d. 204 BCE) attempts to "subject all (Egyptian) Jews to 'poll-tax registration' (λαογραφίαν) in order to process them for 'sale as slaves'" (οἰκετίκην διάθεσιν, 3 Macc 2:28).

32. Berquist, "Resistance," 41–58.

of this imposition, *2 Maccabees* begins, like *Gilgamesh*, with a mundane economic dispute:[33]

- Introducing the Greek-speaking king Seleucus IV (Philopator, d. 175 BCE), the author highlights his willingness to help pay the Jerusalem temple's "expenses";[34]

- One of the temple captains, however, a Benjaminite named Simon,[35] disputes the way in which the "obstructionist" High Priest—a man named Onias[36]—manages "the administration of the city market";[37]

- Unable (or unwilling) to resolve this dispute, Simon goes to the governor of Syria-Phoenicia—a man named Apollonius—and baits him with stories about Jerusalem's "untold wealth";[38]

- The governor forwards the matter to the king, who responds by delegating an emissary—Heliodorus—to travel to Jerusalem and process its "un-countable" wealth;[39]

- From Onias, however, Heliodorus learns that the Temple's wealth amounts to only 400 talents of silver plus a mere 200 talents of gold, most of it earmarked for the care of "widows and orphans";[40]

33. 2 Macc 3:1—4:5 (Gardner, "Leadership," 327–43). Schwartz dates *2 Maccabees* to the 140s BCE (*Maccabees*, 12–14).

34. 2 Macc 3:3 (δαπάνημα, "expenses, revenues").

35. The Bible habitually portrays Benjaminites as ornery and rebellious (Judg 19:14—20:48; 1 Sam 9:1; 2 Sam 16:11; 19:16; 20:1; Esth 2:5; see Blenkinsopp, "Benjamin," 629–45).

36. According to 2 Macc 4:2, Onias III holds both religious and civic titles: "zealot for the laws" (ζηλωτὴν τῶν νόμων) and "benefactor of the city" (εὐεργέτην τῆς πόλεως), the latter being a recognized civic title (Gardner, "Leadership," 330).

37. 2 Macc 3:4 (κατὰ τὴν πόλιν ἀγορανομίας; Stern and Finkielsztejn, "Agoranomos," 469–70). Gardner notes that "like other cities in antiquity, Jerusalem stores its municipal revenues in the temple treasury, which serves as a central bank" ("Leadership," 331), thereby underlining the fact that the primary conflict in *2 Maccabees* is *socioeconomic* (*contra* Goldstein, *Maccabees*, 201). Rosenfeld and Menirav reflect on the complexities of Second Temple economics (*Markets*, 1–26).

38. 2 Macc 3:6 (χρημάτων ἀμυθήτων). Demosthenes uses this phrase to describe Athens' "untold wealth" (see *Philip.* 4:34).

39. 2 Macc 3:6 (ἀναρίθμητος). The root of this word (*sans* alpha privitive) transliterates into English as "arithmetic."

40. 2 Macc 3:10 (χηρῶν καὶ ὀρφανῶν; van der Toorn, "Widow," 19–30).

- Nevertheless Heliodorus appoints a day to audit the books, and the priests in Jerusalem prepare for his "invasion" by praying "to the one who makes the laws about deposits," pleading for those who make these deposits to "be kept safe";[41]

- Fearing that the temple will fall into Gentile "contempt," the inhabitants of Jerusalem rush the streets to protest Heliodorus' arrival;[42]

- Suddenly a heavenly warrior appears (with two heavenly assistants) to protect the temple from Gentile "defilement," mortally wounding Heliodorus in the process;[43]

- Onias then responds to Heliodorus' wounds by miraculously healing him, thereby concluding this "treasury protection" vignette and opening the book on a benevolent note.[44]

Soon afterwards Seleucus IV dies and his infamous brother comes to power—Antiochus IV ("Epiphanes"),[45] a situation which encourages Onias' brother (Jason) to take advantage of the confusion accompanying executive transitions and seize the high priesthood for a relatively small

---

41. 2 Macc 3:15 (παρακαταθημένοις). Isocrates uses this term in a proverb: "Guard more faithfully the secret confided to you than the monies 'entrusted' to you" (lit., "made safe," *Demon.* 1:22).

42. 2 Macc 3:18 (καταφρονήσις). Thucydides warns the Peloponnesians not to focus on the "contemptibility" of their enemies (*Hist.* 1:122); and Cagni argues that the "sin" in *Erra* 5:6 (*ḫitu*) is the "contempt" (*šitutum*, 1:20) shown by the black-headed people (*L'Epopea*, 248).

43. Fischer lists the following reasons for presuming an older Greek story behind this vignette: (a) lack of Hebraisms (suggesting to him an "original Greek composition"); (b) two angelic youths (2 Macc 3:26), paralleling Castor and Pollux, the divine twins of Greco-Roman mythology; and (c) the fact that the Greeks conceive of their high god (Zeus) as willing and able to make himself visible—quite unlike Yahweh, who prefers to remain invisible ("Heliodor," 122–33). Stokholm compares Heliodorus to Kudur–nahhunte, the Elamite king who steals Marduk's statue from Esagila, its temple in Babylon ("Heliodor," 1–28).

44. 2 Macc 3:40 (γαζοφυλακίου τηρήσιν). Himmelfarb compares this divine defense with the divine defense preventing Ptolemy from entering the holy of holies in 3 Macc 1–2 ("Judaism," 20). Knoppers identifies other "treasury protection" stories ("Treasures," 181–208), and Doran shows how the motifs here resonate with temple defense motifs in other "great texts" (*Temple*, 47–51, 72–74, 98–104).

45. 2 Macc 4:7. The son of Antiochus III, Antiochus IV rules from the time of the death of his brother Seleucus IV (175 BCE) until his own death (164 BCE; see Gafni, "Antiochus," 202–4).

bribe (590 talents of silver).[46] The writer of *2 Maccabees* summarily labels this behavior "corruption."[47] To the quadrennial games at Tyre Jason then sends a monetary gift earmarked "for the sacrifice to Heracles,"[48] enlisting Menelaus, brother of the aforementioned temple-captain Simon, to proceed on his behalf and "complete the records of essential business" with the Greeks.[49] Things take a sinister turn, however, when Menelaus double-crosses Jason and purchases the high priesthood for himself, outbidding him by 300 talents. The writer of *2 Maccabees* thus illustrates the depth of Judea's "corruption" by paralleling the despicable behavior of one Judean leader with the despicable behavior of another.[50]

Menelaus' bribe opens up a temporary door to influence with the Greeks, but when he fails to "pay up"[51] Antiochus sends a bill-collector to his door, a "ruler of the citadel named Sostratus."[52] When Menelaus refuses to meet with him, however, his short-lived leadership plunges into free-fall, to which he responds by stealing "golden vessels" from the temple to offer yet another bribe to yet another corruptible "target"—an official named Andronicus.[53] Discovering this sacrilege, the priest Onias

46. 2 Macc 4:1–17 (150 of these talents he gives back to Antiochus IV to erect a gymnasium in Jerusalem). Pausanias argues that every πόλις ("city") must have a municipal office, a theater, an ἀγορά ("marketplace"), a public water supply, and a gymnasium (*Descr.* 10:4:1). Dequeker reads Jason's behavior as an honest attempt to integrate Jewish faith into Hellenistic culture ("Jason," 371–92), but *2 Maccabees* views it as an example of ὑπονοθεύσις ("corruption").

47. 2 Macc 4:7 (ὑπονοθεύω). The nominalized form of this root (νόθος) can mean "corrupted one" (i.e., "bastard"). Medon, e.g., is Oileus' "corrupted son" (νόθος υἱός) via the consort Rhene (Homer, *Il.*2:727).

48. 2 Macc 4:19–20. Disobeying Jason, the envoys use this money to buy warships (Aune, "Herakles," 141–3; Kampen, "Hercules," 143).

49. 2 Macc 4:23.

50. 2 Macc 4:26 (ὑπονοθεύω, same verb, "to corrupt"). Maier argues that alongside the external pressures exerted by "foreign imperialists," internal conflicts amongst the Judeans themselves play a major role, particularly those fixated on relentless disputes over calendrical, hermeneutical, and socioeconomic questions ("Israel," 53–72).

51. 2 Macc 4:27 (εὐτακτέω). In 3 Macc 2:28–33, Ptolemy IV decrees that all rebellious Jews must (a) be entered into the "registry" (λαογραφία); (b) submit to "slave status" (οἰκετίκην διάθεσιν); and (c) be branded with the green ivy leaf (Dionysus' "logo"). Some, however, escape these things by "exchanging money for their lives" (χρήματα περὶ τοῦ ζῆν ἀντικαταλλασσόμενοι, 3:32), a covert allusion to the "big problem" of *bribery* (δωροκοπέω, "to bribe," 3:19; see Cuffari, *Judenfeindschaft*, 218–308).

52. 2 Macc 4:28. In other words, Antiochus turns away from the indigenous religious establishment to the occupational military establishment.

53. 2 Macc 4:23–29 (Nelson, "Andronicus," 247).

publicly accuses Menelaus of "temple-robbery,"[54]and Menelaus responds by having him assassinated.[55]

Seizing the moment, Antiochus responds to this scandal by using it as a pretext to strip the Jerusalem temple of all its "hidden treasures."[56] When this fails to satisfy his financial expectations, he sends his "chief tax-collector"[57] into the Judean countryside to "acquire" even *more* stuff,[58] transforming the Jerusalem Akra (citadel) into a warehouse for incoming "spoil."[59] Dusting off the old "civilization-wilderness" polarity, *1 Maccabees* metaphorically portrays this invasion as the "wildernization"

---

54. According to Plato, "temple-robbing" (ἱεροσύλησις) is as much a crime as kidnapping, burglary, and theft (*Resp.* 1.344b; see Philo, *Jos.* 84; Josephus, *A.J.* 16:164–68; 2 Macc 4:24; Acts 19:37; Rom 3:22). Whether this particular temple-robbery is the trigger for the Maccabean revolt is an unanswerable question (*pace* Harrington, *Maccabean*, 55).

55. 2 Macc 4:30–50. According to Josephus (*B.J.* 7:426–32) a priest named Onias establishes another Jewish temple at Leontopolis (northern Egypt). Rosenberg, following *2 Maccabees'* account that Onias III dies at the hands of the Seleucids, argues that the priest most likely responsible for building the Leontopolis temple is Onias IV ("Onias," 432–33), but Keil challenges the accuracy of this account, arguing that the most likely founder of the Leontopolis temple is Onias III ("Onias III," 221–33). Rainbow, however, views "Onias III" as a figment of Josephus' imagination ("Oniad," 30–52).

56. 1 Macc 1:23 (τοὺς θησαυροὺς τοὺς ἀποκρύφους; note the same ἀπόκρυφος // θησαυρός parallel in LXX Isa 45:3, "hidden // treasure"). Interpreters offer various explanations for Antiochus' behavior: (a) that he is mentally unstable—enough to merit his *other* nickname, ἐπιμανής ("madman," Polybius, *Hist.* 26:1); (b) that he becomes angry at the Jews because they challenge his zeal for Hellenistic culture (Bickermann; Hengel); and (c) that the incessant conflicts between Jason and Menelaus pull him into an internal dispute between rival Jewish factions (Tcherikover). See Marciak, "Antiochus," 61–73.

57. 1 Macc 1:29 (ἄρχοντα φορολογίας). Some identify this taxman with "Apollonius the Mysiarch" in 2 Macc 5:24, reading μυσάρχην as an incorrect transliteration of שׂר מסים ("chief tax-collector"; see Goldstein, *Maccabees*, 211).

58. 1 Macc 1:32 (κληρονομέω). This verb can mean "to inherit" (e.g., 1 Macc 2:57) or "to acquire"; note the parallel κρατεύω in 2:10 ("to seize").

59. 1 Macc 1:35 (σκῦλα; *1–2 Maccabees* repeats some form of this root 23 times). The writer of 1 Macc 1:32 records the "enslavement" of Judeans via another oft-used term (αἰχμαλωτεύω, "to capture"; see 1 Macc 5:13; 8:10; 9:72; 10:33; 15:40)

of Jerusalem,[60] depicting it as the displacement of the city's honor with (what else?) "contempt."[61]

Incensed by these events, the country priest Mattathias puts a profoundly socioeconomic question before his congregation: "What nation has not *acquired* Israel to seize her *spoils*?"[62] Recognizing Jerusalem to be anything but "free," he laments how the Greeks have reduced it to the status of a common "slave."[63] Annoyed by this speech, the Greeks retaliate by attempting to silence him with (what else?) a *bribe* comprised of an unspecified amount of "silver and gold," blithely camouflaging it as a "consignment-gift."[64] Ignoring this bribery-proposal, however, Mattathias takes his congregation and abandons the city for (where else?) the "wilderness."[65]

Judas

Once outside the city walls, however, the Judeans following Mattathias become prey for the slaughter as the Greeks take advantage of the legalistic way many misinterpret the Sabbath laws.[66] After Mattathias dies,

60. 1 Macc 1:39 (ἐρημόω . . . ἐρημός). If this text is alluding to LXX Isa 64:9, its use of singular ἁγίασμα ("sanctuary") would appear to be influenced by LXX's translation of עָרֵי קָדְשְׁךָ ("your holy cities," cited in the plural at *b. Moʿed Qaṭ.* 26a) with singular πόλις ("city"). The decision to use this particular metaphor hardly seems accidental, since the writer intensifies it via the cognate accusative (GKC §117p-r).

61. 1 Macc 1:39 (ἐξουδένωσις; see *Erra* 1:119–20; Gen 25:34; Exod 5:2). According to Josephus the emperor Tiberius, at Herod's request, warns the Jews not to "show contempt" (ἐξουθενίζειν) toward the devotees of other religions (*B.J.* 19:290).

62. 1 Macc 2:10 (κληρονομέω . . . σκῦλα). Mattathias, a priest from the village of Modein (c. 20 miles NW of Jerusalem), is portrayed in this scroll as the first Judean to challenge the Greeks. According to 1 Macc 2:1 he is "the son of Johanan, son of Simeon, a priest of the family of Joarib," but according to Josephus he is "the son of Johanan, the son of Simeon, the son of Hasamonaius, a priest of the family of Joarib" (*A.J.* 12:265).

63. 1 Macc 2:11 (δούλη). Mattathias does not see Israel as παῖς or διάκονος, but as δοῦλος, the lowest rung on the socioeconomic ladder.

64. 1 Macc 2:17–18 (ἀποστολαῖς πολλαῖς). Where this term denotes "apostleship" in *koine* texts (1 Cor 9:2; Gal 2:8), here it denotes the "sending out" of financial payments (see LSJ 220).

65. 1 Macc 2:28 (πόλις); 2:29 (ἔρημος). Notice (a) the overt replication of the "civilization-wilderness" polarity, (b) the peculiar way Mattathias leads people out of "the city" into "the wilderness," and (c) the way in which the Hasmoneans, like the Igigi in *Atrahasis* and the Sibitti in *Erra*, respond negatively to Antiochus' Enlil-istic leadership (Weitzman, "Persecution," 223–30).

66. 1 Macc 2:38 (see CD 10:14–21; Matt 12:1–8). Knowing many Jews refuse to fight on the Sabbath, the Greeks choose *this* day to attack and slaughter them in large numbers (the text claims 1,000 casualties). Afterwards many vow never again to let

however, his son Judas rejects this legalistic mindset, replacing it with a *Realpolitik* mentality more attuned to the thinking of his Greek oppressors.[67] Killing Apollonius and "despoiling" his army, Judas quickly decides to "fight fire with fire" in order to emulate the culture of *acquisition* he publicly opposes.[68] In a stirring speech to his compatriots,[69] he argues (in the spirit of *Exodus* and *Atrahasis*) that violent retaliation, while undesirable in principle, is sometimes unavoidably necessary, especially in situations where innocent civilians have been brutally "despoiled."[70] *2 Maccabees* covertly reflects on the "effectiveness" of this option by comparing the Hasmonean reaction to Seleucid oppression with the Seleucid reaction to Roman oppression, highlighting in the process an inescapable truth—the conquered *always* pays tribute to the conqueror.[71]

Meanwhile, Antiochus promises a full year's salary to any soldier who publicly commits to fighting the Judeans. Observing the depletion of his treasury—particularly the funds formerly supplied by "district taxes"[72] from Judea—he worries, however, that he won't have enough "gifts" to bribe enough officials to insure the success of his campaign. So

---

foreigners twist their laws against them. In fact, according to Heger, "the decision to override the Sabbath law in order to save human life, initiated by the Maccabees and subsequently developed by the Sages, becomes the source of a future hierarchic principle in the legal system" (*Halakhah*, 27). Schwartz sees Jewish unwillingness to fight as another extremist "expression of diasporism" (*Maccabees*, 50; see Batsch, "Temps," 12–35; Nikiprowetzky, "Sabbat," 1–17; Schiffman, *Halakhah*, 77–136).

67. According to Waltz, *Realpolitik* refers to a system in which "success is the ultimate test of policy, and success is defined as preserving and strengthening the state" (*Theory*, 117).

68. According to Josephus, this Apollonius is the governor of Samaria (*A.J.* 12:287), not the Syro-Palestinian governor to whom Simon the Benjamite complains earlier (2 Macc 5:24–26). N.B. how this strategy markedly differs from the strategy depicted in *Esther*, which emphasizes how the Jews, though allotted the right to "despoil" (בזה), refuse to do so (Esth 9:10, 15, 16).

69. See 1 Macc 3:13–14; *A.J.* 12.288. Analyzing the speeches in LXX *Deuteronomy*, *1 Maccabees*, and *Acts of the Apostles*, Soards concludes (with several others) that the speeches in *1 Maccabees* closely resemble those embedded in other Greek histories (*Speeches*, 204–8).

70. 1 Macc 3:20 (σκυλεύω; see *Atr* 1:208–17; Exod 15:1–19). Plato delimits this term to the removal of "arms and weapons" (*Resp.* 469c), but in *Maccabees* it's a synonym for "slavery" (Moore, *Faith*, 301–42).

71. 2 Macc 8:10–11 points out that the market price for "Jewish bodies" (Ἰουδαίων σωμάτων) is 90 slaves per silver talent, and at least once LXX uses αἰχμαλωσία ("captivity") to translate גולה ("exile," Amos 1:15).

72. 1 Macc 3:29 (φόροι τῆς χώρας).

he charges one of his assistants—a man named Lysias—to "redistribute"[73] the property (land and slaves) already "acquired" from Judea,[74] and Lysias responds to this assignment by delegating it to three junior officers (Ptolemy, Nicanor, and Gorgias), who in turn hire a thousand "merchants" to handle details.[75]

Framing his account to make the Hasmoneans look "blameless,"[76] the narrator of 2 Maccabees makes sure to note that after Antiochus' war-plans are discovered, a number of wealthy Judeans sell their property to raise funds to help the Judeans whose property the Greeks specifically "target."[77] To empower these donors Judas delivers another stirring speech in which he asks his audience to reflect with him on two events from their history: (a) their ancestors' victory over 185,000 Assyrians in the eighth century BCE,[78] and (b) their recent victory over 120,000 Galatians.[79] Inspired and empowered by this speech, many Judeans then follow Judas into battle against Nicanor's army, after which they "take back the money of those who came to purchase them as slaves."[80] 1 Maccabees comments on all this by noting that the man the Greeks choose to enslave Israel (Nicanor) ironically turns out to be the very same man defeated by their new hero (Judas Maccabaeus).[81]

73. 1 Macc 3:36 (κατακληροδοτέω; lit., "parcel out by lot").

74. 1 Macc 2:10 (κληρονομέω).

75. 1 Macc 3:41 (lit., "to take the sons of Israel as 'slaves'" [παῖδας]; see 2 Macc 8:34). As Philo makes clear, however, not all slave traders are "kidnappers" (ἀνδραποδίσται); most are simply "men-dealers" (ἀνδραποδοκάπηλοι, Leg. 4.17).

76. Fischer calls 2 Maccabees a "strongly moralizing epitome" ("Maccabees," 443), and Himmelfarb calls it "the first text to present Judaism and Hellenism as opposing categories" ("Judaism," 19).

77. 2 Macc 8:14 (πεπραμένους). Homer uses this term to refer to the exportation of captives to foreign lands as economic commodities (Il. 21:102; Od. 14:297).

78. See 2 Kgs 19:35. Eleazar the priest also mentions the defeat of Sennacherib in his lament-prayer (3 Macc 6:5; see Moore, Faith, 254–59).

79. 2 Macc 8:19–20. Bar-Kochva identifies this battle with the "War of the Brothers" between Seleucus II (Callanicus) and his brother Antiochus (Hierax) in 229 BCE (Maccabaeus, 504).

80. 2 Macc 8:25 (τὰ δὲ χρήματα τῶν παραγεγονότων ἐπὶ τὸν ἀγορασμὸν αὐτῶν ἔλαβον).

81. 2 Macc 8:34–36 (Rappaport, "Nicanor," 247).

Attending to the tithing laws,[82] Judas and his troops then gather at a place of prayer to offer "firstfruits" and "tithes" from *their* "spoils,"[83] redistributing it to widows, orphans, survivors of fallen compatriots,[84] and those who have been "tortured."[85] Defeating a few more Greek squadrons, they repeat this routine, distributing "war trophies"[86] to several more "widows, orphans, the aged, and the tortured."[87] Whether this repetition is literary or historical is a less important question than the fact that the writer of *1 Maccabees* camps on it to plead the case that Maccabean revolt is both religiously *and* politically justifiable.[88]

Ambushing another Greek squadron, Judas warns his troops not to "despoil" them, *not* because it's morally problematic, but because it's militarily foolish. After proving himself victorious on the battlefield, he then *encourages* his troops to plunder the "great wealth" of the Greeks,[89] urging them to seize as much "spoil"[90] as possible by violently con-

---

82. Herman, *Tithe*, 7–37; Jaffee, *Tithing*; Altschuler, "Classification," 1–14.

83. 1 Macc 3:49 (πρωτογενήματα ... δεκάτας). According to 2 Macc 8:28, these tithes come out of the "spoil" (σκῦλος) taken by Hasmoneans—*not* Seleucids—yet many interpreters (a) doubt whether these tithes, if real, actually wind up in the coffers of the Temple; and (b) whether the word מעשר ("tithe") always denotes exactly ten percent (Baumgarten, "Non-Literal," 245–61).

84. 2 Macc 8:28. In another account (3 Macc 3:28) Ptolemy IV decrees that any Egyptian willing to inform against a Jewish neighbor qualifies for (a) the "property" (οὐσία) of those who refuse to inform on their neighbors, plus (b) 2,000 drachmas from the "royal treasury" (βασίλικος). The writer summarily refers to this behavior as living "for the sake of the belly" (γαστρὸς ἕνεκεν, 3 Macc 7:11), a phrase retreaded in GNT as ὁ θεὸς ἡ κοιλία ("the belly is [their] god," Phil 3:19).

85. 2 Macc 8:28 (αἰκίζω). Aeschylus has Prometheus describe himself as "tortured in fetters" (ἐν γυιοπεδαῖς αἰκιζόμενου, *Prom.* 169), and Sophocles has Creon demand that the body of Polyneices be "tortured and eaten by dogs" (πρὸς κυνῶν ἐδεστὸν αἰκισθέν, *Ant.* 206).

86. 2 Macc 8:30 (λάφυρα). Euripides uses this term to describe the "trophies" Herakles seizes from his opponents (*Herc. fur.* 417).

87. 2 Macc 8:30 (Rappaport, "Bacchides," 566–67).

88. To conclude that "the main achievement of the Maccabean revolt ... is the saving of the belief in one God," however, is an overstatement (*contra* Kasher, Review of *Hasmonean*, 421).

89. 1 Macc 4:23 (πλοῦτον μέγαν). According to *2 Maccabees*, Lysias is a Seleucid bureaucrat who levies "tribute" (ἀργυρολόγητος) against the Jerusalem temple, then auctions off the High Priest's office to the highest bidder (the last step in transforming Jerusalem into a Greek πόλις, 2 Macc 11:2).

90. 1 Macc 4:23 (τὴν σκυλείαν).

fronting (like rebellious Igigi or rampaging Sibitti)[91] anyone who dares stand in their way, whether Edomites,[92] Arabs,[93] Transjordanians,[94] or Mediterranean villagers.[95]

Reminding his readers that the Jerusalem temple is not the only bank targeted for Greek invasion,[96] the writer of *1 Maccabees* inserts a vignette about Antiochus' decision to plunder a Persian city "famous for its wealth"[97] since the invasion of Alexander (330 BCE).[98] *Question*: Why does Antiochus rob this temple? *Answer*: Because he needs the money. Having lost so much "abundant spoil" to the Hasmoneans,[99] he now needs to replenish his treasury, and bank-robbing is the easiest way to do it. Returning home, he gets so caught up in the pillage-mentality of his marauding army he starts attacking innocent villages along the way, one of which (Beth-zur)[100] immediately surrenders, having no way to defend itself.[101]

Shifting to the international scene, *1 Maccabees* depicts Judas' admiration for the Romans as an attitude based *not* on their military or

91. *Atr* 1:41–46; *Erra* 1:47–85.

92. 1 Macc 5:3–4.

93. 2 Macc 12:10–16.

94. 1 Macc 5:28, 35.

95. 1 Macc 5:68. Later Judas collects 2,000 silver drachmas to make "atonement" (ἐξιλασμός) for all the victims his troops have killed (2 Macc 12:43–45).

96. Stevens thinks (a) that Egyptian temples do not start loaning money to individuals until the Hellenistic period, and (b) that this is the time when the piel form of שלם begins taking on the meaning, "to repay a loan" (*Temples*, 136–66). Baron and Kahan add that "unlike the ancient temples and medieval churches, neither mosques nor synagogues ever serve as important depositories of funds" ("Economic," 107).

97. 1 Macc 6:1–17. "Elymais" probably refers to Persepolis, the richest city of the Achaemenid empire (Young, "Persepolis," 236; Sobti, "Persepolis," 477–79; Wiesehöfer, *Persia*, 105–14; Kuhrt, *Persian*, 418–65).

98. According to 2 Macc 1:11–17 Antiochus sacks the temple of a Persian goddess named Nanea, but according to Josephus he raids the temple of the Greek goddess Artemis, marries its priestess and takes its "great wealth as dowry" (τὰ χρήματα πλείονα εἰσφερνής, *A.J.* 12:354).

99. 1 Macc 6:6 (σκύλοις πολλοῖς). According to *2 Maccabees*, Antiochus goes to Persia because he thinks, like Gilgamesh, he can "weigh tall mountains in the balances" (2 Macc 9:8; N.B. Sennacherib's similar description of himself in Isa 37:24).

100. As Avi-Yonah points out, Judas re-takes the strategic village of Beth-Zur from the Seleucids about ten years later (1 Macc 4:26–35), only to see it re-taken after two more years ("Beth-Zur," 555).

101. 1 Macc 6:49. The writer adds that Beth-Zur's dwindling food supply is partially the result of a "famine" on the land (λιμός, 1 Macc 6:54; Moore, *Faith*, 139–53).

legal accomplishments,[102] but simply upon the fact that they are "very strong"[103]—strong enough to "enslave" their enemies[104] and make them pay "tribute."[105] Like Cain, the Romans know how to "acquire" possessions from their neighbors (silver and gold mines in Spain; taxes and tribute from Gaul),[106] so that when Judas negotiates an "alliance" with Rome,[107] he does so to "protect" his people from any force that would "enslave Israel completely" (a clear slap at the Seleucids and Ptolemies).[108] Publically displayed bronze tablets set up to memorialize this alliance broadcast the promise that neither party will ever again procure grain, arms, ships, or money from a potentially hostile third party.[109]

Jonathan

After Judas' death, however, this alliance evaporates under the mantle of leadership exercised by his brother Jonathan.[110] Like David son of Jesse

---

102. Petit, *Pax Romana*, 46–73; Huttner, "Civilizationskritik," 447–66; Parchami, *Empire*, 13–58).

103. 1 Macc 8:1 (δυνατοὶ ἰσχύι, repeated twice for emphasis).

104. 1 Macc 8:10 (αἰχμάλω // καταδουλόω).

105. 1 Macc 8:2 (φόρος). According to Herodotus, Croesus is the first barbarian to exact "tribute" from the Greeks (φόρου, *Hist.* 1.6.2).

106. 1 Macc 8:2–8. Other "enslaved" countries include India, Media, Lydia, and Seleucia, but Schäfer documents Rome's particular antipathy toward Judeans (*Judeophobia*, 180–211).

107. 1 Macc 8:17 (συμμαχία; N.B. the earlier συμμαχία with Judea initiated by Ptolemy IV, 3 Macc 3:21). Where ἐπιμαχία refers to a "defensive alliance," συμμαχία refers to an "offensive alliance" (Thucydides, *Hist.* 1:44). Mandell observes that where the Hasmoneans imagine this alliance to resemble a Hebrew ברית ("covenant"), the Romans view it only as an *amicitia* ("suzerainty agreement"; "Maccabees," 202–20).

108. 1 Macc 8:18. Hundreds of years earlier the Judahite king Ahaz makes a similar alliance with another superpower (Assyria) to hold off *his* hostile neighbors, Israel and Syria: "Ahaz sent messengers to King Tiglath-pileser of Assyria, saying, 'I am your servant and your son. Come up, and rescue me from the hand of the king of Syria and the hand of the king of Israel, who are attacking me.' He took silver and gold from the house of Yahweh . . . and sent a 'bribe' (שׁחד) to the king of Assyria. Responding to his request the Assyrian king marched up against Damascus and seized it, taking its people captive" (2 Kgs 16:7–9; see Moore, *Faith*, 221–25).

109. Stern, "Relations," 81–106; Flusser, "Roman," 175–206.

110. According to Josephus, Judas dies on the battlefield at the hand of Bacchides, "a friend of Antiochus Epiphanes . . . entrusted with all of Mesopotamia" (*A.J.* 12:393; see Rappaport, "Bacchides," 566–7; Berridge, "Jonathan," 943–44).

and the legendary Robin of Locksley,[111] Jonathan goes into the "protection business" by inviting his neighbors—especially the rich Nabateans—to "entrust him with their possessions."[112] Like Nabal's reaction to David, however, the Nabateans react with outrage to Jonathan's behavior, one family going so far as to retaliate by assassinating his brother John.[113] Infuriated by this, Jonathan nevertheless decides not to pursue a tit-for-tat vendetta, only take more "spoil" from them.[114]

Meanwhile the new king Demetrius I[115] seizes several Judean villages to provide his troops with more (and more accessible) "food supplies,"[116] triggering a demand from Jonathan that Demetrius return "the captives captured" from all previous incursions.[117] To this Demetrius grudgingly complies, though not because he desires a closer relationship with Jonathan. He complies because he now finds himself challenged at home by a usurper claiming to be the son of Antiochus IV—a man named Alexander Balas.[118] This usurper challenges Demetrius by starting a bidding war for Jonathan's "friendship," promising to (a) release all Judean prisoners, and (b) anoint him high priest.[119] Not to be outdone,

---

111. 1 Sam 25:2–42; see Moore, *Reconciliation*, 23–33; Pollard, *Imagining*, 1–28.

112. 1 Macc 9:35. The origin of the Nabateans is unknown, but by the late fourth century BCE they comprise most of the wealthy middlemen controlling economic access to the Red Sea (Joukowsky, "Nabateans," 716–18).

113. 1 Macc 9:36–38.

114. 1 Macc 9:32–42.

115. Josephus, *A.J.* 12:393. Son of Seleucus IV and nephew of Antiochus IV, Demetrius I comes to power during a difficult time for the Seleucid empire, a time when it finds itself *externally* threatened by the Ptolemies and the Romans and *internally* threatened by the Hasmoneans (Schalit, "Demetrius," 549–50).

116. 1 Macc 9:52 (παραθέσεις βρωμάτων). Polybius describes Hannibal's siege of Iberia as producing enough "abundant supplies" (χορηγιῶν παραθέσεως) to sustain his troops (*Hist.* 3:17:11).

117. 1 Macc 9:72 (τὴν αἰχμαλωσίαν ἣν ἠχμαλώτευσεν).

118. In 1 Macc 10:1 the nickname associated with this character is "Epiphanes," the same as that claimed by his alleged father. Josephus, however, calls him "Balas" (*A.J.* 13:119) which, if deriving from Gk βάλλω, means "scatterer."

119. 1 Macc 10:20. "Friends of the King" enjoy all the privileges of the royal court, including the right to dress accordingly (see 1 Sam 27:6; 1 Macc 2:18; 10:89; Bickermann, *Institutions*, 40–50; Goldstein, *Maccabees*, 232). The fact that these rivals try to outbid each other for Jonathan's "friendship" shows how much power they ascribe to the Hasmoneans.

Demetrius quickly counters this proposal with one of his own, promising Jonathan several "tax exemptions" and "gifts,"[120] specifically,

- to exempt Judea from the "salt tax" and the "crown tax";[121]

- "release" Jerusalem from all "tithes";[122]

- cancel all livestock taxes and free every Judean slave "without reimbursement";[123]

- grant "exemption and release" to every Judean who attends the festivals, sabbaths, new moons, and other holidays;[124]

- help defray temple "expenses" via the tariffs collected at the seaport of Ptolemais;[125]

- grant an annual allowance of 15,000 silver shekels to help pay for "temple services";[126] cancel the 5,000 shekels of silver annually collected "from services rendered at the holy place";[127]

- charge to the king's expense the cost of "rebuilding" and "restoring" the temple complex (as well as the surrounding walls of the city);[128]

- extend a general "pardon" to anyone owing back taxes.[129]

---

120. 1 Macc 10:28 (ἀφέματα ... δόματα).

121. 1 Macc 10:29 (τιμῆς τοῦ ἁλός ... τῶν στεφάνων). Roth and Elon document several Judean taxation practices during this time ("Taxation," 532–58).

122. 1 Macc 10:31 (ἀφίημι ... δεκάται); see Jaffee, *Tithing*; Herman, *Tithe*; Bornstein, "Ma`aserot"; Moore, "Sacrifice."

123. 1 Macc 10:33 (ἀφίημι ἐλεύθεραν δωρεάν).

124. 1 Macc 10:34 (ἀτελείας καὶ ἀφέσεως). N.B. how this decree resembles the *mīšaru* ("release-decree") of Ammiṣaduqa (see *ANET* 526–8; *TDOT* 6:1–7; *CAD* M/2:116–17) as well as the 3-year ἀτέλεια ("exemption") of Cambyses (Herodotus, *Hist.* 3:67).

125. 1 Macc 10:39 (δαπάνη). According to Thucydides, Xerxes warns Pausanias to keep his promises, regardless of "expense" (δαπάνη, *Hist.* 1:129:3)

126. 1 Macc 10:41 (τὰ ἔργα τοῦ οἴκου; lit., "the works of the house").

127. 1 Macc 10:42 (ἀπὸ τῶν χρειῶν τοῦ ἁγίου). In 2 Chron 24:17–27 King Joash dies because he commits the sin of idolatry, but in 2 Kgs 12:1–21 angry priests assassinate him for "mismanaging" their pension fund (Moore, *Faith*, 249).

128. 1 Macc 10:44 (οἰκοδομηθῆναι ... ἐπικαινισθῆναι). In *1 Maccabees* Demetrius blatantly plays the "religion card" to win Jonathan's "friendship," yet Josephus' account marginalizes this (*A.J.* 13:35–57; see Schwartz, "Judaism," 377–91).

129. 1 Macc 10:43 (ἀπολύω; lit., "to release").

In spite of these promises, however, Jonathan rejects Demetrius'
"pie-in-the-sky" proposals, deciding instead to throw his support behind Alexander Balas, a decision he signals publicly in 153 BCE by
donning the high priest's robe at the Feast of Tabernacles.[130] Having
secured Jonathan's "friendship," Alexander then "targets" the king of
Egypt, Ptolemy VI (Philometor),[131] offering him several "gifts worthy of
your position" should he consent to "give me your daughter as wife."[132]
Accepting Alexander Balas' offer, Ptolemy invites his ally Jonathan
to bring "silver and gold and many other gifts" to the upcoming wedding.[133] Manipulating the "field-dweller"-vs.-"city-dweller" polarity to
describe this, the writer of *1 Maccabees* depicts Demetrius' response
to Jonathan via familiar language:[134] "Why do you [Jonathan] assume
authority against us "in the mountains?" If you have confidence in your
forces, come down and meet us, and let us match strength against each
other, for I have on my side the 'power of the cities.'"[135] Empowered by
Alexander Balas' new connection to the Ptolemies, Jonathan not only
ignores Demetrius' threats, he takes "much spoil" from his army.[136]

Dissatisfied with his son-in-law, however, Ptolemy abandons his
"covenant"[137] with Alexander Balas and moves his daughter to the palace of his rival, Demetrius II, thereby exacerbating the internal tensions
growing within the Seleucid regime.[138] Alexander eventually flees to the
"wilderness" to try and escape this "divide-and-conquer" mentality, but
Ptolemy hires an Arab mercenary to cut off his head and mail it back to
him in Egypt.[139]

130. 1 Macc 10:21. In other words, Jonathan deems the priesthood to be more important than all of Demetrius' potential "gifts."

131. Whitehorn, "Ptolemy," 543.

132. 1 Macc 10:51–58. According to Josephus (*A.J.* 13:80–82) the daughter in question is Cleopatra Thea (d. 121 BCE).

133. 1 Macc 10:59–66.

134. Demetrius delivers this response through his lieutenant Apollonius (not the
same Apollonius mentioned in 1 Macc 3:10–12).

135. 1 Macc 10:70–71 (see *Erra* 1:47–60).

136. 1 Macc 10:87 (σκῦλα πολλά).

137. 1 Macc 11:9 (διαθήκη). A διαθήκη-"covenant" is broader and deeper than a
συμμαχία-"alliance" (1 Macc 10:27), yet neither term captures the holistic fullness of
ברית (Moore, "Dreams," 221).

138. Pacwa, "Alexander," 150–1; Gafni, "Alexander," 625.

139. 1 Macc 11:19. Other sources provide different versions of Alexander's death,
but the decapitation in *1 Maccabees* replicates the episode in *GE* in which Gilgamesh

Significantly, Jonathan's response to this treachery is, at least in part, to emulate it.[140] Surrounding the Jerusalem citadel with Hasmonean troops, he bribes Ptolemy with silver and gold in return for his promise to re-classify Judea as a "tax-free" zone.[141] Learning of this conversation, Demetrius II (Ptolemy's new puppet-king) attempts to counter this bribe by laying before Jonathan another set of "pie-in-the-sky" promises: "We confirm the Hasmonean possession of Judea and the three districts of Aphairema and Lydda and Rathamin; adding the latter, with all the region bordering them, to Judea from Samaria.[142] To all those who offer sacrifice in Jerusalem we grant release from the 'royal taxes,' . . . from the crops of the land and the fruit of the trees, as well as any other payments due of the tithes, taxes, salt pit taxes, and crown taxes."[143] In spite of all these promises, however, Jonathan demands one more; viz., that all the Greek soldiers in Jerusalem gather up their gear and leave the city forever. Demetrius promises to comply with this demand, but not without demanding something from Jonathan in return; viz., that he pledge his support against *another* usurper, a *mafioso*-type thug named Trypho.[144] To *this* request Jonathan complies by sending 3000 "stalwart men" to Demetrius, taking "much spoil" from Trypho in the process. Yet when it becomes clear that Demetrius has no intention of removing the Greek soldiers,[145] Jonathan abandons all pretension to "friendship."

---

cuts off Humbaba's head and delivers it to Enlil (*GE* 5:302). According to Josephus, Ptolemy dies soon after receiving this grisly "gift" (*A.J.* 13:119).

140. Whatever his motives, the fact remains that Jonathan, following Judas, pursues a program of *Realpolitik*.

141. 1 Macc 11:28 (ἀφορολόγητος). Plutarch (*Flam.* 10:1–2) juxtaposes this term alongside ἀφρούρητος ("ungarrisoned") to describe another benefactor's attempt to please another weak neighbor.

142. 1 Macc 11:34; see Josephus, *A.J.* 13:127; *B.J.* 3:54–55.

143. 1 Macc 11:35. This list closely resembles the one put forward in 10:38–45. Capdetrey outlines the basic structure of the Seleucid tax code (*Pouvoir*), and Udoh attempts to outline the complexities of the Roman tax code (*Caesar*).

144. Trypho (Τρύφων) means "luxurious" (Plato, *Leg.* 695d) and/or "effeminate" (Aristophanes, *Nub.* 48; *Vesp.* 1455); see McEleney, "Maccabean," 73–80.

145. 1 Macc 11:38–53 (ἀνταποδίδωμι). Doubtless Demetrius reneges on his promise because he wants to punish Jonathan for siding with Alexander Balas, yet, as Thucydides points out, political neighbors often force themselves to "return like for like" (ἴσον ἀνταπόδοτε). Why? Because "he who lends aid in a crisis is most beloved, while he who withholds it is most hated" (*Hist.* 1:43).

Taking advantage of these tensions, Trypho throws his hat into the political ring by declaring himself the mentor of the infant son of the recently beheaded Alexander Balas.[146] Seeking to establish a "friendship" with Jonathan, he sends him an expensive table service plus the following "royal" privileges: to drink from golden cups, to dress in purple, and to wear "the golden buckle."[147] Won over by *these* "gifts," Jonathan duly responds by leading his troops to Gaza and "despoiling" it,[148] pillaging several Arab villages on the way.[149]

Victoriously returning to Jerusalem, he then decides to take advantage of the tensions in his environment by constructing a brick wall around the citadel, thereby prohibiting the Greeks trapped inside from "buying or selling" food.[150] Enraged by these sanctions, Trypho gears up to retaliate, but as soon as he sees the size of Jonathan's army he quickly backs down, deciding instead to (what else?) "give him gifts."[151] Still trying to win Jonathan's "friendship," he invites him to visit his palace in Ptolemais, allegedly to talk peace, and Jonathan walks into his trap. Trypho captures him and, adding insult to injury, offers to sell him back to his brother Simon for 100 talents of silver plus two of Jonathan's sons as "hostages."[152] Leaking the official story that Jonathan's imprisonment is due to his failure to pay his taxes,[153] Trypho then squeezes as much mileage from this situation as he possibly can. Finally, after Simon hands

146. 1 Macc 11:39–40 (according to 11:54 the infant's name, like that of his alleged grandfather, is "Antiochus"). N.B. how the priest Jehoiada similarly works with young King Joash, the only Davidic survivor of Athaliah's purge (2 Kgs 11:1–12).

147. 1 Macc 11:58. By accepting these gifts Jonathan accepts a position at Trypho's court as "Friend of the King" (Bickermann, *Institutions*, 40–50).

148. 1 Macc 11:61 (ἐσκύλευσεν).

149. 1 Macc 12:31 (ἔλαβεν τὰ σκῦλα).

150. 1 Macc 12:36. Comparing the account in *1 Maccabees* with the one in Josephus, Sievers concludes that Jonathan's reason for building the wall is both economic *and* military ("Jerusalem," 195–209).

151. 1 Macc 12:42–43. Ptolemy IV does something similar when he orders "the one in charge of public funds" to give the formerly enslaved Jews of Alexandria enough money to hold a seven-day festival—not to indulge themselves in drunkenness or gluttony, but to celebrate their "salvation" (σωτηρία, 3 Macc 6:36).

152. 1 Macc 13:16. Hostage-taking is common in the ancient world. In addition to the Joseph novella (Gen 37–45), note the examples cited by Snell (*Flight*, 99–116) and Heltzer ("Hostage," 209).

153. 1 Macc 13:15: "We are detaining him because of the 'money' (ἀργύριος) your brother Jonathan owes to the 'royal treasury'" (βασίλικον).

over the money and the hostages, Trypho reneges on his promise and executes Jonathan, burying his body in Gilead.[154]

Simon

This fluid, chaotic situation is the context in which Simon comes to power—the last of the Hasmonean brothers.[155] Appealing to Demetrius II, he tells his old enemy what he thinks he wants to hear; viz., that their enemy Trypho cares nothing about honest government, only the sordid business of "plunder."[156] Publicly supporting his "royal authority,"[157] Simon sends Demetrius a number of "gifts," reminding him "to release ... the things scheduled to be released,"[158] and promising him several fortresses in return. Responding to these gestures, Demetrius *does* promise to release Judea from the "crown tax" and restore "whatever else has been taxed in Jerusalem,"[159] but with regard to the "big problem" in Jerusalem—Greek troops—he does nothing.

Therefore Simon, at his own expense, pays the "back wages" of his militia,[160] empowering *them* to expel the Greek troops from Jerusalem.[161] Reaffirming the Judean-Roman alliance, he sends a spectacular "gift" to his Roman counterpart—a golden shield allegedly weighing one thousand pounds.[162] Impressed by these gestures, Antiochus VII (the new Seleucid king) publicly recognizes the legitimacy of Simon's govern-

154. 1 Macc 13:23 (i.e., near the village of "Baskama"). Josephus calls this village "Basca" (*A.J.* 13:210).

155. Rappaport argues that Judea reaches "independence" under Simon's leadership ("Simon," 601), but Saulnier postpones it to the moment when Simon passes the torch to his son Hyrcanus ("Révolte," 26–29).

156. 1 Macc 13:34 (ἁρπαγή). Thucydides uses this term to describe the "plundering" of Syracuse by the Athenians (*Hist.* 6.52), and Paul uses it to describe the Son's decision not to "plunder" his position as the Father's equal (ἁρπαγμός, Phil 2:6).

157. 1 Macc 13:37. Simon expresses his submission to Demetrius by sending him two very expensive gifts: a "golden crown" and a "palm-rod."

158. 1 Macc 13:37 (ἀφίημι ... ἀφέματα). Note, again, the use of the cognate accusative for emphasis.

159. 1 Macc 13:39.

160. 1 Macc 14:32 (ὀψώνια). Paul uses this term to describe the "wages" of sin (Rom 6:23).

161. 1 Macc 13:49–50. This "independence" does not last very long, though, for in 63 BCE Pompey's legions invade Jerusalem (Josephus, *B.J.* 1:141–58; Nodet, *Crise*, vii).

162. 1 Macc 14:18. This shield is said to weigh "one thousand minas" (approx. 1250 pounds).

ment, affirming "all the tax remissions which the kings before me have granted you, and a release from all the other payments from which they have forgiven you. I permit you to mint your own coins for your country, and I grant freedom to Jerusalem and its sanctuary. All the weapons you have prepared and the strongholds you have built shall remain yours. Every debt you owe the royal treasury, now or in the future, shall be forgiven."[163]

DYSTOPIAN SECTARIAN TEXTS

On the other end of the spectrum the puritan[164] texts from Qumran bear witness to a very different world,[165] the most socioeconomically significant being the *Damascus Document* (CD),[166] the *Rule of the Community* (1QS),[167] the *Habakkuk Commentary* (1QpHab),[168] and the *Thanksgiving Scroll* (1QH).[169] Much has been written about this dystopian litera-

---

163. 1 Macc 15:5–8. Note the constant repetition in this speech of the root ἀφίημι ("to cancel/remit/forgive") which, according to Bultmann, originally means "to release someone from a legal relation, whether office, marriage, obligation, or debt" ("ἀφίημι," 509–12).

164. In this present study "sectarian" and "puritan" are interchangeable terms (yet see Baumgarten, *Flourishing*, 1–15; Regev, "Sectarian," 146–81; Collins, *Beyond*, 69–75).

165. Vermes, *Scrolls*; Wise et al., *Scrolls*; García Martínez and Tigchelaar, *Scrolls*. In addition to biblical and apocryphal texts, these caves yield a treasure trove of texts most interpreters call "sectarian" (VanderKam and Flint, *Scrolls*, 239–54; Schiffman, "Scrolls," 2233–35). Josephus speaks of the "Essenes" as a sect living "the same kind of life as those whom the Greeks call Pythagoreans" (*A.J.* 15:371). With Metzenthin (*Jesaja*, 43), the present study presumes a modified Essene hypothesis like that formulated by the so-called Groningen school (Stegemann, "Essenes," 83–166).

166. Wise, et al., *Scrolls*, 49–78; Baumgarten, "Damascus," 166–70.

167. Wise, et al., *Scrolls*, 112–36; Knibb, "Rule," 793–97. In Murphy's opinion, "the texts of greatest relevance for our inquiry are the sectarian constitutional documents discovered at Qumran" (*Wealth*, 22).

168. Wise, et al., *Scrolls*, 79–88; Bernstein, "Habakkuk," 647–50.

169. Wise, et al., *Scrolls*, 170–89; Puech, "Hodayot," 365–69.

ture[170]—its historical authenticity,[171] its redactoral complexity,[172] its ideological conservatism[173]—yet almost no attention is given to (a) the socioeconomic conflict motifs manipulated by the authors of these texts, or (b) the degree to which these motifs resonate with the socioeconomic conflict motifs manipulated by other "great texts."[174] This is unfortunate because these dystopian texts focus on the same "big problems" of *acquisition, bribery, corruption, deprivation,* and *slavery.*

Damascus Document (CD)

Several passages in the *Damascus Document,* for example, preserve clues to the author's[175] worldview in language molded by the DNA of a dystopian puritan economy.[176] From a "thick analysis" of CD,[177] in fact, it is tempting to conclude that "wealth is at some point an issue in the separation of the *Damascus Document* community from society, in its self-understanding as a community of the 'poor ones,' and in its

170. This literature is "dystopian" because "dystopian authors are far more than doomsday prophets. They warn about what society might realistically become not so much from *default* or the absence of societal planning, but from the very *success* of societal plans conceived on the basis of false views of man" (Hoffecker, "Dystopianism," 46). A few critics, like Alter, view these texts *not* as "great" literature, but as "epigonic" and "derivative" ("Scrolls," 39–40). Murphy, however, argues that the sect responsible for producing this literature is able to "envision a future inversion of the current economic and political structures" (*Wealth,* 22).

171. Brownlee, "Muhammad," 236–39; Fields, "Discovery," 1:208–12; Silberman, "Media," 533.

172. For CD see Davies, *Damascus;* for 1QS see Metso, *Community;* for 1QpHab see Nitzan, *Scroll;* for 1QH see Licht, *Thanksgiving,* 1–52.

173. Grossman, *Reading;* Bockmuehl, "Redaction," 541–60; Feltes, *Gattung;* Hughes, *Allusions.*

174. *Exceptions:* Murphy (*Wealth*); Safrai and Eshel, "Economic," 228–33.

175. Questions about authorship-vs.-editorship are important, but marginal to the present study (see White, "Comparison," 537–53; Davies, *Damascus,* 143–59; Hempel, *Laws,* 187–92; Grossman, *Reading,* 127–61).

176. Lang puts it like this: "Since religious writings often reflect the social milieu of the writer, identifying these reflections increases sociological understanding of the influence of society on religious literature" ("Oppression," 325).

177. Murphy analyzes CD and other Qumran texts through lenses colored by the anthropological insights of Clifford Geertz, particularly his concept of "thick description" (*Interpretation,* 16), her intention being "not simply to count the coins [at Qumran] . . . but . . . to reconstruct in some measure the symbolic world in and against which the sectarian economy functions" (*Wealth,* 24).

organization as a redeemed community."[178] One passage in particular exemplifies this self-understanding as CD, like *1–2 Maccabees*, manipulates the "field-dweller"-vs.-"city-dweller" polarity[179] to indict what the author feels to be a depraved foreign culture of *acquisition*.[180] Adjusting this well-worn polarity to the dualistic mindset of his readers,[181] he rants and raves against this foreign culture for the way it threatens to "invade" his puritan community:[182]

> Whoever decides to live in "camps"[183] according to the "rule of the land"[184] as in ancient times [taking wives and bearing children as *torah* instructs], walks according to the "intention" [lit. "mouth"][185]of *torah* … But all who reject its commandments and statutes will have the "reward"[186] of the wicked "returned"[187] to

178. Murphy, *Wealth*, 45.

179. *Erra* 1:55–56.

180. Paul registers a similar opinion of the Roman economy, criticizing it as a place where "all have turned away, having become altogether worthless" (Rom 3:12, citing Ps 14:1–3).

181. Duhaime, "Dualism," 215–20. Murphy traces the roots of this dualism to internal (biblical) sources, esp. the book of *Deuteronomy* (*Wealth*, 97–99), but Hengel attributes it predominantly to external sources (*Judaism* 1:218–47).

182. The clearest example of dualism occurs in the "two spirits" passage in 1QS 3:13—4:26 (see Frey, "Patterns," 275–335; Kvaalvaag, "Spirit," 159–80).

183. CD 19:2 (מחנות). Although "camps" is not intended to be taken literally, "the most predominant explanatory framework for texts on the disposition of wealth in CD is that the Damascus covenanters are like the post-Exodus wilderness community of Israel. Certain terms originally applied to this community are taken over by the Damascus covenanters [so that] … they become the *camps*, the *congregation*, the *mustered out*" (Murphy, *Wealth*, 93, emphasis added).

184. CD 19:2–3 (סרך הארץ). This is the only occurrence of this phrase at Qumran, though סרך ("rule") not only denotes the fixed regimentation of community life (1QS 5.1; 6.8; 1QM 3.13; 4:9), but plays a definitive role in denoting the parameters of literary structure (N.B. the first–line "titles" of 1QS 1:1, 1QSa 1:1, and 1QM 1:1; see Nötscher, *Terminologie*, 53). Talmud uses סרך to denote regulations like the "rule of immersion" (סרך טבילה, *b. Yom.* 30a) and the "rule of contribution" (סרך תרומה, *b. Ḥul.* 106a).

185. The idiom פי התורה in CD 19:4 parallels the identical idiom in Deut 17:11 (Murphy, *Wealth*, 48–52, 117–37).

186. CD 19:6 (גמול). The primary meaning of this term is "payment," whether positive (Ps 103:2) or negative (Isa 3:11, quoted in *b. Kidd.* 40a), but this is not the only Qumran text to play with the polyphonic possibilities. The Wicked Priest, e.g., "has his reward 'paid back to him' (גמל) because of what he's already 'paid out' (גמל) to the poor" (1QpHab 12:3).

187. CD 19:6 (שוב). Citing Zech 13:7, CD engages the causative form of this word in a satirical curse-formula; i.e., just as the wicked man's reward "returns" (שוב), so also Yhwh's hand "returns" (שוב).

them when God "visits"[188] the land, when the word written by the hand of the prophet Zechariah is fulfilled [which says], "Awake, O sword, against my shepherd![189] ... Strike the shepherd and the flock will scatter, for my hand will turn[190] against the contemptuous, but the poor of the flock[191] will protect[192] him [i.e., the stricken shepherd]."[193]

Having found in the "field-dweller"-vs.-"city-dweller" polarity a recognized vehicle for socioeconomic critique, CD goes on to ponder its significance, adding to its reflections on *Zechariah* a few more from *Hosea*:

These [i.e., the "poor of the flock"] will escape in the "age of visitation,"[194] while those who remain will be delivered up to the sword when the Messiah comes ... This is the judgment: all those who enter into this covenant but abandon its precepts will be "visited" with destruction by the hand of Belial on the day when God "visits."[195] As scripture [*Hosea*] says, "Judah's princes are like those who move the boundary-stone, and I will pour out my wrath upon them like water."[196] This refers to anyone who enters

188. CD 19:6 (פקד). Like גמול, this term has both positive (1 Sam 17:18; 4Q268 1.14; 4Q448 3.4) and negative connotations (Exod 32:34; Jer 9:8).

189. CD 19:7 (citing Zech 13:7). The "shepherd" metaphor in *Zechariah*, regardless of how it originally functions (differing views proposed by Redditt, "Shepherds" vs. Cook, "Metamorphosis"), finds its taproot in the "great texts" of Mesopotamia (e.g., *GE* 6:58–63).

190. CD 19:9 (שוב; see comment on 19:6).

191. CD 19:8–9 (עניי הצון ... צוערים). The term צער can have positive (Jer 49:20) or negative connotations (Jer 30:19; Job 14:21), and just as *Job* relies on an "honor"-vs.-"contempt" polarity, so CD contrasts the צוערים ("contemptuous") with the עניי הצון ("poor of the flock"). Murphy, however, reads the phrases as synonymous parallels (*Wealth*, 35).

192. CD 19:9 (שמר). The appearance of this term echoes the "protection" motif embedded in the Yahwistic imperative animating the "wild man"-vs.-"wise man" stories in *torah*.

193. Rather than launch into a long excursus here on the "stricken shepherd" motif, see Ham (*Coming King*), and Chae (*Jesus*).

194. CD 19:10 (קץ הפקדה). Talmud similarly uses קץ (lit. "end") in the *status constructus* to enunciate eschatological concerns (e.g., קץ משיח, "age of the Messiah," *b. Meg.* 3a).

195. CD 19:14–15 (פקד ... פקד). CD 19:10–19 repeats the "visitation" motif three times, using קץ ("age") and יום ("day") interchangeably.

196. CD 19:16 (גבול). Where *Hosea* indicts Judah's princes for blurring the גבול-boundary protecting Judah from Assyrian "wild men" (Hos 5:11–13), CD indicts the Jerusalem priesthood for *inviting* Greek "wild men" into the holy city (1 Macc 1:41–64).

into the covenant of "repentance,"[197] but refuses to swerve away from the path of treachery, choosing instead to defile himself on the "paths of fornication"[198] with "wicked wealth"[199] . . . arrogantly flaunting his "wealth" and his "profits."[200]

Elsewhere CD lays out its understanding of the boundaries needed to protect the Sabbath from the threat of "contempt": "On the Sabbath no one . . . is to 'lend'[201] anything to his neighbor. He is not to decide anything involving 'wealth' or 'profits,'[202] nor is he to discuss work [generally] or future tasks [specifically]." Two more passages focus on practical economic exchanges and how they are to be conducted (a) between community members internally, and (b) between community members and "foreigners." The first pushes the Mosaic code into uncharted territory: "If something is stolen from the 'wealth of the camp'[203] and no one

197. CD 19:16 (תשובה). CD gravitates to this prophetic *Leitwort* (see Zech 13:7; CD 19:6, 9, 16) in order to challenge his readers to "change loyalties" (Holladay, *Root*, 116).

198. CD 19:17 (דרכי זנות). Just as CD parallels "paths of fornication" with "wicked wealth," so Talmud parallels "paths of death" (דרכי מות) with "lowest rung" (מדריגה התחתונה, *b. Kidd.* 40b).

199. CD 19:17 (הון הרשעה). This line mentions two of the "traps of Belial" listed in CD 4:17–18 (the third being טמא, "defilement"). According to CD 6:15 covenanters must "swear off the wicked wealth which defiles" (להנזר מהון הרשעה הטמא); i.e., the defilement of (a) "special vows" (נדר, see Num 6:2); (b) "devoted things" (חרם); and/or (c) "wealth of the sanctuary" (הון המקדש). Murphy suggests that the phrase "wicked wealth" connotes the headlong pursuit of wealth as "a means of exacting vengeance on neighbors for grudges long borne" (*Wealth*, 37).

200. CD 19:19 (הון . . . בצע). 1QH 18:23 parallels this word-pair alongside another one (הון // יצר בשר, "wealth"//"fleshly inclination"), perhaps to challenge "old wisdom" parallels like Prov 24:4: "By knowledge the rooms (of a house built on wisdom, v. 3) are filled with all precious and pleasant wealth," a proverb one rabbi simplistically interprets as "whoever gets knowledge gets rich" (*b. Sanh.* 92a).

201. CD 10:18 (נשא, lit., "lift up"). One of the Mosaic Code's contributions to ancient Near Eastern law is its stubborn insistence on protecting the poor from poverty as well as the "contempt" so often accompanying it. Deut 24:10–11, for example, reads, "When you make your neighbor a loan (נשא), you shall not enter his house to collect the 'deposit' (עבט; see עבטט in Hab 2:6, cited in 1QpHab 8:8); you shall wait outside until the debtor brings it out to you" (see Lewison, "Usury," 327–39).

202. CD 10:18 (הון . . . בצע, same word-pair found in CD 19:19 and 1QH 18:23). Just as *1–2 Maccabees* criticizes the "profiteer" mentality, and *Gilgamesh* criticizes the "arrogance" mentality [*kadāru, GE* 1:67]), so CD criticizes the hellenized culture of *acquisition*.

203. CD 9:11 (מאד המנחה). The term מאד (translated δύναμις ["power"] in LXX Deut 6:5) can denote "money" in some rabbinic texts (*Tg. Ps.-J.; m. Ber.* 9:5) (Ginzberg, *Jewish*, 41; Murphy, *Wealth*, 48–50).

knows who has taken it, the claimant will 'swear an oath,'[204] and anyone who knows but refuses to identify the culprit will be found 'guilty.'[205] With regard to any debt in need of 'returning,' but without a claimant, the 'returner'[206] will tell the priest about it, and after offering a ram for the guilt-offering,[207] it will go to him and him alone. Otherwise every object left unclaimed will go directly to the priests."[208]

The second tries to apply CD's puritan ideology to what can and cannot be exchanged with "foreigners": "[No one should] stretch out his hand to shed Gentile blood for the sake of 'wealth' or 'profits,'[209] but neither should a Gentile's 'wealth' be seized (except on the advice of the 'Israelite Cabinet')[210] lest it cause him to blaspheme.[211] No one should sell a clean beast or bird to a Gentile because he may then try to offer it in sacrifice [to his gods]. Nor should anyone sell anything to a Gentile from the 'excess'[212] of his granary or his [wine/oil]-press."[213]

204. CD 9:11–12 (ישביע בשבועת); note, again, the use of the cognate accusative.

205. CD 9:12 (אשם). "The extension of guilt beyond the culprit . . . is of biblical origin (Lev 5:1), but the specific application of the precept to stolen property is unique to CD" (Murphy, Wealth, 48).

206. CD 9:13 (שוב . . . משיב). Like CD 19:2–9, CD 9:9–16 engages in wordplay on the root שוב ("to return"; see Moore, "Anomalies," 238–40).

207. CD 9:14 (אשם). Note the polyphonic wordplay on אשם here and in 9:12. Similar wordplay occurs in b. Ber. 5a; b. Shab. 71a; and b. Pes. 31a (covertly alluding, like CD 9:13, to Num 5:7; see Milgrom, "Cultic," 299–308).

208. "While there are still individual owners who may have their property stolen, it is the entire community that is deprived of the property's use, and thus it must be to a communal representative that restitution is made" (Murphy, Wealth, 49). Much like CD, the talmudic order Nezikin ("Damages") addresses a variety of socioeconomic exchanges (Ohrenstein and Gordon, Economic, 57–100; Schiffman, Sectarian, 119).

209. CD 12:7 (הון . . . בצע). This word-pair, though absent from the Hebrew Bible, occurs repeatedly in the Qumran texts (e.g., CD 8:7; 12:7; 19:19; 1QH 18:23, 29–30; 1QpHab 9:5; see Avishur, Word-Pairs, 634–730).

210. CD 12:8 (חבור ישראל). Since the government of Judea is called חבר היהודים ("the Cabinet of the Jews") on Hasmonean coins (Rabin, Zadokite, 61), Hempel suggests that חבור ישראל refers to a governing council in charge of a community much larger than the one inhabited by the Damascus covenanters per se (Law, 70–72, 187–89).

211. According to Tosefta, robbing a Gentile is worse than robbing a Jew because the Gentile is more likely to curse the Name (t. Bab. Qam. 10:15).

212. CD 12:10 (מאד). This is the third term in the Shema triad "heart, soul, strength" in Deut 6:5 (לב-נפש-מאד), and Murphy attends carefully to this sequence (Wealth, 88).

213. Only larger cattle cannot be sold to Gentiles in the rabbinic literature (m. Pes. 4.3; y. Pes. 4.30d; m. Abod. Zar. 1.6; b. Abod. Zar. 15a), but where rabbinic writers worry about Gentiles profiting at the expense of Jews, CD focuses more on the "big problem" of Gentile sacrifice (Murphy, Wealth, 89).

Rule of the Community (1QS)

In the *Rule of the Community,* the most widely attested of the Qumran sectarian texts, a pro-Sadducean[214] writer boldly reinterprets the Shema[215] to address some of the more devious problems he sees threatening his community—a community he sees as quite vulnerable to the depredations generated by the Alexandrian culture of *acquisition*: "All those who 'freely volunteer'[216] for God's truth will bring all their 'knowledge,' 'strength,' and 'wealth'[217] to the 'community of God,'[218] refining their 'knowledge' by the truth of God's statutes,[219] 'measuring' their strength

214. Baumgarten argues that, in spite of the "sons of Zadok" mantra sprinkled throughout the *Rule* (1QS 1:2, 24; 2:3; 5:2, 9; 9:14, 1Q28b 3:22) one can be "Sadducean" in thinking without being an "official" member of the Sadducee party ("Controversies," 157–70). Others feel differently (Schiffman, *Reclaiming*, 73–76; Bernstein, Review of *Reclaiming*," 77–93; Collins, Review of *Reclaiming*, 244–47).

215. Deut 6:4–5. Second Temple worshipers incorporate the Shema into their morning and evening prayers because the simple act of reciting it is considered in some circles to "untie" (פטר) otherwise "binding oaths" (see *b. Ned.* 8a; Blumenthal, "Prayer," 264).

216. 1QS 1:11 (נדב). The nominal form of this root can be translated "freewill offering" (נדבה, Lev 7:16), but in the *Rule* the verbal form most often means "to volunteer." Those who love good and hate evil, for example, "volunteer (נדבים) to carry out God's decrees" (1QS 1:7); participants in the יחד-community "volunteer (מתנדבים) to turn away from evil" (1QS 5:1); those deserving "atonement" (כפר) "volunteer (מתנדבים) to enter Aaron's holiness" (1QS 5:6); those who "volunteer (מתנדבים) to join the covenant community" will be tested to their limits (1QS 5:21–23).

217. This triad (דעת-כוח-הון, "knowledge-strength-wealth") in 1QS 1:11–12 (and 3:2), does not exactly match the triad in Deut 6:5 (לב-נפש-מאד, "heart-soul-strength"), but this hardly negates the fact that (a) "the contribution of wealth to the community is presented ... in word clusters and literary contexts inspired by Deuteronomy," and (b) "the three offerings of 1QS ... are reminiscent of the cluster of commitments enjoined on Israel in Deut 6:5" (Murphy, *Wealth*, 117, 120). In 1QS 5:3 this triad-cluster modulates into תורה-הון-משפט ("law-wealth-judgment"), but note especially that the common term is הון ("wealth").

218. 1QS 1:12 (יחד אל). The word יחד ("community") is morphologically and semantically rooted in what is arguably the most important word in the Shema—אחד ("one," Deut 6:4).

219. 1QS 1:12 (דעת). Contrast the biblical presumption that "the beginning of knowledge (דעת) is the fear of Yahweh" (Prov 1:7), not the affirmation of his "oneness" (Deut 6:4) or the keeping of priestly statutes allegedly based on *torah*.

by his perfect paths,[220] and their wealth by his 'counsel of justice.'"[221] Anyone who refuses to defend the boundaries of this community lacks "the strength to 'turn'[222] his soul around . . . [Therefore] his 'knowledge,' 'strength,' and 'wealth'[223] shall not enter the 'counsel of the community'[224] because he keeps defiling his 'repentance' with evil plotting."[225]

While there are several intertextual parallels between CD and 1QS, the most pertinent here focuses on the problem of *personal vs. corporate wealth*.[226] In one passage of CD, for example, the text affirms that "anyone who lies knowingly about 'money'[227] shall be separated from the pure food for one year and punished for six days."[228] Similarly, the *Rule* affirms that "if anyone is found who knowingly lies about his 'wealth,'[229] he shall be separated from the 'pure food of the Many'[230] for one year and 'fined' one-fourth of his bread."[231]

220. 1QS 1:12 (תכן). *Isaiah* uses this word (here translated "measure") to describe the deity's ability to "measure the heavens with a span" (שמים בזרת תכן, Isa 40:12), and *Job* uses it to describe the deity's ability to "measure the waters in sections" (מים תכן במדה, Job 28:25).

221. 1QS 1:13 (עצת צדקו). This phrase stands in semantic opposition to phrases like עצת חטאין in Talmud ("counsel of sinners," *b. Abod. Zar.* 17b). Substituting הון ("wealth") for the third element of the Shema triad, the *Rule* further qualifies it via the same word used to legitimate the "Cabinet of Israel" in CD 12:8—עצה ("counsel").

222. 1QS 3:1 (משוב). This passage begins and ends with the root שוב ("to return").

223. 1 QS 3:2 (דעת-כוח-הון). This triad replicates the one in 1QS 1:11–12.

224. 1 QS 3:2 (עצת יחד).

225. CD 3:2 (שובה). This line is difficult to translate.

226. GNT addresses the same "big problem" in the Ananias and Sapphira story (Acts 5:1–11).

227. CD 14:20 (ממון). Whereas the man condemned in 1QS 6:25 lies about his "wealth" (הון), the man condemned here lies about his "money" (ממון, "mammon"). Investigating the origin and development of this Aramaic word, Hauck concludes that its negative connotation does not develop fully until the Second Temple period ("μαμωνᾶς," 388).

228. Text reconstructed with the aid of 4QDᵃ 10:1:14, 4QDᵈ 11:1:4–5, and the parallel passage in 1QS 6:24–25 (see Murphy, *Wealth*, 52–53).

229. 1QS 6:24 (הון).

230. 1QS 6:25 (טהרות הרבים). This phrase occurs several times in the Qumran literature (e.g., CD 6:16–17; 7:3; 7:18) and, according to Licht, should be interpreted as an epithet parallel to the one preserved in 1QS 6:20—משקה הרבים ("pure drink of the Many"), an interpretation confirmed by several potsherds and earthen tags from Masada (see Avemarie, "Reconsidered," 215–29).

231. 1QS 6:25 (ענש). This verb occurs several times in this section of 1QS because this is the first of many lists warning that failure to comply will result in a "fine" (ענש).

Habakkuk Commentary (1QpHab)

Like the *Gilgamesh Epic,* the biblical prophecy of *Habakkuk* criticizes the corrupt behavior of Babylonian leaders.[232] In the *Habakkuk Commentary* from Cave 1, however, a clever satirist applies the metaphorical imagery in the biblical prophecy to another bloc of leaders.[233] Where the biblical text condemns the Babylonians for "netting" slaves like schools of fish,[234] the *Habakkuk Commentary* applies this "fishing" metaphor to "the Kittim,"[235] who gather their 'wealth' and 'spoil'[236] like fish from the sea. So when [Habakkuk] says, 'They [the Babylonians] offer sacrifice to their nets and burn incense to their trawls,'[237] this refers to the [Roman] custom of sacrificing to their banners and anointing their weapons as 'objects of worship.'[238] [And when it says,] 'they make their portion fat and their food rich,'[239] this refers to the [Roman] custom of parceling out their yoke—their 'devouring corvée'[240]—on all the peoples in all the lands they perennially ravage."

Where the talmudic tractate *Yoma* uses this term eight times in another set of reflections on the "work"-"rest" polarity (*b. Yom.* 81a), 1QS uses it eighteen times.

232. Gruenthaner thinks the Macedonians are the object of Habakkuk's concern ("Chaldeans," 129–60), but there is little reason to doubt that כסדים in Hab 1:6 refers to the historical Chaldeans (Hess, "Chaldea," 886–87; Roberts, *Habakkuk,* 156).

233. Jemielity discusses the work of several ancient satirists (*Satire;* see Valeta, *Lions*).

234. Hab 1:14–16.

235. Most interpret the cryptic term "Kittim" (כתיאים), occurring forty-two times in these puritan texts (nine times in 1QpHab; eighteen times in the 1QM; fifteen times in other *pesharim*), as a codeword for "the Romans" (Lim, "Kittim," 469; Brooke, "Kittim," 135–59).

236. 1QpHab 6:1 (שלל . . . הון; see also 1QpHab 9:6). LXX often translates שלל with σκῦλος ("spoil"; e.g., 1 Sam 30:20), one of the key socioeconomic terms in *1-2 Maccabees.*

237. Hab 1:16a.

238. 1QpHab 6:5 (מוראם, lit. "feared things"). Roberts comments: "Because his net and seine bring in such an abundance of rich food, the Babylonian worships the tools by which he obtains this abundance as though they were divine. Habakkuk's point is that Babylon worships its military power because its military power brings such a high standard of living to Babylon." The Qumran text applies this text to *its* historical context, but the contemporary practical question is "whether we in our own way deify the means to *our* high standard of living" (*Habakkuk,* 104).

239. Hab 1:16b.

240. 1QpHab 6:7 (מסס מאכלם). Legal texts document the depredations of corvée slavery as early as the third millennium (Wilcke, *Law,* 21, 35), and literary texts refer

In column after column the author of 1QpHab goes out of his way to "name the names" of his enemies, even while being very careful to conceal the actual names under a veil of rhetorical camouflage:[241]

> Surely "'wealth"[242] will "corrupt"[243] the "Boastful Man" who stretches his gullet wide like Sheol, but who, like Death, is never satisfied.[244] All the nations and peoples will gather before him and "taunt" him,[245] making him the butt of their jokes as they exclaim, "Look at the man who enriched himself with others' possessions! How long can his debt keep piling up?"[246] *Interpretation:* This refers to the Wicked Priest[247] who at first proves to be trustworthy, but whose heart turns haughty as he "rules" over Israel, "corrupting" *torah* for the sake of "riches,"[248] robbing and hoarding

---

to it as well (e.g., *GE* 1:63–72; see Sterba, "Organization," 21). The term מאכל (from the root אכל, "to devour") intertextually reprises the language depicting other "devourers" in other "great texts" (e.g., Ishtar, *GE* 6:68). Following 1 Kgs 9:10–28, some argue that Solomon never imposes the "corvée" (מס) on indigenous Hebrews, but most see this as special pleading (Moore, *Faith*, 200).

241. The identities of the individuals known only as מורה הצדק ("Teacher of Righteousness," 1QpHab 1:13; 2:2; 5:10; 7:4; 8:3; 9:9–10; 11:5), איש הכזב ("Man of Lies," 2:2; 5:11), מטיף הכזב ("Spouter of Lies," 10:9), and הכהן הרשע ("Wicked Priest," 8:8; 9:9; 11:4; 12:2, 7) remain under "dispute after nearly fifty years of study" (Bernstein, "Habakkuk," 649; see Eshel, *Scrolls*, 29–62).

242. 1QpHab 8:3 (הון). This *pesher* preserves a tradition morphologically indistinguishable, but semantically distinguishable from MT Hab 2:5 (which reads היין, "wine"), yet the Qumran text must be taken seriously because it's approx. 1000 years older than the primary manuscript upon which MT is based (Codex Leningradensis). Young suggests that the process by which the text of the Hebrew Bible stabilizes is similar to the process by which the text of *Gilgamesh* stabilizes ("Stability," 173–84).

243. 1QpHab 8:3 (בגד).

244. This line may originally refer to Death's ability to "devour" all challengers (*CAT* 1.5:1:1–8; Blenkinsopp, "Death," 472–83) before later evolving into a metaphor for "insatiable greed."

245. 1QpHab 8:6 (משל). This verb can mean "to taunt" (Hab 2:6) or "to rule" (Dan 11:4). 1QpHab 8:9 plays on both meanings.

246. 1QpHab 8:7–8 (עד מתי יכביד עלו עבטט).

247. Van der Woude argues that the "Wicked Priest" could be one of several historical figures—Judas Maccabaeus, Alcimus, Jonathan, Simon, Johannes Hyrcanus, or Alexander Jannaeus ("Wicked," 349–59). Eshel identifies him with Judas' brother Jonathan (*Scrolls*, 29–62), but Lim argues that cryptic epithets like "Wicked Priest" (1QpHab 9:9; 11:4; 12:2, 8) and "Man of Lies" (1QpHab 2:2; 5:11) are probably different titles for the same person ("Liar," 45–51).

248. 1QpHab 8:9–11 (משל-בגד-הון). This "rule-corrupt-wealth" triad chiastically reverses the הון-בגד-משל ("wealth-corrupt-rule") triad in Hab 2:5–6, but the "wealth-

the "wealth" of violent men who stand in open rebellion before God ... and incurring serious additional guilt for embezzling the "peoples' wealth."[249]

Although the commentator's critique grows with every *ad hominem* accusation, none are based on the original historical context of *Habakkuk*:

> Will not your "creditors"[250] suddenly rise up? Will not those who scare you wake up and make you "*their* spoils?"[251] Since you are the "despoiler" of many nations, all the rest of the peoples will "despoil" you.[252] This refers to the priest who rebels against the precepts [of God][253] ... and the last priests of Jerusalem who accumulate "wealth" and "profits"[254] from "despoiling"[255] the peoples. In the last days, however, their "wealth" and their "spoil" will go into the hands of the army of the Kittim—for *they* are the "rest of the peoples."[256]

---

acquirers" (מקני הון) in 1QS 11:2 are the last in a list which includes the "Haughty of Spirit" (רמי רוח), the "Bending Men" (אנשי מטהה, i.e., the men who bend *torah* to suit their own desires), the "Finger Pointers" (שולחי אצבע), and the "Speakers of Futility" (מדברי און, 11:1–2).

249. 1QpHab 8:12 (הון עמים). García Martínez translates "public money" (*Scrolls*, 17).

250. 1QpHab 8:14 (נשכיך). The primary meaning of נשך is "to bite" (Num 21:8); thus the one who "lends at interest" is the one who "takes bites" out of debtors (see Deut 23:20).

251. 1QpHab 8:14 (משיסות למו). LXX Hab 2:7 translates διαπαργή ("plunder").

252. 1QpHab 8:15 (וישלוכה ... שלותה). These lines, a direct citation from Hab 2:7–8, preserve the repetition of שלל ("despoil") in the biblical text.

253. Doubtless this priest is the "Wicked Priest" (כהן הרשע) referred to repeatedly (1QpHab 9:9; 11:4; 12:2, 8).

254. 1QpHab 9:5 (הון ... בצע). As mentioned above, this word-pair recurs several times in this dystopian literature (CD 8:7; 12:7; 19:19; 1QH 18:23, 29–30).

255. 1QpHab 9:5 (שלל). Two things occur here: (a) the author of *Habakkuk* satirically manipulates the "plunder-vs.-protection" polarity; and (b) the author of the *Habakkuk Commentary* re-applies this polarity to engage what he imagines to be the needs of *his* audience.

256. This prophecy, of course, comes to pass when the Romans lay siege to Jerusalem in 66 CE (Josephus, *B.J.* 6:220–70).

Thanksgiving Scroll (1QH)

The brooding poems in the *Thanksgiving Scroll*,[257] though predominantly comprised of laments like those in the biblical books of *Jeremiah* and *Job*,[258] nevertheless preserve two passages in which the socioeconomic conflict motif-trajectory abruptly breaks through the literary skin. The first of these occurs in a hymn preserved on column 6: "I pledge upon my soul an oath not to sin against you, nor to do anything evil in your eyes … I will not lift my face to evil. I will not accept a 'bribe.'[259] I will not 'exchange'[260] your truth for wealth, nor any of your 'judgments' for a 'bribe.'"[261] The second seeks an answer to the perennial question, "Who is my protector?" "You have not given me 'wealth' or 'profits' as my 'staff,'[262] nor have you made the 'fleshly inclination' my refuge.[263] The 'wealth' of

257. Sukenik (*Scrolls*) first labels this scroll הודיות (*hodayôt*, "thanksgivings") in 1947, but this in no way implies that 1QH is bereft of קינה ("lament"). In 1QH 19:22, for example, an insertion above the line reads "I have sighed on the 'harp of lament' (כנור קינה) for every sorrow" (see 1QH 17:4; Jer 7:29; 9:9, 19). Burrows sees in 1QH a "type known as the individual psalm of complaint in the Old Testament … combined with the note of thanksgiving in some of the poems" (*Scrolls*, 380), and Puech summarizes: sometimes 1QH "takes the form of thanksgiving, or praise, or lament, or supplication" ("Hodayot," 367).

258. Moore, "Terror," 662–75; "Laments," 228–52.

259. 1QH 6:19 (שוחד). Rabbi Yohanan ben Zakkai asks his students, "If I were to be taken before a human king … whose anger … with me does not last forever, and who if he imprisons me does not imprison me forever, and who if he puts me to death does not put me to everlasting death, and whom I can … 'bribe with mammon' (לשחדו בממון), then I would weep. But now that I am going before the supreme King of Kings, the Holy One who lives forever, whose anger … is an everlasting anger, who if he imprisons me imprisons me forever, who if he puts me to death puts me to death forever, and whom I cannot … 'bribe with mammon' (לשחדו בממון), shall I not weep?" (*b. Ber.* 28b).

260. 1QH 6:20 (מור). Jeremiah makes a similar comparison via a similar metaphor: "My people 'exchange' (מור) their 'glory' (כבוד) for something which does not 'profit'" (יעל, Jer 2:11).

261. 1QH 6:20 (שוחד … משפט). The Hebrew Bible also contrasts שחד ("bribe") with משפט ("justice," 1 Sam 8:3; Mic 3:11), and on one occasion parallels "taking a bribe from the innocent" with "lending money at interest" (Ps 15:5).

262. 1QH 18:23 (משען … הון … בצע). The 23rd Psalm uses the feminine form of this noun in the line, "Your rod and your 'staff' (משענת) comfort me" (Ps 23:4).

263. 1QH 18:23 (יצר בשר). Second Temple theologians often contrast two "inclinations"—an "evil"/"fleshly" inclination vs. a "good"/"spiritual" inclination—as in the prayer, "May the 'good inclination' (יצר טוב) have sway over me, but not the 'evil inclination'" (יצר הרע, *b. Ber.* 60b). Marcus documents the history of this dualism ("Inclination," 606–21).

mighty men is [found] in the 'abundance of [their] luxuries'; i.e., the abundance of [their] grain, wine, and oil.[264] They take pride in their 'possessions' and 'acquisitions'[265] ... But to the sons of your truth you give 'insight'[266] ... The soul of your servant loathes 'wealth' and 'profits'[267] and [rejoices not] in 'luxurious affluence.'"[268]

SUMMARY

Jewish literature in the Second Temple period can be read from any number of angles, but most relevant here is the bifocalized way in which these Hebraic texts respond to the Hellenistic culture of *acquisition* imposed over Syria-Palestine by Alexander the Great. Where *1–2 Maccabees* covertly describes the aftermath of this invasion in gory detail, the puritan texts from Qumran denigrate it as the source of all "blasphemy," "wickedness," and "poverty." Where *1–2 Maccabees* indirectly focuses on the "big problems" of "taxation," "slavery," and "despoliation" from a *Realpolitik* perspective, the dystopian texts from Qumran boldly condemn as "greedy," "rebellious," and "eternally damned" anyone who dares to engage this "foreign" economic system. Most importantly, where *1–2 Maccabees* tepidly winks at Jewish participation in the "big problems" of *bribery* and *corruption*, the Qumran texts aggressively condemn the "Wicked Priest" and his associates for abandoning the Yahwistic imperative.

How do the Nazarenes react to these "big problems" in the parabolic texts ascribed to *their* Teacher? To that question we now turn.

---

264. 1QH 18:24 (חיל ... רוב ... עדנים). In Gen 2:15 עדן refers to the garden of "Eden" (lit., garden of "luxury"; see 1QH 14:16).

265. 1QH 18:25 (מקנה ... קנין). The name "Cain" (קין) derives from the root קנה ("to acquire").

266. 1QH 18:27 (שׂכל). Ezra thanks God for raising up a "man of insight" (איש שׂכל) to lead worship in the new temple (Ezra 8:18). Similarly the intellectual leader of the Qumran covenanters is called the "Instructor" (משׂכיל—same root: שׂכל—1QS 3:13; 9:12, 21; 1QH 20:11), a leader who "abandons" the "wealth" (הון) of the "Men of the Pit" much like "a servant (who) abandons his wealth to a master" (1QS 9:22–23).

267. 1QH 18:29 (הון ... בצע). N.B. that this word-pair both begins and concludes this passage.

268. 1QH 18:30 (רום עדנים). Contrast this worldview with that which seeks to "drink from the river of (God's) luxuries" (נחל עדניך תשקם, *b. Sanh.* 100a, citing Ps 36:9).

5

Socioeconomic Conflict Motifs in the Greek New Testament

T HE GREEK NEW TESTAMENT incorporates many of the same socioeconomic conflict motifs as those manipulated in the "great texts"
preceding it, even though those animating the Pauline correspondence[1]
do not function in exactly the same way as those found in the Gospels,[2]
and those animating the Pastoral Epistles[3] do not function in exactly the
same way as those manipulated by the apocalyptic scroll of *Revelation.*[4]
The following pages do not attempt to identify every socioeconomic motif in the Greek New Testament—such a task deserves a separate study—
but they do attempt to explain how the socioeconomic conflict motifs
in the more ancient texts shape and inform the Nazarene stewardship
parables preserved in the *Gospel of Luke.*[5]

1. Meggitt, *Paul*; Theissen, "Social," 65–84; Byron, *Slavery.*

2. Oakman argues, for example, that the "Jesus traditions retain an echo of a vigorous critique of political economy and its exploitative monetary system in the interests
of urging the alternative 'network' of the kingdom of God, with exchanges of goods
organized through principles of generalized reciprocity" ("Money," 347).

3. Adapting and extending the socioeconomic insights of Spicq (*Épîtres*), Kidd
argues that the concern of the Pastoral Epistles is "to help social superiors (esp. upper-
class heads of households) relate to the rest of the community of faith" (*Wealth*, 196), a
conclusion Fee takes with "full seriousness" (Review of *Wealth*, 353).

4. Bauckham, "Economic"; Taylor, "Monetary," 580–96; Fernández, "Judgment."

5. Metzger observes (*Consumption*, 13) that several of the parables in the Lukan
"travel narrative" (Luke 9:51—19:27) share similar characters (wealthy men), similar
settings (elite residences), and a common motif (overconsumption).

Like Islam and Christianity, Judaism is a "religion of the book,"[6] but like most "book religions"[7] the *priests* in this religious system interpret the "sacred book" very differently than do the *sages*.[8] Where the former tend to rely on a type of interpretation called *halakah*, the latter gravitate to that which the rabbis call *haggadah*.[9] The first of these terms refers to a "particular law or decision in a given instance, as in the frequent expression 'a halakah (given) to Moses on Sinai.'[10] [Later it] develops into a generic term for the whole legal system of Judaism, embracing all the detailed laws and observances."[11] The second, however, denotes any attempt to "investigate and interpret the *meaning*, the *values*, and the *ideas* which underlie the specific distinctions which govern religious life. In line with the accepted tendency to define *haggadah* as 'that which is not *halakah*,' one could say that the relation between *haggadah* and *halakah* is similar to the relation between theory and practice."[12]

These distinctions help delineate not only the methods used to create the apocryphal, pseudepigraphal, and rabbinic texts of Second Temple Judaism,[13] but the contents and shape of the texts gathered into the library now called the Greek New Testament.[14] In the *Letter to the Hebrews,* for example, a rabbinically-trained educator[15] describes Jesus of Nazareth as "the *high priest* of our confession," then lays out the implications of this title in what can only be described as a systematic *halakic*

6. Sloyan, *Religions*. Moingt argues that Christianity is not so much a "religion of the book" as a religion based on the life of Jesus Christ—who then becomes the lens through which its "sacred book" is interpreted ("Livre," 355–64).

7. Weber, *Judaism*, 169–218.

8. Blenkinsopp, *Leadership*; Grabbe, *Specialists*; Fishbane, *Interpretation*.

9. The word הלכה (from הלך, "to walk") refers to "the legal side of Judaism" as distinct from הגדה (from נגד, "to tell"), which refers to "the nonlegal material, particularly of the rabbinic literature" (Jacobs, "Halakhah," 251).

10. הלכה למשה מסיני (*b. Shab.* 28b).

11. Jacobs, "Halakhah," 251.

12. Wald, "Aggadah," 454.

13. Evans, *Ancient*; Stahlberg, *Fictions*; Neusner, *Praxis*.

14. Addressing all the issues surrounding the formation of the GNT is not possible here, not least because "no surviving documents either in the church or in Judaism offer clear answers ... [and] scholars with impeccable academic and ecclesiastical credentials have difficulty agreeing on these matters" (McDonald, *Canon*, 4). See Brown, *Introduction*, 1–96; Achtemeier, et al., *Introducing*, 589–608.

15. Aberbach, *Education*, 1–16.

treatise.[16] In the Gospels, however, the predominant description of Jesus is that of a "*wise sage.*"[17] Why? Because like other rabbis of his time, this one knows how to balance *halakah* with *haggadah* in his approach to Torah interpretation.[18] In fact, approximately one-third of the material ascribed to him in the Gospels comes packaged in a format the Hebrews call *mashal* (and the Greeks call *parabolē*).[19] "The parables of Jesus are intimately related to the religious heritage, culture, language, agricultural life and social concerns of the Jewish people during the Second Temple period ... Even if Jesus is not the first parabolic teacher, his masterful use of the parable helps to account for his phenomenal popularity and success. Indeed, he is a master of *haggadah*."[20]

Given these facts, it's important to recognize that some of the most creative attempts to address the "big problems" of the Syro-Palestinian economy in the Second Temple period are preserved within the *Gospel of Luke*.[21]

THE PARABLE OF THE GOOD SAMARITAN (LUKE 10:25–37)

In the Parable of the Good Samaritan, for example, Jesus addresses a pressing *halakic* question from a *haggadic* perspective. Rather than consult Torah only for the purpose of defining boundaries (e.g., to generate yet another list of attributes distinguishing "neighbors" from

16. Heb 3:1 (ἀρχιερέα τῆς ὁμολογίας ἡμῶν). See Tönges, "Epistle," 89–105; Gray, "Brotherly," 335–51; DeSilva, *Bearing*; Whitlark, *Enabling*.

17. Witherington, *Jesus*, 147–210. The most common title ascribed to Jesus in the Gospels is "rabbi" (Matt 26:25, 49; Mark 9:5; 11:21; 14:45; John 1:38, 49; 3:2, 26; 4:31; 6:25; 9:2; 11:8).

18. Stern, *Parables*, 152–84. Cheong has a table illustrating the relationship between *halakah* and *haggadah* (*Dialogic*, 65).

19. Heb משל; Gk παραβολή; Scott, *Parable*, 8–30.

20. Young, *Jesus*, 3. Scott defines a parable as "a *mašal* that employs a short narrative fiction to reference a symbol ... The hearing and grasping of a parable is a process leading a hearer through a series of stages. We expect it as a *mašal* to be laid beside something; we know that its literal first level is for the sake of an unexpressed something else, that it is the expression for an unknown content. But just understanding the narrative is not sufficient ... It is in laying a narrative beside a symbol that parable occurs, for symbol is implicated in the parable's discourse. The kingdom makes parable religious; the narrative discloses the kingdom; together they create parable" (*Parable*, 8, 62).

21. Metzger, *Consumption*, 12–13; Long, *Stewardship*. Though wealth and possessions are dealt with throughout *Luke*, the present analysis focuses only on the parables.

"foreigners"),[22] he tells a story designed (a) to draw biblically illiterate listeners inductively into the heart of Torah, then (b) challenge them to wrestle with its Yahwistic imperative.[23] This is not the only way to read this parable, of course, just one marginalized over a long history of interpretation.[24]

Thus when a lawyer asks him,[25] "What must I do to inherit eternal life," Jesus responds with another question, "How do *you* read Torah?" To this his questioner responds by quoting the Shema: "You shall love the Lord your God with all your heart and all your soul and all your mind and all your strength."[26] Then he quotes *another* command from Torah—"You shall love your neighbor as yourself"—and Jesus applauds the holistic nature of his response.[27] The conversation takes a critical turn, however, when the lawyer persistently asks, "but who *is* my neighbor?"

As the previous chapter of this study tries to show, this is one of the most hotly debated questions in Second Temple Judaism, particularly at Qumran—i.e., "Who is to be included in the *yaḥad*-community, and who is to be excluded?"[28] Indeed, this question pulsates at the heart of

---

22. Such a list appears in the *Halakic Letter* from Cave 4 (4QMMT; Schiffman, "Miqtsat," 558–60).

23. Fitzmyer, *Luke* 2:882–90; Gregory, "Agape," 16–42; Knowles, "Victim," 145–74.

24. Cadwallader points to three approaches dominating contemporary discussion. Some approach it as the "Parable of the Man who Fell Among Thieves"; others read it as the "Parable of the Wounded Man"; and still others approach it as the "Parable of the Good Samaritan" ("Samaritan," 7–15). This is not to suggest that "sociological and cultural-anthropological studies (fail to) illuminate the Gospels at many points," nor that these newer studies fail to "affect a reading of the parables especially where Jesus addresses economic topics" (Blomberg, *Parables*, 161; see Malina, *Origins*, 1–19).

25. *Luke* has a negative view of "lawyers" (νόμικοι) because from the author's perspective they hinder the learning process (Luke 11:52), refuse to engage questions honestly (14:3–4), burden the uninitiated with cryptic "legalese" (11:46), choose only to "test" rather than "learn" (10:25), and refuse baptism (7:30).

26. Luke 10:27 (citing Deut 6:4–5). As noted above, devout Jews cite the Shema at least twice a day in the Second Temple period (see *m. Ber.* 1.1–4; *b. Ned.* 8a; Blumenthal, "Prayer," 264), and the sectarian texts from Qumran often dwell on the socioeconomic implications. The addition of a fourth element (διανοία, "mind") is unique to the Gospels (in Matt 22:37 "mind" replaces "strength"; in Mark 12:30 "mind" is inserted between "soul" and "strength"; in Luke 10:27 "mind" is tacked on after "heart," "soul," and "strength").

27. Luke 10:27 (citing Lev 19:18). The Nazarene teaches that "eternal life" is obtainable (a) when *both* methods—halakah and haggadah—are applied to Torah interpretation, and (b) when holistic interpretation leads to genuine behavioral change.

28. Safrai and Eshel, "Economic," 228–33.

all communities, even those considering themselves to be more or less "global."[29] When the puritans at Qumran address it, they delimit their responses to narrow *halakic* categories reinforced by nativistic fears resistant to the "big problem" of *foreign invasion*.[30] Repeatedly in the Qumran texts the leaders of the *yaḥad* warn their members not to engage in socioeconomic transactions with foreigners, often to the point of threatening different kinds of penalties against those who ignore these warnings.[31]

Jesus challenges (a) this approach to Torah interpretation, and (b) this definition of "economy."[32] Instead of preaching another *halakic* sermon on the importance of "maintaining proper boundaries," however, he "clarifies the law by means of narrative exegesis,"[33] telling this lawyer a short story about a hapless traveler attacked by pirates.[34] Parading before his interrogator a couple of *halakic* "solutions" to the "big problem" encountered by this traveler (metaphorically symbolized by the "priest" and the "Levite"), he challenges this lawyer to come up with a practical, concrete way to redeem the wounded man from his socioeconomic "crisis."[35]

29. Walker, "*Neighbor*," 3–15.

30. Flusser, "Qumran," 193–201. See Moore, "Monocultural," 41–45.

31. See CD 9:9–16; 12:6–11; 1QS 6:24–25; Schiffman, *Halakhah*, 22–32.

32. Gk οἰκονομία. In another Lukan parable an indignant landlord orders his manager to "Show me the books on the 'economy' (οἰκονομία) you're mismanaging" (Luke 16:2).

33. Green, *Luke*, 426. Sandmel reads this parable as "not in itself anti-Jewish, but in the total context of Luke it does lend itself to a possible alignment with other anti-Jewish passages"—but this analysis fails to distinguish between the *various* Judaisms of the Second Temple period (*Anti-Semitism*, 77).

34. According to v. 30 he falls into the hands of λησταῖς ("robbers/bandits/pirates/terrorists"). Horsley and Hanson interpret this term against a grid defined by the "historical peasant" model ("Banditry," 48–87), but Mattila ("Jesus," 291–313) argues that the social-scientific concept of "peasant" is problematic. Why? Because it owes too much to the unresolved debate between Alexander Chayanov (*Theory*) and the Agrarian-Marxists of the early twentieth century—a debate largely ignored today by the wholesale assimilation of Chayanov's anticollectivist perspective into Western scholarship. As even Lenin himself recognizes, however, Chayanov's analysis is too microeconomic to account for (a) the marked socioeconomic inequalities which often exist among members of the same "peasant" community; and (b) the great multiplicity of economic strategies often employed by "peasants" to procure their livelihoods.

35. Van Dyke lists several of the dangers lurking on the Jerusalem-Jericho road (*Out-of-Doors*, 119–37).

The "priest" and the "Levite," like the Qumran covenanters, avoid touching the wounded traveler because of the possibility that it might—to quote the language of the *Damascus Document*—"render them unfit to eat the pure food."[36] Richard Bauckham, however, points to another, deeper problem. Underneath the conflict on the surface of this parable lies a "conflict" within Torah itself. The levitical command to "avoid defilement" might easily be made to contradict—at least in some minds—the equally levitical command to "love your neighbor."[37] Interpreters must therefore figure out how to prioritize these commands. But how, exactly? Priestly lawyers spend their days arguing such questions,[38] but the Nazarene's position is unequivocally clear. Whenever the *halakic* principle of "love"[39] appears to conflict with the *halakic* principle of "cultic purity,"[40] *the former takes precedence over the latter*.[41] By thus prioritizing the disparate elements within Torah Jesus of Nazareth seeks not only to restore his audience's understanding of Torah,[42] he also tries to help them understand the holistic balance between "acquisition" and "protection" within the Yahwistic imperative:

CREATION = ACQUISITION *plus* PROTECTION.

The decision to cast the hero of this parable as a Samaritan highlights this prioritization strategy. By shining the spotlight on a "hated foreigner" Jesus tries to focus attention on the underlying conditions at

36. CD 6:16–17; 7:3; 7:18; 1QS 6:25. The priest and the Levite do not want to defile themselves by touching a possible corpse (Lev 21:11; see Harrington, "Holiness," 124–35; Fitzmyer, *Luke* 2:882–85).

37. Lev 21:11 vs. Lev 19:18; see Bauckham, "Scrupulous," 475–89.

38. One of the most celebrated examples is a document reconstructed from six fragments from Cave 4 called the *Halakic Letter* (abbreviated 4QMMT because of its other title, *Miqsat Ma`asei Ha-Torah*, מקצת מעשי התורה, "Some Rulings Pertaining to the Torah") in which a spokesperson for the Qumran sect lays out approximately twenty areas of disagreement with the Jerusalem priesthood over how to interpret Torah (see Schiffman, "Miqsat," 558–60).

39. Lev 19:18 (אהבה).

40. Lev 21:11 (טמא). Note that טמא is one of the "three traps of Belial" (CD 4:15–18).

41. As Rappaport points out, this remains a minority position among many "people of the book" ("Religion," 147–49).

42. Gregory explores the global possibilities of Jesus' *agape*-ethic ("Agape," 16–42), and Mendham explores the similarities between the *agape*-ethic of Søren Kierkegaard and the *eudaimonia*-ethic of Alasdair MacIntyre ("Eudaimonia," 591–625).

least partially responsible for this "big problem" in Roman Judea.[43] Many southern Judeans, for well-known historical reasons,[44] hold their northern Israelite neighbors in "contempt,"[45] *especially* the Samaritans.[46] Thus the *really* radical twist to the story is that, rather than cast the hero as a "victim," or even as an "enemy," Jesus chooses to cast a "foreign invader" as the *hero* of this now-famous tale. Like Gilgamesh and Jacob, this hero looks nothing like the miracle-performing priest Onias, or the *Realpolitik* warrior Judas Maccabaeus, or the Qumranian "Teacher of Righteousness."[47] No, *this* hero looks more like the displaced "foreigner" who goes *incognito* to save his *retenu*-family from starvation (Joseph), or the widowed "foreigner" who offers herself to an inebriated stranger on a public threshing-floor to redeem the name of her dead husband (Ruth).[48] By casting its hero as a "hated foreigner," this parable helps future storytellers find ways to help future audiences resist the nativistic fears which always try to turn neighbors into "competitors," visitors into "invaders," and foreigners into "children of darkness."[49]

What Jesus formulates from *his* reading of Torah, in other words, is an understanding of "neighbor" diametrically opposed to those championed by his nativist contemporaries. This tale does not "play the Samaritan card" for "shock value," nor does it try to paint Christianity as "politically correct" on the issue of "minority rights."[50] It simply points out how self-destructive it is to prioritize the *halakic* principle of "cultic purity" over the *halakic* principle of "love" by challenging readers to (a)

---

43. Horsley and Hanson ascribe the reasons for banditry to several factors, both internal and external ("Banditry," 63–69).

44. At the root of this prejudice (explicitly noted in John 4:9) lies a specific historical event: the Assyrian conquest of Samaria in the eighth century BCE, after which the Assyrians repopulate it with foreign peoples worshiping foreign gods (2 Kgs 17:24–41; Josephus, *A.J.* 11:290, 306–12; Dexinger, "Samaritaner," 67–140).

45. Smith, *Palestinian*; Zangenberg, et al., *Religion*.

46. Purvis, *Samaritan*, 4–8; Anderson and Giles, *Keepers*, 9–103.

47. 2 Macc 3:1—4:38; 4 Macc 3:19—4:14; 1QpHab 7:1–14; Abel, *Histoire* 1:108–206.

48. Lichtheim, *Literature*, 222–35; Moore, "Moabite," 203–17.

49. N.B. the disparaging epithet "children of darkness" (בני חשך) in the *War Scroll* (1QM 1:1, 10, 16; 3:6, 9), applied not just to pagan "foreigners," but to *anyone* outside the puritan "community" (יחד).

50. Griffiths ("Politics," 85–114) and Esler ("Reduction," 325–57) wrestle with these and other possibilities.

interpret Torah from a holistic perspective, and (b) apply the results to the "neighbor-vs.-foreigner" debate.[51]

THE PARABLE OF THE RICH FOOL (LUKE 12:13–21)

Continuing on the road to Jerusalem, Jesus encounters another request; viz., that he "command"[52] a man's brother to divide up their family's "inheritance."[53] Like the sibling rivalry stories in Torah, the situation behind this request focuses squarely on the "big problem" of *primogeniture* (though the text gives no specifics),[54] yet in lieu of a *halakic* sermonic response Jesus tells a *haggadic* story about a rich man's behavior doubtless driven (or at least influenced) by proverbial sentiments drawn from the *Wisdom of Ben Sira*:[55] "One becomes rich through diligence and 'greed,'[56] and this is the 'value' of his reward:[57] when he says, 'I have found rest, and now I shall feast on my goods,' he does not know when the time will come when he will leave them to others at his death."[58]

Just like the conversation setting up the Parable of the Good Samaritan, this conversation begins with a response *to* a question *with* a question: "Who appointed me 'judge' and 'arbitrator' over you?"[59] Where the first of these juridical titles denotes the decision-making process generally,[60] the second denotes the title of a financial official in a few

51. Lev 21:11. This משל intertextually resonates with *Erra* and the Joseph novella because each features (a) unfortunate victims dealing with (imminent) socioeconomic collapse from which (b) an unconventional savior provides redemption.

52. The term εἰπέ is the aorist imperative of λέγω ("to speak").

53. Luke 12:13 (κληρονομία). Though usually translated "inheritance," this term most often means "acquisition" in *1–2 Maccabees* (e.g., 1 Macc 1:32; 2:10).

54. Metzger, however, interprets this parable alongside the "Parable of the Two Sons" (Luke 15:11–32; *Consumption*, 26–76).

55. The apocryphal book of *Sirach*, often introduced in Talmud with the authoritative phrase, "as it is written," is included in LXX, but not in the Hebrew Bible (Segal and Bayer, "Ben-Sira," 376–78).

56. Sir 11:18 (σφιγγία). This rare word is not the same word for "greed/covetousness" in Luke 12:15 (πλεονεξία).

57. Sir 11:18 (αὕτη ἡ μερὶς τοῦ μισθοῦ αὐτοῦ), translating μερὶς in light of μεριστής (Luke 12:14).

58. Sir 11:18–19 (see *1 En.* 97:8–10). Malherbe situates this parable in its most plausible literary-historical context in order to argue that the most effective translation of πλεονεξία is "covetousness" ("Christianization," 123–35).

59. Luke 12:14 (κριτής . . . μεριστής).

60. According to Isa 30:18 (LXX), Yahweh is the only true κριτής ("judge").

older texts.[61] Whether Jesus (or Luke) has this specific connotation in mind is not determinable, yet the fact that this economic connotation adorns the term centuries prior to Jesus' ministry deserves at least some consideration.

At any rate, the parable which follows begins by describing the field of a "wealthy" man as extremely "fruitful."[62] Responding to this fruitfulness, this prosperous farmer does something which at first seems rather odd. He talks to himself—not to God, but to *himself*: "He 'dialogued'[63] with himself, [asking], 'What should I do? I have no place to warehouse my crops.' Then he said, 'I will do this: I will tear down my storage sheds and build bigger ones, and there I will warehouse my grain and my "treasures."[64] And I will say to my soul, "Soul, you have 'many treasures'[65] laid up for many years. Eat. Drink. Cheer up. Relax.""[66] Just as Erra and Yaṣṣib talk to themselves,[67] the rich man's self-directed conversation gives him a vehicle for weighing the pros and cons of his decision. Unlike Erra and Yaṣṣib, however, he does not decide to go to war, nor does he thank God for the blessings from which he so abundantly profits. What he does do, however, reveals how radically he fails to recognize the depth of the "crisis" before him; viz., (a) that he has yet to understand the boundaries of his mortality;[68] and (b) that he

61. Pippidi notes this nuance in inscriptional data discovered on what is now the east coast of Romania some three hundred years before the writing of the *Gospel of Luke* (*Inscriptiones* 1:6).

62. Luke 12:16 (ἀνθρώπου τινὸς πλουσίου εὐφόρησεν ἡ χώρα). To illustrate the relevance of this parable, N.B. Josephus' account of a contemporary nationalist named John of Gischala (d. 73 CE), a *Realpolitik* businessman who manipulates the "fruitfulness" (εὐφορήκυιας) of the olive oil market in order to "gather a large sum of money," which he then uses to arm Sibitti-like zealots against the Romans (*B.J.* 2:592; Rappaport, "Gischala," 477–93).

63. Luke 12:17 (διελογίζετο ἐν ἑαυτῷ, lit., "he had dialogue with himself"; see Luke 20:14). People talk to themselves a lot in the Lukan parables.

64. Luke 12:18 (τὰ ἀγαθά μου). When the adjective ἀγαθός ("good") appears in the neuter plural, it becomes a substantive denoting "good things"; i.e., "possessions"/"treasures" (Sir 14:4; Wis 7:11)

65. Luke 12:19 (πολλὰ ἀγαθὰ).

66. Luke 12:17–19.

67. Erra talks to his "heart" (Akk *libbu*, Erra 2 C10:38); Yaṣṣib talks to his "genie" (Ug *ggn*, CAT 1.16:6:26); the rich man "dialogues with himself" (διελογίζετο ἐν ἑαυτῷ, Luke 12:17). In 12:19 he speaks to his "soul" (ψυχή), saying (in so many words), "O soul, *now* you're living the good life."

68. Gilgamesh faces the same crisis of "mortality" because "the central theme of the *Gilgamesh Epic* . . . is the problem of death" (Heidel, *Gilgamesh*, 250–51).

has yet to understand the meaning of the Yahwistic imperative. Instead he decides (like Gilgamesh) (a) to "wrest the boon of immortality" away from the divine world;[69] and, like the "rabble" in the wilderness,[70] (b) replace the Yahwistic imperative with the latest (hellenized) version of the "deprivation myth."[71] The result? Instead of using his "treasures" to "protect" the helpless, he spends his days obsessing over how to hoard more and more "spoil."

This investment strategy presumes, however, (a) that there's always going to be a "future," fully enjoyable without restriction; and (b) that "hoarding spoils" is synonymous with "investing wisely." As he does elsewhere in the Lukan travel narrative,[72] Jesus boldly challenges these presumptions, indicting this narcissistic materialist for defining the "good life" in categories alien to the Yahwistic imperative.[73] In this way Jesus carefully defines what covetousness really means.[74] *Interpretation:* Like Ishtar, this rich man defines the "good life" in categories allergic to the pursuit of *wisdom*.[75] No matter how much wealth he's given, it's never enough. Thus his unwillingness to deal with the crisis of his prosperity— and it is a crisis[76]—ultimately leads him to make the fateful decision to equate his life with his possessions.[77]

69. Abusch, "Development," 619.

70. Num 11:4.

71. Van der Spek asks, "Did the Hellenistic kings pursue economic policies aimed at increasing their subjects' prosperity? My answer must be no. Their policies were primarily directed toward their own wealth, prestige, and power. Everything else was secondary" ("Hellenistic," 433).

72. "Fear not, little flock, for it is your Father's good pleasure to give you the kingdom. Sell your possessions, and give alms. Make purses for yourselves that do not wear out, an unfailing treasure (θησαυρός) in heaven, where no thief comes near and no moth destroys. For where your treasure (θησαυρός) is, there your heart will be also" (Luke 12:32–34).

73. Compare the "good life" in *GE* 1:233 vs. Deut 10:13.

74. Luke 12:15 (πλεονεξία; Malherbe, "Christianization") Note the close similarity between the "3 traps of Belial" ("fornication-wealth-impurity," CD 4:17–18) and the triad of "fornication-impurity-covetousness" (Eph 5:3, 5). In 5:5 πλεονεξία ("covetousness") is synonymous with εἰδωλαλάτρης ("idolatry").

75. N.B. the parallel contrasts between Ninsun-vs.-Ishtar in *Gilgamesh* and Lady Wisdom-vs.-Lady Folly in *Proverbs*.

76. Keister and Moller document this crisis ("Wealth," 63–81).

77. Luke 12:15 (ἡ ζωὴ αὐτοῦ… τῶν ὑπαρχόντων αὐτῷ).

Investing everything in the deprivation myth, this man chooses to ignore exactly one-half of the Yahwistic imperative, the same half Cain ignores—*protection*.[78] Interpreting his prosperity merely as an opportunity to hoard more "spoils," he replicates the behavior of the Seleucid king Antiochus IV (Epiphanes), the "hated foreigner" who builds warehouses for all the "spoils" he takes from Judea in his attempt to "wildernize" Jerusalem.[79] Like the victim traveling the road to Jericho, however, the crisis of his mortality unexpectedly breaks in ("Fool! Tonight your soul is required of you!"),[80] thereby forcing him to realize (a) that he is not the Creator, and (b) that everything he "owns" is soon to be given over to someone else. In short, the rich man's problem is not his desire to acquire, only his desire to acquire *at any cost*.[81]

THE PARABLE OF THE MASTER AND HIS SLAVES (LUKE 12:35–48)

In this passage Jesus uses a pedagogical form Peter specifically calls a "parable,"[82] though few interpreters follow the fisherman's lead. Instead, some describe this part of the Lukan travel narrative as an amorphous list of "sayings about vigilance and faithfulness,"[83] while others describe it as a preview of *Luke's* "eschatological discourse."[84] Yet this parable, like no other in the Gospels, engages the master-slave polarity embedded in other "great texts" (like *Atrahasis* and *Exodus*) from two perspectives: (a) "watchfulness"; and (b) "prudence."[85]

Like the "Parable of the Bridesmaids" in the *Gospel of Matthew*,[86] this tale presumes (a) a wedding banquet context, and (b) the impor-

78. Gen 4:1–16.

79. 1 Macc 1:39 (ἐρημόω . . . ἐρημός). Bluntly put, the rich man cannot tell the difference between "blessings" and "spoils."

80. Luke 12:20.

81. See Eccl 5:10: "The lover of money will not be satisfied with 'money' (כסף, lit., "silver"), nor the lover of wealth with 'abundance' (המון, "noise, din, turmoil, abundance," *HAL* 240). This also is 'emptiness' (הבל)."

82. Luke 12:41 (παραβολή).

83. Fitzmyer, *Luke* 2:xiv.

84. Johnson and Harrington, *Luke*, 205; Green, *Luke*, 497.

85. Luke 12:37, 42 (γρηγορέω . . . φρόνις). The second of these terms (adjectivally presented as φρόνιμος) appears here and in the "Parable of the Prudent Manager" (Luke 16:8 uses the adverbial form φρονίμως, "shrewdly").

86. Matt 25:1–13. Either Luke or Matthew switch the order of these two vignettes

tance of "watchfulness" among slaves/employees/attendants.[87] Where
the Matthean parable features a master disciplining his slaves for failing to be "watchful," however, the Lukan parable depicts a master so de-
lighted by the "watchfulness" he sees in his servants, he does something
totally unexpected. *He* decides to serve *them*. A more obvious rejection
of the "slavery-is-essential-to-economic-survival" ideology is difficult to
imagine.[88]

Where *Atrahasis* goes so far as to promote the use of bribery to
validate this ideology, however, Jesus redefines this venerable socioeconomic institution. That is, where his audience defines "slavery" as an institution in which "slaveholders" use "slaves" to "gain power,"[89] Jesus turns
the "master-slave" relationship on its head in order to illustrate one of
the central paradoxes of the new economy he envisions for his disciples.[90]
Responding to Peter, again he answers a question with a question: "Who
is the faithful and prudent 'manager'[91] whose master will put in charge
of his slaves to give them their food-ration at the proper time? Blessed is
that slave whom his master finds so doing when he comes. I tell you the
truth—he will put that slave in charge of all his possessions."[92] In addition to the quality of "watchfulness," in other words, this master expects
his employees to manage his business affairs.[93] He wants them, like the
retenu-slave Joseph, to be "prudent"[94] in the way they manage his posses-

---

as Luke 12:35–40 nominally parallels Matt 25:1–13, and Luke 12:41–48 closely parallels
Matt 24:45–51.

87. The "watchman" motif has a long history in the prophetic literature (see Ezek
3:16–21; 33:1–9; Brownlee, "Ezekiel," 392–408).

88. *Atr* 1:243; Sterba, "Organization," 21; Moore, *Faith*, 200.

89. Patterson, *Slavery*, 337.

90. Whether this vision ever becomes reality is difficult to say. Perplexed by the paradoxical way Paul uses the slavery metaphor (both positively and negatively), Glancy
suggests that Paul's use of the slavery motif "hides" some aspects as it "highlights" others (*Slavery*, 9–38). Palmer discusses the paradoxical nature of Christian discipleship
generally ("Scarcity," 94–115).

91. Luke 12:42 (οἰκονόμος).

92. Luke 12:42–43. The wording of Luke 12:44 reflects the LXX wording of Gen
39:4.

93. This is the first of two "managerial" parables in the Lukan travel narrative, the
other being the "Parable of the Dishonest Manager" (Luke 16:1–13).

94. The term φρόνιμος can be translated either "prudent" or "wise," depending on
context. Sophocles uses the term to describe Ajax's return to "sanity" after months of
rage (*Ajax* 259). Plato uses it to contrast the "wise" (φρόνιμος) and "foolish" (ἄφρων)

sions.[95] Anyone who fulfills the potential of this job description is to be rewarded. Anyone who abuses it is to be punished.

In this way Jesus challenges the myth that all slaves are nothing more than angry "wild men" and all masters are capricious "Enlils." Moreover, he radically deconstructs the "master-slave" polarity in order to re-define "economy" within the covenantal categories issuing out of the Yahwistic imperative. Where "masters" in the Hellenized Palestinian economy try "to influence public attitudes and deflect attempts to interfere with proprietary claims on their slaves,"[96] *this* master promises to "serve" any slave who decides to practice "watchfulness" and "prudence."[97] Thus, where the Graeco-Roman world often stereotypes "slaves" as mindless creatures who "act dumb ... lie ... steal ... run away ... injure ... kill ... and engage in armed revolt,"[98] *these* slaves, empowered by *this* master, are challenged to live and work within a very different set of socioeconomic values.

THE PARABLES OF THE LOST SHEEP AND THE LOST COIN (LUKE 15:3–10)

The situation triggering these two parables (again) returns to the "neighbor"-vs.-"foreigner" polarity, the firewall behind which so many Judeans hide themselves whenever nativistic fear trumps neighborly compassion. Enfranchised religionists like the "scribes and Pharisees," for example, often relegate all "tax-collectors" to the category of "hated foreigners."[99] Responding to this caste mentality Jesus launches two powerful parables.[100] The first, about a shepherd losing one of his sheep, focuses on one of the most important staple businesses of the Syro-

---

elements inside every "soul" (ψυχή, *Soph.* 247a). Compare the *nēmequ*-vs.-*kadāru* polarity in *Gilgamesh* and the Lady Wisdom-vs.-Lady Folly polarity in *Proverbs*.

95. Gen 39:4. In spite of the chronological gap, this parable explores the same "master-slave" dynamic as that structuring the Joseph novella and *Atrahasis*.

96. Patterson, *Slavery*, 173.

97. This master is not "enslaved" (δουλόω); he simply "serves" (διακονέω), a dynamic well-illustrated by the foot-washing episode (John 13:1–20).

98. Patterson, *Slavery*, 173.

99. Luke 15:1 (τελώνης). Polybius (d. 120 BCE) has one of his characters describe another character as a "vulgar tax-collector," using a term for "vulgar" which originally means "of the class of artisans" (βαναύσος, *Hist.* 12:13:9).

100. Actually he tells three, but *Luke* uses the first two to introduce a much longer third one (Luke 15:11–32).

Palestinian economy, using well-known pastoral images to help his audience understand his teaching. In Ps 77:20, for example, Yahweh is the Great Shepherd who faithfully feeds his flock, even though Isa 53:6 describes this flock as hopelessly gone "astray."[101]

Yet again, rather than enter into a *halakic* argument with these religionists over the problems to which tax-collectors are vocationally susceptible (like bribery),[102] Jesus tells a short story about a shepherd who unexpectedly loses one of his sheep from a flock of one hundred.[103] Now, unexpectedly losing 1% of one's business income may not seem like a "big problem" to most Westerners, but to Palestinian shepherds struggling to eke out a living such a loss can do great damage (if nothing else, make it that much more difficult to pay the "livestock tax").[104] But Jesus does not delve into any of these details. He simply cites a well-known socioeconomic dilemma to illustrate the care with which all shepherds know they must treat their flocks, whether or not they choose in the process to emulate the example of the Good Shepherd.[105]

In terms of percentages, the "Parable of the Lost Coin" raises the stakes considerably. Here a distracted woman, for reasons never stated, loses her (daily? weekly?) grocery allowance. Distressed and desperate, she searches diligently for it until finally she finds it, calling her neighbors over to celebrate its recovery. Both of these parables use common economic situations to illustrate (a) the inherent value of people, regardless of socioeconomic "class,"[106] and (b) the joy of recovering something valuable whenever it becomes, for whatever reason, "lost." The twist comes in the difficult-to-define notion of "value." No one in these sto-

---

101. Heil argues that "Ezekiel 34 in particular contains the entire semantic field needed for the implied reader to appreciate fully the . . . shepherd metaphor" ("Ezekiel," 699; see *GE* 6:58–63).

102. "We too have our *publicani*: postmasters in village shops, contractors who arrange to clean government offices and the builders who erect them, concerns which supply clothing or equipment to the armed forces, hospitals, public corporations, and so on" (Stockton, Review of *Publicans*, 97).

103. Shepherds thus afflicted often wonder whether the loss of their property is due to "straying," "thievery," "disease," "wolves," or all of the above (Heil, "Ezekiel," 701–2).

104. 1 Macc 10:33; Roth and Elon, "Taxation," 533.

105. See ὁ ποιμήν ὁ καλὸς ("the good shepherd") in John 10:1–18 and רעה אחד ("one shepherd") in Ezek 34:23.

106. Mani documents how this caste mentality still defines the reality of contemporary Indian life, where "brahmanical pseudo-religion" still draws power from well-oiled "engines of oppression" (*Debrahmanising*, 45–84).

ries, for example, loses an expensive gold ring or precious Torah scroll
… only a single sheep and a single coin. Behind this text, however, it's
important to identify the lingering prejudices pervading its hearers, particularly the fact that most enfranchised Judeans consider *shepherds*, like
the *retenu*-herdsmen of ancient Egypt, to be "unclean"[107]—not to mention their attitudes toward *women*.[108]

Jesus addresses these prejudices head-on. In order for his disciples
to interpret Torah properly, he argues, first they must learn (a) how to
balance "cultic purity" with "love," and (b) learn how to recognize that
which is *most* valuable.[109] With these parables *Luke* therefore (a) exposes
the flaws in contemporary Judean interpretation of Torah, even as he (b)
encourages those scapegoated by their nativistic leaders to keep trying
to recover their losses.[110]

THE PARABLE OF THE TWO BROTHERS (LUKE 15:11–32)

Contemporary interpreters analyze this well-known vignette from a
variety of angles.[111] Some argue that the type-scenes within it resemble
those habitually handed down from teacher to student in traditional
Graeco-Roman schools, especially those focusing on "the father with
two sons, one moral and the other immoral."[112] Others find parallels and
precedents in the rabbinic literature,[113] still others in the Hebrew Bible.[114]

In the 1977 film *Jesus of Nazareth* filmmaker Franco Zeffirelli focuses on the second part of the story in which the joyful father tries to
persuade his oldest son to celebrate his brother's return.[115] Thus, instead
of reading the story as "The Parable of the Prodigal Son," Zeffirelli reads

---

107. Even as ancient Israelite shepherds are "abhorrent" (תועבה) to the Egyptians
(Gen 46:34), Josephus parallels "shepherds" (τοῖς ποίμεσι) with "the polluted" (τοῖς
μιαροῖς, *C. Ap.* 1:266).

108. Lev 12:1–8; 11Q19 48:16; Gruber, "Purity," 65–76.

109. Bauckham, "Scrupulous," 475–89.

110. Pöhlmann discusses the parables in Luke 15 against the economic ideas of
Hesiod, Xenophon, Aristotle, the Pythagoreans, and the Stoics (*Verlorene*, 1–48).

111. For a list of options, see Scott, *Parable*, 99–125.

112. Rau, *Reden*, 216–94.

113. Aus, "Fame," 443–69.

114. Bailey, *Finding*, 194–212; Drury, *Tradition*, 143–47; Aus, *Weihnachtsgeschichte*,
126–73.

115. Talbert, *Luke*, 275.

it as "The Parable of the Two Brothers," imagining Jesus telling it to his disciples in order to reconcile "Matthew" (portrayed as worldly, but spiritually hungry) to "Peter" (portrayed as well-meaning, but nativistically fearful).[116]

In *Hear Then the Parable,* however, Bernard Brandon Scott focuses on the first part of the story in which the younger son leaves home but eventually finds his way back, reminding his readers (a) that sibling rivalry is a well-known motif in the Hebrew Bible (Cain and Abel; Ishmael and Isaac, Esau and Jacob; Aaron and Moses, etc.), and (b) that at least one sage considers it unwise for patriarchal donors to pass on their inheritance before death: "To son or wife, to brother or friend, do not give power over yourself as long as you live. Do not give your property to another, lest you change your mind and have to ask for it back. While you are still alive and have breath in you, do not let anyone take your place. For it is better that your children should ask from you than that you should look to the hands of your sons."[117] As this quotation from *Sirach* illustrates, Second Temple rabbis take the institution of *primogeniture* very seriously, even though they often find themselves bound to discuss it only within *halakic* categories:

> This is the order of inheritance: If a man die and have no son, then you shall cause his inheritance to pass unto his daughter.[118] ... If a man assign his goods to his sons he must write, "From today and after my death"[119] ... If he leaves elder sons and younger sons, the elder sons may not care for themselves [out of the common inheritance] at the cost of the younger sons, nor may the younger sons claim maintenance at the cost of the elder sons. They must all share alike.[120]

Yet the issue here is truly a "*big* problem"—one of the biggest, in fact, within the "great literature"—and the trajectory upon which it operates is rooted in some very old socioeconomic polarities. Just as the Matthean Jesus appeals to *halakic* categories to reframe contemporary

116. *Jesus of Nazareth;* screenplay by Anthony Burgess; directed by Franco Zeffirelli (London: ITC Entertainment, 1977).

117. Sir 33:19–21.

118. *Torah* sets this precedent with the ruling passed on to the daughters of Zelophehad (Num 27:8).

119. On this phrase see *b. Git.* 72a.

120. *m. Bab. Bat.* 8.2–8.

discussion about divorce,[121] so the Lukan Jesus appeals to *haggadic* categories to re-frame contemporary discussion about primogeniture. Just as the "wild man"-vs.-"wise man" stories in *Genesis* persistently focus on the balanced nature of the "acquisition"-"protection" polarity, so this parable aims at a similar goal: "In a parable, something other and something more is pointed to by the concrete picture, and it's up to the hearer to figure out the something other and something more. This is typical of 'devious' Oriental wisdom, and such wisdom abounds in the parables of Jesus."[122]

Like Cain, one of the brothers in this story seeks to "acquire"; like Abel, the other endures the consequences of his brother's decision.[123] Like Gilgamesh, one brother reacts poorly to life "beyond the boundaries" (the "far country");[124] like Enkidu, the other loudly complains, even while chafing against those very same boundaries.[125] Like the Igigi, one party wants to be "free" from the drudgery of mundane work; like the Annunaki, the other expects everyone to work hard.[126] Like Enki, one party wants to be *creative*; like Enlil, the other wants only to be *careful*.[127] Like Lot, one party craves *independence*; like Abraham, the other craves some semblance of *interdependence*.[128] Like Esau, one brother finds himself driven by *hunger*; like Jacob, the other finds himself driven by *contempt*.[129] Like *Gilgamesh*, one brother becomes "lost"; also like *Gilgamesh*, someone turns his life around enough, essentially, to become "found."[130]

121. Meier, "Divorce," 74–181.

122. Malina, *Insights*, 5.

123. Gen 4:1–16. The term διασκορπίζω in Luke 15:13 ("to squander") often appears in LXX to indicate the "scattering" of peoples and persons resistant to the Yahwistic imperative (Num 10:34; Deut 20:3; Jer 9:18; Ezek 11:16; Neh 1:8; Tob 13:5). Thus, when the younger brother goes into a "far country," he "scatters" his family's inheritance.

124. Luke 15:13 (χώραν μαχρὰν). The younger brother takes his father's fortune "into a far country," but rather than associate this "country" with a geographical location, the intertextual parallels suggest a focus on the younger brother's "lostness" (ἀπόλλυμι, v. 32) because, like Gilgamesh, he finds himself in an "unprotected" place where "monsters" prowl.

125. *GE* 5:70–75. Aus reflects on these parallels, but not from an intertextual perspective (*Weihnachtsgeschichte*, 126–73).

126. *Atr* 1:1–6; *Ee* 6:10; Komoróczy, "Work," 19.

127. *Atr* 1:208–17.

128. Gen 13:1–18.

129. Gen 25:19—33:17.

130. The "lost-found" polarity shapes the larger literary structure of all three parables in Luke 15: lost *sheep*, lost *coin*, lost *son* (Bailey, *Finding*, 109–93).

In short, the "Parable of the Two Sons" (a) reprises many of the same socioeconomic conflict motifs manipulated within the "great literature" which precedes it; and (b) re-interprets these motifs to a new audience facing old challenges.

THE PARABLE OF THE PRUDENT MANAGER (LUKE 16:1–13)

In this parable Jesus challenges his audience to engage a story about a corrupt business manager who embezzles funds: "Once there was a rich man who had a manager, and charges were brought to him that this man was 'squandering' his property.[131] So he summoned him and said, 'What is this that I hear about you? Show me the books on the economy you're mismanaging. No longer can you be my manager.'"[132] To cushion the blow of unemployment, however, the manager develops a containment strategy like that devised by the clay-based creatures in *Atrahasis*; i.e., he starts cutting side deals. Where the clay-based creatures in *Atrahasis* cut side deals to neutralize *their* master,[133] this manager starts cutting side deals with his master's clients in order to enhance his chances for future employment. This behavior does not at first glance seem "appropriate,"[134] yet like *Atrahasis*, the *Gospel of Luke* focuses not so much on surface behavior as under-the-surface intentions. Thus, even though this manager still loses his job, one cannot help but admire the "shrewdness" he displays under pressure.[135]

Jesus' *haggadic* approach to Torah really shines in this passage. This parable does not refer directly to Torah, nor does its primary authority-figure play anything more than a minor role. Most of the action takes place in the heart of the dishonest manager who successfully uses bribery as a "last resort."[136] Just as Enki goes out of his way to bypass Enlil, so this manager goes out of his way to bypass his master. Similarly Jesus

131. Luke 16:1 (διασκορπίζω). Jesus uses this verb to describe the younger son's behavior in the foregoing parable (Luke 15:13).

132. Luke 16:1–2. The words translated "manager" (οἰκονόμος) and "economy" (οἰκονομία) come from the same Gk root: οἶκος + νόμος ("house" + "law").

133. In *Atr* 1:376–83 Enki recommends to the *amēlūtū* that they cut a deal with Namtara in order to neutralize Enlil.

134. Some companies require their executives to sign non-compete agreements to stem the loss of clients to competitors (Garrison and Stevens, "Sign," 103–26).

135. Luke 16:8 (φρονίμως); the adjectival form appears in 12:42 (φρόνιμος).

136. *Atr* 1:182–83; Gen 38:1–26; Josh 2:1–21; Esth 5–7.

goes out of his way to tell an "inappropriate" story not easily outlined on a *halakic* grid, but one teeming with insights to which every listener can relate, even when it necessitates relearning and reimagining basic concepts like "power," "grace," "justice," and "law."

THE PARABLE OF THE POUNDS (LUKE 19:11–27)

This parable revisits the "master-slave" polarity introduced earlier in the "Parable of the Master and his Slaves."[137] It also shares several attributes with the "Parable of the Talents" in the *Gospel of Matthew*,[138] but what most distinguishes it from the Matthean parable is the motif of *kingship*.[139] The origin and intention of this motif is disputed,[140] but it is important to recognize here (a) that this is not the first mention of the slavery motif in *Luke*, nor (b) is this the first mention of the slavery motif in the "great literature." Where the "Parable of the Master and His Slaves" focuses on the attributes of "watchfulness" and "prudence," this one focuses on the motif of "productivity."[141] In fact, the word Luke uses to describe this "productivity" is a term Xenophon highlights in one of his historical dialogues:[142]

> *Dercylidas:* "Tell me, Meidias, did your father leave you master of his property?" *Meidias:* "Yes, indeed." *Dercylidas:* "And how many

137. Luke 12:35–48.

138. Matt 25:14–30.

139. That is, the "master" in the Lukan parable goes into a "far country" to receive a "kingly appointment" (βασιλεία, Luke 19:12, 15). Jülicher (*Gleichnisreden* 2:485) interprets this to mean that Luke refers to an allegory about a "throne pretender," a hypothesis still popular in older scholarly circles. Intratextually, of course, it's ironic that *Luke* uses βασιλεία instead of *Matthew* in this context (Burger, *Davidssohn*, 72–106; Kingsbury, *Matthew*, 96–103).

140. Some trace the "Parable of the Pounds" in its entirety to Jesus himself (Jeremias, *Parables*, 58–60; Crossan, *Parables*, 103), but others view the "royalty" attribute as something (perhaps an "allegory") created (or replicated) by the author of *Luke* (McGaughy, "Fear," 236–37). Some try to draw connections between the details in Luke 19:11–27 and Josephus' account of the journey of Archelaus to Rome to confirm his father's "royal appointment" (*A.J.* 17:213–23; *B.J.* 2:16–19; Jeremias, *Parables*, 59), but others disagree (e.g., Weinert, "Parable," 505–7).

141. Luke 19:16 (προσεργάζομαι).

142. The context of this conversation is a fifth century (BCE) conflict between a Persian warrior named Dercylidas who confiscates the possessions of a Greek man named Meidias (Xenophon, *Hellenica* 3:1:1–28).

houses did he have? How many farms? How many pastures?"
Meidias: (starts reciting a list of his "possessions" . . .) *Dercylidas:*
(interrupting) "Tell me, Meidias, to whom did Mania belong?"[143]
Meidias: "She belonged to Pharnabazus."[144] *Dercylidas:* "Then
don't her possessions belong to Pharnabazus?" *Meidias:* "Uh
. . . yes." *Dercylidas:* "Then they must now be ours since we are
victorious, and Pharnabazus has become our enemy. So, lead the
way to the place where the possessions of Mania—or rather of
Pharnabazus—are stored."

Confiscating Mania's possessions, Dercylidas then declares: "Gentlemen,
we have earned pay for the army (about 8,000 men) for almost a year;
and if we earn anything more, that, too, 'shall be produced.'"[145]

SUMMARY

The Teacher of Righteousness from Qumran and the Teacher of righteousness from Nazareth live in an historical era in which the end of
days is widely believed to be "at hand."[146] Both identify many kinds of
corruption they believe to be threatening the health of their respective
constituents.[147] Both view the entrenched corruption in Jerusalem as an
especially "big problem." The historical background against which each
leader operates is ambivalently fluid, and this creates a perfect take-over
environment for "foreign invasion."

The Qumranian Teacher has a priestly background, so naturally he
gravitates to *halakic* methods of *Torah* interpretation to deal with this
"big problem." Only occasionally do the texts from Qumran depict him
as a *prophet/sage*,[148] yet when they do they betray little of the haggadic
insight peppering the pages of Talmud and midrash. In the words attributed to the Nazarene teacher, however, one finds ambiguity and irony
and surprise and many other types of *haggadic* qualities. Manipulating
well-known metaphors and characters he tells stories about sheep, shep-

---

143. Mania is the wife of Zeneus, satrap of the region of Aeolis, and mother–in–law
of Meidias.

144. When Pharnabazus appoints Mania as satrap after her husband's death Meidias
becomes so angry he strangles her to death, then confiscates her family's assets.

145. Xenophon, *Hellenica* 3:1:28 (προσεργάζομαι).

146. Angel, *Chaos*, 99–161.

147. Ibid., 37–73, 99–161.

148. E.g., 1QpHab 7:1–8.

herds, lost coins, lost sons, rich employers, slaves, desperate managers, prudent managers, overstuffed warehouses, insensitive priests, desensitized Levites, "good" Samaritans, wounded travelers, and desperate pirates in order to create pedagogical situations designed to encourage his listeners to make wiser socioeconomic decisions. Deeply knowledgeable of Torah, he nevertheless quotes from it only when absolutely necessary, never overpowering or condescendingly cornering his listeners into making simplistic decisions rooted in fear or prejudice or ignorance or inexperience. Instead his goal is to help them find their way back to the canons of the Yahwistic imperative.

6

Conclusions and Applications

THE INTRODUCTION TO THIS book raises two questions: (1) How can a study of ancient Near Eastern socioeconomic conflict motifs help us understand the Bible? and (2) How can a literary-historical study of the Bible help us understand the socioeconomic values so deeply embedded in Western culture? Here at the conclusion it is now time to revisit these questions in order to ask whether the foregoing analysis offers any help toward addressing them more intelligently.

Responding to the first question it now seems appropriate to conclude, in light of the above survey, (a) that several of the socioeconomic conflict motifs within the "great literature" of the ancient Near East help shape the form and contents of the Hebrew Bible, and (b) that the Hebrew literary trajectory created by repetitive usage of these motifs penetrates deep into the Second Temple literature of the Hasmoneans, the Essenes, and the Nazarenes. Most of the motifs on this trajectory make their first appearance in the sophisticated mythopoeic critiques generated by the Mesopotamian scribes responsible for compiling together the epics of *Gilgamesh, Atrahasis,* and *Erra,* even though, as the above discussion repeatedly points out, this is hardly an exhaustive list. The Canaanites and the Egyptians—just to name two other scribal cultures—use similar motifs in their "great literature" to critique *their* economies.[1]

Working within this specific literary-historical context, the scribes responsible for compiling the Hebrew Bible therefore already have at their disposal a well-known array of socioeconomic conflict motifs. The

---

1. As Koch points out, it's more than a little "plausible" that a very old relationship exists between the Hebrew and Egyptian scribal cultures. Why? Because both focus on "the desirability of following basic norms that are necessary for the preservation of community and its participants" ("Ṣādäq," 53).

book of *Genesis* draws from this array to address the "big problems" of *acquisition* and *protection*, manipulating its "wild man"-vs.-"wise man" stories from several angles in order to address several socioeconomic issues. The book of *Exodus* boldly addresses the "big problem" of *slavery*, proposing a response less dependent on the ambivalent fence-sitting attitude of *Atrahasis* than the Yahwistic socioeconomic principle of *redemption*. The book of *Numbers* follows suit with several episodes designed to engage, however covertly and carefully, the "big problem" of *deprivation*. Finally, *Deuteronomy's* farewell speech identifies several "big problems" threatening the newly-formed boundaries of the Hebrew *covenant community*. Following Walter Burkert's observation that the "great literature" of a given culture always focuses on what it perceives to be its "universal imperative,"[2] this book suggests that the "universal imperative" in the Hebrew Bible can be boiled down to the following equation:

CREATION = ACQUISITION + PROTECTION.

Alexander's campaign is not the first "foreign invasion" to disrupt the Syro-Palestinian economy, but the culture of *acquisition* it imports over the Fertile Crescent sorely tests Judea's commitment to the Yahwistic imperative. On one end of the ideological continuum, the Hasmoneans respond to the Hellenistic invasion by focusing on external political matters, significantly ignoring its internal dynamics and thereby encouraging various degrees of syncretistic assimilation. On the other end of the continuum, puritan groups like the Qumran covenanters deal with the Alexandrian culture of *acquisition* by restricting Torah interpretation to legalistic categories governed almost entirely by the priestly principles of *halakic* reflection, thereby reducing Torah to little more than a litmus test for putting "foreigners" in their socio-political and socioeconomic "place." Among other rabbis, Jesus of Nazareth responds to this one-sidedness by re-interpreting Torah within *haggadic* as well as *halakic* categories in order to help his disciples rediscover the Yahwistic imperative in its original form.

Now to the second question: "How can a literary-historical study of the Bible help us understand the socioeconomic values so deeply embedded in contemporary Western culture?" In many ways this is a more difficult question, not simply because it is harder to implement than to theorize, to make application than to explain, but because the level of

2. Burkert, *Structure*, 16–22.

uncertainty about the future health of the global economy remains frustratingly high.[3] However, though the footnotes sprinkled throughout the foregoing chapters often nibble at the challenge of application, it is time to take a few larger bites.

First, *corruption* continues to be a "big problem" in the contemporary global economy. Whether it is as big a problem now as it was in the economies of the ancient Near East is not immediately determinable, of course, yet researchers *are* successfully quantifying it within various segments of the contemporary global community.[4] One of the most comprehensive of these attempts is the annual Corruption Perceptions Index (CPI) published by an organization called Transparency International (TI).[5] According to TI's 2008 CPI, for example, the most corrupt countries in the world are Somalia, Iraq, Myanmar, and Haiti (the least corrupt being Denmark, New Zealand, Sweden and Singapore).[6] These results differ only slightly from those published in previous CPIs, where, for example, Bangladesh, Nigeria, Paraguay and Madagascar are the most corrupt countries (2001), and Chad, Bangladesh, Turkmenistan and Myanmar are the most corrupt a few years later (2005).[7] Whether or not one agrees with all the details in these findings (or the methods by which they are reached), it does not take a rocket scientist to figure out from these surveys that the poorer the country, the greater the possibility of socioeconomic *corruption*.[8]

Moreover, a fairly recent poll of North American voters suggests that contemporary American attitudes toward corruption also tend to be "heavily conditioned by socioeconomic background."[9] Exactly why is not readily determinable,[10] yet several studies show that upper-class

3. MacGillivray, *Globalization*, 5.

4. For recent introductions to this research see Fisman and Miguel, *Gangsters*; Mishra, *Corruption*; Rose-Ackerman, *Corruption*; Elliott, *Corruption*.

5. Go to www.transparency.org.

6. Go to www.transparency.org/policy_research/surveys_indices/cpi/2008.

7. Go to www.transparency.org/policy_research/surveys_indices/cpi/2001.

8. Whether these higher corruption levels are a cause or an effect of poverty is a much-debated question. To understand the statistical methods used by TI in its CPI surveys, go to http://www.transparency.org/policy_research/surveys_indices/cpi.

9. Redlawsk and McCann, "Corruption," 261.

10. Redlawsk and McCann conclude that "the term 'corruption' is fundamentally ambiguous in American politics. It means different things to different individuals, and these divergent understandings can have markedly different political implications" ("Corruption," 262).

folk ("Annunaki") tend to think more legalistically about the problem than do their lower-class neighbors ("Igigi").[11] Researchers propose several possible explanations for this result,[12] but the only reason for citing it here is to illustrate how much the literary scenarios preserved in the "great literature" of the ancient Near East—the literary environment in which the Bible first comes to life—still resonate with contemporary (postmodern) reality. What these results suggest, in other words, is that the greater the awareness of this literature, the easier it is to understand why (a) no "single term is more frequently employed" in contemporary socioeconomic literature than the word *corruption*;[13] and (b) why global organizations like Transparency International give so much attention to it.[14]

Second, *bribery* remains a "big problem" today, not least because it is so difficult to define it within a pluralized global context.[15] Michael Philips addresses this problem by (a) defining "bribery" from an exhaus-

11. Johnston, "Corruption," 367–91. Redlawsk and McCann report (a) that "law-breaking" is more problematic for lower-class respondents than "favoritism," and further, (b) that "favoritism" is less problematic for upper-class respondents than actual "law-breaking" ("Corruption," 262).

12. "It may well be that what lower and middle status people regard as illegitimate favors and advantages are seen by higher status groups as merely the fruits of merit and expertise ... The legitimacy of special favors and privileges, it seems, has much to do with whether one views them from above or below" (Johnston, "Corruption," 387).

13. Brooks, "Corruption," 1.

14. In addition to TI, the following organizations regularly measure the impact of bribery and corruption on the global economy: the Bertelsmann Foundation (www.bertelsmann-stiftung.de/cps/rde/xchg/SID-0A000F0A-D2A7CCFB/bst_engl/hs.xsl/307.htm), the World Bank (http://web.worldbank.org/WBSITE/EXTERNAL/EXTABOUTUS/IDA/0,,contentMDK:20941073~pagePK:51236175~piPK:437394~theSitePK:73154,00.html), the *Economist* Intelligence Unit (www.eiu.com/), Freedom House (www.freedomhouse.org/template.cfm?page=1), Global Insight (www.globalinsight.com/), Merchant International Group (www.merchantinternational.com/investigations.php), the International Institute for Management Development (http://www.imd.ch/), Political and Economic Risk Consultancy (http://www.asiarisk.com/), and the World Economic Forum (http://www.weforum.org/en/index.htm). Other organizations have headquarters "on the field"; e.g., the Asian Development Bank (www.adb.org/About/default.asp), and the African Development Bank (www.afdb.org/).

15. "It is not easy to define exactly what constitutes bribery and other corrupt practices. Clear-cut cases do exist, but greyer areas arise in connection with facilitation payments, gifts and hospitality, conflicts of interest and use of intermediaries" (Gordon and Miyake, "Bribery," 162). See Argandoña, "Corruption," 251–64; Manion, "Corruption," 167–95; Beekun and Badawi, "Islamic Perspective," 131–45.

tively deductive perspective,[16] and (b) distinguishing it from other practices like "extortion" and "gift-giving."[17] Others define it more inductively; e.g., by comparing hundreds of corporate codes of conduct in order to ascertain the greatest areas of procedural overlap,[18] or by reimagining bribery *not* as a two-party, but as a *three*-party transaction: (a) the bribe-payer; (b) the bribe-taker; and (c) the employer from whom bribe-taking employees withdraw their "loyalty."[19]

Transparency International publishes a Bribe Payers Index based on surveys of the behavior of senior business executives operating in twenty-six countries.[20] Unlike other inductive analyses focusing on the values and behaviors of bribe-*takers*, however, the TI Bribe Payers Index focuses on the values and behaviors of bribe-*payers*: "Corruption and bribery are complex transactions that involve both someone who offers a benefit, often a bribe, and someone who accepts, as well as a variety of specialists or intermediaries to facilitate the transaction. By perpetuating the 'abuse of entrusted power for private gain' [TI's definition of 'corruption'] both the bribe-payer and bribe-taker cause damage in a number of

---

16. Philips defines "bribery" in three stages: "P is bribed by R if and only if (a) P accepts payment from R to act on R's behalf, (b) P's act on R's behalf consists in violating some rule or understanding constitutive of a practice in which P is engaged, and (c) either P's violation is a violation of some official duty P has by virtue of his participation in that practice or P's violation significantly affects the interests of persons or organizations whose interests are typically connected to that practice" ("Bribery," 625–26).

17. Philips, "Bribery," 629–36. By blurring the boundaries between "bribery" and "gift-giving," for example, some observers label inflated CEO salaries as simply another form of "bribery" (e.g., Bishop, "Salaries," 1–11).

18. Gordon and Miyake, "Bribery," 161–73.

19. As D'Andrade puts it, "If we think of bribing as a form of employing then the person bribed has two separate employers. In that situation he can only act as a faithful agent of both if he is able to strictly separate the times he acts as agent for each employer … But typically bribes are offered to obtain the reverse of what a person would otherwise do as an employee. Think of the most common examples: the person bribed acts against the interests of his original employer by substituting the second (bribing) employer's desires for his presumed concern for the first employer's business" ("Bribery," 242).

20. These countries are Argentina, Brazil, Chile, the Czech Republic, Egypt, France, Germany, Ghana, Hungary, India, Indonesia, Japan, Malaysia, Mexico, Morocco, Nigeria, Pakistan, the Philippines, Poland, Russia, Senegal, Singapore, South Africa, South Korea, the United Kingdom and the United States (Riaño and Hodess, "Report," 14–15).

ways. Ultimately, their corrupt dealings create extreme inequity, both in markets and in societies."[21]

Questions: Is it merely coincidental that the academic and organizational institutions most effectively identifying the problems of *corruption* and *bribery* in the global economy are headquartered in *Western* countries? Is it merely coincidental that the individuals leading these institutions are uniformly trained at *Western* schools using *Western* curricula? Is it merely coincidental that these curricula operate on the basis of a value system rooted (directly or indirectly) in the principles of the Judeo-Christian heritage? And is it merely coincidental that the ideological center of the Judeo-Christian tradition is the Bible?[22]

Third, *slavery* remains a surprisingly "big problem" in the global economy, however concealed it might be from the eyes of the general public. The foregoing chapters do not attempt to examine its historical origins,[23] only (a) the tortuously ambivalent ways in which "great texts" like *Atrahasis* try to justify it; (b) the straightforward way documents like *Exodus* try to challenge it; (c) the way in which early "foreign invaders" try to institutionalize it; and (d) the way in which early Nazarene literature tries to redefine it.

Yet slavery is still a "big problem." According to one source, in fact, "there are more slaves today than at any time in human history."[24]

> For our purposes, let's say that the center of the moral universe is in Room S-3800 of the UN Secretariat in Manhattan. From here, you are some five hours from being able to negotiate the sale, in broad daylight, of a healthy boy or girl. Your slave will come in any color you like, as Henry Ford said, as long as it's black. Maximum age: fifteen. He or she can be used for anything. Sex or domestic labor are the most frequent uses . . . You are living at a time when there are more slaves than at any point in history.[25]

21. Riaño and Hodess, "Report," 2.

22. In Gunkel's words, "the gods of the Babylonians passed away when their time came. The hearts of the heathen turned to little Judah when the time was fulfilled. This enormous historical event, under whose influence the whole of world history stands, must have had a most mighty cause" (*Israel*, 55).

23. Dandamaev, *Slavery*; Stolper, "Registration," 80–101; Baker, "Degrees," 18–26; Chirichigno, *Debt-Slavery*; Gelb, "Freedom," 84–85.

24. Skinner, "Enslaved," 62.

25. Skinner, *Crime*, 1–2.

Of course, the slavery *business* is not something with which most readers of this book have much knowledge or interest,[26] but this hardly implies that Westerners live fully emancipated lives. In fact, the *form* of slavery which most readily plagues the lives of contemporary Westerners, the one which most readily and thoroughly bridges the Grand Canyon separating *this* world from the ancient world, is *debt-slavery*. Classically defined, debt-slavery is a "form of bondage resulting from a situation of debtor insolvency."[27] Often it appears in two forms, *internal* and *external*. Internally, for example, "whoever breaks a taboo (especially relative to mourning) or offends a man, or accidentally causes a fire, or destroys wealth, has to provide compensation in the form of appropriate payment; if he is unable to do so, he is put into a form of bondage to the injured party."[28] Externally, however, communities throughout the world experience this phenomenon whenever they are forced to experience the results of war/invasion/colonization.[29]

Better known among most readers of this book, however, are two types of "debt-slavery" which have proven themselves to be most prone to attack the socioeconomic stability of both friends and family; viz., (a) catastrophic *divorce,* and (b) catastrophic *illness.* With regard to the first type of "slavery," everyone reading these lines probably knows somebody who has suffered some degree of financial pain as a direct result of catastrophic *divorce.* Researchers routinely document this reality as the dark side of the "divorce revolution."[30] One influential study, for example, reports a 73 percent decline in the income of divorced women within the first year of marital divorce, a startling statistic which is rendered even more startling by the corollary report that the income of divorced

26. See Tucker, "Slaves," 572–629. Bechard reports that "against their will, children are trafficked mostly into the international sex trade for prostitution, sex tourism, and pornography. Outside of sexual exploitation children are used for organ harvesting, forced labor, soldiers in rebel armies, domestic servitude, street beggers and camel jockeys. Whatever their purpose, whatever act they are forced to perform, the victims of child trafficking become, by any definition, slaves" (*Unspeakable,* 2).

27. Testart, "Debt Slavery," 175.

28. Ibid., 173.

29. Alfred Kroeber documents this phenomenon among the Yurok tribe of northern California in the first half of the twentieth century (*Handbook,* 1–97); Smith and Dale document it for the Ila-speaking tribes of central Africa (*Rhodesia*).

30. Weitzman, *Divorce,* 337–39.

men actually *increases* by 42 percent.[31] Many challenge these numbers, of course, re-calculating the drop in women's income as "only" about 27 percent, and the increase in men's income as "only" about 10 percent.[32] Still others, however, rely on the data gathered by the Survey of Labor and Income Dynamics (SLID), and suggest that the "dramatic drop" in divorced women's income corresponds to a relatively "slight drop" in the income of divorced men,[33] then climbs to about 80 percent of divorced men's income after one year. Regardless of the possibilities, however, the socioeconomic "slavery" experienced by millions of Americans (like the soccer mom outside my office door) ranges anywhere from "significant" to "severe."

Second, catastrophic *illness* contributes to Western "debt-slavery" among millions of people within aging nations like the U.S.[34] According to a report of the U.S. Subcommittee on Health and Long-Term Care of the House Select Committee on Aging, in fact, the degree to which American citizens experience financial ruin from catastrophic illness is downright alarming. Each year (according to this already-dated report),[35] about twenty million Americans fall victim to catastrophic illness. Of this number, about five million go without health care while "countless others suffer great financial hardship,"[36] struggling to pay for whatever health care they can find.[37] Of course, the challenge of designing and implementing a health care system which fairly and equitably addresses this "big problem" is one of the greatest challenges of the twenty-first century, yet until or unless something happens to change the *status quo*, millions of Americans will continue to suffer this type of *slavery* as well.[38]

31. Ibid., 266–68.

32. Peterson, "Divorce," 528–36.

33. Gadalla, "Impact," 55–65. More can be learned about SLID at www.statcan.gc.ca/cgi-bin/imdb/p2SV.pl?Function=getSurvey&SDDS=3889&lang=en&db=imdb&adm=8&dis=2.

34. Schultz and Binstock, *Aging Nation*, 223–36.

35. Bacon, "Long-Term," 146–54.

36. Ibid., 147.

37. Defining "poverty" is to some extent a subjective enterprise, but in 2009 the U.S. Dept. of Health and Human Services set the "poverty line" for a household of four at $22,050 (http://aspe.hhs.gov/poverty/09poverty.shtml).

38. Folland, *Economics*, 281–308; Feldstein, *Health*, 412.

Fourth, *addiction* is a persistently "big problem" in many Western families, causing in some cases a great deal of pain.[39] Different types of addiction generate different types of pain, of course,[40] and researchers take a variety of positions on the "nature-vs.-nurture" debate,[41] yet according to the book of *Numbers* and the *Gospel of Luke* no addiction is identifiable apart from the volitional choices individuals make with regard to the "deprivation myth," particularly when these choices lead to lifestyles where "work" and "rest" conflict and clash.

Much more might be said, but perhaps enough *has* been said to show that the socioeconomic conflict motifs embedded within the primary literature of the Judeo-Christian tradition remain an enormously untapped resource for postmodern Westerners seeking to learn how to identify and address the socioeconomic problems so dramatically affecting their daily lives. Whether this readership will engage this literature from perspectives akin to the Hasmoneans, Essenes, or Nazarenes is another question for another book.

39. See the essays published from two different conferences, the first in the UK (Vuchinich and Heather, *Choice*), and the second in the U.S. (Chaloupka, *Substance*).

40. Four of the most common are *drug addiction* (Needle, "Costs," 1125–43), *sexual addiction* (Schneider, "Rebuilding," 288–94), *food-addiction* (Morrill and Chinn, "Obesity," 353–66) and *work-addiction* (Killinger, *Workaholics*).

41. Nestler and Aghajanian, "Molecular," 58–63; Billard and Dayananda, "Addiction," 649–62.

Bibliography

Abel, Félix-Marie. *Histoire de la Palestine depuis la conquête d'Alexandre jusqu'à l'invasion arabe.* Paris: Gabalda, 1952.

———. *Les Livres des Maccabees.* Paris: Gabalda, 1949.

Abela, Anthony M. "Genesis 13: Abraham Discovers the Land as God's Gift." *Melita Theologica* 38 (1987) 53–80.

Aberbach, Moses. *Jewish Education and History: Continuity, Crisis and Change.* London: Routledge, 2009.

Abrahams, Israel, and Cecil Roth. "Cassuto, Umberto." In *EJ* 4:510–11.

Abusch, Tzvi. *Babylonian Witchcraft Literature.* Atlanta: Scholars, 1987.

———. "Ishtar." In *DDD* 452–56.

———. "Ishtar's Proposal and Gilgamesh's Refusal." *History of Religions* 26 (1986) 143–87.

———. "The Development and Meaning of the Epic of Gilgamesh: An Interpretive Essay." *JAOS* 121 (2002) 614–22.

Achcar, Gilbert. *The Clash of Barbarisms: The Making of the New World Disorder.* Boulder, CO: Paradigm, 2006.

Achtemeier, Paul, et al. *Introducing the New Testament: Its Literature and Theology.* Grand Rapids: Eerdmans, 2001.

Ackerman, Kenneth D. *Young J. Edgar: Hoover, The Red Scare, and the Assault on Civil Liberties.* New York: Carroll and Graf, 2007.

Ackerman, Susan. "The Queen Mother and the Cult in Ancient Israel." *JBL* 112 (1993) 385–401.

———. *When Heroes Love: The Ambiguity of Eros in the Stories of Gilgamesh and David.* New York: Columbia University Press, 2005.

———. "Why Is Miriam Also among the Prophets? (and Is Zipporah among the Priests?)." *JBL* 121 (2002) 47–80.

Adam, A. K. M. *Faithful Interpretation: Reading the Bible in a Postmodern World.* Minneapolis: Fortress, 2006.

Adams, Peter J. *Fragmented Intimacy: Addiction in a Social World.* New York: Springer, 2008.

Adams, Robert McCormick. "Early Civilization, Subsistence, and Environment." In *City Invincible: A Symposium on Urbanization and Cultural Development in the Ancient Near East,* edited by Carl H. Kraeling and Robert McCormick Adams, 269–95. Chicago: University of Chicago Press, 1960.

Adler, Jonathan E. "Lying, Deceiving, or Falsely Implicating." *Journal of Philosophy* 94 (1997) 435–52.

Agarwal, Bina. *A Field of One's Own: Gender and Land Rights in South Asia.* Cambridge: Cambridge University Press, 1994.

Aguilar, Mario I. "Maccabees—Symbolic Wars and Age Sets: The Anthropology of War in *1 Maccabees.*" In *Ancient Israel: The Old Testament in Its Social Context,* edited by Philip Esler, 240–53. Minneapolis: Fortress, 2006.

Ahiakpor, James C. *Classical Macroeconomics: Some Modern Variations and Distortions.* New York: Routledge, 2003.

Ahituv, Shmuel. *Handbook of Ancient Hebrew Inscriptions.* Jerusalem: Mosad Bialik, 1992.

Ahroni, Reuben. "Why Did Esau Spurn the Birthright? A Study in Biblical Interpretation." *Judaism* 29 (1980) 323–31.

Aitken, Kenneth T. "The Wooing of Rebekah: A Study in the Development of the Tradition." *JSOT* 30 (1984) 3–23.

Alberts, Robert H. "Shame: A Dynamic in the Etiology of Violence." *Dialog* 36 (1997) 254–65.

Albright, William Foxwell. "Gilgamesh and Engidu: Mesopotamian Genii of Fecundity." *JAOS* 40 (1920) 307–35.

———. "The Archaeological Results of an Expedition to Moab and the Dead Sea." *BASOR* 14 (1924) 2–12.

———. *Yahweh and the Gods of Canaan.* Garden City, NY: Doubleday, 1968.

Alcorn, Randy C. *Money, Possessions, and Eternity.* Wheaton: Tyndale House, 2003.

Alexander, Bruce K. *The Globalization of Addiction: A Study in Poverty of the Spirit.* New York: Oxford University Press, 2010.

Alexander, T. D. "Are the Wife/Sister Incidents of Genesis Literary Compositional Variants?" *VT* 62 (1992) 145–53.

"Alexander the Great." In *EWB* 1:137–41.

Alford, C. Fred. *Whistleblowers: Broken Lives and Organizational Power.* Ithaca: Cornell University Press, 2002.

Allen, James P. *The Ancient Egyptian Pyramid Texts.* Atlanta: Society of Biblical Literature, 2005.

Al-Rawi, F. N. H. and J. A. Black. "The Second Tablet of Išum and Erra." *Iraq* 51 (1989) 111–22.

Alster, Bendt. "*Ilu awilum* : *We-e i-la,* 'Gods : Men' versus 'Man : God': Punning and the Reversal of Patterns in the *Atrahasis Epic.*" In *Riches Hidden in Secret Places: Ancient Near Eastern Studies in Memory of Thorkild Jacobsen,* edited by Tzvi Abusch, 35–40. Winona Lake, IN: Eisenbrauns, 2002.

Alt, Albrecht. "Anteil des Königtums an der sozialen Entwicklung in den Reichen Israel und Juda." In *Kleine Schriften zur Geschichte des Volkes Israel,* 348–72. Munich: Beck, 1968.

———. "The God of the Fathers." 1929. Translated by Robert A. Wilson. In *Essays on Old Testament History and Religion,* 1–77. Sheffield: JSOT, 1989.

Alter, Robert. "How Important Are the Dead Sea Scrolls?" *Commentary* 93 (1992) 34–41.

———. *The Art of Biblical Narrative.* New York: Basic, 1981.

———. "Sacred History and the Beginnings of Prose Fiction." *Poetics Today* 1 (1980) 143–62.

Altschuler, D. "On the Classification of Judaic Laws in the *Antiquities* of Josephus and the *Temple Scroll* of Qumran." *AJS Review* 7 (1982) 1–14.

Amador, Hester. *Academic Constraints in Rhetorical Criticism of the New Testament: An Introduction to a Rhetoric of Power.* Sheffield: Sheffield Academic, 1999.

Anderson, Robert T., and Terry Giles. *The Keepers: An Introduction to the History and Culture of the Samaritans*. Peabody, MA: Hendrickson, 2002.

Angel, Andrew R. *Chaos and the Son of Man: The Hebrew* Chaoskampf *Tradition in the Period 515 BCE to 200 CE*. London: T. & T. Clark, 2006.

Annus, Amar, and Alan Lenzi. *Ludlul bēl nēmeqi: The Standard Babylonian Poem of the Righteous Sufferer*. Helsinki: Neo-Assyrian Text Corpus Project, 2010.

Appadurai, Arjun. "Grassroots Globalization and the Research Imagination." *Public Culture* 12 (2000) 1–19.

————. *Modernity at Large: Cultural Dimensions of Globalization*. Minneapolis: University of Minnesota Press, 1996.

Appleby, Joyce Oldham. *Inheriting the Revolution: The First Generation of Americans*. Cambridge, MA: Harvard Belknap, 2001.

ApRoberts, Ruth. *The Biblical Web*. Ann Arbor: University of Michigan Press, 1994.

Arbel, Vita Daphna. *Beholders of Divine Secrets: Mysticism and Myth in the Hekhalot and Merkevah Literature*. Albany: State University of New York, 2003.

Archi, Alfonso. "'Debt' in an Archaic Palatial Economy: The Evidence from Ebla." In *Debt and Economic Renewal in the Ancient Near East*, edited by Michael Hudson and Marc van de Mieroop, 95–108. Bethesda, MD: CDL, 2002.

————. "Further Concerning Ebla and the Bible." *BA* 44 (1981) 145–54.

Arendt, Hannah. *On Revolution*. New York: Viking, 1963.

Argandoña, Antonio. "Corruption and Companies: The Use of Facilitating Payments." *JBE* 60 (2005) 251–64.

Arndt, H. W. "The 'Trickle-Down' Myth." *Economic Development and Cultural Change* 32 (1982) 1–10.

Arneth, Martin. *"Sonne der Gerechtigkeit": Studien zur Solarisierung der Jahwe-Religion im Lichte von Psalm 72*. Wiesbaden: Harrassowitz, 2000.

Arnold, Bill. "What Has Nebuchadnezzar to Do with David?" In *Mesopotamia and the Bible*, edited by Mark W. Chavalas and K. Lawson Younger, Jr., 330–55. Grand Rapids: Baker, 2002.

Artzi, Pinchas. "Some Unrecognized Syrian Amarna Letters." *JNES* 27 (1968) 163–71.

Asenjo, Bill. "Addiction." In *GEM* 1:50–53.

Assmann, Jan. *Die Mosaische Unterscheidung: Der Preis des Monotheismus*. München: Hanser, 2003.

————. "Isis." In *DDD* 456–58.

Attridge, Harold W. "Historiography." In *Jewish Writings of the Second Temple Period*, edited by Michael Edward Stone, 157–84. Assen: Van Gorcum, 1984.

Aune, David E. "Heracles." In *ABD* 3:141–43.

Aus, Roger David. *Weihnachtsgeschichte—Barmherziger Samariter—Verlorener Sohn: Studien zu ihrem jüdischen Hintergrund*. Berlin: Institut Kirche und Judentum, 1988.

————. "Luke 15:11–32 and R. Eliezer ben Hyrcanus's Rise to Fame." *JBL* 104 (1985) 443–69.

Avemarie, Friedrich. "טהרות הרבים and משקה הרבים: Jacob Licht Reconsidered." In *Legal Texts and Legal Issues: Proceedings of the Second Meeting of the International Organization for Qumran Studies, Cambridge 1995, Published in Honour of Joseph M. Baumgarten*, edited by Moshe Bernstein et al., 215–29. Leiden: Brill, 1997.

Avishur, Yitzhak. *Stylistic Studies of Word-Pairs in Biblical and Ancient Semitic Literatures*. Neukirchen-Vluyn: Neukirchener, 1984.

Avi-Yonah, Michael. "Beth Zur." In *EJ* 3:555.

Avruch, Kevin. "Reciprocity, Equality, and Status-Anxiety in the Amarna Letters." In *Amarna Diplomacy: The Beginnings of International Relations*, edited by Raymond Cohen and Raymond Westbrook, 154–64. Baltimore: Johns Hopkins, 2000.

Bachvarova, Mary R. "Relations between God and Man in the Hurro-Hittite *Song of Release*." *JAOS* 125 (2005) 45–58.

Bacon, Peter W., et al. "Long-Term Catastrophic Care: A Financial Planning Perspective." *Journal of Risk and Insurance* 56 (1989) 146–54.

Bahrani, Zainab. "The Hellenization of Ishtar: Nudity, Fetishism, and the Production of Cultural Differentiation in Ancient Art." *Oxford Art Journal* 19 (1996) 3–16.

Bailey, John A. "Initiation and the Primal Woman in Gilgamesh and Genesis 2–3." *JBL* 89 (1970) 137–50.

Bailey, Kenneth E. *Finding the Lost: Cultural Keys to Luke 15*. St. Louis, MO: Concordia, 1992.

Bailkey, Nels M. "A Babylonian Philosopher of History." *Osiris* 9 (1950) 106–30.

Baines, John. "Egyptian Myth and Discourse: Myth, Gods, and the Early Written and Iconographic Record." *JNES* 50 (1991) 81–105.

———. "Interpreting Sinuhe." *Journal of Egyptian Archaeology* 68 (1982) 31–44.

Baker, David L. *Tight Fists or Open Hands: Wealth and Poverty in Old Testament Law*. Grand Rapids: Eerdmans, 2009.

Baker, H. "Degrees of Freedom: Slavery in Mid-First Century Babylonia." *WA* 33 (2001) 18–26.

Bakhtin, Mikhail. *Problems of Dostoevsky's Poetics*. Minneapolis: University of Minnesota Press, 1984.

Balentine, Samuel E. "'For No Reason.'" *Int* 57 (2003) 349–69.

Bar, Shaul. *A Letter That Has Not Been Read: Dreams in the Hebrew Bible*. Cincinnati: Hebrew Union College Press, 2001.

Bard, Kathryn A. "The Egyptian Predynastic: A Review of the Evidence." *Journal of Field Archaeology* 21 (1994) 265–88.

Bar-Kochva, Bezalel. *Judas Maccabaeus: The Jewish Struggle against the Seleucids*. Cambridge: Cambridge University Press, 1989.

Baron, Salo W. and Arcadius Kahan. "Economic History." In *EJ* 6:95–138.

Barré, Michael L. "'Wandering About' as a *Topos* of Depression in Ancient Near Eastern Literature and the Bible." *JNES* 60 (2001) 177–87.

Barron, Bruce. *The Health and Wealth Gospel: What's Going On Today in a Movement that Has Shaped the Faith of Millions*. Downers Grove, IL: InterVarsity, 1987.

Barron, Patrick. "The Separation of Wild Animal Nature and Human Nature in Gilgamesh: Roots of a Contemporary Theme." *Papers on Language and Literature* 38 (2002) 377–94.

Bassler, Jouette. *God and Mammon: Asking for Money in the New Testament*. Nashville: Abingdon, 1991.

Batsch, Christophe. "Temps de la guerre et respect du sabbat dans Judith." In *Le Temps et les Temps dans les littératures juives et chrétiennes au tournant de notre ère*, edited by Christian Grappe and Jean-Claude Inglaere, 12–35. Leiden: Brill, 2006.

Batto, Bernard. *Slaying the Dragon: Mythmaking in the Biblical Tradition*. Louisville: Westminster John Knox, 1992.

———. "The Covenant of Peace: A Neglected Ancient Near Eastern Motif." *CBQ* 49 (1987) 187–211.

Bauckham, Richard. "The Scrupulous Priest and the Good Samaritan: Jesus' Parabolic Interpretation of the Law of Moses." *NTS* 44 (1998) 475–89.

———. "The Economic Critique of Rome in Revelation 18." In *Images of Empire*, edited by Loveday Alexander, 47–90. Sheffield: Sheffield Academic, 1991.

Baumgarten, Albert I. *The Flourishing of Jewish Sects in the Maccabean Era: An Interpretation.* Leiden: Brill, 1997.

———. "The Pharisaic *Paradosis.*" *HTR* 80 (1987) 63–77.

Baumgarten, Joseph M. "Damascus Document." In *EDSS* 1:166–70.

———. "On the Non-Literal Use of the מעשר/ δεκάτη." *JBL* 103 (1984) 245–61.

———. "The Pharisaic-Sadducean Controversies about Purity and the Qumran Texts." *JJS* 31 (1980) 157–70.

Beaulieu, Paul-Alain. *The Pantheon of Uruk in the Neo-Babylonian Period.* Leiden: Brill/ Styx, 2003.

Bechard, Raymond. *Unspeakable: The Hidden Truth Behind the World's Fastest-Growing Crime.* New York: Compel, 2006.

Beck, Martin. *Elia und die Monolatrie.* Berlin: de Gruyter, 1999.

Beckman, Gary. "The Hittite Gilgamesh." In *The Epic of Gilgamesh*, edited by Foster et al., 157–67. New York: Norton, 2001.

———. "The Religion of the Hittites." *BA* 52 (1989) 98–108.

Bediako, K. "John Mbiti's Contribution to African Theology." In *Religious Plurality in Africa: Essays Presented to John S. Mbiti,* edited by Jacob K. Olupona and Sulayman S. Nyang, 367–90. Berlin: Mouton/de Gruyter, 1993.

Beekun, Rafik I., and Jamal A. Badawi. "Balancing Ethical Responsibility among Multiple Organizational Stakeholders: The Islamic Perspective." *JBE* 60 (2005) 131–45.

Beinhocker, Eric D. *The Origin of Wealth: Evolution, Complexity, and the Radical Remaking of Economics.* Cambridge: Harvard Business School, 2006.

Bell, Carol. *The Evolution of Long Distance Trading Relationships across the LBA/Iron Age Transition on the Northern Levantine Coast: Crisis, Continuity and Change.* Oxford: Archaeopress, 2006.

Belsey, Catherine. *Shakespeare and the Loss of Eden: Construction of Family Values in Early Modern Culture.* New Brunswick, NJ: Rutgers University Press, 1999.

Benedict, Ruth. *Patterns of Culture.* Boston: Houghton Mifflin, 1959.

Ben-Reuven, Sara. "Measure for Measure in the Story of *Joseph.*" *Beit Mikra* 49 (2004) 185–90.

Bentley, Colene. "Family, Humanity, Polity: Theorizing the Basis and Boundaries of Political Community in *Frankenstein.*" *Criticism* 47 (2005) 325–51.

Benjamin. Don C. *Deuteronomy and City Life.* Lanham, MD: University Press of America, 1983.

Bentham, Jeremy. *The Rationale of Reward.* London: Hunt, 1825.

Bergmann, Claudia D. "We Have Seen the Enemy and He is only a 'She': The Portrayal of Warriors as Women." *CBQ* 69 (2007) 651–72.

Berkman, John. "The Consumption of Animals and the Catholic Tradition," *Logos: A Journal of Catholic Thought and Culture* 7 (2004) 174–90.

Berlejung, Angelika, and Bernd Janowski. *Tod und Jenseits im alten Israel und in seiner Umwelt: theologische, religionsgeschichtliche, archäologische, und ikonograpische Aspekte.* Tübingen: Mohr Siebeck, 2009.

Berlin, Adele. "Ethnopoetry and the Enmerkar Epics." *JAOS* 103 (1982) 17–24.

Bernal, Martin. *Black Athena: The Afroasiatic Roots of Classical Civilization.* New Brunswick: Rutgers University Press, 1987.

Bernheimer, Richard. *Wild Men in the Middle Ages: A Study in Art, Sentiment, and Demonology.* Cambridge, MA: Harvard University Press, 1952.

Bernstein, Moshe. "Pesher Habakkuk." In *EDSS* 2:647–50.

———. Review of *Reclaiming the Dead Sea Scrolls,* by Lawrence Schiffman. *AJS Review* 22 (1997) 77–93.

Berquist, Jon. "Resistance and Accomodation in the Persian Empire." In *In the Shadow of Empire: Reclaiming the Bible as a History of Faithful Resistance,* edited by Richard A. Horsley, 41–58. Louisville: Westminster John Knox, 2008.

Berridge, John M. "Jonathan." In *ABD* 3:942–44.

Bethge, Eberhard. *Dietrich Bonhoeffer: A Biography.* Minneapolis: Fortress, 2000.

Beuken, W. A. M. "Exodus 16:5, 23: A Rule Regarding the Keeping of the Sabbath," *JSOT* 32 (1985) 3–14.

Beye, Charles Rowan. "The Rhythm of Hesiod's *Works and Days.*" *Harvard Studies in Classical Philology* 76 (1972) 23–43.

Bickermann, Elias J. *Institutions des Séleucides.* Paris: P. Geuthner, 1938.

Biddle, Mark. "Ancestral Motifs in 1 Samuel 25: Intertextuality and Characterization." *JBL* 121 (2002) 617–38.

Billard, L. and P. W. A. Dayananda. "A Drug Addiction Model." *Journal of Applied Probability* 25 (1988) 649–62.

Bishop, John Douglas. "Crossing the Boundaries of Obligation: Are Corporate Salaries a Form of Bribery?" *JBE* 55 (2004) 1–11.

Blake, William. *The Complete Writings of William Blake: With Variant Readings,* edited by Geoffrey Keynes. London: Oxford University Press, 1972.

Blauner, Bob. *Resisting McCarthyism: To Sign or Not To Sign California's Loyalty Oath.* Palo Alto: Stanford University Press, 2009.

Blenkinsopp, Joseph. "Benjamin Traditions Read in the Early Persian Period." In *Judah and the Judeans in the Persian Period,* edited by Oded Lipschitz and Manfred Oeming, 629–45. Winona Lake, IN: Eisenbrauns, 2006.

———. "Judah's Covenant with Death (Isa xxviii 14–22)." *VT* 50 (2000) 472–83.

———. *Judaism, the First Phase: The Place of Ezra and Nehemiah in the Origins of Judaism.* Grand Rapids: Eerdmans, 2009.

———. *Sage, Priest, Prophet: Intellectual and Religious Leadership in Ancient Israel.* Louisville: Westminster John Knox, 1995.

———. *The Pentateuch: An Introduction to the First Five Books of the Bible.* New York: Doubleday, 1992.

———. *Treasures Old and New: Essays in the Theology of the Pentateuch.* Grand Rapids: Eerdmans, 2004.

Blight, David W. *Frederick Douglass' Civil War: Keeping Faith in Jubilee.* Baton Rouge, LA: Louisiana State University Press, 1989.

Blomberg, Craig L. *Interpreting the Parables.* Downers Grove, IL: InterVarsity, 1990.

Bloom, Allan David. *The Closing of the American Mind: How Higher Education has Failed Democracy and Impoverished the Souls of Today's Students.* New York: Simon & Schuster, 1987.

Bloxham, Eleanor. *Economic Value Management: Application and Techniques.* Hoboken, NJ: Wiley, 2002.

Blumenthal, H. Elchanan. "Night Prayer." In *EJ* 15:264.

Boadt, Lawrence. "Divine Wonders Never Cease: The Birth of *Moses* in God's Plan of Exodus." In *Preaching Biblical Texts: Expositions by Jewish and Christian Scholars,* edited by Frederick C. Holmgren and Herman E. Schalmaan, 46–61. Grand Rapids: Eerdmans, 1995.

Boccaccini, Gabriel. *Beyond the Essene Hypothesis: The Parting of the Ways between Qumran and Enochic Judaism.* Grand Rapids: Eerdmans, 1998.

Bockmuehl, M. "Redaction and Ideology in the Rule of the Community." *RevQ* 18 (1998) 541–60.

Bodi, Daniel. *The Book of Ezekiel and the Poem of Erra.* Göttingen: Vandenhoeck und Ruprecht, 1991.

Boehmer, Rainer M. "Uruk 1980–1990: A Progress Report," *Antiquity* 65 (1991) 465–78.

Boellstorff, Tom. *Coming of Age in Second Life: An Anthropologist Explores the Virtually Human.* Princeton: Princeton University Press, 2008.

Böhl, Franz Marius Theodor de Liagre. "Das problem der ewigen Lebens im Zyklus und Epos des Gilgamesch." In *Opera Minora*, 234–62. Groningen: Wolters, 1953.

Bokser, Baruch M. "Unleavened Bread and Passover." In *ABD* 6:755–65.

Bolle, Kees. "Myth: An Overview." In *ER* 9:6359–71.

Bornstein, David Joseph. "Ma`aserot." In *EJ* 13:313–14.

Botha, P. "Isaiah 37:21–35: Sennacherib's Siege of Jerusalem as a Challenge to the Honour of Yahweh." *OTE* 13 (2000) 269–82.

Bottéro, Jean. "Akkadian Literature." In *CANE* 4:2293–303.

———. "Désordre économique et annulation des dettes en Mésopotamie à l'époque paléo-babylonienne." *JESHO* 4 (1961) 113–67.

———. *Everyday Life in Ancient Mesopotamia.* Baltimore: Johns Hopkins Press, 2001.

———. *Religion in Ancient Mesopotamia.* Chicago: University of Chicago Press, 2001.

Bowditch, Phebe Lowell. *Horace and the Gift Economy of Patronage.* Berkeley: University of California Press, 2001.

Boyer, Paul. *When Time Shall Be No More: Prophecy Belief in Modern American Culture.* Cambridge, MA: Belknap, 1992.

Boyle, Charles R. "Am I My Brother's Keeper? The Semantics of Responsibility." *Lexington Theological Quarterly* 9 (1974) 89–99.

Branigan, Keith. *Urbanism in the Aegean Bronze Age.* Sheffield: Sheffield Academic, 2000.

Braulik, Georg. "The Political Impact of the Festival: Biblical Statements." *Skrif en Kerk* 20 (1999) 326–39.

Breck, John. *The Shape of Biblical Language: Chiasmus in the Scriptures and Beyond.* Crestwood, NY: St. Vladimir's Seminary, 1994.

Breitbart, Sidney. "The *Cain* and Abel Narratives: Problems and Lessons." *JBQ* 32 (2004) 122–24.

Brett, Mark G. *Genesis: Procreation and the Politics of Identity.* London: Routledge, 2000.

Brettler, Marc Zvi. *How to Read the Bible.* Philadelphia: Jewish Publication Society, 2005.

Brinkman, John Anthony. "Gilgamesh Epic." In *NCE* 6:222–24.

———. *A Political History of Post-Kassite Babylonia.* Rome: Pontifical Biblical Institute, 1968.

Brooke, George J. "The Kittim in the Qumran Commentaries." In *Images of Empire*, edited by Loveday Alexander, 135–59. Sheffield: JSOT, 1991.

Brooks, Robert C. "The Nature of Political Corruption." *Political Science Quarterly* 24 (1909) 1–22.

Brown, A. S. "Aphrodite and the Pandora Complex." *Classical Quarterly* 47 (1997) 26–47.

Brown, Raymond E. *An Introduction to the New Testament*. New York: Doubleday, 1997.

———. *The Epistles of John*. Garden City, NY: Doubleday, 1982.

Brown, Stephen G. "The Structure of Ecclesiastes." *Evangelical Review of Theology* 14 (1990) 195–208.

Brown, William P. *Seeing the Psalms: A Theology of Metaphor*. Louisville: Westminster John Knox, 2002.

Brownlee, William H. "Ezekiel's Parable of the Watchman and the Editing of Ezekiel." *VT* 28 (1978) 392–408.

———. "Muhammad Ed-Deeb's Own Story of his Scroll Discovery." *JNES* 16 (1957) 236–39.

Brueggemann, Walter. *Deep Memory, Exuberant Hope: Contested Truth in a Post-Christian World*. Minneapolis: Fortress, 2000.

———. *In Man We Trust*. Atlanta: John Knox, 1972.

———. "Pharaoh as Vassal: A Study of Political Metaphor." *CBQ* 57 (1995) 27–51.

———. *Theology of the Old Testament*. Minneapolis: Fortress, 1987.

———. "The Kerygma of the Priestly Writers." *ZAW* 84 (1972) 397–414.

———. *The Land*. Minneapolis: Fortress, 2002.

———. *Words That Linger, Texts that Explode*. Minneapolis: Fortress, 2000.

Brutti, Maria. *The Development of the High Priesthood During the Pre-Hasmonean Period: History, Ideology, Theology*. Leiden: Brill, 2006.

Bryan, Betsy M. "The Egyptian Perspective on Mitanni." In *Amarna Diplomacy: The Beginnings of International Relations*, edited by Raymond Cohen and Raymond Westbrook, 71–84. Baltimore: Johns Hopkins University Press, 2000.

Brzezinski, Zbigniew. *Out of Control: Global Turmoil on the Eve of the 21st Century*. New York: MacMillan, 1993.

Buchan, James. *Frozen Desire: The Meaning of Money*. New York: Farrar, Strauss, Giroux, 1997.

Buchholz, Todd G. "Biblical Laws and the Economic Growth of Ancient Israel." *Journal of Law and Religion* 6 (1988) 389–427.

Budge, Ernest Alfred Wallis. *The Book of the Cave of Treasures*. London: Religious Tract Society, 1927.

Bultmann, Rudolf. "ἀφίημι." In *TDNT* 1:509–12.

Burger, Christoph. *Jesus als Davidssohn. Eine traditionsgeschichtliehe Untersuchung*. Göttingen: Vandenhoeck and Ruprecht, 1970.

Burgess, Ann Wolbert, et al. *Victimology: Theories and Applications*. Sudbury, MA: Jones and Bartlett, 2009.

Burke, Aaron A. *"Walled Up to Heaven": The Evolution of Middle Bronze Age Fortification Strategies in the Levant*. Winona Lake, IN: Eisenbrauns, 2008.

Burkert, Walter. *Structure and History in Greek Mythology and Ritual*. Berkeley: University of California Press, 1979.

Burrows, Millar. *More Light on the Dead Sea Scrolls*. New York: Viking, 1958.

Butler, Sally A. L. *Mesopotamian Conceptions of Dreams and Dream Rituals*. Münster: Ugarit, 1998.

Butting, Klara. "Abel steh auf! Die Geschichte von Kain und Abel—und Schet (Gen 4.1–26)." *Bibel und Kirche* 58 (2003) 16–19.

Butzer, K. "Environmental Change in the Near East and Human Impact on the Land." In *CANE* 1:123–52.

Byron, John. "Living in the Shadow of Cain: Echoes of a Developing Tradition in James 5:1–6." *NT* 48 (2006) 261–74.

―――. *Slavery Metaphors in Early Judaism and Pauline Christianity*. Tübingen: Mohr Siebeck, 2003.

Cadwallader, Alan H. "Where to Now, Good Samaritan?" *St. Mark's Review* 196 (2004) 7–15.

Cagni, Luigi. *L'Epopea di Erra*. Roma: Istituto di Studi del Vicino Oriente, 1969.

―――. *The Poem of Erra*. Malibu: Undena, 1977.

Cahill, Thomas. *The Gifts of the Jews*. New York: Talese/Doubleday, 1998.

Caine, Ivan. "Numbers in the Joseph Narrative." *Jewish Civilization: Essays and Studies* 1 (1979) 3–17.

Cameron, Rondo E., and Larry Neal. *A Concise Economic History of the World*. 4th ed. New York: Oxford, 2003.

Capdetrey, Laurent. *Le pouvoir séleucide: territoire, administration, finances d'un royaume hellénistique*. Rennes: Presses universitaires de Rennes, 2007.

Caplice, Richard I. *The Akkadian Namburbi Texts: An Introduction*. Los Angeles: Undena, 1974.

Carlyle, Thomas. *Chartism*. London: Fraser, 1840.

Carmichael, Calum M. *The Origins of Biblical Law: The Decalogues and the Book of the Covenant*. Ithaca: Cornell University Press, 1992.

Carr, Edward Hallett. *A History of Soviet Russia*. Baltimore: Penguin, 1966.

Carroll, Michael P. "Leach, Genesis, and Structural Analysis: A Critical Evaluation." *American Ethnologist* 4 (1977) 663–77.

Chae, Young S. *Jesus as the Eschatological Davidic Shepherd: Studies in the Old Testament, Second Temple Judaism, and in the Gospel of Matthew*. Tübingen: Mohr/Siebeck, 2006.

Chalcraft, David J. *Sectarianism in Early Judaism: Sociological Advances*. London: Equinox, 2007.

Chaloupka, Frank J., et al. *The Economic Analysis of Substance Use and Abuse: An Integration of Econometric and Behavioral Economic Research*. Chicago: University of Chicago Press, 1999.

Chan, A. "Goddesses in Chinese Religions." In *Goddesses in Religions and Modern Debate*, edited by Larry Hurtado, 9–81. Atlanta: Scholars, 1990.

Chaney, Marvin. "Bitter Bounty: The Dynamics of Political Economy Critiqued by the Eighth-Century Prophets." In *Reformed Faith and Economics*, edited by Robert L. Stivers, 15–30. New York: University Press of America, 1989.

Chavalas, Mark William, and Murray R. Adamthwaite. "Archaeological Light on the Old Testament." In *The Face of Old Testament Studies*, edited by David W. Baker and Bill T. Arnold, 59–96. Grand Rapids: Baker, 1999.

Chayanov, Alexander. *The Theory of Peasant Cooperatives*, 1919. Reprint. London: I. B. Tauris, 1991.

Cheong, C.-S. Abraham. *A Dialogic Reading of The Steward Parable in Luke 16:1–9*. New York: Lang, 2001.

Chesson, Meredith, and G. Philip. "Tales of the City? 'Urbanism' in the Early Bronze Age Levant from Mediterranean and Levantine Perspectives." *Journal of Mediterranean Archaeology* 16 (2003) 3–16.

Childs, Brevard. *Exodus*. Philadelphia: Westminster, 1974.

―――. *Introduction to the Old Testament as Scripture*. Philadelphia: Fortress, 1979.

Chiodi, Silvia Maria. "An." In *ER* 1:301–3.

Chirichigno, Gregory C. *Debt-Slavery in Israel and the Ancient Near East.* Sheffield: Sheffield Academic, 1993.

Chu, C. Y. Cyrus. "Primogeniture." *Journal of Political Economy* 99 (1991) 78–99.

Clapp, Rodney. *The Consuming Passion: Christianity and the Consumer Culture.* Downers Grove, IL: InterVarsity, 1998.

Clements, Ronald E. "The Enduring Value of the Old Testament: An Interesting Quest." *BI* 16 (2008) 25–42.

Clifford, Richard J. *Creation Accounts in the Ancient Near East and in the Bible.* Washington: Catholic Biblical Association, 1994.

Cobb, John B. *Sustaining the Common Good: A Christian Perspective on the Global Economy.* Cleveland: Pilgrim, 1994.

Cogan, Mordechai. *The Raging Torrent: Historical Inscriptions from Assyria and Babylonia Relating to Ancient Israel.* Jerusalem: Carta, 2008.

Cohen, Art. "Godard/Lang/Godard—The Film-Within-the-Film: Finite Regress and Other Semiotic Strategies." *American Journal of Semiotics* 9 (1992) 115–29.

Cohen, Samy. *The Resilience of the State: Democracy and the Challenge of Globalization.* Boulder, CO: Rienner, 2006.

Cohen, Sande, and R. L. Rutsky. *Consumption in an Age of Information.* New York: Berg, 2005.

Cohn, Robert L. "Negotiating with the Natives: Ancestors and Identity in Genesis." *HTR* 96 (2003) 147–66.

Cole, Douglas. "Myth and Anti-Myth: The Case of *Troilus and Cressida.*" *Shakespeare Quarterly* 31 (1980) 76–84.

Cole, John W., and Eric R. Wolf. *The Hidden Frontier: Ecology and Ethnicity in an Alpine Valley.* New York: Academic, 1974.

Collins, John J. *Beyond the Qumran Community: The Sectarian Movement of the Dead Sea Scrolls.* Grand Rapids; Eerdmans, 2009.

———. "Introduction to Volume 1." In *EoA* 1:xiii–xvii.

———. Review of *Reclaiming the Dead Sea Scrolls,* by Lawrence Schiffman. *DSD* 2 (1995) 244–47.

———. *The Bible after Babel: Historical Criticism in a Postmodern Age.* Grand Rapids: Eerdmans, 2005.

———. "The Exodus and Biblical Theology." In *Jews, Christians, and Theology of the Hebrew Scriptures,* edited by Alice Ogden Bellis and Joel S. Kaminsky, 247–61. Atlanta: Society of Biblical Literature, 2000.

Colpe, Carsten. "Syncretism." In *ER* 13:8926–34.

Comor, Edward A. *The Global Political Economy of Communication: Hegemony, Telecommunication, and the Information Economy.* New York: St. Martin's, 1994.

Congreve, William. *The Mourning Bride.* Dublin: Powell, 1735.

Cook, Stephen L. "The Metamorphosis of a Shepherd: The Tradition History of Zech 11:17 + 13:7–9." *CBQ* 55 (1993) 453–66.

Cooper, Jerrold S. *The Curse of Agade.* Baltimore: Johns Hopkins, 1983.

———. Review of *Das altorientalische Menschenbild und die sumerischen und akkadischen Schöpfungsmythen,* by Giovanni Pettinato. *JAOS* 93 (1973) 581–85.

Coote, Robert B. "Tribalism: Social Organization in the Biblical Israels." In *Ancient Israel: The Old Testament in Its Social Context,* edited by Philip F. Esler, 35–49. Minneapolis: Fortress, 2006.

Copeland, Morris Albert. *Fact and Theory in Economics—The Testament of an Institutionalist: Collected Papers of Morris A. Copeland.* Edited by Chandler Morse. Ithaca, NY: Cornell University Press, 1958.

Corn, Alfred. *Incarnation: Contemporary Writers on the New Testament.* New York: Viking, 1990.

Coser, Lewis A. "Some Social Functions of Violence." *Annals of the American Academy of Political and Social Science* 364 (1966) 8–18.

Cotterill, Anne. "'Rebekah's Heir': Dryden's Late Mystery of Genealogy." *Huntington Library Quarterly* 63 (2000) 212.

Covey, Stephen R. *The Seven Habits of Highly Effective People.* New York: Simon and Schuster, 1989.

Cowgill, George L. "Origins and Development of Urbanism: Archaeological Perspectives." *Annual Review of Anthropology* 33 (2004) 525–49.

Crook, Zeba A. "Reciprocity: Covenantal Exchange as a Test Case." In *Ancient Israel: The Old Testament in Its Social Context*, edited by Philip F. Esler, 78–91. Minneapolis: Augsburg Fortress, 2006.

Cross, Frank Moore. "Prose and Poetry in the Mythic and Epic Texts from Ugarit." *HTR* 67 (1974) 1–15.

———. "Reuben, First-Born of Jacob." *ZAW* 100 (1988) 46–65.

———. "The 'Olden Gods' in Ancient Near Eastern Creation Myths." In *From Epic to Canon*, 73–83. Baltimore: Johns Hopkins, 1999.

———. "The Priestly Houses of Early Israel." In *Canaanite Myth and Hebrew Epic*, 195–215. Cambridge: Harvard University Press, 1973.

Crossan, John Dominic. *In Parables: The Challenge of the Historical Jesus.* New York: Harper and Row, 1973.

Cryer, Frederick H. *Divination in Ancient Israel and Its Ancient Near Eastern Environment: A Sociohistorical Investigation.* Sheffield: JSOT, 1994.

Cuffari, Anton. *Judenfeindschaft in Antike und Altem Testament.* Hamburg: Philo, 2007.

Cuthbertson, Gilbert Morris. *Political Myth and Epic.* East Lansing, MI: Michigan State University Press, 1975.

Dalley, Stephanie. *Myths from Mesopotamia: Creation, the Flood, Gilgamesh, and Others.* Oxford: Oxford University Press, 2009.

Damrosch, David. *The Narrative Covenant: Transformations of Genre in the Growth of Biblical Literature.* San Francisco: Harper and Row, 1987.

Dandamaev, Muhammad A. *Slavery in Babylonia from Nabopolassar to Alexander the Great.* DeKalb, IL: Northern Illinois University Press, 1984.

———. *Vavilonskie Pisci.* Moscow: Nauka, 1983.

D'Andrade, Kendall. "Bribery." *JBE* 4 (1985) 239–48.

Dasgupta, Partha. *Economics: A Very Short Introduction.* Oxford: Oxford University Press, 2006.

Davenport, Tracy. "An Anti-Imperialist Twist to the 'Gilgamesh Epic.'" In *Gilgamesh and the World of Assyria*, edited by Joseph Azize and Noel Weeks, 1–23. Leuven: Peeters, 2006.

Davidson, Jo Ann. "World Religions and the Vegetarian Diet." *Journal of the Adventist Theological Society* 14 (2003) 114–30.

Davies, Eryl W. "The Morally Dubious Passages of the Hebrew Bible: An Examination of Some Proposed Solutions." *Currents in Biblical Research* 3 (2005) 197–228.

Davies, Philip R. *Scribes and Schools: The Canonization of the Hebrew Scriptures.* Louisville: Westminster John Knox, 1998.

———. *The Damascus Covenant: An Introduction to the "Damascus Document."* Sheffield: JSOT, 1982.

Davies, William David. *Christian Origins and Judaism.* London: Darton, Longman, and Todd, 1962.

Davis, John B. *The Theory of the Individual in Economics: Identity and Value.* New York: Routledge, 2003.

Day, Peggy L. "Anat." In *DDD* 36–43.

———. "Anat: Ugarit's 'Mistress of Animals.'" *JNES* 51 (1992) 181–90.

Deist, Ferdinand E. *The Material Culture of the Bible: An Introduction.* Sheffield: Sheffield Academic, 2000.

Denning-Bolle, Sara. *Wisdom in Akkadian Literature: Expression, Instruction, Dialogue.* Leiden: Ex Oriente Lux, 1992.

Dequeker, Luc. "Jason's Gymnasium in Jerusalem (2 Macc 4:7–17): The Failure of a Cultural Experiment." *Bijdragen* 54 (1993) 371–92.

Derby, Josiah. "The Daughters of Zelophehad Revisited." *JBQ* 25 (1997) 169–71.

Derfler, Steven L. *The Hasmonean Revolt: Rebellion or Revolution?* Lewiston, NY: Mellen, 1989.

DeSilva, David Arthur. *Bearing Christ's Reproach: The Challenge of Hebrews in an Honor Culture.* Richland Hills, TX: Bibal, 1999.

Detienne, Marcel. "Forgetting Delphi between Apollo and Dionysus." *Classical Philology* 96 (2001) 147–58.

Dexinger, Ferdinand. "Der Ursprung der Samaritaner im Spiegel der frühen Quellen." In *Die Samaritaner*, edited by Ferdinand Dexinger and Reinhard Pummer, 67–140. Darmstadt: Wissenschaftliche Buchgesellschaft, 1992.

Diakonoff, Igor M. "Socio-Economic Classes in Babylonia and the Babylonian Concept of Social Stratification." In *Gesellschaftsklassen im alten Zweistromland und in den abgrenzenden Gebieten*, edited by Dietz Otto Edzard, 41–52. Munich: Bayerische Akademie Wissenschaft, 1972.

———. "The Rise of the Despotic State in Ancient Mesopotamia." In *Ancient Mesopotamia*, 173– 203. Moscow: Nauka, 1969.

Dietrich, Manfred, et al. *The Cuneiform Alphabetic Texts from Ugarit, Ras Ibn Hani and Other Places.* Münster: Ugarit, 1995.

Dietrich, Walter. "Synchronie und Diachronie in der Exegesis der Samuelbücher—Eine Einführung." In *David und Saul im Widerstreit—Diachronie und Synchronie im Wettstreit: Beiträge zur Auslegung des ersten Samuelbuches*, edited by W. Dietrich, 9–14. Göttingen: Vandenhoeck & Ruprecht, 2004.

Dillmann, August. *Die Genesis.* Leipzig: Hirzel, 1892.

Dirck, Brian R. *Lincoln Emancipated: The President and the Politics of Race.* DeKalb, IL: Northern Illinois University Press, 2007.

Dobbs-Alsopp, Frederick William. *Lamentations.* Louisville: Westminster John Knox, 2002.

Dodds, Eric Robertson. *The Greeks and the Irrational.* Berkeley: University of California Press, 1951.

Donner, Herbert, and Wolfgang Röllig. *Kanaanische und aramäische Inschriften.* Wiesbaden: Harrassowitz, 2002.

Doran, Robert. *Temple Propaganda: The Purpose and Character of 2 Maccabees.* Washington, DC: Catholic Biblical Association, 1981.

Douglas, Mary. *In the Wilderness: The Doctrine of Defilement in the Book of Numbers.* Sheffield: Sheffield Academic, 1993.

Downing, Christine, and Paola Ceccarelli. "Athena." In *ER* 1:586–88.

Drosnin, Michael. *The Bible Code.* New York: Simon and Schuster, 1997.

Droysen, Johann Gustav. *Geschichte des Hellenismus.* Hamburg: Perthes, 1877–78.

Drury, John. *Tradition and Design in Luke's Gospel.* London: Darton, Longmann, and Todd, 1976.

Duchrow, Ulrich. "Biblical Perspectives on Empire: A View from Western Europe." *The Ecumenical Review* 46 (Jan 1994) 21–27.

Duhaime, Jean. "Dualism" in *EDSS* 1:215–20.

Dumbrell, William J. *Covenant and Creation: An Old Testament Covenantal Theology.* Exeter: Paternoster, 1984.

Dürr, Hans Peter. *Dreamtime: Concerning the Boundary between Wilderness and Civilization.* New York: Blackwell, 1985.

Dyck, J. van. "Le motif cosmique dans la pensée sumérienne." *Acta Orientalia* 28 (1964) 1–59.

———. "Une insurrection générale au pays de Larsa avant l'avenement de Nûradad." *JCS* 19 (1965) 1–25.

Earle, Carville V. "A Staple Interpretation of Slavery and Free Labor." *Geographical Review* 68 (1968) 51–65.

Edens, Christopher. "Dynamics of Trade in the Ancient Mesopotamian 'World System.'" *American Anthro-pologist* 94 (1992) 118–39.

Edwards, Rem B. *Pleasures and Pains: A Theory of Qualitative Hedonism.* Ithaca, NY: Cornell, 1979.

Edzard, Dietz Otto. *Die "Zweite Zwischenzeit" Babyloniens.* Wiesbaden: Harrassowitz, 1957.

———. "Irra (Erra) Epos." In *RlA* 5:166–70.

———. "Kleine Beiträge zum Gilgameš Epos." *Or* 54 (1985) 46–55.

Eissfeldt, Otto. *Der Maschal in alten Testament.* Giessen, Töpelmann, 1924.

———. *The Old Testament: An Introduction.* New York: Harper and Row, 1965.

Ekelund, Robert Burton. *Sacred Trust: The Medieval Church as an Economic Firm.* New York: Oxford University Press, 1996.

Eldredge, John. *Wild at Heart: Discovering the Secret of a Man's Soul.* Nashville: Nelson, 2001.

Elgvin, Torleif. Review of *Wealth in the Dead Sea Scrolls and the Qumran Community,* by Catherine Murphy. *JSS* 49 (2004) 348–51.

Eliade, Mircea. "Preface." In *ER* 1.x–xi.

———. *The Myth of the Eternal Return: Cosmos and History,* 1954. Reprint. Princeton: Princeton University Press, 2005.

———. *The Quest: History and Meaning in Religion.* Chicago: University of Chicago Press, 1969.

———. *The Sacred and the Profane.* New York: Harcourt, Brace, Jovanovich, 1959.

Elliott, Kimberly Ann. *Corruption and the Global Economy.* Washington, DC: Institute of International Economics, 1997.

Ellis, Peter F. "Maccabees, Books of." In *NCE* 9:5–9.

El-Saady, Hassan. "Reflections on the Goddess Tayet." *Journal of Egyptian Archaeology* 80 (1994) 213–17.

Eltis, Walter Alfred. *The Classical Theory of Economic Growth.* New York: Palgrave, 2000.

Erchak, Gerald Michael. *The Anthropology of Self and Behavior.* Piscataway, NJ: Rutgers University Press, 1992.

Ernst, Carl W. *Following Muhammad: Rethinking Islam in the Contemporary World.* Chapel Hill: University of North Carolina, 2004.

Eshel, Hanan. *The Dead Sea Scrolls and the Hasmonean State.* Grand Rapids: Eerdmans, 2008.

Esler, Philip F. *Ancient Israel: The Old Testament in its Social Context.* Minneapolis: Fortress, 2006.

———. "Jesus and the Reduction of Intergroup Conflict: The Parable of the Good Samaritan in the Light of Social Identity Theory." *BI* 8 (2000) 325–57.

Esposito, John L. and Dalia Mogahed. *Who Speaks for Islam? What A Billion Muslims Really Think.* New York: Gallup, 2008.

Euben, Roxanne L. "Premodern, Antimodern, or Postmodern? Islamic and Western Critiques of Modernity." *The Review of Politics* 59 (1997) 429–59.

Evans, Craig. *Ancient Texts for New Testament Studies: A Guide to the Background Literature* Peabody, MA: Hendrickson, 2005.

Eyre, Christopher I. "The Agricultural Cycle, Farming, and Water Management in the Ancient Near East." In *CANE* 1:175–90.

Falkenstein, Adam. "Fluch über Akkade." *ZA* 57 (1965) 43–124.

Fall, Patricia L., et al. "Seeds of Civilization: Bronze Age Rural Economy and Ecology in the Southern Levant." *Annals of the Association of American Geographers* 88 (1998) 107–25.

Fee, Gordon D. Review of *Wealth and Beneficence in the Pastoral Epistles*, by Reggie Kidd. *JBL* 111 (1992) 352–54.

———. *The Disease of the Health and Wealth Gospels.* Vancouver: Regent College, 1985.

Feldman, Louis H. *Jew and Gentile in the Ancient World: Attitudes and Interactions from Alexander to Justinian.* Princeton: Princeton University Press, 1993.

———. "Josephus' Portrayal of the Hasmoneans Compared with *1 Maccabees*." In *Josephus and the History of the Greco-Roman Period: Essays in Memory of Morton Smith*, edited by Fausto Parente and Joseph Sievers, 41–68. Leiden: Brill, 1994.

Feldman, Marian H. *Diplomacy by Design: Luxury Arts and an "International Style" in the Ancient Near East, 1400–1200 BCE.* Chicago: University of Chicago Press, 2006.

Feldstein, Paul J. *Health Care Economics.* Florence, KY: Delmar Cengage Learning, 2004.

Feltes, Heinz. *Die Gattung des Habakukkommentars von Qumran. Eine Studie zum frühen jüdischen Midrasch.* Würzburg: Echter, 1986.

Ferguson, Niall. *The Ascent of Money: A Financial History of the World.* New York: Penguin, 2008.

Fernández, Dagoberto Ramírez. "The Judgment of God on the Multinationals: Revelation 18." In *Subversive Scriptures: Revolutionary Readings of the Christian Bible in Latin America*, edited by Leif Vaage, 75–100. Valley Forge, PA: Trinity, 1997.

Fichtner, Paula S. *Protestantism and Primogeniture in Early Modern Germany.* New Haven: Yale, 1989.

Fields, Weston W. "Discovery and Purchase." In *EDSS* 1:208–12.

————. *Sodom and Gomorrah: History and Motif in Biblical Narrative*. Sheffield: Sheffield Academic, 1997.

Finley, Moses I. *The Ancient Economy*. Berkeley: University of California, 1973.

Firestone, Reuven. "Difficulties in Keeping a Beautiful Wife: The Legend of Abraham and Sarah in Jewish and Islamic Tradition." *JJS* 42 (1991) 196–214.

————. "Prophethood, Marriageable Consanguinity, and Text: The Problem of Abraham and Sarah's Kinship Relationship and the Response of Jewish and Islamic Exegesis." *JQR* 83 (1993) 331–47.

Fischer, Irmtraud. "Was kostet der Exodus? Monetäre Metaphern für die zentrale Rettungserfahrung Israels in einer Welt der Sklaverei." *Jahrbüch für Biblische Theologie* 21 (2006) 25–44.

Fischer, Thomas. "Heliodor im Tempel zu Jerusalem—ein 'hellenistischer' Aspekt der 'frommen Legende.'" In *Prophetie und geschichtliche Wirklichkeit im alten Israel: Festschrift für Siegfried Herrmann zum 65 Geburtstag*, edited by Rüdiger Liwak and Siegfried Wagner, 122–33. Stuttgart: Kohlhammer, 1991.

————. "Maccabees, Books of." In *ABD* 4:439–50.

————. *Seleukiden und Makkabaeer*. Bochum: Brockmeyer, 1980.

Fishbane, Michael. *Biblical Interpretation in Ancient Israel*. Oxford: Clarendon, 1985.

————. *Biblical Myth and Rabbinic Mythmaking*. New York: Oxford University Press, 2005.

Fisman, Raymond, and Edward Miguel. *Economic Gangsters: Corruption, Violence and the Poverty of Nations*. Princeton: Princeton University Press, 2008.

Fitzenreiter, Martin. "Grabdekoration und die Interpretation funerärer Rituale im Alten Reich." In *Social Aspects of Funerary Culture in the Egyptian Old and Middle Kingdoms*, edited by Harco Willems, 67–140. Leuven: Peeters, 2001.

Fitzmyer, Joseph A. *The Gospel according to Luke*. New York: Doubleday, 1981.

Flanagan, J. "Chiefs in Israel." *JSOT* 20 (1981) 47–73.

Fleming, Daniel E. "Ur: After the Gods Abandoned Us." *The Classical World* 97 (2003) 5–18.

Flusser, David. "Gnosticism." In *EJ* 7:650–51.

————. "The Roman Empire in Hasmonean and Essene Eyes." In *Judaism of the Second Temple Period, Vol. I: Qumran and Apocalypticism*, 175–206. Grand Rapids: Eerdmans, 2007.

————. "The Social Message from Qumran." In *Judaism and the Origins of Christianity*, 193–201. Jerusalem: Magnes, 1988.

Foakes, R. A. *Shakespeare and Violence*. Cambridge: Cambridge University Press, 2003.

Fohl, Hans. *Tragische Kunst bei Herodot: Inaugural-Dissertation zur Erlangung der Doktorwürde der höhen philosophischen Fakultät der Universität Rostock*. Leipzig: Robert Noske, 1913.

Fohrer, Georg. *Introduction to the Old Testament*. Nashville: Abingdon, 1968.

Folland, Sherman, et al. *Economics of Health and Health Care*. Upper Saddle River, NJ: Prentice-Hall, 2009.

Fontenrose, Joseph E. *The Ritual Theory of Myth*. Berkeley: University of California Press, 1966.

Forest, Jean-Daniel. "L'Épopée de Gilgamesh, ses origines et sa postérité." In *Gilgamesh and the World of Assyria*, edited by Joseph Azize and Noel Weeks, 25–36. Leuven, Peeters, 2007.

Forster, Edwin Morgan. *Aspects of the Novel.* New York: Harcourt, Brace, Jovanovich, 1927.

Fort, Timothy L. *Prophets, Profits, and Peace: The Positive Role of Business in Promoting Religious Tolerance.* New Haven: Yale, 2008.

Foster, Benjamin. *Before the Muses: An Anthology of Akkadian Literature.* Bethesda, MD: CDL, 2005.

———. "Ea and Saltu." In *Ancient Near Eastern Studies in Memory of Jacob J. Finkelstein,* edited by Maria de Jong Ellis, 79–84. Hamden, CT: Academy of Arts and Sciences, 1977.

———. "*Gilgamesh*: Sex, Love, and the Ascent of Knowledge." In *Love and Death in the Ancient Near East: Essays Presented to Marvin A. Pope,* edited by John H. Marks and Robert M. Good, 21–42. Guilford, CT: Four Quarters, 1987.

———. "In Search of Akkadian Literature." In *Before the Muses: An Anthology of Akkadian Literature,* 1–47. Bethesda, MD: CDL, 2005.

———, et al. *The Epic of Gilgamesh.* New York: Norton, 2001.

Fox, Michael V. "Wisdom in the Joseph Story." *VT* 51 (2001) 26–41.

Fox-Genovese, Elizabeth. "Literary Criticism and the Politics of the New Historicism." In *The Postmodern History Reader,* edited by Keith Jenkins, 84–102. London: Routledge, 1997.

Frazier, James. *The Golden Bough.* London: MacMillan, 1911.

Frankena, Rintje. "Untersuchungen zum Irra-Epos." *BiOr* 14 (1957) 2–10.

Frankl, Razelle. *Televangelism: The Marketing of Popular Religion.* Carbondale, IL: Southern Illinois University Press, 1987.

Freedman, David Noel. "The Real Story of the Ebla Tablets: Ebla and the Cities of the Plain." *BA* 41 (1978) 143–64.

Fretheim, Terence E. *Abraham: Trials of Family and Faith.* Charleston: University of South Carolina Press, 2007.

Frey, Jörg. "Different Patterns of Dualistic Thought in the Qumran Library: Reflections on Their Background and History." In *Legal Texts and Legal Issues: Proceedings of the Second Meeting of the International Organization for Qumran Studies, Cambridge, 1995, Published in Honor of Joseph Baumgarten,* edited by Moshe Bernstein, et al., 275–335. Leiden: Brill, 1997.

Frick, Frank S. "The Political and Ideological Interests of Female Sexual Imagery in Hosea 1–3." In *To Break Every Yoke: Essays in Honor of Marvin L. Chaney,* edited by Robert B. Coote and Norman K. Gottwald, 200–208. Sheffield: Phoenix, 2007.

Friedberg, Maurice. *A Decade of Euphoria: Western Literature in Post-Stalin Russia, 1954–64.* Bloomington: Indiana University Press, 1976.

Friedman, Benjamin M. *The Moral Consequences of Economic Growth.* New York: Knopf, 2005.

Friedman, Milton. *Capitalism and Freedom.* Chicago: University of Chicago Press, 1962.

Friedman, Richard E. "An Essay on Method." In *Le-David Maskil: A Birthday Tribute to David Noel Freedman,* edited by Richard E. Friedman and William H. Propp, 1–16. Winona Lake, IN: Eisenbrauns, 2004.

Friedrich, Johannes. "Die hethitischen Bruckstücke des Gilgameš-Epos." *ZA* 39 (1930) 1–82.

Fritz, Volkmar. "'Solange die Erde steht': vom Sinn der jahwistischen Fluterzählung in Gen 6–8." *ZAW* 94 (1982) 599–614.

Frolov, Serge, and Vladimir Orel. "The House of Yahweh," *ZAW* 108 (1996) 254–57.

Frye, Northrop. *The Great Code: The Bible and Literature*. New York: Harcourt, 1982.

————, and Jay Macpherson. *Biblical and Classical Myths: The Mythological Framework of Western Culture*. Toronto: University of Toronto Press, 2004.

Frykholm, Amy Johnson. *Rapture Culture: Left Behind in Evangelical America*. New York: Oxford University Press, 2007.

Frymer-Kensky, Tikva. *In the Wake of the Goddesses: Women, Culture, and the Biblical Transformation of Pagan Myth*. New York: Free, 1992.

————. "Marduk." In *ER* 8:5702–3.

————. "Patriarchal Family Relationships and Near Eastern Law." *BA* 44 (1981) 209–14.

————. "The Atrahasis Epic and its Significance for Our Understanding of Genesis 1–9." *BA* 40 (1977) 147–55.

————, and Giovanni Pettinato. "Enuma Elish." In *ER* 4:2809–12.

————, and Pietro Mander. "Ashur." In *ER* 1:548–9.

Fung, Yiu-Wing. *Victim and Victimizer: Joseph's Interpretation of His Destiny*. Sheffield: Sheffield Academic, 2000.

Fuye, F. Alotte de la. *Documents Présargoniques*. Paris: Leroux, 1908.

Gabel, John B., et al. *The Bible as Literature: An Introduction*. New York: Oxford, 2000.

Gadalla, Tahany M. "Impact of Marital Dissolution on Men's and Women's Incomes: A Longitudinal Study." *JDR* 50 (2009) 55–65.

Gadamer, Hans Georg. *Hegels Dialektik*. Tübingen: Mohr (Siebeck), 1971.

Gafni, Isaiah M. "Alexander Balas." In *EJ* 1:625.

————. "Antiochus." In *EJ* 2:202–4.

————. "Josephus and 1 Maccabees." In *Josephus, the Bible, and History*, edited by Louis H. Feldman and Gōhei Hata, 116–31. Detroit: Wayne State University Press, 1989.

Galbraith, John Kenneth. *The Affluent Society*. Boston: Houghton Mifflin, 1958.

Galil, Gershon. *The Lower Stratum Families in the Neo-Assyrian Period*. Leiden: Brill, 2007.

Galling, Kurt. *Die Erwählungstraditionen Israels*. Giessen: Töpelmann, 1928.

García Martínez, Florentino, and Elbert J. C. Tigchelaar. *The Dead Sea Scrolls Study Edition*. Leiden: Brill, 1998.

Gardiner, Alan Henderson. *Notes on the Story of Sinuhe*. Paris: Librairie Honoré Champion, 1916.

Gardner, Gregg. "Jewish Leadership and Hellenistic Civic Benefaction in the Second Century BCE." *JBL* 126 (2007) 327–43.

Gardner, Iain. "Docetism." *ER* 4:2381.

Gardner, John, et al. *Gilgamesh*. New York: Knopf, 1984.

Garelli, Paul. *L'Assyrologie*. Paris: Presses Universitaires de France, 1972.

Garr, W. Randall. "The Grammar and Interpretation of Exodus 6:3." *JBL* 111 (1992) 385–408.

Garrison, M., and C. Stevens. "Sign This Agreement Not to Compete or You're Fired! Noncompete Agreements and the Public Policy Exception to Employment at Will." *Employee Responsibilities and Rights Journal* 15 (2003) 103–26.

Geertz, Clifford. *The Interpretation of Cultures*. New York: Basic, 1973.

Gelb, Ignace. "From Freedom to Slavery." In *Gesellschaftsklassen im alten Zweistromland und in den abgrenzenden Gebieten*, edited by Dietz Otto Edzard, 81–92. München: Bayerischen Akademie der Wissenschaften, 1972.

————. "On the Alleged Temple and State Economies in Ancient Mesopotamia." In *Studi in Onore di Edoardo Volterra*, 137–54. Milan: Giuffrè, 1969.

————. "Prisoners of War in Early Mesopotamia." *JNES* 32 (1973) 70–98.

————. "Quantitative Evaluation of Slavery and Serfdom." In *Kramer Anniversary Volume: Cuneiform Studies in Honor of Samuel Noah Kramer*, edited by Barry L. Eichler, 195–207. Neukirchen-Vluyn: Neukirchener, 1976.

Geller, Markham J. "Freud, Magic, and Mesopotamia: How the Magic Works." *Folklore* 119 (1997) 1–7.

————. "The Influence of Ancient Mesopotamia on Hellenistic Judaism." In *CANE* 1:43–54.

Geller, Stephen A. "Manna and Sabbath: A Literary-Theological Reading of Exodus 16." *Int* 59 (2005) 5–16.

Gennep, Arnold Van. *Les rites de passage*. Paris: Nourry, 1909.

George, Andrew R. *The Babylonian Gilgamesh Epic: Introduction, Critical Edition, and Cuneiform Texts*. Oxford: Oxford University Press, 2003.

————. "The Epic of Gilgamesh: Thoughts on Genre and Meaning." In *Gilgamesh and the World of Assyria: Proceedings of the Conference Held at Mandelbaum House, University of Sydney, 21–23 July 2004*, edited by Joseph Azize and Noel Weeks, 46–51. Leuven: Peeters, 2007.

————. *The Epic of Gilgamesh: The Babylonian Epic Poem and Other Texts in Akkadian and Sumerian*. New York: Penguin, 2000.

————, and F. N. H. al-Rawi. "Tablets from the Sippar Library VI: *Atra-hasīs*." *Iraq* 58 (1996) 147–90.

Gerstenberger, Erhard. *Theologies in the Old Testament*. Minneapolis: Fortress, 2002.

Geschiere, Peter. *The Modernity of Witchcraft: Politics and the Occult in Postcolonial Africa*. Charlottesville: University of Virginia Press, 1997.

Gibbon, Edward. *History of the Decline and Fall of the Roman Empire*, 1792. Reprint. New York: Knopf, 1993.

Gibson, John C. L. *Textbook of Syrian Semitic Inscriptions*. 3 vols. Oxford: Clarendon, 1982.

Gills, Barry K. "Democratizing Globalization and Globalizing Democracy." *Annals of the American Academy of Political and Social Science* 581 (2002) 158–71.

Gilula, Mordechai. "The Smiting of the First-Born—An Egyptian Myth?" *Tel Aviv* 4 (1977) 94–95.

Ginzberg, Eli. *Studies in the Economics of the Bible*. Philadelphia: Jewish Publication Society of America, 1932.

————. "Studies in the Economics of the Bible." *JQR* 22 (1932) 343–408.

Ginzberg, Louis. *An Unknown Jewish Sect*. New York: Jewish Theological Seminary of America, 1976.

Gittlen, Barry, ed. *Sacred Time, Sacred Place: Archaeology and the Religion of Israel*. Winona Lake, IN: Eisenbrauns, 2001.

Givens, Terryl L. *By the Hand of Mormon: The American Scripture that Launched a New World Religion*. New York: Oxford University Press, 2003.

Glancy, Jennifer A. *Slavery in Early Christianity*. Minneapolis: Fortress, 2006.

Glass, Zipporah G. "Land, Slave Labor and Law: Engaging Ancient Israel's Economy." *JSOT* 91 (2000) 27–39.

Glassner, Jean-Jacques, and Benjamin Foster. *Mesopotamian Chronicles*. Atlanta: Scholars, 2004.

Glazer, Myron P., and Penina M. Glazer. *Whistleblowers: Exposing Corruption in Government and Industry.* New York: Basic, 1990.

Glazov, Yuri. *The Bridling of the Tongue and the Opening of the Mouth in Biblical Prophecy.* Sheffield: Sheffield Academic, 2001.

Gnuse, Robert. "From Prison to Prestige: The Hero Who Helps a King in Jewish and Greek Literature." *CBQ* 72 (2010) 31–45.

Godelier, Maurice. *The Enigma of the Gift.* Chicago: University of Chicago Press, 1999.

Goedicke, Hans. Review of *Die Erzählung des Sinuhe*, by Roland Koch. *JNES* 52 (1993) 236.

Goetze, Albrecht. "Historical Allusions in the Old Babylonian Omen Texts." *JCS* 1 (1947) 253–65.

———. *Kulturgeschichte Kleinasiens.* München: Beck'sche, 1957.

Gold, Mark S., and Michael J. Herkov. "Addiction and Dependence." In *EBio* 1:62–68.

Goldingay, John. *Old Testament Theology.* 3 vols. Downers, Grove, IL: InterVarsity, 2003–2009.

Goldman, Michael. *Imperial Nature: The World Bank and Struggles for Social Justice in the Age of Globalization.* New Haven: Yale, 2005.

Goldman, Shalom. *The Wiles of Women/The Wiles of Men: Joseph and Potiphar's Wife in Ancient Near Eastern, Jewish, and Islamic Folklore.* Albany: SUNY, 1995.

Goldstein, Jonathan A. *1 Maccabees.* New York: Doubleday, 1976.

Gonzalez, Justo L. *Faith and Wealth: A History of Early Christian Ideas on the Origin, Significance, and Use of Money.* Eugene, OR: Wipf & Stock, 1990.

Goodblatt, David M. *Elements of Ancient Jewish Nationalism.* Cambridge: Cambridge University Press, 2006.

Goodkin, Richard E. *Birth Marks: The Tragedy of Primogeniture in Pierre Corneille, Thomas Corneille, and Jean Racine.* Philadelphia: University of Pennsylvania Press, 2000.

Goodnick, Benjamin. "Korah and his Aspirations." *JBQ* 28 (2000) 177–81.

———. "Rebekah's Deceit or *Isaac's* Great Test." *JBQ* 23 (1995) 221–28.

Gordon, Cyrus H., and Gary Rendsburg. *The Bible and the Ancient Near East.* New York: Norton, 1998.

Gordon, Kathryn, and Maiko Miyake. "Business Approaches to Combating Bribery: A Study of Codes of Conduct." *JBE* 34 (2001) 161–73.

Görg, Manfred. "Kain und das 'Land Nod.'" *Biblische Notizen* 71 (1994) 5–12.

Gottwald, Norman K. *The Hebrew Bible: A Socio-Literary Introduction.* Philadelphia: Fortress, 1985.

———. *The Politics of Ancient Israel.* Louisville: Westminster John Knox, 2001.

———. *The Tribes of Yahweh.* Maryknoll: Orbis, 1979.

Gould, Roger V. "Collective Violence and Group Solidarity: Evidence from a Feuding Society." *American Sociological Review* 64 (1999) 356–80.

Gourevitch, Victor. *The Social Contract and Other Later Political Writings of Jean-Jacques Rousseau.* Cambridge: Cambridge University Press, 1997.

Grabbe, Lester L. *Did Moses Speak Attic? Jewish Historiography and Scripture in the Hellenistic Period.* Sheffield: Sheffield Academic, 2001.

———. *Priests, Prophets, Diviners, Sages: A Socio-Historical Study of Religious Specialists in Ancient Israel.* Valley Forge, PA: Trinity, 1995.

———. "Reflections on the Discussion." In *Can a "History of Israel" Be Written?* Edited by Lester L. Grabbe, 188–96. London: T. & T. Clark, 2004.

Graf, David F. "Hegra." In *ABD* 3:113–14.

Graf, Fritz. "Violence." In *ER* 14:9595–600.

Grafton, David D. Review of *Following Muhammad*, by Carl W. Ernst. *JAAR* 73 (2005) 528–31.

Grajetzki, Wolfram. *The Middle Kingdom of Ancient Egypt: History, Archaeology and Society*. London: Duckworth, 2006.

Gray, John. "Baal's Atonement." *UF* 3 (1971) 61–70.

———. "Canaanite Kingship in Theory and Practice." *VT* 2 (1952) 193–220.

Gray, Patrick. "Brotherly Love and the High Priest Christology of Hebrews." *JBL* 122 (2003) 335–51.

Green, Barbara. *"What Profit For Us?" Remembering the Story of Joseph*. Lanham, MD: University Press of America, 1996.

Green, Joel B. *The Gospel of Luke*. Grand Rapids: Eerdmans, 1997.

Greenburg, Moshe. *The Hab/piru*. New Haven: American Oriental Society, 1955.

———. "Sabbatical Year and Jubilee." In *EJ* 17:625–26.

Greene, John T. *Balaam and His Interpreters*. Atlanta: Scholars, 1992.

———. *The Role of the Messenger and Message in the Ancient Near East*. Atlanta: Scholars, 1989.

Greengus, Samuel. "Legal and Social Institutions of Ancient Mesopotamia." In *CANE* 1:469–84.

———. "The Old Babylonian Marriage Contract." *JAOS* 89 (1969) 505–32.

Greenspahn, Frederick E. "A Mesopotamian Proverb and Its Biblical Reverberations." *JAOS* 114 (1994) 33–38.

———. *When Brothers Dwell Together: The Preeminence of Younger Siblings in the Hebrew Bible*. New York: Oxford University Press, 1994.

Greenstein, Edward L. "Kirta." In *UNP* 9–48.

———. "The Firstborn Plague and the Reading Process," in *Pomegranates and Golden Bells: Studies in Biblical, Jewish, and Near Eastern Ritual, Law, and Literature in Honor of Jacob Milgrom*, edited by David P. Wright, et al., 555–68. Winona Lake, IN: Eisenbrauns, 1995.

———. "Wordplay, Hebrew." In *ABD* 6:968–71.

Gregory, Eric. "Agape and Special Relations in a Global Economy: Theological Resources." In *Global Neighbors: Christian Faith and Moral Obligation in Today's Economy*, edited by Douglas A. Hicks and Mark R. Valeri, 16–42. Grand Rapids: Eerdmans, 2008.

Gresseth, Gerald K. "The Gilgamesh Epic and Homer." *The Classical Journal* 70 (1975) 1–18.

Griffiths, John Gwyn. "Hellenistic Religions." In *ER* 6:3900–913.

———. *The Origins of Osiris and His Cult*. Leiden: Brill, 1980.

Griffiths, Richard Owen. "The Politics of the Good Samaritan." *Political Theology* 1 (1999) 85–114.

Grillet, Bernard, and Michel Lestienne. *La Bible d'Alexandrie: premier livre des Regnes*. Paris: Cerf, 1997.

Grintz, Yehoshua M. "Apocrypha and Pseudipigrapha." In *EJ* 2:258–61.

———. "Maccabees, First Book of." In *EJ* 13:316–17.

Groneberg, Brigitte. *Lob der Ishtar: Gebet und Ritual an die altbabylonischen Venusgöttin*. Gröningen: STYX, 1997.

———. "Towards a Definition of Literature as Applied to Akkadian Literature." In *Mesopotamian Poetic Language: Sumerian and Akkadian,* edited by Marianna E. Vogelzang and Herman L. J. Vanstiphout, 59–84. Groningen: Styx, 1996.

Grosby, Steven Elliott. *Biblical Ideas of Nationality: Ancient and Modern.* Winona Lake, IN: Eisenbrauns, 2002.

Grossman, Maxine L. *Reading for History in the Damascus Document: A Methodological Study.* Leiden: Brill, 2002.

Grotanelli, Cristiano. "The Story of *Combabos* and the *Gilgamesh* Tradition." In *Mythology and Mythologies: Methodological Approaches to Intercultural Influences: Proceedings of the Second Annual Symposium of the Assyrian and Babylonian Intellectual Heritage Project held in Paris, France, Oct. 4–7, 1999,* edited by Robert M. Whiting, 19–27. Helsinki: Neo-Assyrian Text Corpus Project, 2001.

Gruber, Mayer I. "Purity and Impurity in Halakic Sources and Qumran Law." In *Wholly Woman, Holy Blood: A Feminist Critique of Purity and Impurity,* edited by Kristin De Troyer, et al., 65–76. Harrisburg, PA: Trinity, 2003.

———. "The Tragedy of Cain and Abel: A Case of Depression." *JQR* 69 (1978) 89–97.

Gruen, Erich S. *Heritage and Hellenism: The Reinvention of Jewish Tradition.* Berkeley: University of California Press, 1998.

Gruenthaner, Michael J. "Chaldeans or Macedonians? A Recent Theory on the Prophecy of Habakkuk." *Bib* 8 (1927) 129–60.

Grumach, Irene. "Ramses." In *EJ* 17:89.

Grüneberg, Keith Nigel. *Abraham, Blessing, and the Nations: A Philological and Exegetical Study of Genesis 12:3 in its Narrative Context.* Berlin: de Gruyter, 2003.

Guinan, Michael. *The Pentateuch.* Collegeville, MN: Liturgical, 1990.

Gunkel, Hermann. *Israel and Babylon: The Babylonian Influence on Israelite Religion,* 1903. Translated by K. C. Hanson. Eugene, OR: Cascade, 2009.

———. *Genesis.* Göttingen: Vandenhoeck und Ruprecht, 1901.

Gunton, Colin. *A Brief Theology of Revelation.* New York: T. and T. Clark, 2005.

Güterbock, Hans G. "A View of Hittite Literature." *JAOS* 84 (1964) 107–15.

Guyette, Fred. "Joseph's Emotional Development." *JBQ* 32 (2004) 181–88.

Haas, Peter Jerome. *Morality after Auschwitz: The Radical Challenge of the Nazi Ethic.* Philadelphia: Fortress, 1988.

Hackett, Jo Ann. "Rehabilitating Hagar: Fragments of an Epic Pattern." In *Gender and Difference in Ancient Israel,* edited by Peggy L. Day, 12–27. Minneapolis: Fortress, 1989.

———. *The Balaam Text from Deir Allā.* Chico, CA: Scholars Press, 1980.

Hallo, William W. "Gutium." *RlA* 3 (1957–71) 717–19.

———. "Sharecropping in the Edict of Ammi-ṣaduqa." In *Hesed ve-Emet: Studies in Honor of Ernest S. Frerichs,* edited by Jodi Magness & Seymour Gitin, 205–16. Atlanta: Scholars, 1998.

———. "The First Purim." *BA* 46 (1983) 19–29.

Halpern, Baruch. *The First Historians: The Hebrew Bible and History.* San Francisco: Harper & Row, 1988.

Halverson, John. "The World of *Beowulf.*" *English Literary History* 36 (1969) 593–608.

Ham, Clay Alan. *The Coming King and the Rejected Shepherd: Matthew's Reading of Zechariah's Messianic Hope.* Sheffield: Phoenix, 2005.

Hammond, John Craig. "'They Are Very Much Interested in Obtaining an Unlimited Slavery': Rethinking the Expansion of Slavery in the Louisiana Purchase Territories." *Journal of the Early Republic* 23 (2003) 353–80.

Handy, Lowell. *Among the Host of Heaven: The Syro-Palestinian Pantheon as Bureaucracy.* Winona Lake, IN: Eisenbrauns, 1994.

Hanson, K. C. "When the King Crosses the Line: Royal Deviance in Levantine Ideologies." *Biblical Theology Bulletin* 26 (1996) 11–25.

———, and Douglas E. Oakman. *Palestine in the Time of Jesus: Social Structures and Social Conflicts.* 2nd ed. Minneapolis: Fortress, 2008.

Hardmeier, Christof. "Wirtschaftliche Prosperität und Gottvergessenheit: Die theologische Dimension wirtschaftlicher Leistungskraft nach Dtn 8." *Leqach* 4 (2004) 15–24.

Harkins, Angela Kim. "Cain and Abel in the Light of Envy: A Study in the History of Interpretation of Envy in Genesis 4:1–16." *JSP* 12 (2001) 62–84.

Harrington, Daniel J. *The Maccabean Revolt: Anatomy of a Biblical Revolution.* Wilmington, DE: Michael Glazier, 1988.

Harrington, Hannah K. "Holiness and Law in the Dead Sea Scrolls." *DSS* 8 (2001) 124–35.

Harris, James Rendel. *The Cult of the Heavenly Twins.* Cambridge: Cambridge University Press, 1906.

Harris, Rivkah. *Gender and Aging in Mesopotamia.* Norman: University of Oklahoma, 2000.

———. "Images of Women in the Gilgamesh Epic." In *Lingering Over Words: Studies in Ancient Near Eastern Literature in Honor of William L. Moran,* edited by Tzvi Abusch et al., 219–30. Atlanta: Scholars, 1990.

———. "Inanna-Ishtar as Paradox and a Coincidence of Opposites." *History of Religions* 30 (1991) 261–78.

———. Review of *The Goddess Anat,* by Neal Walls. *JAOS* 115 (1995) 718–19.

———. "The Conflict of Generations in Ancient Mesopotamian Myths," *Comparative Studies in Society and History* 34 (1992) 621–35.

Harrison, Robert Pogue. *Forests: The Shadow of Civilization.* Chicago: University of Chicago Press, 1992.

Hasel, George F. "Sabbath." In *ABD* 5:849–56.

Hattem, Willem C. van. "Once Again: Sodom and Gomorrah." *BA* 44 (1981) 87–92.

Hauck, Friedrich. "μαμῶνας." In *TDNT* 4:388–90.

Hausman, Daniel H. "Economics, Philosophy of." In *Routledge Encyclopedia of Philosophy.* London: Routledge, 1998. No pages. Online: www.rep.routledge.com/article/R005.

Heard, R. Christopher. *Dynamics of Diselection: Ambiguity in Genesis 12–36 and Ethnic Boundaries in Post-Exilic Judah.* Atlanta: Society of Biblical Literature, 2001.

Hecht, William Charles. "Gilgamesh and Hippolytus: An Archetypal Exploration." MA thesis, California State University, 1995.

Heger, Paul. *The Pluralistic Halakhah: Legal Innovations in the Late Second Commonwealth and Rabbinic Periods.* Berlin: de Gruyter, 2003.

Heichelheim, Fritz M. Review of *Social and Economic History of the Hellenistic World,* by Mikhail Roztovtzeff. *The Economic Journal* 52, 205 (March 1942) 59–61.

Heidel, Alexander. *The Babylonian Genesis: The Story of Creation.* Chicago: University of Chicago Press, 1963.

———. *The Gilgamesh Epic and Old Testament Parallels.* Chicago: University of Chicago Press, 1949.

Heil, John Paul. "Ezekiel 34 and the Narrative Strategy of the Shepherd and Sheep Metaphor in Matthew." *CBQ* 55 (1993) 698–708.

Heimpel, Wolfgang. *Letters to the King of Mari.* Winona Lake, IN: Eisenbrauns, 2003.

Heinegg, Peter. Review of *God Is Not Great,* by Christopher Hitchens. *Cross Currents* 57 (2007) 467–70.

Heinz, Marlies, and Marian H. Feldman. *Representations of Political Power: Case Histories from Times of Change and Dissolving Order in the Ancient Near East.* Winona Lake, IN: Eisenbrauns, 2007.

Held, George F. "Parallels Between the *Gilgamesh Epic* and Plato's *Symposium.*" *JNES* 42 (1983) 133–41.

Heltzer, Michael. "A Guarantee Hostage in the Story of Joseph (Gen 42:44) and in Middle-Assyrian Times." *ZABR* 8 (2002) 207–10.

Helyer, Larry. "Abraham's Eight Crises." *Bible Review* 11 (1995) 20–27.

———. "The Separation of Abram and Lot: Its Significance in the Patriarchal Narratives." *JSOT* 26 (1983) 77–88.

Hempel, Charlotte. *The Laws of the Damascus Document: Sources, Tradition, and Redaction.* Leiden: Brill, 1998.

Hendel, Ronald. "Of Demigods and the Deluge: Toward an Interpretation of Genesis 6:1–4." *JBL* 106 (1987) 13–26.

———. *Remembering Abraham: Culture, Memory, and History in the Hebrew Bible.* New York: Oxford University Press, 2005.

———. Review of *Sodom and Gomorrah,* by Weston Fields. *JBL* 118 (1999) 126–28.

———. "The Exodus in Biblical Memory." *JBL* 120 (2001) 601–22.

———. *The Epic of the Patriarch: The Jacob Cycle and the Narrative Traditions of Canaan and Israel.* Atlanta: Scholars, 1987.

———. "The Flame of the Whirling Sword: A Note on Gen 3:24." *JBL* 104 (1985) 671–74.

———. "When God Acts Immorally: Is the Bible a Good Book?" *Bible Review* 7, 3 (1991) 35–50.

Hengel, Martin. *Judaism and Hellenism.* Philadelphia: Fortress, 1974.

———. "Judaism and Hellenism Revisited." In *Hellenism in the Land of Israel,* edited by John Collins and Gregory Sterling, 6–37. Notre Dame: University of Notre Dame Press, 2001.

Henninger, Joseph. "Zum Problem der Venussterngottheit bei den Semiten." *Anthropos* 71 (1976) 129–68.

Henze, Matthias. *The Madness of King Nebuchadnezzar: The Ancient Near Eastern Origins and Early History of Interpretation of Daniel 4.* Leiden: Brill, 1999.

Herman, Menahem. *Tithe as Gift: The Institution in the Pentateuch and in light of Mauss's Prestation Theory.* San Francisco: Mellen Research University Press, 1991.

Herrmann, Wolfgang. "El." In *DDD* 274–80.

Herzog, Ze'ev. *Archaeology of the City: Urban Planning in Ancient Israel and Its Social Implications.* Tel Aviv: Emery and Claire Yass Publications in Archaeology, 1997.

Heschel, Abraham Joshua. *The Sabbath: Its Meaning for Modern Man.* New York: Farrar, Strauss, & Young, 1951.

Heslam, Peter Somers. *Globalization and the Good.* Grand Rapids: Eerdmans, 2004.

Hess, Richard. "Chaldea." In *ABD* 1:886–87.

Hesselbein, Frances, et al. *The Community of the Future*. San Francisco: Jossey-Bass, 1998.

Hiebert, Theodore. "Babel: Babble or Blueprint? Calvin, Cultural Diversity, and the Interpretation of Genesis 11:1–9." In *Reformed Theology: Identity and Ecumenicity II: Biblical Interpretation in the Reformed Tradition*, edited by Wallace M. Alston, Jr. and Michael Welker, 127–45. Grand Rapids: Eerdmans, 2007.

Higgins, W. E. "Double-Dealing Ares in the *Oresteia*." *Classical Philology* 73 (1978) 24–35.

Himmelfarb, Gertrude. "Telling It As You Like It: Postmodernist History and the Flight from Fact." In *The Postmodern History Reader*, edited by Keith Jenkins, 158–74. New York: Routledge, 1997.

Himmelfarb, Martha. "Judaism and Hellenism in 2 Maccabees." *Poetics Today* 19 (1998) 19–40.

Hirsch, Eric D. "The Bible." In *The New Dictionary of Cultural Literacy*, edited by Eric D. Hirsch et al., 1–26. Boston: Houghton Mifflin, 1993.

Hitchens, Christopher. *God Is Not Great: How Religion Poisons Everything*. New York: Twelve Books, 2007.

Hobson, John M. *The Eastern Origins of Western Civilization*. Cambridge: Cambridge University Press, 2004.

Hodges, Richard. *Towns and Trade in the Age of Charlemagne*. London: Duckworth, 2000.

Hoffecker, W. Andrew. "A Reading of *Brave New World*: Dystopianism in Historical Perspective." *Christianity and Literature* 29 (1980) 46–62.

Hoffman, W. Michael. *Emerging Global Business Ethics*. Westport, CT: Quorum, 1994.

Hoffner, Harry A. *Hittite Myths*. Atlanta: Scholars, 1990.

Hoftijzer, Jacob. *Die Verheissungen an die drei Erzvater*. Leiden: Brill, 1956.

Holladay, William L. *The Root שוב in the Old Testament with Particular Reference to its Usages in Covenantal Contexts*. Leiden: Brill, 1958.

Hollis, Susan Tower. "Ancient Israel as the Land of Exile and the 'Otherworld' in Ancient Egyptian Folktales and Narratives." In *Boundaries of the Ancient Near Eastern World: A Tribute to Cyrus H. Gordon*, edited by Meir Lubetski et al., 320–37. Sheffield: Sheffield Academic, 1998.

———. *The Ancient Egyptian "Tale of Two Brothers": The Oldest Fairy Tale in the World*. Norman, OK: University of Oklahoma Press, 1990.

Holman, Susan R. *Wealth and Poverty in Early Church and Society*. Grand Rapids: Baker, 2008.

Homer-Dixon, Thomas. *Environment, Scarcity, and Violence*. Princeton: Princeton University Press, 2001.

Hooke, Samuel Henry. "Cain and Abel." *Folklore* 50 (1939) 58–65.

———. *Myth and Ritual: Essays on the Myth and Ritual of the Hebrews in Relation to the Culture Pattern of the Ancient East*. London: Blackwell, 1933.

Hopkins, Clark. "Assyrian Elements in the Perseus-Gorgon Story." *American Journal of Archaeology* 38 (1934) 341–58.

———. Review of *Institutions des séleucides*, by Elias Bickerman." *American Historical Review* 45 (1939) 105–6.

Hopkins, David C. "'All Sorts of Field Work': Agricultural Labor in Ancient Palestine." In *To Break Every Yoke: Essays in Honor of Marvin L. Chaney*, edited by Robert Coote and Norman Gottwald, 149–72. Sheffield: Phoenix, 2007.

———. "Pastoralists in Late Bronze Age Palestine: Which Way Did They Go?" *BA* 56 (1993) 200–11.

Hoppe, Leslie. *There Shall Be No Poor Among You: Poverty in the Bible.* Nashville: Abingdon, 2004.

Horsley, Richard A., and John S. Hanson. "Ancient Jewish Social Banditry." In *Bandits, Prophets, and Messiahs*, 48–87. Harrisburg, PA: Trinity, 1999.

Hosseini, Khalid. *The Kite Runner.* New York: Riverhead, 2003.

Hout, Theo van den. *The Purity of Kingship: An Edition of CHT 569 and Related Hittite Oracle Inquiries of Tudhaliya IV.* Leiden: Brill, 1998.

Howard, David M. *Joshua.* Nashville: Broadman and Holman, 1998.

Hudson, Michael. "Mesopotamia and Classical Antiquity." In *Land Value Taxation around the World. Annual Supplement to The American Journal of Economics and Sociology*, edited by Robert V. Andelson. Oxford: Blackwell, 2000.

———. "Reconstructing the Origins of Interest-Bearing Debt and the Logic of Clean Slates." In *Debt and Economic Renewal in the Ancient Near East*, edited by Michael Hudson & Marc van de Mieroop, 3–15. Bethesda, MD: CDL, 2002.

———. "The Dynamics of Privatization, from the Bronze Age to the Present." In *Privatization in the Ancient Near East and Classical World*, edited by Michael Hudson and Baruch Levine, 1–26. Cambridge, MA: Peabody Museum of Archaeology and Ethnology, 1996.

———, and Baruch A. Levine. *Privatization in the Ancient Near East and Classical World.* Cambridge, MA: Peabody Museum of Archaeology and Ethnology, 1996.

Huffmon, Herbert B. "Cain, the Arrogant Sufferer." In *Biblical and Related Studies Presented to Samuel Iwry*, edited by Ann Kort and Scott Morschauser, 109–114. Winona Lake, IN: Eisenbrauns, 1985.

Hughes, Julie A. *Scriptural Allusions and Exegesis in the Hodayot.* Leiden: Brill, 2006.

Hughes, Richard T., and C. Leonard Allen. *Illusions of Innocence: Protestant Primitivism in America.* Chicago: University of Chicago Press, 1988.

Huizinga, Johan. "On a Definition of History." *Communications of the Royal Netherlands Academy of Sciences* 68 (1929) 14–23.

Hull, John M. "Bargaining with God: Religious Development and Economic Socialization." *Journal of Psychology and Theology* 27 (1999) 241–49.

Humphreys, W. Lee. "Novella." In *Saga, Legend, Tale, Novella, Fable: Narrative Forms in Old Testament Literature*, edited by George W. Coats, 82–96. Sheffield: JSOT, 1985.

Huntington, Samuel P. *The Clash of Civilizations and the Remaking of World Order.* New York: Simon and Schuster, 1998.

Hurowitz, Victor Avigdor. "Finding New Life in Old Words." In *Gilgamesh and the World of Assyria*, edited by Joseph Azize and Noel Weeks, 67–78. Leuven: Peeters, 2007.

Hurvitz, Avi. "The Historical Quest for Ancient Israel and the Linguistic Evidence of the Hebrew Bible: Some Methodological Observations." *VT* 47 (1997) 301–15.

Husser, Jean-Marie. *Dreams and Dream Narratives in the Biblical World.* Sheffield: Sheffield Academic, 1999.

Hutter, Manfred. *Altorientalische Vorstellungen von der Unterwelt: literar- und religionsgeschichtliche Überlegungen zu "Nergal und Ereskigal."* Göttingen: Vandenhoeck und Ruprecht, 1985.

Huttner, Ulrich. "Zur Civilizationskritik in der frühen Kaiserzeit: die Diskreditierung der 'pax Romana.'" *Historia: Zeitschrift der Alte Geschichte* 49 (2000) 447–66.

Hutton, Rodney. "Korah." In *ABD* 4:100–101.

Ingraffia, Brian D. *Postmodern Theory and Biblical Theology: Vanquishing God's Shadow.* Cambridge: Cambridge University Press, 1996.

Ipsen, Avaren. *Sex Working and the Bible.* London: Equinox, 2009.

Isaac, Benjamin. Review of *The History of the Jewish People in the Age of Jesus Christ*, by Emile Schürer. *Journal of Roman Studies* 79 (1989) 244–45.

Iser, Wolfgang. "Staging as an Anthropological Category." *New Literary History* 23 (1992) 877–88.

Izre'el, Shlomo. *Adapa and the South Wind: Language Has the Power of Life and Death.* Winona Lake, IN: Eisenbrauns, 2001.

Jacobs, Louis. "Halakhah." In *EJ* 8:251–58.

———. "Judaism." In *EJ* 11:511–20.

———. "Passover." In *ER* 10:7003–5.

———. "Shabbat." In *ER* 12:8256–58.

Jacobsen, Thorkild. "*Inuma Ilu Awilum.*" In *Essays on the Ancient Near East in Honor of Jacob Joel Finkelstein*, edited by Maria de Jong Ellis, 113–17. Hamden, CT: Archon, 1977.

———. "Mesopotamian Religions: An Overview." In *ER* 9:5946–63.

———. "Primitive Democracy in Ancient Mesopotamia." *JNES* 2 (1943) 159–72.

———. "The Assumed Conflict Between the Sumerians and the Semites in Early Mesopotamian History." *JAOS* 59 (1939) 485–95.

———. *"The Harps That Once"... Sumerian Poetry in Translation.* New Haven: Yale, 1987.

———. "The Historian and the Sumerian Gods." *JAOS* 114 (1994) 145–53.

———. "The Investiture and Anointing of Adapa in Heaven." *AJSLL* 46 (1930) 201–3.

———. "The Name Dumuzi." *JQR* 76 (1985) 41–45.

———. *The Treasures of Darkness: A History of Mesopotamian Religion.* New Haven: Yale, 1974.

———. "Two *bal-bal-e* Dialogues." In *Love and Death in the Ancient Near East: Essays in Honor of Marvin H. Pope* edited by John. Henry Marks and Robert McClive Good, 57–63. Guilford, CT: Four Quarters, 1987.

Jaffee, Martin S. *Mishnah's Theology of Tithing: A Study of Tractate מעשרת.* Chico, CA: Scholars, 1981.

Jafri, Amir H. *Honour Killing: Dilemma, Ritual, Understanding.* Oxford: Oxford University Press, 2008.

Jager, Bernd. "The Birth of Poetry and the Creation of a Human World: An Exploration of the Epic of Gilgamesh." *Journal of Phenomenological Psychology* 32 (2001) 131–54.

Janowski, Bernd. "Jenseits von Eden. Gen 4,1–16 und die nichtpriesterliche Urgeschichte." In *Die Dämonen: Die Dämonologie der israelitische-judische und frühchristlichen Literatur im Kontext ihrer Umwelt*, edited by Armin Lange, et al., 37–59. Tübingen: Mohr Siebeck, 2003.

Janthial, Dominique. *L'oracle de Nathan et l'unité du livre d'Isaïe.* Berlin: de Gruyter, 2004.

Jarman, Mark. "When the Light Came On: The Epic *Gilgamesh.*" *The Hudson Review* 58 (2005) 329–34.

Jaruzelska, Izabela. *Amos and the Officialdom in the Kingdom of Israel. The Socio-Economic Position of the Officials in the Light of the Biblical, the Epigraphic and Archaeological Evidence.* Poznan: Wydawnictwo Naukowe Uniwersytetu im Adama Mickiewicza, 1998.

Jason, Heda. *Ethnopoetry: Form, Content, Function.* Bonn: Linguistica Biblica, 1977.

Jasper, David. *A Short Introduction to Hermeneutics.* Louisville: Westminster John Knox, 2004.

Jastrow, Marcus. Review of *Vater, Sohn und Fursprecher in der Babylonischen Gottesvorstellung,* by H. Zimmern. *American Journal of Theology* 2 (1897) 468–74.

Jeansonne, Sharon Pace. "The Characterization of Lot in Genesis," *Biblical Theology Bulletin* 18 (1988) 123–29.

Jeffrey, David L. *People of the Book: Christian Identity and Literary Culture.* Grand Rapids: Eerdmans, 1996.

Jemielity, Thomas. *Satire and the Hebrew Prophets.* Louisville: Westminster John Knox, 2002.

Jeremias, Alfred. *Handbuch der altorientalischen Geisteskultur.* Berlin: de Gruyter, 1929.

Jeremias, Joachim. *The Parables of Jesus.* New York: Scribners, 1972.

Jha, Prem Shankar. *The Perilous Road to the Market: The Political Economy of Reform in Russia, India, and China.* London: Pluto, 2002.

Joannès, Francis. "Private Commerce and Banking in Achaemenid Babylon." In *CANE* 3:1475–85.

Johns, Kenneth D. *Televangelism: A Powerful Addiction.* New York: XLibris, 2006.

Johnson, Luke Timothy. *Sharing Possessions: Mandate and Symbol of Faith.* Philadelphia: Fortress, 1981.

———, and Daniel Harrington. *The Gospel of Luke.* Collegeville, MN: Liturgical, 2006.

Johnston, Michael. "Right and Wrong in American Politics: Popular Conceptions of Corruption." *Polity* 18 (1986) 367–91.

Jones, David W., and Russell S. Woodbridge. *Health, Wealth, and Happiness: Has the Prosperity Gospel Overshadowed the Gospel of Christ?* Grand Rapids: Kregel, 2011.

Jonker, Louis C. *Exclusivity and Variety: Perspectives on Multidimensional Exegesis.* Kampen: Kok Pharos, 1996.

Jorgenson, Dale W. and Kevin J. Stiroh. *Raising the Speed Limit: US Economic Growth in the Information Age.* Paris: Organization for Economic Cooperative Development, 2000.

Joukowsky, Martha Sharp. "Nabateans." In *EJ* 14:716–18.

Jülicher, Adolph. *Die Gleichnisreden Jesu.* Tübingen: Mohr Siebeck, 1910.

Jung, Carl. *Memories, Dreams, Reflections.* New York: Random House, 1961.

———. *Modern Man in Search of a Soul.* London: Routledge and Kegan Paul, 1933.

Kaiser, Otto. "Die Bindung Isaaks: Untersuchungen zur Eigenart und Bedeutung von Genesis 22." In *Zwischen Athen und Jerusalem,* 199–224. Berlin: de Gruyter, 2003.

Kallet, Lisa. *Money and the Corrosion of Power in Thucydides: The Sicilian Expedition and Its Aftermath.* Berkeley: University of California Press, 2002.

Kaminsky, Joel. "Reclaiming a Theology of Election: Favoritism and the Joseph Story." *Perspectives in Religious Studies* 31 (2004) 135–52.

———. *Yet I Loved Jacob: Reclaiming the Biblical Concept of Election.* Nashville: Abingdon, 2007.

Kamionkowski, S. Tamar. "The Savage Made Civilized: An Examination of Ezekiel 16:8." In *Every City Shall Be Forsaken: Urbanism and Prophecy in Israel and the Ancient Near East,* edited by Lester L Grabbe and Robert Haak, 176–81. Sheffield: Sheffield Academic, 2001.

Kammenhuber, Annelies. *Orakelpraxis, Träume und Vorzeichenschau bei den Hethitern.* Heidelberg: Winter, 1976.

Kampen, John. "Hercules." In *ABD* 3:143.

Karabell, Zachary. *Peace Be Upon You: The Story of Muslim, Christian, and Jewish Coexistence.* New York: Knopf, 2007.

Kasher, Aryeh. Review of *The Hasmonean Revolt: Rebellion or Revolution?*, by Steven L. Derfler. *JQR* 83 (1993) 419–21.

Kasper, Sherryl Davis. *The Revival of Laissez-Faire in American Macroeconomic Theory: A Case Study of the Pioneers.* Northampton, MA: Elgar, 2002.

Kass, Leon R. Review of *Assimilation vs. Separation: Joseph the Administrator and the Politics of Religion in Biblical Israel,* by Aaron Wildavsky. *Commentary* 96 (1993) 58–61.

Katz, Stan J., and Aimee Liu. *Codependency Conspiracy: How to Break the Recovery Habit and Take Control of Your Life.* New York: Warner, 1991.

Keel, Othmar. *Corpus der Stempelsiegel: Amulette aus Palastina/Israel von den Anfangen bis zur Perserzeit.* Freiburg: Universitätsverlag, 1995.

Keeley, Lawrence H. *War Before Civilisation: The Myth of the Peaceful Savage.* New York: Oxford, 1997.

Keil, Volkmar. "Onias III—Märtyrer oder Tempelgründer?," *ZAW* 97 (1985) 221–33.

Keiser, Clarence Elwood. *Selected Temple Documents of the Ur Dynasty.* New Haven: Yale, 1919.

Keister, Lisa A., and Stephanie Moller. "Wealth Inequality in the United States." *ARS* 26 (2000) 63–81.

Kelly, Wyn. "Melville's Cain." *American Literature* 55 (1983) 24–40.

Kemp, Barry J. "Unification and Urbanization of Ancient Egypt." In *CANE* 2:679–90.

Kermally, Sultan. *When Economics Means Business: The New Economics of the Information Age.* London: Financial Times Pitman, 1999.

Kessler, Rainer. *Statt und Gesellschaft im vorexilischen Juda vom 8 Jahrhundert bis zum Exil.* Leiden: Brill, 1992.

Keynes, John Maynard. *The General Theory of Employment, Interest and Money.* New York: Harcourt, Brace, 1936.

Khalidi, Tarif. *The Muslim Jesus: Saying and Stories in Islamic Literature.* Cambridge: Harvard, 2001.

Khan, Tamira S. *Beyond Honour: A Historical Materialist Explanation of Honour Related Violence.* Oxford: Oxford University Press, 2006.

Kidd, Reggie M. *Wealth and Beneficence in the Pastoral Epistles: A "Bourgeois" Form of Early Christianity?* Atlanta: Scholars, 1990.

Killinger, Barbara. *Workaholics: The Respectable Addicts.* Toronto: Key Porter, 2004.

Kilmer, Anne Draffkorn. "A Note on an Overlooked Word-Play in Akkadian *Gilgamesh.*" In *Zikir Šumim: Assyriological Studies Presented to F. R. Krause on the Occasion of His Seventieth Birthday,* edited by Fritz R. Krause and G. van Driel, 128–32. Leiden: Brill, 1982.

———. "More Wordplay in Akkadian Poetic Texts." In *Puns and Pundits: Wordplay in the Hebrew Bible and Ancient Near Eastern Literature,* edited by Scott Noegel, 89–101. Bethesda, MD: CDL, 2000.

———. "The Mesopotamian Concept of Overpopulation and its Solution as Represented in the Mythology." *Or* 41 (1972) 160–77.

———. "The Mesopotamian Counterparts of the Biblical Nephilim." In *Perspectives on Language and Text: Essays and Poems in Honor of Francis I. Andersen's Sixtieth*

Birthday, edited by Edgar W. Conrad and Edward G. Newing, 29–43. Winona Lake, IN: Eisenbrauns, 1987.

Kim, Henry S. "Archaic Coinage as Evidence for the Use of Money." In *Money and Its Uses in the Ancient Greek World*, edited by Andrew Meadows and Kirsty Shipton, 7–22. New York: Oxford University Press, 2004.

Kim, Young Yun. "Intercultural Communication." In *ECI* 2:452–59.

King, J. Robin. "The Joseph Story and Divine Politics: A Comparative Study of a Biographical Formula from the Ancient Near East." *JBL* 106 (1987) 577–94.

Kingsbury, Jack Dean. *Matthew: Structure, Christology, Kingdom.* Philadelphia: Fortress, 1975.

Kirk, Geoffrey Stephen. *Myth: Its Meaning and Functions in Ancient and Other Cultures.* Berkeley: University of California Press, 1970.

Kirsch, J. *A History of the End of the World.* San Francisco: HarperOne, 2007.

Kitching, Gavin. "Globalism and Globalization." In *ESTE* 2:874–77.

Klay, Robin, et al. "American Evangelicalism and the National Economy, 1870–1997." In *More Money, More Ministry: Money and Evangelicals in Recent North American History*, edited by Larry Eskridge and Mark A. Noll, 15–38. Grand Rapids: Eerdmans, 2000.

Klein, Jacob. "A New Look at the 'Oppression of Uruk' Episode in the Gilgamesh Epic." In *Riches Hidden in Secret Places: Ancient Near Eastern Studies in Memory of Thorkild Jacobsen*, edited by Tzvi Abusch, 187–201. Winona Lake, IN: Eisenbrauns, 2002.

Klein, Melanie. *The Psycho-Analysis of Children.* London, Hogarth, 1949.

Klein, William W., et al. *Introduction to Biblical Interpretation.* Nashville: Thomas Nelson, 2004.

Klinger, Elmar. "Revenge and Retribution." In *ER* 11.7779–84.

Kloos, Carola. *Yahweh's Combat with the Sea: A Canaanite Tradition in the Religion of Ancient Israel.* Leiden: Brill, 1986.

Kluger, Rivkah S. *The Archetypal Significance of Gilgamesh.* Einsiedeln: Daimon, 1991.

Klunzinger, Marlene, and Michael S. Moore. "Codependency and Pastoral Care: A Report from the Trenches." *ResQ* 38 (1996) 159–74.

Knibb, Michael. "Rule of the Community." In *EDSS* 2:793–97.

Knoppers, Gary. "Dissonance and Disaster in the Legend of Kirta." *JAOS* 114 (1994) 572–82.

———. "Greek Historiography and the Chronicler's History: A Reexamination." *JBL* 122 (2003) 627–50.

———. "Treasures Won and Lost: Royal [Mis]appropriations in Kings and Chronicles." In *The Chronicler as Author: Studies in Text and Texture*, edited by M. Patrick Graham and Steven L. McKenzie, 181–208. Sheffield: Sheffield Academic, 1999.

Knowles, Michael P. "What was the Victim Wearing? Literary, Economic, and Social Contexts for the Parable of the Good Samaritan." *BI* 12 (2004) 145–74.

Knudtzon, Jørgen Alexander. *Assyrische Gebete an den Sonnengott.* Leipzig: Pfeiffer, 1893.

Koch, Klaus. "Die hebräische Gott und die Gotteserfahrungen der Nachbarvölker: Inklusiver und exklusiver Monotheismus im Alten Testament." In *Der Gott Israels und die Götter des Orients: Religionsgeschichtliche Studien II zum 80 Geburtstag von Klaus Koch*, edited by Friedhelm Hartenstein and Martin Rösel, 9–41. Göttingen: Vandenhoeck und Ruprecht, 2007.

———. "Molek astral." In *Mythos im alten Testament und seiner Umwelt. Festschrift für Hans-Peter Müller*, edited by Armin Lange et al., 29–50. Berlin: de Gruyter, 1999.

———. "Sädäq und Ma'at: Konnektive Gerichtigkeit in Israel und Agypten?" In *Gerechtigkeit: Richten und Retten in der abendländischen Tradition und ihren altorientalistischen Ursprüngen*, edited by Jan Assmann et al., 37–64. München: Fink, 1998.

———. "Šaddaj: Zum Verhältnis zwischen israelitischer Monolatrie und nordwest-semitischen Polytheismus." *VT* 26 (1976) 299–332.

———. *Was ist Formgeschichte?* Neukirchen-Vluyn: Neukirchener, 1964.

Kofoed, Jens Bruun. *Text and History: Historiography and the Study of the Biblical Text.* Winona Lake, IN: Eisenbrauns, 2005.

Komoróczy, G. "Work and Strike of Gods: New Light on the Divine Society in the Sumero-Akkadian Mythology." *Oikumene* 1 (1976) 9–37.

Kowalewski, David. *Deep Power: The Political Ecology of Wilderness and Civilization.* Huntington, NY: Nova Science, 2000.

König, Eduard. *Die Genesis.* Gütersloh: Bertelsmann, 1925.

Kramer, Kenneth. "Sacred Traditions and Texts." In *World Scriptures: An Introduction to Comparative Religions*, 7–17. New York: Paulist, 1986.

Kramer, Samuel Noah. *Sumerian Mythology.* Philadelphia: American Philosophical Society, 1944.

———. "The Epic of Gilgamesh and Its Sumerian Sources." *JAOS* 64 (1944) 7–23.

———. "The Weeping Goddess: Sumerian Prototypes of the Mater Dolorosa." *BA* 46 (1983) 69–80.

———, and John Maier. *Myths of Enki, the Crafty God.* New York: Oxford University Press, 1989.

———, and Thorkild Jacobsen. "Gilgamesh and Agga." *American Journal of Archaeology* 53 (1949) 1–18.

Kratz, Reinhard. *Die Komposition der erzählenden Bücher der Alten Testaments: Grundwissen der Bibelkritik.* Göttingen: Vandenhoeck und Ruprecht, 2000.

Kraus, Fritz Rudolph. *Königliche Verfügungen in Altbabylonischer Zeit.* Leiden: Brill, 1984.

Kroeber, Alfred Louis. *Handbook of the Indians of California.* U.S. Bureau of American Ethnology Bulletin, 1–97. Washington: Smithsonian Institution, 1925.

Krugman, Paul R. *The Great Unraveling.* London: Penguin, 2004.

Kugel, James L. "Qohelet and Money." *CBQ* 51 (1989) 32–49.

Kuhrt, Amélie. *The Ancient Near East.* 2 vols. London: Routledge, 1995.

———. *The Persian Empire: A Corpus of Sources of the Achaemenid Period.* London: Routledge, 2007.

Kunin, Seth. *The Logic of Incest: A Structuralist Analysis of Hebrew Mythology.* Sheffield: Sheffield Academic, 1995.

Kuran, Timor. *Islam & Mammon: The Economic Predicaments of Islamism.* Princeton: Princeton University Press, 2005.

Kushner, Harold S. *When Bad Things Happen to Good People.* New York: Schocken, 1981.

Kuyt, Annelies, and Gerold Necker. *Orient als Grenzbereich? Rabbinisches und ausserrabbinisches Judentum.* Wiesbaden: Harrassowitz, 2007.

Kvaalvaag, R. "The Spirit in Human Beings in Some Qumran Non-Biblical Texts." In *Qumran Between the Old and New Testaments*, edited by Frederick H. Cryer and Thomas L. Thompson, 159–80. Sheffield: Sheffield Academic, 1998.

Lachmann, Richard. *Capitalists in Spite of Themselves: Elite Conflict and Economic Transitions in Early Modern Europe*. New York: Oxford University Press, 2000.

LaHaye, Tim, and Jerry Jenkins. *Left Behind: A Novel of the Earth's Last Days*. Wheaton, IL: Tyndale House, 1995.

Lambert, Wilfrid G. "A Catalogue of Texts and Authors." *JCS* 16 (1962) 59–77.

———. *Babylonian Wisdom Literature*. Oxford: Clarendon, 1960.

———. "Myth and Ritual as Conceived by the Babylonians." *JSS* 13 (1968) 104–12.

———. Review of *Das Era Epos*, by F. Gössmann." *AfO* 18 (1957–58) 400–401.

———. Review of *The Evolution of the Gilgamesh Epic*, by Jeffrey Tigay. *JBL* 104 (1985) 115–17.

———. "The Mesopotamian Background of the Hurrian Pantheon." *RHA* 36 (1978) 129–34.

———, and Alan R. Millard. *Atra-Ḥasīs: The Babylonian Story of the Flood*. Oxford: Oxford University Press, 1969.

Lanckau, Jörg. *Der Herr der Träume: Eine Studie zur Funktion des Traumes in der Josefsgeschichte der Hebräischen Bible*. Zürich: Theologischer, 2006.

Lang, Bernhard. *Wisdom and the Book of Proverbs: A Goddess Redefined*. New York: Pilgrim, 1986.

Lang, Graeme. "Oppression and Revolt in Ancient Palestine: The Evidence in Jewish Literature from the Prophets to Josephus." *Sociological Analysis* 49 (1989) 325–42.

Langdon, Stephen. *Sumerian Liturgical Texts*. Philadelphia: University Museum, 1917.

Lange, Astrid. *Was die Rechten Lesen: Fünfzig rechtsextreme Zeitschriften, Ziele, Inhalte, Taktik*. München: Beck, 1993.

Laniak, Timothy. *Shepherds After My Own Heart: Pastoral Traditions and Leadership in the Bible*. Downers Grove: InterVarsity, 2006.

Lapsley, Jacqueline. "'Am I Able to Say Just Anything?' Learning Faithful Exegesis from Balaam." *Int* 60 (2006) 22–31.

Lasine, Stuart. *Knowing Kings: Knowledge, Power and Narcissism in the Hebrew Bible*. Atlanta: Society of Biblical Literature, 2001.

LaSor, William et al. *Old Testament Survey*. 2nd ed. Grand Rapids: Eerdmans, 1996.

Laughland, John. Review of *Frozen Desire: The Meaning of Money*, by James Buchan. *National Review* 49 (Nov 10, 1997) 54–55.

Launderville, Dale. *Piety and Politics: The Dynamics of Royal Authority in Homeric Greece, Biblical Israel, and Old Babylonian Mesopotamia*. Grand Rapids: Eerdmans, 2003.

Leach, Edmund Ronald. *Genesis as Myth and Other Essays*. London: Cape, 1969.

Leahy, Anthony. "Ethnic Diversity in Ancient Egypt." In *CANE* 1:225–34.

Leemans, W. F. *The Old Babylonian Merchant: His Business and Social Position*. Leiden: Brill, 1950.

Lefkowitz, Mary R. and Guy MacLean Rogers. *Black Athena Revisited*. Chapel Hill: University of North Carolina Press, 1996.

Leick, Gwendolyn. *Sex and Eroticism in Mesopotamian Literature*. London: Routledge, 1994.

Lemche, Niels Peter. "*Andurārum* and *Mīšarum*: Comments on the Problem of Social Edicts and their Application in the Ancient Near East." *JNES* 38 (1979) 11–22.

———. *Ancient Israel: A New History of Israelite Society*. Sheffield: JSOT, 1988.

———. "Bare Bones: Putting Flesh on the Economics of Ancient Israel." In *The Origins of the Ancient Israelite States*, edited by Volkmar Fritz and Philip Davies, 121–39. Sheffield: Sheffield Academic, 1996.

———. "Our Most Gracious Sovereign: On the Relationship between Royal Mythology and Economic Oppression in the Ancient Near East." In *Ancient Economy in Mythology: East and West*, edited by Morris Silver, 109–34. Savage, MD: Rowan & Littlefield, 1991.

———. "The Manumission of Slaves—the Fallow Year—the Sabbatical Year—the Jobel Year." *VT* 26 (1976) 38–59.

Lemmelijn, Bénédicte. "Setting and Function of Exod 11:1–10 in the Exodus Narrative." In *Studies in the Book of Exodus*, edited by Marc Vervenne, 443–60. Leuven: Peeters, 1996.

Lenski, Gerhard Emmanuel. *Power and Privilege: A Theory of Social Stratification*. New York: McGraw-Hill, 1966.

Lenzi, Alan. *Secrecy and the Gods: Secret Knowledge in Ancient Mesopotamia and Biblical Israel*. Helsinki: University of Helsinki, 2008.

Lerner, Berel Dov. "Timid Grasshoppers and Fierce Locusts: An Ironic Pair of Biblical Metaphors." *VT* 49 (1999) 545–48.

Leuenberger, Martin. *Segen und Segenstheologien im alten Israel: Untersuchungen zu ihren religions- und theologiegeschichtlichen Konstellationen und Transformationen*. Zürich: Theologischer, 2008.

Levenson, Jon. "Liberation Theology and the Exodus." In *Jews, Christians, and the Theology of the Hebrew Scriptures*, edited by Alice Ogden Bellis and Joel S. Kaminsky, 215–30. Atlanta: Society of Biblical Literature, 2000.

———. *The Death and Resurrection of the Beloved Son: The Transformation of Child Sacrifice in Judaism and Christianity*. New Haven: Yale University Press, 1993.

Levinson, Joshua. "An-other Woman: Joseph and Potiphar's Wife: Staging the Body Politic." *JQR* 87 (1997) 269–301.

Leventhal, Allan M., and Christopher R. Martell. *The Myth of Depression as Disease*. Westport, CT: Praeger, 2005.

Levin, Yigal. "Joseph, Judah, and the 'Benjamin Conundrum.'" *ZAW* 116 (2004) 223–41.

Levine, Baruch A. "Firstborn." In *EJ* 7:45–48.

———. *Numbers 21–36*. New York: Doubleday, 2000.

———. "On the Semantics of Land Tenure in Biblical Literature: The Term אחזה." In *The Tablet and the Scroll: Near Eastern Studies in Honor of William Hallo*, edited by Mark E. Cohen et al., 134–40. Bethesda, MD: CDL, 1993.

———, and Jean Michel de Tarragon. "Dead Kings and Rephaim: The Patrons of the Ugaritic Dynasty." *JAOS* 104 (1984) 649–59.

Levine, Étan. "The Syriac Version of Genesis IV 1–16." *VT* 26 (1976) 70–78.

Levine, Lee I. *Judaism and Hellenism in Antiquity: Conflict or Confluence?* Seattle: University of Washington Press, 1998.

Levine, Molly Myerowitz. Review of *Black Athena Revisited*, by Mary Lefkowitz and Guy Rogers. *Classical Philology* 93 (1998) 345–63.

Levison, John R., and Priscilla Pope-Levison, eds. *Return to Babel: Global Perspectives on the Bible*. Louisville: Westminster John Knox, 2004.

Lévi-Strauss, Claude. *Structural Anthropology*. New York: Basic, 1976.

———. *The Raw and the Cooked*. Chicago: University of Chicago Press, 1983.

———. *Totemism*. Boston: Beacon, 1963.

Levy, David M. *How the Dismal Science Got Its Name: Classical Economics and the Ur-Text of Racial Politics*. Ann Arbor: University of Michigan Press, 2001.

Lewin, Moshé. *Political Undercurrents in Soviet Economic Debates: From Bukharin to the Modern Reformers*. Princeton: Princeton University Press, 1974.

Lewis, Jack P. "The Offering of Abel (Gen 4:4): A History of Interpretation." *JETS* 37 (1994) 481–96.

Lewis, Theodore J. *Cults of the Dead in Ancient Israel and Ugarit*. Atlanta: Scholars, 1989.

———. "First-Born of Death." In *DDD* 332–35.

Lewison, Martin. "The Ethics of Usury: Conflict of Interest?" *JBE* 22 (1999) 327–39.

Licht, Jacob. מגלתה הודיות: *The Thanksgiving Scroll*. Jerusalem: Mosad Bialik, 1957.

Lichtheim, Miriam. *Ancient Egyptian Literature*. Berkeley: University of California Press, 1973.

Lilla, Mark. *The Stillborn God: Religion, Politics, and the Modern West*. New York: Knopf, 2007.

Lim, Timothy L. "Kittim." In *EDSS*, 1:469–71.

———. "The Wicked Priest or the Liar?" In *The Dead Sea Scrolls in Their Historical Context*, edited by Timothy L. Lim, et al., 45–51. Edinburgh: T. & T. Clark, 2000.

Lincoln, Abraham. *The Emancipation Proclamation, January 1, 1863*. Washington, DC: National Archives and Records Administration, 1986.

Lincoln, Bruce. "Cattle." In *ER* 3:1464–68.

———. *Priests, Warriors, and Cattle: A Study in the Ecology of Religions*. Berkeley: University of California Press, 1981.

Lipiński, Eduard. "Adad." In *ER* 1:27–29.

Lipton, Diana. *Longing for Egypt and Other Unexpected Biblical Tales*. Sheffield: Phoenix, 2008.

———. Review of *Power and Marginality in the Abraham Narrative*, by Hemchand Gossai. *VT* 47 (1997) 423.

Lisca, Peter. *John Steinbeck: Nature and Myth*. New York: Crowell, 1978.

Litke, Joel. "Korah and His Fall: Observations on Holiness." *JBQ* 36 (2008) 118–20.

Liverani, Mario. *International Relations in the Ancient Near East*. New York: Palgrave, 2001.

———. *Prestige and Interest: International Relations in the Near East*. Padova: Sargon, 1990.

———. "The Great Powers Club." In *Amarna Diplomacy: The Beginnings of International Relations*, edited by Raymond Cohen and Raymond Westbrook, 15–27. Baltimore: Johns Hopkins, 2000.

Long, D. Stephen. *Divine Economy: Theology and the Market*. New York: Routledge, 2000.

Long, Roswell Curtis. *Stewardship Parables of Jesus*. Nashville: Cokesbury, 1931.

Long, V. Philips. *Israel's Past in Present Research: Essays on Israelite Historiography*. Winona Lake, IN: Eisenbrauns, 1999.

———. *The Art of Biblical History*. Grand Rapids: Zondervan, 1994.

Longino, Michèle. Review of *Birth Marks: The Tragedy of Primogeniture in Pierre Corneille, Thomas Corneille, and Jean Racine*, by Richard E. Goodkin. *The French Review* 75 (2002) 966–67.

Loretz, Oswald. "Die prophetische Kritik des Rentenkapitalismus. Grundlagen-Probleme der Prophetenforschung." *UF* 7 (1975) 271–78.

Lowell, Lee. *Get Rich With Options: Four Winning Strategies Straight from the Exchange Floor.* Hoboken, NJ: Wiley, 2009.

Lowery, Richard H. *Sabbath and Jubilee.* St. Louis, MO: Chalice, 2000.

Lowry, S. Todd. Review of *Xenophon Oeconomicus* by Sarah Pomeroy. *SEJ* 63 (1997) 828–29.

———. *The Archaeology of Economic Ideas: The Classical Greek Tradition.* Durham: Duke University Press, 1987.

Luciani, Joseph J. *The Power of Self-Coaching: The Five Essential Steps to Creating the Life You Want.* Hoboken, NJ: Wiley, 2004.

MacCary, W. Thomas. *Childlike Achilles: Ontogeny and Phylogyny in the Iliad.* New York: Columbia University Press, 1982.

MacGillivray, Alex. *A Brief History of Globalization: The Untold Story of Our Incredible Shrinking Planet.* Philadelphia: Running, 2006.

Machacek, D. "Prosperity Theology." In *Contemporary American Religion, vol. 2,* edited by Wade Clark Roof, 560–62. New York: MacMillan, 2000.

Machinist, Peter. "Rest and Violence in the Poem of Erra." *JAOS* 103 (1983) 221–26.

MacIntosh, A. A. "Exodus 8:19, Distinct Redemption, and the Hebrew Roots פדה and פדד." *VT* 21 (1971) 548–55.

MacKinnon, M. "Calvinism and the Infallible Assurance of Grace: The Weber Thesis Reconsidered." *BJS* 39 (1988) 143–77.

———. "Weber's Explanation of Calvinism: The Undiscovered Provenance of Capitalism." *BJS* 39 (1988) 178–210.

Mafico, Temba L. J. *Yahweh's Emergence as "Judge" Among the Gods: A Study of the Hebrew Root שפט.* Lewiston, NY: Mellen, 2006.

Magnanini, Suzanne. "Foils and Fakes: The Hydra in Giambattista Basile's Dragon-Slayer Tale *Lo mercante.*" *Marvels and Tales* 19 (2005) 167–96.

Maier, Johann. "Israel als Gegenüber der Diadochenreiche." In *Israel as Gegenüber: Vom Alten Orient bis in die Gegenwart,* edited by Folker Siegert, 53–72. Göttingen: Vandenhoeck & Ruprecht, 2000.

Malherbe, Abraham. "The Christianization of a Topos." *NT* 38 (1996) 123–35.

Malina, Bruce J. *Christian Origins and Cultural Anthropology.* Atlanta: John Knox, 1986.

———. *The New Testament World: Insights from Cultural Anthropology.* Louisville: Westminster John Knox, 2001.

Malthus, Thomas. *Essay on the Principle of Population.* Edited by Philip Appleman. 1798. Reprint, Norton, 2003.

Ma 'lūf, L. "Ibn Sīnā's *Kitab al-Siyāsa.*" In *Traités inédits d'anciens philosophes arabes,* edited by Ishâq ibn Honein, 1–18. Beirut: Imprimerie Catholique, 1911.

Malul, Meir. " 'āqēb 'Heel' and 'āqab 'To Supplant' and the Concept of Succession in the Jacob-Esau Narratives." *VT* 46 (1996) 190–212.

Mandell, Sara R. "Did the *Maccabees* Believe That They Had a Valid Treaty with Rome?" *CBQ* 53 (1991) 202–20.

Mandle, Jay R. *Globalization and the Poor.* Cambridge: Cambridge University Press, 2003.

Mandolfo, Carleen. "'You Meant Evil Against Me': Dialogic Truth and the Character of Jacob in Joseph's Story." *JSOT* 28 (2004) 449–65.

Mangum, Garth L., et al. *The Persistence of Poverty in the United States.* Baltimore: Johns Hopkins, 2003.

Mani, Braj Ranjan. *Debrahmanising History: Dominance and Resistance in Indian Society.* New Delhi: Manohar, 2005.

Manion, Melanie. "Corruption by Design: Bribery in Chinese Enterprise Licensing." *JLEO* 12 (1996) 167–95.

Mann, Michael. *The Sources of Social Power.* Cambridge: Cambridge University Press, 1986.

Mann, Samuel J. "Joseph and his Brothers: A Biblical Paradigm for the Optimal Handling of Traumatic Stress." *Journal of Religion and Health* 40 (2001) 335–42.

Marciak, Michal. "Antiochus IV Epiphanes and the Jews." *Polish Journal of Biblical Research* 5 (2006) 61–73.

Marcovich, Miroslav. "From Ishtar to Aphrodite." *Journal of Aesthetic Education* 30 (1996) 43–59.

Marcus, David. "Israelite Law." In *ER* 7:4734–37.

———. "Traditional Jewish Responses to the Question of Deceit in Genesis 27." In *Jews, Christians, and the Theology of the Hebrew Scriptures*, edited by Alice Ogden Bellis and Joel Kaminsky, 293–305. Atlanta, Society of Biblical Literature, 2000.

———, and Giovanni Pettinato. "Enlil." In *ER* 4:2799–801.

Marcus, Joel. "The Evil Inclination in the Epistle of James." *CBQ* 44 (1982) 606–21.

Marglin, Frédérique Apffel. "Hierodouleia." In *ER* 6.3966–70.

Martin, Dale B. *The Pedagogy of The Bible.* Louisville: Westminster John Knox, 2008.

Martola, Nils. *Capture and Liberation. A Study in the Composition of the First Book of Maccabees.* Åbo: Åbo Akademie, 1984.

Marx, Alfred. *Les systèmes sacrificiels de l'Ancien Testament: Formes et fonctions du culte sacrificiel à Yhwh.* Leiden: Brill, 2005.

Marx, Karl. *Das Kapital: Kritik der politischen Ökonomie.* Hamburg: Meissner, 1872.

Marx, Karl, and Friederich Engels. *A Manifesto of the Communist Party*, 1848. Reprint, Peking: Foreign Languages, 1973.

Massey, Denise McLain. "Addiction and Spirituality." *Review and Expositor* 91 (1994) 9–80.

Matthews, Victor Harold. *Pastoral Nomadism in the Mari Kingdom.* Cambridge, MA: ASOR, 1978.

———. "The Unwanted Gift: Implications of Obligatory Gift Giving in Ancient Israel." *Semeia* 87 (1999) 91–104.

———, and Don C. Benjamin. *Old Testament Parallels: Laws and Stories from the Ancient Near East.* New York: Paulist, 1997.

Mattila, Sharon Lea. "Jesus and the 'Middle Peasants'? Problematizing a Social-Scientific Concept." *CBQ* 72 (2010) 291–313.

Maul, Stefan M. *Das Gilgamesch-Epos.* München: Beck, 2005.

Mauss, Armand L., and Philip L. Barlow. "Church, Sect, and Scripture: The Protestant Bible and Mormon Sectarian Retrenchment." *Sociological Analysis* 52 (1991) 397–414.

Mauss, Marcel. *The Gift: Forms and Functions of Exchange in Archaic Societies.* Translated by Ian Cunnison, 1925. New York: Norton, 1967.

Mayer, Werner R. "Ein Mythos von der Eschaffung des Menschen und des Königs." *Or* 56 (1987) 55–68.

McAfee, Eugene Clifford. "The Patriarch's Longed-for Son: Biological and Social Reproduction in Ugaritic and Hebrew Epic." PhD diss., Harvard University, 1996.

McCarthy, Dennis. "The Symbolism of Blood and Sacrifice." *JBL* 88 (1969) 166–76.

McCoy, Bowen H. "The Parable of the *sadhû.*" *Harvard Business Review* 75 (1983) 103–8.

McDonald, Lee. *The Biblical Canon: Its Origin, Transmission, and Authority.* Peabody, MA: Hendrickson, 2007.

McEleney, Neil J. "The Maccabean Revolt: A Struggle to Remain Faithful." *The Bible Today* 25 (1987) 73–80.

McFague, Sally. *Life Abundant: Rethinking Theology and Economy for a Planet in Peril.* Minneapolis: Fortress, 2001.

McFarland, L., et al. *21st Century Leadership: Dialogues with 100 Top Leaders.* Provo, UT: Executive Excellence, 1994.

McGaughy, Lane C. "The Fear of Yahweh and the Mission of Judaism: A Postexilic Maxim and Its Early Christian Expansion in the Parable of the Talents." *JBL* 94 (1975) 235–45.

McGeough, Kevin M. *Exchange Relationships at Ugarit.* Leuven: Peeters, 2007.

McGurn, W. "Pulpit Economics." *First Things: A Journal of Religion, Culture, and Public Life* 122 (April 2002) 21–25.

McNutt, Paula. "In the Shadow of Cain." *Semeia* 87 (1999) 45–64.

McRae, William J. "Bread from Heaven: An Exposition of Exodus 16." *Emmaus Journal* 7 (1998) 217–29.

Meador, Keith G., and Shaun C. Henson. "Growing Old in a Therapeutic Culture." *Theology Today* 57 (2000) 185–202.

Meeker, Joseph W. *The Comedy of Survival: Studies in Literary Ecology.* New York: Scribner's, 1972.

Meeks, M. Douglas. *God the Economist: The Doctrine of God and Political Economy.* Minneapolis: Fortress, 1989.

Meggitt, Justin J. *Paul, Poverty, and Survival.* Edinburgh: T. & T. Clark, 1998.

Meier, John. "Jesus' Teaching on Divorce." In *A Marginal Jew: Rethinking the Historical Jesus, Vol. 4,* 74–181. New Haven: Yale University Press, 2009.

Meinhold, Arndt. "Die Geschichte des Sinuhe und die alttestamentliche Diasporanovelle." *Wissenschaftliche Zeitschrift der Ernst-Moritz-Albert Universität* 20 (1971) 277–81.

Melchior-Bonnet, Sabine. "Mirrors." In *ER* 9:6063–65.

Mellinkoff, Ruth. *The Mark of Cain.* Berkeley: University of California Press, 1981.

Melville, Herman. *The Confidence Man: His Masquerade,* 1857. Reprint, Indianapolis: Bobbs-Merrill, 1967.

Mendelsohn, Isaac. *Slavery in the Ancient Near East.* Oxford: Oxford University Press, 1949.

———. *Legal Aspects of Slavery in Babylonia, Assyria and Palestine.* Williamsport, PA: Bayard, 1932.

Mendham, Matthew D. "Eudaimonia and Agape in MacIntyre and Kierkegaard's *Works of Love:* Beginning Unpolemical Enquiry." *JRE* 35 (2007) 591–625.

Merton, Robert K. "The Role-Set: Problems in Sociological Theory." *BJS* (1957) 106–20.

Metso, Sarianna. *The Textual Development of the Qumran Community Rule.* Leiden: Brill, 1997.

Mettinger, Tryggve N. D. *The Riddle of Resurrection: "Dying and Rising Gods" in the Ancient Near East.* Stockholm: Almqvist and Wiksell, 2001.

Metzenthin, Christian. *Jesaja-Auslegung in Qumran.* Zurich: Theologischer, 2010.

Metzger, James A. *Consumption and Wealth in Luke's Travel Narrative.* Leiden: Brill, 2007.

Meyer, Michaela D. "Utilizing Mythic Criticism in Contemporary Narrative Culture." *Communication Quarterly* 51 (2003) 518–29.

Meyers, Carol L. *Exodus*. Cambridge: Cambridge University Press, 2005.

Michalowski, P. "The Unbearable Lightness of Enlil." In *Intellectual Life of the Ancient Near East: Papers Presented at the 43rd Rencontre Assyriologique Internationale Prague, July 1–5, 1996*, edited by Jiri Prosecky, 237–47. Prague: Oriental Institute, 1998.

Michèle Daviau, Paulette M., et al. *Excavations at Tell Jawa*. Leiden: Brill, 2002.

Michell, Humfrey. *The Economics of Ancient Greece*. New York: Barnes and Noble, 1957.

Mikesell, Marvin W. "The Deforestation of Mount Lebanon." *Geographical Review* 59 (1969) 1–28.

Milgrom, Jacob. "The Cultic אשם: A Philological Analysis." In *Proceedings of the Sixth World Congress of Jewish Studies*, 299–308. Jerusalem: World Union of Jewish Studies, 1977.

Mill, John Stuart. "On the Definition of Political Economy and the Method of Investigation Proper to It," 1836. Reprint. *The Collected Works of John Stuart Mill*. Toronto: University of Toronto, 1967.

———. *Principles of Political Economy*, 1848. Reprint, Kitchener, Ontario: Batoche, 2001.

Miller, Arthur. *The Crucible*, 1953. Reprint, New York: Penguin, 2003.

Mirguet, Francoise. "Numbers 16: The Significance of Place—An Analysis of Spatial Markers." *JSOT* 32 (2008) 311–30.

Mirowski, Philip. *Machine Dreams: Economics Becomes a Cyborg Science*. Cambridge: Cambridge University Press, 2002.

Mishra, Ajit. *The Economics of Corruption*. New York: Oxford University Press, 2005.

Mitchell, Christopher Wright. *The Meaning of BRK "To Bless" in the Old Testament*. Sheffield: JSOT, 1991.

Mitchell, Stephen. *Gilgamesh: A New English Version*. New York: Free, 2004.

Moberly, R. W. L. *The Old Testament of the Old Testament: Patriarchal Narratives and Mosaic Yahwism*. Minneapolis: Fortress, 1992.

Mobley, Gregory. *The Empty Men: The Heroic Tradition of Ancient Israel*. New York: Doubleday, 2005.

———. "The Wild Man in the Bible and the Ancient Near East." *JBL* 116 (1997) 217–33.

Moe-Lobeda, Cynthia D. "Refuting the False Gospel of Globalization." *The Other Side* 38 (2002) 16–21.

Moingt, Joseph. "Le livre et l'evenement." *Études* 401 (2004) 355–64.

Momigliano, Arnoldo Dante. *Essays on Ancient and Modern Judaism*. Chicago: University of Chicago Press, 1994.

———. "Hellenism." In *EJ* 8:784–91.

———. "Rostovtzeff's Twofold History of the Hellenistic World." *Journal of Hellenic Studies* 63 (1943) 116–17.

Monroe, Christopher Mountfort. *Scales of Fate: Trade, Tradition, and Transformation in the Eastern Mediter-ranean ca. 1350–1175 BCE*. Münster: Ugarit, 2009.

Moore, George Foot. *Judaism in the First Centuries of the Christian Era: The Age of the Tannaim*. Cambridge: Harvard University Press, 1954.

Moore, Michael S. "Abraham." In *EHJ* 2–3.

———. "Bathsheba's Silence." In *Inspired Speech: Prophecy in the Ancient Near East: Essays Presented in Honor of Herbert B. Huffmon*, edited by John Kaltner and Louis Stulman, 336–46. New York: Continuum, 2004.

———. "America's Monocultural Heritage." *Fides et Historia* 15 (1982) 39–53.

———. "Big Dreams and Broken Promises: Solomon's Treaty with Hiram in its International Context." *BBR* 14 (2004) 205–21.

———. *Faith Under Pressure: A Study of Biblical Leaders in Conflict.* Siloam Springs: Leafwood, 2003.

———. "*Haggōël*: The Cultural Gyroscope of Ancient Hebrew Society." *ResQ* 23 (1980) 27–35.

———. "Jehu's Coronation and Purge of Israel," *VT* 53 (2003) 97–114.

———. "Job's Texts of Terror." *CBQ* 55 (1993) 662–75.

———. "Numbers." In *The Transforming Word*, edited by Mark W. Hamilton, 185–202. Abilene: Abilene Christian University Press, 2009.

———. "Prophet or Magician? Reflections on the Balaam Story." *The Bible Today* 39 (2001) 17–21.

———. *Reconciliation: A Study of Biblical Families in Conflict.* Joplin, MO: College, 1994.

———. Review of *Amos and the Officialdom in the Kingdom of Israel: The Socioeconomic Position of the Officials in the Light of the Biblical, the Epigraphic and Archaeological Evidence*, by Izabela Jaruzelska. *JBL* 119 (2000) 758–60.

———. Review of *Authorizing an End*, by Donald Polaski. *BBR* 13 (2003) 294–96.

———. "Ruth." In *Joshua, Judges, Ruth*, edited by J. Gordon Harris et al., 293–383. Peabody, MA: Hendrickson, 2000.

———. "Ruth the Moabite and the Blessing of Foreigners." *CBQ* 60 (1998) 203–17.

———. "Sacrifice, Tithes, Offerings." In *EHJ* 533–36.

———. "Searching in Sheba." *ResQ* 44 (2002) 33–42.

———. *The Balaam Traditions: Their Character and Development.* Atlanta: Scholars, 1990.

———. "The Laments in Jeremiah and 1QH: Mapping the Metaphorical Trajectories." In *Uprooting and Planting: Essays on Jeremiah for Leslie Allen*, edited by John Goldingay, 228–52. New York: Continuum, 2007.

———. "To King or Not to King: A Canonical-Historical Approach to Ruth." *BBR* 11 (2001) 27–41.

———. "Two Textual Anomalies in Ruth." *CBQ* 59 (1997) 324–43.

———. "Wise Women or Wisdom Woman: A Biblical Study of Women's Roles." *ResQ* 35 (1993) 147–58.

Moorey, Peter Roger S. *Ancient Mesopotamian Materials and Industries.* Oxford: Clarendon, 1994.

———, and C. Leonard Woolley. *Ur of the Chaldees.* Ithaca, NY: Cornell University Press, 1982.

Moran, William. "*Atrahasis*: The Babylonian Story of the Flood." *Bib* 40 (1971) 51–61.

———. "Mesopotamia: History." In *NCE* 9:525–38.

———. "Ovid's *Blanda Voluptas* and the Humanization of Enkidu." *JNES* 50 (1991) 121–27.

———. Review of *Altorientalischen Literaturen*, by Wolfgang Röllig et al. *JAOS* 100 (1980) 189–90.

———. "Rilke and the Gilgamesh Epic." *JCS* 32 (1980) 208–10.

———. "Some Considerations of Form and Interpretation in Atrahasis." In *Language, Literature, and History: Philological and Historical Studies Presented to Erica Reiner,* edited by Francesca Rochberg-Halton, 245–55. New Haven: American Oriental Society, 1987.

———. *The Amarna Texts.* Baltimore: Johns Hopkins, 1992.

———. "The Creation of Man in *Atrahasis* I 192–248." *BASOR* 200 (1970) 48–56.

———. "The Epic of Gilgamesh: A Document of Ancient Humanism." *Bulletin of the Canadian Society for Mesopotamian Studies* 22 (1991) 15–22.

———. "The *Gilgamesh Epic*: A Masterpiece from Ancient Mesopotamia." In *CANE* 4:2327–36.

Morgan, David T. *The New Brothers Grimm and Their "Left Behind" Fairy Tales.* Macon, GA: Mercer University Press, 2006.

Morrill, Allison C., and Christopher D. Chinn. "The Obesity Epidemic in the United States." *Journal of Public Health Policy* 25 (2004) 353–66.

Morris, Brian. *Anthropological Studies in Religion: An Introductory Text.* Cambridge: Cambridge University Press, 1987.

Morse, J. Mitchell. "Jacob and Esau in Finnegan's Wake." *Modern Philology* 52 (1954) 123–30.

Moskowitz, Eva S. *In Therapy We Trust: America's Obsession with Self-Fulfillment.* Baltimore: Johns Hopkins University Press, 2001.

Mouton, Alice. *Rêves hittites. Contribution à une histoire et une anthropologie du rêve en Anatolie ancienne.* Leiden: Brill, 2007.

Mugerauer, Robert. "Literature as Reconciliation: The Art of Hypothetical Vision." *Soundings* 58 (1975) 407–15.

Mullen, E. Theodore. *The Divine Council in Canaanite and Early Hebrew Literature.* Atlanta: Scholars, 1980.

Müller, Hans-Peter. "Entmythologisierung und Altes Testament." *NZSTR* 35 (1993) 1–27.

Murnane, William J. "The History of Ancient Egypt: An Overview," *CANE* 2:691–717.

Murphy, Catherine. *Wealth in the Dead Sea Scrolls and in the Qumran Community.* Leiden: Brill, 2002.

Murphy, Roland. *The Wisdom Literature: Job, Proverbs, Ruth, Canticles, Ecclesiastes and Esther.* Grand Rapids: Eerdmans, 1981.

Nakane, Chie. *Kinship and Economic Organization in Rural Japan.* London: Athlone, 1967.

Napier, A. David. *Masks, Transformation and Paradox.* Berkeley: University of California Press, 1986.

Nebelsick, Harold P. Review of *The Meaning of Creation: Genesis and Modern Science,* by Conrad Hyers. *Theology Today* 44 (1987) 264–66.

Needle, Richard, et al. "Costs and Consequences of Drug Use: A Comparison of Health Care Utilization and Social-Psychological Consequences for Clinical and Nonclinical Adolescents and their Families." *International Journal of Addiction* 23 (1988) 1125–43.

Nelson, Russell D. "Andronicus." In *ABD* 1:247.

Nemet-Nejat, Karen Rhea. *Daily Life in Ancient Mesopotamia.* Peabody, MA: Hendrickson, 2002.

Nestler, Eric J., and George K. Aghajanian. "Molecular and Cellular Basis of Addiction." *Science* 278 (Oct 3, 1997) 58–63.

Neusner, Jacob. *Praxis and Parable: The Divergent Discourses of Rabbinic Judaism.* Lanham, MD: University Press of America, 2006.

———. *The Economics of the Mishnah.* Chicago: University of Chicago Press, 1990.

Newman, Jay. *Biblical Religion and Family Values: A Problem in the Philosophy of Culture.* Westport, CT: Praeger, 2001.

Newsom, Carol A. *The Book of Job: A Contest of Moral Imaginations.* New York: Oxford University Press, 2003.

Nickelsburg, George W. E. *Ancient Judaism and Christian Origins: Diversity, Continuity, and Transformation.* Minneapolis: Fortress, 2003.

Niditch, Susan. *A Prelude to Biblical Folklore: Underdogs and Tricksters.* Champaign, IL: University of Illinois Press, 2004.

Niehaus, Isak A. "Perversion of Power: Witchcraft and the Sexuality of Evil in the South African Lowveld." *Journal of Religion in Africa* 32 (2002) 269–99.

Nikiprowetzky, Vladimir. "Le sabbat et les armes dans l'histoire ancienne d'Israël." *REJ* 159 (2000) 1–17.

Nilson, Sherrill V. "Gilgamesh in Relationship: A Feminist, Kleinian Hermeneutic of the Contemporary Epic." PhD diss., California Institute of Integral Studies, 2001.

Nissinen, Martti, et al. *Prophets and Prophecy in the Ancient Near East.* Atlanta: Society of Biblical Literature, 2003.

Nitzan, Bilhah. פשר הבקוק: *A Scroll from the Wilderness of Judaea.* Jerusalem: Bialik Institute, 1986.

Nodet, Étienne. *A Search for the Origins of Judaism: From Joshua to the Mishnah.* Sheffield: Sheffield Academic, 1997.

———. *La crise maccabéenne: historiographie juive et traditions bibliques.* Paris: Cerf, 2005.

———. "La dédicace, les maccabées et le messiée." *RB* 93 (1986) 321–75.

Noegel, Scott B. *Nocturnal Ciphers: The Allusive Language of Dreams in the Ancient Near East.* New Haven: American Oriental Society, 2007.

———. "The Significance of the Seventh Plague," *Bib* 76 (1995) 532–39.

Nolan, James L. *The Therapeutic State: Justifying Government at Century's End.* New York: NYU Press, 1998.

Noonan, John T., and Dan M. Kahan. "Bribery." In *Encyclopedia of Crime and Justice*, edited by Joshua Dressler, 105–11. New York: MacMillan, 2002.

North, Douglas C. *Structure and Change in Economic History.* New York: Norton, 1981.

North, Gary. *Foundations of Christian Scholarship.* Vellocito, CA: Ross House, 1976.

Noth, Martin. *A History of Pentateuchal Traditions*, 1948. Translated by Bernhard W. Anderson. Englewood Cliffs, NJ: Prentice-Hall, 1972.

Nötscher, Friedrich. *Zur theologischen Terminologie der Qumrantexte.* Bonn: Hanstein, 1956.

Nunn, John Francis. *Ancient Egyptian Medicine.* Norman: University of Oklahoma Press, 1996.

Nussbaum, Martha. "Aristotle, Politics, and Human Capabilities." *Ethics* 111 (2000) 102–40.

———. "Fears for Democracy in India," *Chronicle of Higher Education* 53 (May 18, 2007) B6.

Nye, Robert A. "Honor and Shame." In *EESH* 5:103–13.

Oakman, Douglas E. "Biblical Hermeneutics: Marcion's Truth and a Developmental Perspective." In *Ancient Israel: The Old Testament in Its Social Context*, edited by Philip F. Esler, 267–82. Minneapolis: Fortress, 2006.

————. "Money in the Moral Universe of the New Testament." In *The Social Setting of Jesus and the Gospels*, edited by Bruce Malina, et al., 335–48. Minneapolis: Fortress, 2002.

O'Brien, Conor Cruise. *The Long Affair: Thomas Jefferson and the French Revolution.* Chicago: University of Chicago Press, 1998.

O'Brien, Dennis P. *The Classical Economists Revisited.* Princeton: Princeton University Press, 2004.

Oded, Bustanay, and Shimon Gibson. "Canaan." In *EJ* 4:391–93.

Oden, Robert A. "The Contendings of Horus and Seth: A Structural Interpretation." *History of Religions* 18 (1979) 352–69.

Ogden Bellis, Alice, and Joel Kaminski. *Jews, Christians, and the Theology of the Hebrew Scriptures.* Atlanta: Society of Biblical Literature, 2000.

Ohrenstein, Roman A. and Barry Gordon, *Economic Analysis in Talmudic Literature: Rabbinic Thought in the Light of Modern Economics.* Leiden: Brill, 1992.

Ollenburger, Ben C. "Jubilee: 'The Land is Mine; You are Aliens and Tenants with Me.'" In *Reclaiming the Old Testament: Essays in Honour of Waldemar Janzen*, edited by Gordon M. Zerbe, 208–34. Winnipeg: CMBC, 2001.

Olson, Dennis T. "Power and Leadership: Moses and the Manna Story." *Princeton Seminary Bulletin* 25 (2004) 316–31.

————. *The Death of the Old and the Birth of the New: The Framework of the Book of Numbers and the Pentateuch.* Chico, CA: Scholars, 1985.

Oort, Johannes van. *Jerusalem and Babylon: A Study into Augustine's "City of God" and Sources of His Doctrine of the Two Cities.* Leiden: Brill, 1991.

Oosthuizen, Rudolph de wet. Review of *Genesis: The Story We Haven't Heard*, by P. Borgman. *RBL* (www.bookreviews.org) 2004.

Omura, Masako. "Stamp Seals from Kaman-Kalehöyük Dated from the 1st Millenium B.C." In *Essays on Ancient Anatolia and Its Surrounding Civilizations*, edited by Takahito Mikasa, 43–58. Wiesbaden: Harrassowitz, 1995.

Oppenheim, A. Leo. *Ancient Mesopotamia: Portrait of a Dead Civilization.* Chicago: University of Chicago Press, 1977.

————. *The Interpretation of Dreams in the Ancient Near East.* Philadelphia: American Philosophical Society, 1956.

Orlin, Eric M. "Politics and Religion: Politics and Ancient Mediterranean Religions." In *ER* 11:7275–79.

Osteen, Joel. *Become a Better You: Seven Keys to Improving Your Life Every Day.* New York: Free, 2007.

Otto, Eckhart. "Die Paradieserzählung Genesis 2–3: Eine nachpriesterschriftliche Lehrerzählung in ihrem religionshistorischen Kontext." In *"Jedes Ding hat seine Zeit . . ." Studien zur israelitischen Weisheit: Festschrift für Diethelm Michel zum 65. Geburtstag*, edited by Anja Angela Diesel et al., 167–92. Berlin: de Gruyter, 1996.

————. *Krieg und Frieden in der Hebraischen Bibel und im Alten Orient.* Stuttgart: Kohlhammer, 1999.

————. *Mose.* Stuttgart: Katholisches Bildwerkung, 2000.

————. "Soziale Restitution und Vertragsrecht: *mīšarum, (an)-durāru(m), kirenzi, parā tarnumar, šemitta* und *derôr* in Mesopotamien, Syrien, in der hebräischen Bibel und die Frage des Rechtstransfers im alten Orient." *RA* 92 (1998) 125–60.

Pacwa, Mitchell C. "Alexander." In *ABD* 1:150–51.

Page, Denys Lionel. *Homeric Odyssey.* Oxford: Clarendon, 1955.

Palmer, Parker J. "A World of Scarcity, A Gospel of Abundance." In *The Promise of Paradox: A Celebration of Contradictions in the Christian Life*, 94–115. San Francisco: Jossey-Bass, 2008.

Paradise, Jonathan. "Marriage Contracts of Free Persons at Nuzi." *JCS* 39 (1987) 1–36.

Parchami, Ali. *Hegemonic Empire: The Pax Romana, Brittanica, and Americana*. London, Routledge, 2009.

Pardee, Dennis. Review of *The Goddess Anat in Ugaritic Myth*, by Neal H. Walls. *JBL* 113 (1994) 505–6.

Parish, Peter J. *Slavery: History and Historians*. Boulder, CO: Westview, 1990.

Parker, Simon B. "The Historical Composition of *KRT* and the Cult of El." *ZAW* 89 (1977) 161–75.

———. *The Pre-Biblical Narrative Tradition: Essays on the Ugaritic Poems* Keret *and* Aqhat. Atlanta: Scholars, 1989.

———. "Ugaritic Literature and the Bible." *Near Eastern Archaeology* 63 (2000) 228–31.

———. *Ugaritic Narrative Poetry*. Atlanta: Scholars, 1997.

Parkinson, R. *The Tale of Sinuhe and Other Ancient Egyptian Poems*. New York: Oxford University Press, 1999.

Parpola, Simo. *Assyrian Prophecies*. Helsinki: Helsinki University Press, 1997.

———. *Letters from Assyrian Scholars to the Kings Esarhaddon and Assurbanipal*. Winona Lake, IN: Eisenbrauns, 2007.

———. "The Assyrian Tree of Life." *JNES* 52 (1993) 161–208.

———. "The Esoteric Meaning of the Epic of Gilgamesh." In *Intellectual Life in the Ancient Near East: Papers Presented at the 43rd Rencontre Assyriologique Internationale*, edited by Jiři Prosecky, 318–27. Prague: Academy of Sciences of the Czech Republic, 1998.

Patterson, Orlando. *Slavery and Social Death: A Comparative Study*. Cambridge, MA: Harvard University Press, 1982.

Paul, Shalom. "The 'Plural of Ecstasy' in Mesopotamian and Biblical Love Poetry." In *Solving Riddles and Untying Knots: Biblical, Epigraphic, and Semitic Studies in Honor of Jonas C. Greenfield*, edited by Ziony Zevit et al., 585–98. Winona Lake, IN: Eisenbrauns, 1995.

Payne, Ruby K. *A Framework for Understanding Poverty*. Highlands, TX: aha-Process, 2005.

Pelikan, Jaroslav. *Luther's Works*. St. Louis: Concordia, 1958.

Perdue, Leo. *Reconstructing Old Testament Theology: After the Collapse of History*. Minneapolis: Augsburg Fortress, 2005.

Perelman, Michael. *The Invention of Capitalism: Classical Political Economy and the Secret History of Primitive Accumulation*. Durham: Duke University Press, 2000.

Perlitt, Lothar. "Die Aporie der gegenwärtigen Pentateuchdiskussion und die Joseferzählung der Genesis." *BZ* 29 (1985) 31–48.

Perry, T. Anthony. "Cain's Sin in Genesis 4:1–7: Oracular Ambiguity and How to Avoid It." *Prooftexts* 25 (2005) 258–75.

Petersen, David. "Genesis and Family Values," *JBL* 124 (2005) 5–23.

———. *The Roles of Israel's Prophets*. Sheffield: JSOT, 1981.

Peterson, Richard R. "A Re-evaluation of the Economic Consequences of Divorce." *ASR* 61 (1996) 528–36.

Petit, Paul. *Pax Romana*. Berkeley: University of California Press, 1976.

Pettinato, Giovanni. "Ebla and the Bible." *BA* 43 (1980) 203–16.

————. *Ebla, A New Look at History*. Baltimore: Johns Hopkins University Press, 1991.

————. *Das altorientalische Menschenbild und die sumerischen und akkadischen Schöpfungsmythen*. Heidelberg: Winter, 1971.

————. "Die Bestrafung des Menschengeschlechts durch die Sintflut." *Or* 37 (1968) 165–200.

————. "Mesopotamian Religions: An Overview." In *ER* 9:5963–67.

Philips, Michael. "Bribery." *Ethics* 94 (1984) 621–36.

Picchioni, S. A. *Il poemetto di Adapa*. Budapest: ELTE Sokszorositóüzemében, 1981.

Pippidi, D. M. *Inscriptiones Daciae et Scythiae Minoris Antiquae. Series Altera: Inscriptiones Scythiae Minoris Graecae et Latinae*. Bucharest: Romanian Academy, 1983.

Pientka, Rosel. *Die spätaltbabylonische Zeit: Abiešuh bis Samsuditana—Quellen, Jahresdaten, Geschichte*. Münster: Rhema, 1998.

Pinnock, Clark. "Pursuit of Utopia, Betrayal of the Poor." *Crux* 23 (1987) 5–14.

Pirson, Ron. *The Lord of the Dreams: A Semantic and Literary Analysis of Genesis 37–50*. New York: Sheffield Academic, 2002.

————. "The Two-Fold Message of Potiphar's Wife." *SJOT* 18 (2004) 248–59.

Pitard, Wayne Thomas. "Aram-Naharaim." In *ABD* 1:341.

Pleins, J. David. "Murderous Fathers, Manipulative Mothers, and Rivalrous Siblings: Rethinking the Architecture of Genesis-Kings." In *Fortunate the Eyes That See: Essays in Honor of David Noel Freedman in Celebration of His Seventieth Birthday*, edited by Astrid Beck et al., 121–36. Grand Rapids: Eerdmans, 1995.

Pöhlmann, Wolfgang. *Der Verlorene Sohn und das Haus: Studien zu Lukas 15.11–32 im Horizont der antiken Lehre von Haus, Erziehung und Ackerbau*. Tübingen: Mohr Siebeck, 1993.

Polanyi, Karl. *The Livelihood of Man*. New York: Academic, 1977.

Polaski, Donald. *Authorizing an End: The Isaiah Apocalypse and Intertextuality*. Leiden: Brill, 2000.

————. "What Mean These Stones? Inscriptions, Textuality and Power in Persia and Yehud." In *Approaching Yehud: New Approaches to the Study of the Persian Period*, edited by Jon L. Berquist, 37–48. Atlanta: Society of Biblical Literature, 2007.

Pollard, Anthony James. *Imagining Robin Hood: the Late-Medieval Stories in Historical Context*. London: Routledge, 2004.

Pollard, Arthur. *Satire*. London: Methuen, 1982.

Pomeroy, Sarah B. *Xenophon, Oeconomicus: A Social and Historical Commentary*. Oxford: Clarendon, 1995.

Porton, Gary G. "Diversity in Postbiblical Judaism." In *Early Judaism and Its Modern Interpreters*, edited by Robert G. Kraft and George W. E. Nickelsburg, 57–80. Atlanta: Scholars, 1986.

Posner, R. "A Theory of Primitive Society, with Special Reference to Law." *Journal of Law and Economics* 23 (1980) 1–53.

Postgate, J. Nicholas. *Early Mesopotamia: Society and Economy at the Dawn of History*. London: Routledge, 1994.

————. Review of *L'Épopée de Gilgamesh*, by R. Tournay and A. Shaffer. *VT* 46 (1996) 575–76.

————. Review of *The Book of Ezekiel and the Poem of Erra*, by Daniel Bodi. *VT* 43 (1993) 137.

Potts, Alex. *Flesh and the Ideal. Winckelmann and the Origins of Art History*. New Haven: Yale University Press, 1994.

Pounds, Norman J. *An Economic History of Medieval Europe*. London: Longman, 1994.

Preuss, Horst Dietrich. *Old Testament Theology.* Louisville: Westminster John Knox, 1995.

Pritchard, James Bennett. *Ancient Near Eastern Texts Relating to the Old Testament.* Princeton: Princeton University Press, 1969.

Propp, William Henry. "Symbolic Wounds: Applying Anthropology to the Bible." In *Le-David Maskil: A Birthday Tribute for David Noel Freedman,* edited by Richard Friedman and William Propp, 17–24. Winona Lake, IN: Eisenbrauns, 2004.

Prothero, Roland E. *The Works of Lord Byron: Letters and Journals.* London: Murray, 1922.

Provan, Iain. *1 and 2 Kings.* Peabody, MA: Hendrickson, 1995.

Pryor, Frederick L. "Simulation of the Impact of Social and Economic Institutions on the Size Distribution of Income and Wealth." *American Economic Review* 63 (1973) 50–72.

Puech, Emile. "Hodayot." In *EDSS* 1:365–69.

Purvis, James D. *The Samaritan Pentateuch and the Origin of the Samaritan Sect.* Cambridge, MA: Harvard University Press, 1968.

Puzo, Mario. *The Godfather.* New York: Signet, 1969.

Pyper, Hugh S. "The Enticement to Re-Read: Repetition as Parody in 2 Samuel." *BibInt* 1 (1993) 153–66.

Quiñones, Ricardo J. *The Changes of Cain: Violence and the Lost Brother in Cain and Abel Literature.* Princeton: Princeton University Press, 1991.

Rabin, Chaim. *The Zadokite Documents.* Oxford: Clarendon, 1958.

Rabinowitz, Louis Isaac. "Famine and Drought." In *EJ* 6:707–8.

Rad, Gerhard von. *Das erste Buch Mose.* Göttingen: Vandenhoeck und Ruprecht, 1958.

———. "Josephsgeschichte und ältere Chokma." *VTSup* 3 (1953) 120–27.

———. *Old Testament Theology.* New York: Harper and Row, 1962.

———. *Wisdom in Israel.* London: SCM, 1972.

Rainbow, Paul. "The Last Oniad and the Teacher of Righteousness." *JJS* 48 (1997) 30–52.

Rainey, Anson F. "Unruly Elements in Late Bronze Canaanite Society." In *Pomegranates and Golden Bells: Studies in Biblical, Jewish, and Near Eastern Ritual, Law, and Literature in Honor of Jacob Milgrom,* edited by David P. Wright et al., 481–96. Winona Lake, IN: Eisenbrauns, 1995.

Rajak, Tessa. "Jews and Greeks: The Invention and Exploitation of Polarities in the Nineteenth Century." In *The Jewish Dialogue with Greece and Rome: Studies in Cultural and Social Interaction,* 535–57. Leiden: Brill, 2001.

Rand, Herbert. "David and Ahab: A Study of Crime and Punishment." *JBQ* 24 (1996) 90–97.

Rangarajan, L. N. *The Arthashastra of Kautilya.* New York: Penguin, 1992.

Rapoport, David C. "Moses, Charisma, and Covenant." *Western Political Quarterly* 32 (1979) 123–43.

Rappaport, David. "Religion and Terror: Thugs, Assassins, and Zealots." In *International Terrorism: Characteristics, Causes, Controls,* edited by Charles W. Kegley, 147–49. New York: St. Martin's, 1990.

Rappaport, Uriel. "Bacchides." In *ABD* 1:566–67.

———. "John of Gischala: From Galilee to Jerusalem." *JJS* 33 (1982) 477–93.

———. "Nicanor." In *EJ* 15:247.

———. "Simon the Hasmonean." In *EJ* 18:601.

Rasmussen, Larry. *Economic Anxiety and Christian Faith.* Minneapolis: Augsburg, 1981.

Rau, Eckhard. *Reden in Vollmacht, Hintergrund, Form und Anliegen der Gleichnisse Jesu.* Göttingen: Vandenhoeck & Ruprecht, 1990.

Ray, Larry. "Post-Communism: Postmodernity or Modernity Revisited?" *BJS* 48 (1997) 543–60.

Redford, Donald B. *Akhenaten, the Heretic King.* Princeton: Princeton University Press, 1984.

———. *A Study of the Biblical Story of Joseph.* Leiden: Brill, 1970.

Redditt, Paul. "Israel's Shepherds: Hope and Pessimism in Zechariah 9–14." *CBQ* 51 (1989) 631–42.

Redlawsk, David P., and James A. McCann. "Popular Interpretation of 'Corruption' and Their Partisan Consequences." *Political Behavior* 27 (2005) 261–83.

Reeder, Greg. "Running the *Heb-Sed.*" *KMT: A Modern Journal of Ancient Egypt* 4, 4 (1993–94) 60–71.

Regev, Eyal. "Comparing Sectarian Practice and Organization: The Qumran Sects in Light of the Regulations of the Shakers, Hutterites, Mennonites and Amish." *Numen* 51 (2004) 146–81.

Reiner, Erica. "Die akkadische Literatur." In *Neues Handbuch der Literatur-Wissenschaft: Altorientalische Literaturen,* edited by Wolfgang Röllig, 1.151–210. Wiesbaden: Athenaion, 1978.

Reis, Pamela Tamarkin. "Uncovering Jael and Sisera: A New Reading." *SJOT* 19 (2005) 24–47.

Rendsburg, Gary A. "Notes on Genesis xxxv." *VT* 34 (1984) 361–66.

Resic, Sanimir. *American Warriors in Vietnam: Warrior Values and the Myth of the War Experience during the Vietnam War 1965–1973.* Malmö: Team Offset and Media, 1999.

Riaño, Juanita, and Robin Hodess. "Transparency International's 2008 Bribe Payers Report," 1–21. Online: www.transparency.org/publications/publications/bribe_payers_index_2008.

Richard, Suzanne. *Near Eastern Archaeology: A Reader.* Winona Lake, IN: Eisenbrauns, 2003.

Richards, Alan, and John Waterbury. *A Political Economy of the Middle East.* Boulder, CO: Westview, 2007.

Riches, David. "The Obligation to Give: An Interactional Sketch." In *The Structure of Folk Models,* edited by Ladislav Holy and Milan Stuchlik, 209–31. New York: Academic, 1981.

Ricoeur, Paul. "Myth: Myth and History." In *ER* 9:6373–80.

———. *The Symbolism of Evil.* Boston: Beacon, 1967.

Riemann, Paul A. "Am I My Brother's Keeper?" *Int* 24 (1970) 482–91.

Ries, Julien. "Blessing." In *ER* 2:247–50.

Ringgren, Helmer. "גאל." In *TDOT* 2:350–55.

Robbins, Lionel. *An Essay on the Nature and Significance of Economic Science.* London: Macmillan, 1932.

Roberts, Jimmy Jack McBee. "Erra: Scorched Earth." *JCS* 24 (1971) 11–16.

———. *Nahum, Habakkuk and Zephaniah.* Louisville: Westminster John Knox, 1991.

———. *The Earliest Semitic Pantheon: A Study of the Semitic Deities Attested in Mesopotamia Before Ur III.* Baltimore: Johns Hopkins University Press, 1972.

———. "The Hand of Yahweh." *VT* 21 (1971) 244–51.

———. "The Mari Prophetic Texts in Transliteration and English Translation." In *The Bible and the Ancient Near East*, 157–253. Winona Lake, IN: Eisenbrauns, 2002.

Robinson, Bernard P. "Zipporah to the Rescue: A Contextual Study of Exodus iv 24–6." *VT* 36 (1986) 447–61.

Roche, Carole. "The Lady of Ugarit." *Near Eastern Archaeology* 63 (2000) 214–15.

Rohrlich, Ruby. "State Formation in Sumer and the Subjugation of Women." *Feminist Studies* 6 (1980) 76–102.

Rorty, Richard. "Texts and Lumps." *New Literary History* 17 (1985) 1–16.

Rose-Ackerman, Susan. *Corruption and Government: Causes, Consequences and Reform.* Cambridge: Cambridge University Press, 1999.

Roseberry, William. "Political Economy." *Annual Review of Anthropology* 17 (1988) 161–85.

Rosenberg. Joel C. *The Last Days: A Novel.* Wheaton, IL: Tyndale House, 2006.

Rosenberg, Stephen G. "Onias, Temple of." In *EJ* 15:432–33.

Rosenfeld, Ben Tsiyon, and Joseph Menirav. *Markets and Marketing in Roman Palestine.* Leiden: Brill, 2005.

Ross, Allen P. *Holiness to the Lord: A Guide to the Exposition of the Book of Leviticus.* Grand Rapids: Baker, 2002.

Rostovtzeff, Mikhail. *The Social and Economic History of the Ancient World.* Oxford: Clarendon, 1941.

Roth, Cecil, and Menahem Elon. "Taxation." In *EJ* 19:532–58.

Roth, Martha. "The Dowries of the Women of the Itti-Marduk-Balatu Family." *JAOS* 111 (1991) 19–37.

Rouland, Robert. "Sociological Norms and the Heroic Epic." *Journal of Comparative Literature and Aesthetics* 12–13 (1989–90) 90–99.

Rowe, Ignacio Márquez. "How Can Someone Sell His Own Fellow to the Egyptians?" *VT* 54 (2004) 335–43.

Rowley, Harold Henry. *The Biblical Doctrine of Election.* London: Lutterworth, 1950.

Rowton, M. B. "The Woodlands of Ancient Western Asia." *JNES* 26 (1967) 261–77.

Rubio, Gonzalo. "Inanna and Dumuzi: A Sumerian Love Story." *JAOS* 121 (2001) 268–74.

Rudman, Dominic. "A Little Knowledge Is a Dangerous Thing: Crossing Forbidden Boundaries in Gen 3–4." In *Studies in the Book of Genesis: Literature, Redaction, and History*, edited by André Wénin, 461–66. Leuven: Peeters, 2001.

Ruppel, Karl August. *Theologie und Wirtschaft: Konzepte protestantischer Wirstschaftsethik zwischen Aufklärung und Industrialisierung.* Hildesheim: Olms, 1999.

Ruppert, Lothar. "Abram und Lot: Zwei ungleiche 'Bruder.'" In *Schöpfungsplan und Heilsgeschichte: Festschrift für Ernst Haag*, edited by Renate Brandscheidt and Theresia Mende, 235–50. Trier: Paulinus, 2002.

Sabbath, Roberta S. "General Introduction." In *Sacred Tropes: Tanakh, New Testament, and Qur'an as Literature and Culture,* edited by Roberta S. Sabbath, 1–12. Leiden: Brill, 2009.

Safire, William. *The First Dissident: The Book of Job in Today's Politics.* New York: Random House, 1992.

Safrai, Zeev. *The Economy of Roman Palestine.* London: Routledge, 1994.

———, and Hanan Eshel. "Economic Life." In *EDSS* 1:228–33.

Saghieh, Muntaha. *Byblos in the Third Millenium B.C.: A Reconstruction of the Stratigraphy and a Study of the Cultural Connections.* Warminster: Aris and Phillips, 1983.

Sahlins, Marshall David. *Stone Age Economics.* Hawthorne, NY: Aldine de Gruyter, 1972.

Said, Edward W. *Culture and Imperialism.* New York: Vintage, 1994.

Sakenfeld, Katharine Doob. "Zelophehad's Daughters." *Perspectives on Religious Studies* 15 (1988) 37–47.

Sallaberger, Walter. *Das Gilgamesch-Epos: Mythos, Werk und Tradition.* Munich: Beck, 2008.

———. "Der 'Prolog' des Codex Lipit-Ishtar." In *"Gerechtigkeit und Recht zu üben" (Gen 18,19): Studien zur altorientalischen und biblischen Rechtsgeschichte, zur Religionsgeschichte Israels und zur Religionssoziologie. Festschrift für Eckart Otto zum 65. Geburtstag,* edited by Reinhard Achenbach and Martin Arneth, 7–33. Wiesbaden: Harrassowitz, 2009.

Samuel, Alan. *From Athens to Alexandria: Hellenism and Social Goals in Ptolemaic Egypt.* Louvain: Studia Hellenistica, 1983.

Sanders, James A. *Canon and Community: A Guide to Canonical Criticism.* Philadelphia: Fortress, 1987.

Sandmel, Samuel. *Anti-Semitism in the New Testament?* Philadelphia, Fortress, 1978.

Sandoval, Timothy. *The Discourse of Wealth and Poverty in the Book of Proverbs.* Leiden: Brill, 2007.

Santayana, George. *The Life of Reason.* New York: Scribner's Sons, 1906.

Santiko, Hariani. "The Goddess Durgā in the East Javanese Period." *Asian Folklore Studies* 56 (1997) 209–26.

Sarachek, Bernard. "Greek Concepts of Leadership." *Academy of Management Journal* 11 (1968) 39–48.

Sarna, Nahum, et al. "Cain." In *EJ* 4.340–42.

———. *Understanding Genesis.* New York: Schocken, 1972.

Sasson, Jack M. "The Servant's Tale: How Rebekah Found a Spouse." *JNES* 65 (2006) 241–65.

Saulnier, Stéphane. "La révolte." *MB* 43 (1986) 26–29.

Savignac, Jean de. "La sagesse du Qôhéléth et l'épopée de Gilgamesh." *VT* 28 (1978) 318–23.

Schäfer, Peter. *Judeophobia: Attitudes Toward the Jews in the Ancient World.* Cambridge: Cambridge University Press, 1998.

Schaffer, Aaron. "Gilgamesh, the Cedar Forest, and Mesopotamian History." *JAOS* 103 (1983) 307–13.

Schalit, Abraham. "Demetrius I Soter." In *EJ* 5:549–50.

Schams, Christine. *Jewish Scribes in the Second-Temple Period.* Sheffield: Sheffield Academic, 1998.

Scharbert, Josef. "ברך." In *TDOT* 2:279–308.

Scheff, Thomas J. "Shame and the Social Bond: A Sociological Theory." *Sociological Theory* 18 (2000) 84–99.

Schein, Seth L. *The Mortal Hero: An Introduction to Homer's Iliad.* Berkeley: University of California Press, 1984.

Scherer, Andreas Georg. "Is the Selfish Man Wise? Considerations of Context in Proverbs 10:1—22:16 with Special Regard to Surety, Bribery, and Friendship." *JSOT* 76 (1997) 59–70.

Schiffman, Lawrence H. "Dead Sea Scrolls." In *ER* 4:2233–35.

———. "Miqtsat Ma`asei Ha-Torah." In *EDSS* 1:558–60.

———. *Reclaiming the Dead Sea Scrolls.* New York: Doubleday, 1995.

———. *Sectarian Law in the Dead Sea Scrolls: Courts, Testimony, and the Penal Code.* Chico, CA: Scholars, 1983.

———. *The Halakhah at Qumran.* Leiden: Brill, 1975.

Schippe, Cullen, and Chuck Stetson, eds. *The Bible and Its Influence.* Fairfield, VA: Bible Literary Project, 2005.

Schloen, J. David. *The House of the Father as Fact and Symbol: Patrimonialism in Ugarit and the Ancient Near East.* Winona Lake, IN: Eisenbrauns, 2001.

———. "The Exile of Disinherited Kin in *CAT* 1.12 and *CAT* 1.23." *JNES* 52 (1993) 209–20.

Schmithals, W. "Zum Problem der Entmythologisierung bei Rudolf Bultmann." *ZTK* 92 (1995) 166–206.

Schmitt, Richard. *Alienation and Freedom.* Boulder, CO: Westview, 2002.

Schneidau, Herbert. *Sacred Discontent: The Bible and Western Tradition.* Baton Rouge: Louisiana State University Press, 1976.

Schneider, Jennifer P. "Rebuilding the Marriage During Recovery from Compulsive Sexual Behavior." *Family Relations* 38 (1989) 288–94.

Schniedewind, William. *How the Bible Became a Book: The Textualization of Ancient Israel.* New York: Cambridge University Press, 2004.

Scholem, Gershom Gerhard. *Ursprung und Anfänge der Kabbala.* Berlin: Walter deGruyter, 1962.

Schorn, Ulrike. *Ruben und das System der zwölf Stämme Israels: Redaktionsgeschichtliche Untersuchungen zur Bedeutung des Erstgeborene Jakobs.* Berlin: de Gruyter, 1997.

Schottroff, Willy. *Der altisraelitisch Fluchspruch.* Neukirchen-Vluyn: Neukirchener, 1969.

Schultz, James H., and Robert H. Binstock. *Aging Nation: the Economics and Politics of Growing Older in America.* Baltimore: Johns Hopkins University Press, 2008.

Schultze, Quentin. *Communicating for Life: Christian Stewardship on Community and Media.* Grand Rapids: Baker, 2000.

———. *Televangelism and American Culture: The Business of Popular Religion.* Grand Rapids: Baker, 1991.

Schwartz, Daniel R. *2 Maccabees.* Berlin: de Gruyter, 2008.

Schwartz, Regina M. *The Curse of Cain: The Violent Legacy of Monotheism.* Chicago: University of Chicago Press, 1997.

Schwartz, Seth. "A Note on the Social Type and Political Ideology of the Hasmonean Family." *JBL* 112 (1993) 305–9.

———. "The 'Judaism' of Samaria and Galilee in Josephus' Version of the Letter of Demetrius I to Jonathan." *HTR* 82 (1989) 377–91.

Scott, Bernard Brandon. *Hear Then the Parable: A Commentary on the Parables of Jesus.* Minneapolis: Fortress, 1989.

Seaford, Richard. *Money and the Early Greek Mind: Homer, Philosophy, Tragedy.* Cambridge: Cambridge University Press, 2004.

Seely, Paul. "The Firmament and the Water Above. Part I: The Meaning of רקיע in Gen 1:6–8." *WTJ* 53 (1991) 227–40.

Segal, Moshe Zevi, and Bathja Bayer. "Ben Sira, Wisdom of." In *EJ* 3:376–78.

Sefati, Yitzhak. *Love Songs in Sumerian Literature: A Critical Edition of the Dumuzi-Inanna Songs.* Ramat Gan: Bar-Ilan University, 1998.

Segal, Charles. "The Raw and the Cooked in Greek Literature: Structures, Values, Metaphor." *The Classical Journal* 69 (1974) 289–308.

Segovia, Fernando F. and Mary Ann Tolbert, eds. *Teaching the Bible: The Discourses and Politics of Biblical Pedagogy.* Maryknoll, NY: Orbis, 1998.

Sethe, Kurt. *Die altagyptischen Pyramidtexte.* Leipzig: Hinrichs, 1908.

Seow, Choon Leong. "The Syro-Palestinian Context of Solomon's Dream." *HTR* 77 (1984) 141–52.

Shapiro, Aharon H. "Moses: Henry George's Inspiration." *AJES* 47 (1988) 493–501.

Sharon, Diane M. "Some Results of a Structural Semiotic Analysis of the Story of Judah and Tamar." *JSOT* 29 (2005) 289–318.

Shavit, Yaacov. *Athens in Jerusalem: Classical Antiquity and Hellenism in the Making of the Modern Secular Jew.* London: Littman Library, 1997.

Shelley, Mary. *Frankenstein; Or The Modern Prometheus,* 1817. Reprinted. Oxford: Oxford University Press, 1969.

Shemesh, Yael. "A Gender Perspective on the Daughters of Zelophehad: Bible, Talmudic Midrash, and Modern Feminist Midrash." *BI* 15 (2007) 80–109.

Sherwood, Yvonne. *A Biblical Text and Its Afterlives: The Survival of Jonah in Western Culture.* Cambridge: Cambridge University Press, 2000.

Shields, M. "To Seek but Not to Find: Old Meanings for *Qohelet* and *Gilgamesh.*" In *Gilgamesh and the World of Assyria,* edited by Joseph Azize and Noel Weeks, 129–46. Leuven: Peeters, 2006.

Shipp, Mark. *Of Dead Kings and Dirges: Myth and Meaning in Isaiah 14:4b–21.* Leiden: Brill, 2003.

Shulman, George M. "The Myth of Cain: Fratricide, City-Building, and Politics." *Political Theory* 14 (1986) 215–38.

Sicherman, Harvey, and Gilad J. Gevaryahu. "Foremost in Rank and Foremost in Power": Conflict over the Firstborn in Israel." *JBQ* 31 (2002) 17–25.

Sider, Ronald J. *Rich Christians in an Age of Hunger: Moving from Affluence to Generosity.* 4th ed. Nashville: Thomas Nelson, 2005.

Siebert-Hommes, Jopie. "Die Geburtsgeschichte des Mose innerhalb des Erzählzusammenhangs von *Exodus* i und ii." *VT* 42 (1992) 398–404.

Sievers, Joseph. "Jerusalem, the Akra, and Josephus." In *Josephus and the History of the Graeco-Roman Period: Essays in Memory of Morton Smith,* edited by Fausto Parente and Joseph Sievers, 195–209. Leiden: Brill, 1994.

Sigrist, R. Marcel. "Nippur entre Isin et Larsa de Sin-iddinam à Rim-Sin." *Or* 46 (1977) 363–74.

———. "Offrandes dans le temple de Nusku à Nippur." *JCS* 29 (1977) 169–83.

Silberman, Lou H. "Chosen People." In *EJ* 4:669–72.

Silberman, Neil Asher. "Media." In *EDSS* 2:533.

Silver, Morris. *Ancient Economy in Mythology.* Savage, MD: Rowman & Littlefield, 1991.

———. *Economic Structures of Antiquity.* Westport, CT: Greenwood, 1995.

———. *Economic Structures of the Ancient Near East.* Totowa, NJ: Barnes & Noble, 1986.

———. *Prophets and Markets: The Political Economy of Ancient Israel.* Boston: Kluwer-Nijhoff, 1983.

———. "Karl Polanyi and Markets in the Ancient Near East: The Challenge of the Evidence." *Journal of Economic History* 43 (1983) 795–829.

———. *Taking Ancient Mythology Economically.* New York: Brill, 1992.

Simundson, Daniel J. *The Message of Job: A Theological Commentary.* Minneapolis: Augsburg, 1986.

Sitzler, Dorothea. *Vorwurf gegen Gott: ein religiöses Motiv im Alten Orient*. Wiesbaden: Harrassowitz, 1995.

Sjöberg, Åke W. "*In-nin šà-gu-ra*: A Hymn to the Goddess Inanna." *ZA* 65 (1976) 161–253.

Skinner, E. Benjamin. *A Crime So Monstrous: Face-to-Face with Modern-Day Slavery*. New York: Free, 2008.

———. "A World Enslaved." *Foreign Policy* 165 (2008) 62–67.

Skinner, John. *A Critical and Exegetical Commentary on Genesis*. Edinburgh: T. & T. Clark, 1930.

Sklair, Leslie. *Globalization: Capitalism and Its Alternatives*. Oxford: Oxford University Press, 2002.

Slanski, Kathryn E. "Classification, Historiography and Monumental Authority: The Babylonian Entitlement *narûs* (*kudurrus*)." *JCS* 52 (2000) 95–114.

Sloyan, Gerard Stephen. *Religions of the Book*. Lanham, MD: University Press of America, 1996.

Smart, James D. *The Strange Silence of the Bible in the Church*. Philadelphia: Westminster, 1970.

Smith, Adam. *An Enquiry into the Nature and Causes of the Wealth of Nations*, 1776. Reprint, New York: Smith, 1948.

Smith, Edwin William, and Andrew Murray Dale. *The Ila-Speaking Peoples of Northern Rhodesia*. New Hyde Park, NY: University, 1920.

Smith, Gary Scott. "Evangelicals Confront Corporate Capitalism: Advertising, Consumerism, Stewardship, and Spirituality, 1880–1930." In *More Money, More Ministry: Money and Evangelicals in Recent North American History*, edited by Larry Eskridge and Mark A. Noll, 39–80. Grand Rapids: Eerdmans, 2000.

Smith, Mark S. *The Early History of God: Yahweh and the Other Deities of Ancient Israel*. Grand Rapids: Eerdmans, 2002.

———. *The Memoirs of God: History, Memory and the Experience of the Divine in Ancient Israel*. Minneapolis: Fortress, 2004.

———. "The Near Eastern Background of Solar Language for Yahweh." *JBL* 109 (1990) 29–39.

———. *The Origins of Biblical Monotheism: Israel's Polytheistic Background and the Ugaritic Texts*. New York: Oxford University Press, 2001.

———. *The Pilgrimage Pattern in Exodus*. Sheffield: Sheffield Academic, 1997.

———. *The Ugaritic Baal Cycle: Volume I, Introduction with Text, Translation and Commentary of CAT 1.1–2*. Leiden: Brill, 1994.

———, and Wayne Pitard. *The Ugaritic Baal Cycle: Volume II, Introduction with Text, Translation and Commentary of CAT 1.3–4*. Leiden: Brill, 2009.

Smith, Morton. *Palestinian Parties and Politics that Shaped the Old Testament*. London: SCM Press, 1987.

Snaith, Norman Henry. "The Daughters of Zelophehad." *VT* 16 (1966) 124–27.

Snell, Daniel C. *Flight and Freedom in the Ancient Near East*. Leiden: Brill, 2001.

———. *Life in the Ancient Near East*. New Haven: Yale, 1997.

———. "Methods of Exchange and Coinage in Ancient Western Asia." In *CANE* 3:1487–97.

Soards, Marion L. *The Speeches in Acts: Their Content, Context, and Concerns*. Louisville: Westminster John Knox, 1994.

Sobti, Manu P. "Persepolis." In *EMA* 4:477–79.

Sommerfeld, Walter. *Der Aufstieg Marduks. Die Stellung Marduks in der babylonischen Religion des zweiten Jahrtausends v. Chr.* Kevelaer: Butzon und Bercker, 1982.

Soden, Wolfram von. "'Als die Götter (auch noch) Mensch waren.' Einige Grundgedanken des altbabylonischen Atramhasis-Mythus." *Or* 38 (1969) 413–21.

———. "Etemenanki vor Asarhaddon nach der Erzählung vom Turmbau zu Babel und dem Erra-Mythos." *UF* 3 (1971) 253–63.

———. *The Ancient Orient: An Introduction to the Study of the Ancient Near East.* Grand Rapids; Eerdmans, 1994.

Soelle, Dorothy. "Peace Needs Women." *USQR* 38 (1983) 83–91.

Solé, Robert, and Dominique Valbelle. *The Rosetta Stone: The Story of the Decoding of Hieroglyphics.* London: Profile, 2002.

Spalinger, Anthony. "Orientations on Sinuhe." *Studien zur Ältägyptischen Kultur* 25 (1998) 311–39.

Sparks, Kenton L. *God's Word in Human Words: An Evangelical Appropriation of Critical Biblical Scholarship.* Grand Rapids: Baker, 2008.

Speiser, Ephraim Avigdor. *Genesis.* Garden City: Doubleday, 1964.

———. "The Epic of Gilgamesh." In *ANET* 72–99.

Spek, Robartus J. van der. "The Hellenistic Near East." In *The Cambridge Economic History of the Greco-Roman World*, edited by Walter Scheidel, et al., 409–33. Cambridge: Cambridge University Press, 2008.

Spero, Shubert. "Jacob and Esau: The Relationship Reconsidered." *JBQ* 32 (2004) 245–50.

Spicq, Ceslas. *Saint Paul: Les Épîtres pastorales.* Paris: Gabalda, 1969.

Spieckermann, Hermann. "*Dies irae*: der alttestamentliche Befund und seine Vorgeschichte." *VT* 39 (1989) 194–208.

———. "Wrath and Mercy as Crucial Terms of Theological Hermeneutics." In *Divine Wrath and Divine Mercy in the World of Antiquity*, edited by Reinhard G. Kratz and Hermann Spieckermann, 1–18. Tübingen: Mohr Siebeck, 2008.

Spier, Hedwige. "The Motive for the Suppliants' Flight." *The Classical Journal* 57 (1962) 315–17.

Spina, Frank A. "The 'Ground' for Cain's Rejection (Gen 4): אדמה in the Context of Gen 1–11." *ZAW* 104 (1992) 319–32.

Spindler, Michael. *American Literature and Social Change: William Dean Howells to Arthur Miller.* Bloomington: Indiana University Press, 1983.

Stahlberg, Lesleigh Cushing. *Sustaining Fictions: Intertextuality, Midrash, Translation, and the Literary Afterlife of the Bible.* London: T. & T. Clark, 2008.

Stanfield, J. Ron. *The Economic Thought of Karl Polanyi: Lives and Livelihood.* New York: St. Martin's, 1986.

Stansell, Gary. "Wealth: How Abraham Became Rich." In *Ancient Israel: The Old Testament in Its Social Context*, edited by Philip Esler, 92–110. Minneapolis: Fortress, 2006.

Starr, Chester G. "An Overdose of Slavery." *Journal of Economic History* 18 (1958) 17–32.

Stecker, Robert. "Pragmatism and Interpretation." *Poetics Today* 14 (1993) 181–91.

Stearns, Peter N. *Consumerism in World History: The Global Transformation of Desire.* London: Routledge, 2001.

Steele, L. "Mesopotamian Elements in the Proem of Parmenides? Correspondences between the Sun-Gods Helios and Shamash." *Classical Quarterly* 52 (2002) 583–88.

Stefanini, Ruggero. "Enkidu's Dream in the Hittite 'Gilgamesh.'" *JNES* 28 (1969) 40–47.

Stegemann, Hartmut. "The Qumran Essenes." In *The Madrid Qumran Congress*, edited by J. T. Barrera et al., 83–166. Leiden: Brill, 1992.

Steger, Manfred. *Globalization: A Very Short Introduction*. Oxford: Oxford University Press, 2003.

Stein, G. *Rethinking World Systems: Diasporas, Colonies, and Interaction in Uruk Mesopotamia*. PhD diss., University of Arizona, 1999.

Steinberg, Naomi A. "Gender Roles in the Rebekah Cycle." *USQR* 39 (1984) 175–88.

———. *Kinship and Marriage in Genesis: A Household Economics Perspective*. Minneapolis: Fortress, 1993.

Steinkeller, Piotr. "On Rulers and Officials in the Ancient Near East." In *Priests and Officials in the Ancient Near East*, edited by Kazuko Watanabe, 103–37. Heidelberg: Carl Winter, 1999.

Stendahl, Krister. "The Bible as a Classic and the Bible as Holy Scripture." *JBL* 103 (1984) 3–10.

———. "Biblical Theology, Contemporary." In *IDB* 1:418–32.

Sterba, Richard L. "The Organization and Management of the Temple Corporations in Ancient Mesopotamia." *Academy of Management Review* 1 (1976) 16–26.

Stern, David. *Parables in Midrash: Narrative and Exegesis in Rabbinic Literature*. Cambridge, Harvard University Press, 1991.

Stern, Harold S. "The Knowledge of Good and Evil." *VT* 8 (1958) 405–18.

Stern, Menahem. "The Relations Between the *Hasmonean* Kingdom and Ptolemaic Egypt in View of the International Situation During the 2nd and 1st Centuries BCE." *Zion* 50 (1985) 81–106.

———, and Gérald Finkielsztejn. "Agoranomos." In *EJ* 1:469–70.

Stern, Philip D. "The Origin and Significance of the 'Land Flowing with Milk and Honey.'" *VT* 42 (1992) 554–57.

Sternberg, Meir. "The Bible's Art of Persuasion: Ideology, Rhetoric, and Poetics in Saul's Fall." *HUCA* 54 (1983) 45–82.

———. *The Poetics of Biblical Narrative: Ideological Literature and the Drama of Reading*. Bloomington: Indiana University Press, 1985.

Stevens, Marty E. *Temples, Tithes, and Taxes*. Peabody, MA: Hendrickson, 2006.

Steymans, Hans Ulrich. *Deuteronomium 28 und die adê zur Thronfolgeregelung Asarhaddons: Segen und Fluch im Alten Orient und in Israel*. Freiburg: Universitätsverlag, 1996.

Stiglitz, Joseph E. "Information and the Change in the Paradigm in Economics." *The American Economic Review* 92 (2002) 460–501.

Stockton, David. Review of *Publicans and Sinners: Private Enterprise in the Service of the Roman Republic*, by Ernst Badian. *The Classical Review* 25 (1975) 96–98.

Stokholm, Niels. "Zur Überlieferung von Heliodor, Kuturnahhunte and anderen missglückten Tempelräubern." *Studia Theologica* 22 (1968) 1–28.

Stol, Marten. "Private Life in Ancient Mesopotamia." In *CANE* 485–501.

Stoll, Steven. "Agrarian Anxieties." *Harper's Magazine* 321 (July 2010) 6–8.

Stolper, Matthew W. *Entrepreneurs and Empire: The Murašû Archive, the Murašû Firm, and Persian Rule in Babylonia*. Leiden: Nederlands Historisch-Archaeologisch Instituut te Istanbul, 1985.

———. "Registration and Taxation of Slave Sales in Achaemenid Babylonia." *ZAVA* 79 (1989) 80–101.

Stone, Jerome Arthur. *The Minimalist Vision of Transcendence: A Naturalist Philosophy of Religion*. Albany: SUNY, 1992.

Sukenik, Eleazar. *The Dead Sea Scrolls of the Hebrew University*. Jerusalem: Magnes, 1955.

Suter, Kevin. "Christians and Personal Wealth." *AJT* 3 (1989) 643–50.

Swartz, Michael. "Judaism: An Overview." In *ER* 7:4968–88.

Swift, Louis J. "Iustitia and Ius Privatum: Ambrose on Private Property." *American Journal of Philology* 100 (1979) 176–87.

Szpakowska, Kasia Maria. *Behind Closed Eyes: Dreams and Nightmares in Ancient Egypt*. Swansea: Classical Press of Wales, 2003.

Taggar-Cohen, Ada. "Law and Family in the Book of Numbers: The Levites and the *tidennutu* Documents from Nuzi." *VT* 48 (1998) 74–94.

Tadmor, Hayim. "The 'People' and the Kingship in Ancient Israel." In *Jewish Society Through the Ages*, edited by Hayim Hillel Ben-Sasson and Shmuel Ettinger, 46–68. New York: Schocken, 1971.

Tafsir al-Jalalayn. Dār al-Qalam: al-Qāhirah, 1966.

Takács, Sarolta A. "Isis." In *ER* 7:4557–60.

Talbert, Charles H. *Reading Luke: A Literary and Theological Commentary on the Third Gospel*. New York: Crossroad, 1982.

Talon, Philippe. *The Standard Babylonian Creation Myth Enūma Eliš*. Helsinki: Neo-Assyrian Text Corpus Project, 2005.

Tarn, William Woodthorpe. *Hellenistic Civilization*. Cleveland, OH: World, 1961.

Tate, W. Randolph. *Biblical Interpretation: An Integrated Approach*. Peabody, MA: Hendrickson, 2008.

Taylor, Barry. *Society and Economy in Early Modern Europe, 1450–1789: A Bibliography of Post-War Research*. Manchester: Manchester University Press, 1989.

Taylor, Deborah Furlan. "The Monetary Crisis in Revelation 13:17 and the Provenance of the Book of Revelation." *CBQ* 71 (2009) 580–96.

Taylor, J. "Solar Worship in the Bible and Its World." PhD diss., Yale University, 1989.

Tcherikover, Victor. *Hellenistic Civilization and the Jews*. Philadelphia: Jewish Publication Society, 1961.

————. "Palestine under the Ptolemies." *Mizraim* 4/5 (1937) 48–51.

Terrien, Samuel. *The Elusive Presence*, 1978. Reprint, Eugene, OR: Wipf & Stock, 2000.

Testart, Alain. "The Extent and Significance of Debt Slavery." *Revue française de sociologie* 43 (2002) 173–204.

Theissen, Gerd. *The Bible and Contemporary Culture*. Minneapolis: Fortress, 2007.

————. "The Social Structure of Pauline Communities: Some Critical Remarks on J. Meggitt's *Paul, Poverty and Survival*." *JSNT* 84 (2001) 65–84.

Thiel, Winfried. *Gedeutete Geschichte*. Neukirchen-Vluyn: Neukirchener, 2005.

Tickamyer, Ann. "Wealth and Power: A Comparison of Men and Women in the Property Elite." *Social Forces* 60 (1981) 463–81.

Tigay, Jeffrey. *The Evolution of the Gilgamesh Epic*. Philadelphia: University of Pennsylvania Press, 1982.

Tilly, Charles. "Since Gilgamesh." *Social Research* 53 (1986) 391–410.

Todaro, Michael P. *Economic Development in the Third World*. London: Longman, 1977.

————, and Stephen C. Smith. *Economic Development*. London: Longman Group, 2009.

Tolkien, J. R. R. "Beowulf, the Monsters and the Critics." In *Modern Writings on Major English Authors*, edited by James R. Kreuzer and Lee Cogan, 1–32. Indianapolis: Bobbs-Merrill, 1963.

———. *The Lord of the Rings: The Two Towers*, 1954. Reprint. New York: Ballentine, 1994.

Tönges, Elke. "'The Epistle to the Hebrews as a 'Jesus-Midrash.'" In *Hebrews: Contemporary Methods—New Insights*, edited by Gabriella Gelardini, 89–105. Leiden: Brill, 2005.

Toorn, Karel van der. "Did Ecclesiastes Copy Gilgamesh?" *Bible Review* 16 (2000) 22–30.

———. *Family Religion in Babylonia, Syria and Israel*. Leiden: Brill, 1996.

———. *Sin and Sanction in Israel and Mesopotamia*. Assen: van Gorcum, 1985.

———. "The Public Image of the Widow in Ancient Israel." In *Between Poverty and the Pyre: Moments in the History of Widowhood*, edited by Jan Bremmer and Lourens van den Bosch, 19–30. London: Routledge, 1995.

———. "Why Wisdom Became a Secret: On Wisdom as a Written Genre." In *Wisdom Literature in Mesopotamia and Israel*, edited by Richard Clifford, 21–32. Atlanta: Society of Biblical Literature, 2007.

Tournay, Raymond. "À propos du verbe הין." *Revue biblique* 101 (1994) 321–25.

Towner, W. Sibley. *The Rabbinic "Enumeration of Scriptural Examples": A Study of a Rabbinic Pattern of Discourse with Special Reference to Mekhilta d'R. Ishmael*. Leiden: Brill, 1973.

Townsend, Joan. "Fact, Fallacy, and Revitalization Movement." In *Goddesses in Religions and Modern Debate*, edited by Larry Hurtado, 179–203. Atlanta: Scholars, 1990.

Tracy, Brian. *Getting Rich Your Own Way*. Hoboken, NJ: Wiley, 2004.

Trigger, Bruce G. *Understanding Early Civilizations: A Comparative Study*. Cambridge: Cambridge University Press, 2003.

Trimpe, Birgit. *Von der Schöpfung bis zur Zerstreuung: Intertextuelle Interpretationen der biblischen Urgeschichte (Gen 1–11)*. Osnabrück: Universitätsverlag Rasch, 2000.

Tucker, Lee. "Child Slaves in Modern India: The Bonded Labor Problem." *Human Rights Quarterly* 19 (1997) 572–629.

Tucker, W. Dennis. "Revisiting the Plagues in Psalm CV." *VT* 55 (2005) 401–11.

Turner, Edith, and Pamela R. Frese. "Marriage." In *ER* 8:5724–27.

Turner, Frederick W. *Beyond Geography: The Western Spirit against the Wilderness*. New York: Viking, 1980.

Turner, Victor Witter. *The Ritual Process: Structure and Anti-Structure*. Chicago: Aldine, 1969.

Tyler, Stephen A. *The Unspeakable: Discourse, Dialogue, and Rhetoric in the Postmodern World*. Madison: University of Wisconsin Press, 1987.

Udoh, Fabian E. *To Caesar What is Caesar's: Tribute, Taxes and Imperial Administration in Early Roman Palestine*. Providence: Brown University Press, 2005.

Ungnad, Arthur, and Hugo Gressman. *Das Gilgamesh-Epos*. Göttingen: Vandenhoeck und Ruprecht, 1911.

Uphill, E. P. "Pithom and Raamses: Their Location and Significance." *JNES* 27 (1968) 291–316.

Valeta, David M. *Lions and Ovens and Visions: A Satirical Reading of Daniel 1–6*. Sheffield: Phoenix, 2008.

Vallet, Ronald E. *Stepping Stones of the Steward: A Faith Journey Through Jesus' Parables*. Grand Rapids: Eerdmans, 1994.

Vancil, Jack. "The Symbolism of the Shepherd in Biblical, Intertestamental, and New Testament Material." PhD diss., Dropsie College, 1975.

Van de Mieroop, Marc. *A History of the Ancient Near East.* London: Blackwell, 2003.

———. *The Ancient Mesopotamian City.* New York: Oxford, 1999.

VanderKam, James, and Peter Flint. *The Meaning of the Dead Sea Scrolls: Their Significance for Understanding the Bible, Judaism, Jesus, and Christianity.* San Francisco: HarperOne, 2004.

Van Drimmelen, Rob. *Faith in a Global Economy: A Primer for Christians.* Geneva: World Council of Churches, 1998.

Van Dyke, Henry. *Out-of-Doors in the Holy Land.* New York: Scribner's Sons, 1908.

Vanhoozer, Kevin J. "Scripture and Tradition." In *The Cambridge Companion to Postmodern Theology,* edited by Kevin J. Vanhoozer, 149–69. Cambridge: Cambridge University Press, 2003.

Van Nortwick, Thomas. *Somewhere I Have Never Traveled: The Second Self and the Hero's Journey in Ancient Epic.* Oxford: Oxford University Press, 1992.

Van Seters, John. "Abraham." In *ER* 1:13–17.

———. *Abraham in History and Tradition.* New Haven: Yale, 1975.

———. *In Search of History: Historiography in the Ancient World and the Origins of Biblical History.* New Haven: Yale, 1983.

Vanstiphout, Herman L. "Inanna/Ishtar as a Figure of Controversy." In *Struggles of Gods: Papers of the Groningen Work Group for the Study of the History of Religions,* edited by Hans Gerhard Kippenberg, et al., 225–37. Berlin: de Gruyter, 1984.

Vaughn, Andrew G. "'And Lot Went with Him': Abraham's Disobedience in Genesis 12:1–4a." In *David and Zion: Biblical Studies in Honor of J. J. M. Roberts,* edited by Bernard F. Batto and Kathryn L. Roberts, 111–23. Winona Lake, IN: Eisenbrauns, 2004.

Veblen, Thorstein. *Absentee Ownership and Business Enterprise in Recent Times.* New York: Huebsch, 1923.

Veenker, Ronald A. "Forbidden Fruit: Ancient Near Eastern Sexual Metaphors." *HUCA* 70–71 (2000) 57–73.

Veith, G. "'Wait Upon the Lord': David, Hamlet, and the Problem of Revenge." In *The David Myth in Western Literature,* edited by Raymond-Jean Frontain and Jan Wojcik, 70–83. West Lafayette, IN: Purdue University Press, 1980.

Velde, Herman te. *Seth, God of Confusion: A Study of His Role in Egyptian Mythology and Religion.* Leiden: Brill, 1977.

———. "Theology, Priests, and Worship in Ancient Egypt." In *CANE* 3:1731–49.

Vermes, Geza. *The Complete Dead Sea Scrolls in English.* New York: Penguin, 2004.

Volk, Konrad. *Inanna und Šukaletuda: Zur historisch-politischen Deutung eines sumerischen Literaturwerkes.* Wiesbaden: Harrassowitz, 1995.

von Franz, Marie-Luise. *Projection and Re-Collection in Jungian Psychology.* La Salle, IL: Open Court, 1980.

Von Hendy, Andrew. *The Modern Construction of Myth.* Bloomington: Indiana University Press, 2002.

Veitch, Jonathan. *American Superrealism: Nathanael West and the Politics of Representation in the 1930s.* Madison: University of Wisconsin Press, 1997.

Vernant, Jean Pierre. *Myth and Society in Ancient Greece.* London: Harvester, 1980.

Vuchinich, Rudolph Eugene, and Nick Heather. *Choice, Behavioural Economics, and Addiction.* Oxford: Elsevier, 2003.

Vulpe, Nicola. "Irony and the Unity of the *Gilgamesh Epic*." *JNES* 53 (1994) 275–83.

Wachlin, Mary Goughnour. "The Bible: Why We Need to Teach It; How Some Do." *The English Journal* 87 (March 1998) 31–36.

Wahl, Harald Martin. "Die Jakobserzählung der Genesis und der Jubiläen im Vergleich: Zur Auslegung der Genesis im 2. Jahrhundert v. Chr und mit Anmerkungen der Pentateuchforschung." *VT* 44 (1994) 524–46.

Wald, Stephen G. "Aggadah." In *EJ* 1:454–64.

Walker, Christopher, and Michael Dick. *The Induction of the Cult Image in Ancient Mesopotamia: The Mesopotamian Mīs Pî Ritual.* Helsinki: Helsinki University Press, 2001.

Walker, Thomas W. "Who is My *Neighbor*? An Invitation to See the World with Different Eyes." In *Global Neighbors: Christian Faith and Moral Obligation in Today's Economy,* edited by Douglas A. Hicks and Mark R. Valeri, 3–15. Grand Rapids: Eerdmans, 2008.

Wallis, Louis. Review of *Studies in the Economics of the Bible*, by Eli Ginzberg. *American Journal of Sociology* 39 (1933) 270–71.

Walls, Neal H. *Desire, Discord and Death: Approaches to Ancient Near Eastern Myth.* Boston: ASOR, 2001.

———. *The Goddess Anat in Ugaritic Myth.* Atlanta: Scholars, 1992.

Waltke, Bruce K. "Cain and His Offering." *WTJ* 48 (1986) 363–72.

Walton, John. *Ancient Near Eastern Thought and the Old Testament.* Grand Rapids: Baker, 2006.

———. "The Imagery of the Substitute King Ritual in Isaiah's Fourth Servant Song." *JBL* 122 (2003) 734–43.

Waltz, Kenneth Neal. *Theory of International Politics.* New York: Random House, 1979.

Wander, Nathaniel. "Structure, Contradiction, and 'Resolution' in Mythology: Father's Brother's Daughter Marriage and the Treatment of Women in Genesis 11:50." *JANES* 13 (1981) 75–99.

Waschke, Ernst-Joachim. "Zum Verhältnis von Ruhe und Arbeit in den biblischen Schöpfungsgeschichten Gen 1–3." In *"Gerechtigkeit und Recht zu üben" (Gen 18,19): Studien zur altorientalischen und biblischen Rechtsgeschichte, zur Religionsgeschichte Israels und zur Religionssoziologie. Festschrift für Eckart Otto zum 65. Geburtstag,* edited by Reinhard Achenbach and Martin Arneth, 69–80. Wiesbaden: Harrassowitz, 2009.

Wasserman, Nathan. *Style and Form in Old Babylonian Literary Texts.* Leiden: Brill, 2003.

Weber, Clifford. "The Dionysus in Aeneas." *Classical Philology* 97 (2002) 322–43.

Weber, Max. *Ancient Judaism,* 1921. Reprint. New York: Simon & Schuster, 1967.

———. *The Methodology of the Social Sciences.* New York: Free, 1949.

———. *The Protestant Ethic and the Spirit of Capitalism.* Translated by Talcott Parsons, 1920. Reprint. New York: Scribner's, 1958.

Wehr, Hans, and J. Milton Cowan. *A Dictionary of Modern Written Arabic.* Ithaca, NY: Cornell University Press, 1966.

Weimar, Peter. "Zur Freiheit geschaffen." *Bibel und Kirche* 34 (1979) 86–90.

Weinert, Francis D. "Parable of the Throne Claimant Reconsidered." *CBQ* 39 (1977) 505–14.

Weinfeld, Moshe. "Ancient Near Eastern Patterns in Prophetic Literature." *VT* 27 (1977) 178–95.

———. *Deuteronomy 1–11.* New York: Doubleday, 1991.

———. "Sarah and Abimelech Against the Background of Assyrian Law and the Genesis Apocryphon." In *Mélanges bibliques et orientaux en l'honneur de M. Mathias Delcor*, edited by André Caquot et al., 431–6. Neukirchen-Vluyn: Neukirchener, 1985.

———. "The Worship of Molech and the Queen of Heaven and its Background." *UF* 4 (1972) 133–54.

Weinstock, Stefan. *Divus Julius*. Oxford: Clarendon, 1971.

Weippert, Helga. "Das Wort vom neuen Bund in Jeremia XXXI 31–34." *VT* 29 (1979) 336–51.

Weippert, Manfred. "Libanon." In *RlA* 6 (1980–3) 644–45.

———. "Semitische Nomaden des zweiten Jahrtausends." *Bib* 55 (1974) 265–80, 427–33.

Weitzman, Lenore J. *The Divorce Revolution: The Unexpected Social and Economic Consequences for Women and Children in America*. New York: Free, 1985.

Weitzman, Steven. "Plotting Antiochus' Persecution." *JBL* 123 (2004) 219–34.

Welbourn, Frederick Burkewood. Review of *The Structural Study of Myth and Totemism*, by Edmund Leach." *Journal of Religion in Africa* 1 (1968) 233–34.

Wellhausen, Julius. *Prolegomena zur Geschichte Israels*. Berlin: Reimer, 1883.

Wells, Bruce. "What Is Biblical Law? A Look at Pentateuchal Rules and Near Eastern Practice." *CBQ* 70 (2008) 223–43.

Wenham, Gordon J. "Method in Pentateuchal Source Criticism." *VT* 41 (1991) 84–109.

Went, Robert. *The Enigma of Globalization: A Journey to a New Stage of Capitalism*. New York: Routledge, 2002.

Westbrook, Raymond. "A Sumerian Freedman." In *Literatur, Politik, und Recht in Mesopotamien: Festschrift für Claus Wilcke*, edited by Walter Sallaberger et al., 333–40. Wiesbaden: Harrassowitz, 2003.

Westenholz, Aage. *Old Sumerian and Old Akkadian Texts in Philadelphia II: The "Akkadian" Texts, the Enlilemaba Texts, and the Onion Archive*. Copenhagen: University of Copenhagen Museum Tusculanum, 1987.

———, and U. Koch-Westenholz. "Enkidu—The Noble Savage?" In *Wisdom, Gods, and Literature: Studies in Assyriology in Honour of W. G. Lambert*, edited by A. R. George and I. Finkel, 437–51. Winona Lake, IN: Eisenbrauns, 2000.

Westenholtz, Joan Goodnick, and Aage Westenholtz. *Cuneiform Inscriptions in the Collection of the Bible Lands Museum Jerusalem: The Old Babylonian Inscriptions*. Leiden: Brill, 2006.

Westermann, Claus. *Elements of Old Testament Theology*. Atlanta: John Knox, 1982.

———. *Genesis 1–11*. Darmstadt: Wissenschaftliche Buchgesellschaft, 1976.

———. *Genesis 12–36*. Neukirchen-Vluyn: Neukirchener, 1981.

———. *The Promises to the Fathers: Studies on the Patriarchal Narratives*. Philadelphia: Fortress, 1979.

Wettengel, Wolfgang. *Die Erzählung von den beiden Brüdern: Der Papyrus d'Orbiney und die Königsideologie der Ramessiden*. Göttingen: Vandenhoeck und Ruprecht, 2003.

Whedbee, J. William. *The Bible and the Comic Vision*. Minneapolis: Fortress, 2002.

White, Sidnie. "A Comparison of the 'A' and 'B' Manuscripts of the Damascus Document." *RevQ* 12 (1987) 537–53.

Whitehorn, John. "Ptolemy." In *ABD* 5:541–44.

Whitelam, Keith. *The Invention of Ancient Israel: The Silencing of Palestinian History*. London: Routledge, 1996.

Whiteley, Peter M. "Indians of the Southwest." In *ER* 10:6720–30.

Whitlark, Jason A. *Enabling Fidelity to God: Perseverance in Hebrews in Light of Reciprocity Systems in the Ancient Mediterranean World.* Milton Keynes, UK: Paternoster, 2008.

Whybray, Roger N. *The Making of the Pentateuch: A Methodological Study.* Sheffield: Sheffield Academic, 1987.

Wiesel, Elie. "He Who Kills, Kills His Brother." *Bible Review* 14, 1 (1998) 20–21.

Wiesehöfer, Josef. *Ancient Persia.* London: I. B. Tauris, 2006.

Wiethoff, William E. *A Peculiar Humanism: The Judicial Advocacy of Slavery in High Courts of the Old South.* Athens: University of Georgia Press, 1996.

Wiggermann, Franciscus Antonio Maria. "An Unrecognized Synonym of Sumerian sukkal, 'Vizier.'" *ZA* 78 (1989) 225–40.

———. "Theologies, Priests, and Worship in Ancient Mesopotamia." In *CANE* 3:1857–81.

Wilcke, Claus. *Early Ancient Near Eastern Law: A History of Its Beginnings. The Early Dynastic and Sargonic Periods.* Winona Lake, IN: Eisenbrauns, 2007.

Wildavsky, Aaron. *Assimilation vs. Separation: Joseph the Administrator and the Politics of Religion in Biblical Israel.* New Brunswick, NJ: Transaction, 1993.

Willi-Plein, Ina. "Genesis 27 als Rebekkageschichte." *TZ* 45 (1989) 315–34.

Williams, David Salter. *The Structure of 1 Maccabees.* Washington: Catholic Biblical Association, 1999.

Williams, James G. "Number Symbolism and Joseph as a Symbol of Completion." *JBL* 98 (1979) 86–87.

Williams, Michael James. *Deception in Genesis: An Investigation into the Morality of a Unique Biblical Phenomenon.* New York: Lang, 2001.

Williamson, Thad, et al. *Making a Place for Community: Local Democracy in a Global Era.* London: Routledge, 2002.

Willis, Thayer Cheatham. *Navigating the Dark Side of Wealth: A Life Guide for Inheritors.* Nashport, OH: New Concord, 2005.

Wilson, Lindsay. *Joseph, Wise and Otherwise: The Intersection of Wisdom and Covenant in Genesis 37–50.* Milton Keynes, UK: Paternoster, 2004.

Winckler, John J. *The Constraints of Desire: The Anthropology of Sex and Gender in Ancient Greece.* London: Routledge, 1990.

Wintermute, O. S. "Jubilees: A New Translation and Introduction." In *OTP* 2:35–142.

Wise, Michael, et al. *The Dead Sea Scrolls: A New Translation.* San Francisco: HarperCollins, 2005.

Witherington, Ben. *Jesus the Sage: The Pilgrimage of Wisdom.* Minneapolis: Augsburg Fortress, 2000.

Wittfogel, Karl August. *Oriental Despotism: A Comparative Study of Total Power.* New Haven: Yale, 1957.

Wolff, Hans Walter. "The Kerygma of the Yahwist." In *The Vitality of Old Testament Traditions*, edited by Walter Brueggemann and Hans Walter Wolff, 41–66. Richmond, VA: John Knox, 1975.

Wolff, Hope Nash. "Gilgamesh, Enkidu, and the Heroic Life." *JAOS* 89 (1969) 392–98.

Wong, Fook-Kong. "Manna Revisited: A Study of the Mythological and Interpretative Contexts of Manna." PhD diss., Harvard University, 1998.

Woude, A. S. van der. "Wicked Priest or Wicked Priests: Reflections on the Identification of the Wicked Priest in the Habakkuk Commentary." *JJS* 33 (1982) 349–59.

Wright, Christopher J. H. *Deuteronomy.* Peabody, MA: Hendrickson, 1996.

Wright, Mary, and Dennis Pardee. "Literary Sources for the History of Palestine and Syria: Contacts between Egypt and Syro-Palestine during the Old Kingdom." *BA* 51 (1988) 143–61.

Wright, G. R. H. "Dumuzi at the Court of David." *Numen* 28 (1981) 54–63.

Wuthnow, Robert. *The Crisis in the Churches: Spiritual Malaise, Fiscal Woe.* New York: Oxford, 1997.

Wyatt, Nicholas. "Epic in Ugaritic Literature." In *A Companion to Ancient Epic,* edited by John Miles Foley, 246–54. Oxford: Blackwell, 2005.

Xeravits, Géza G., and József Zsengellér. *The Books of the Maccabees: History, Theology, Ideology.* Leiden: Brill, 2007.

Yacoub, J. "The Dignity of the Individual and of Peoples: The Contribution of Mesopotamia and of Syriac Heritage." *Diogenes* 54 (2007) 19–37.

Yoffee, Norman. "Political Economy in Early Mesopotamian States." *Annual Review of Anthropology* 24 (1995) 281–311.

Young, Brad. *Jesus and His Jewish Parables.* Tulsa, OK: Gospel Research Foundation, 1999.

Young, Ian M. "Textual Stability in Gilgamesh and the Dead Sea Scrolls." In *Gilgamesh and the World of Assyria,* edited by Joseph Azize and Noel Weeks, 173–84. Leuven: Peeters, 2008.

Young, T. Cuyler. "Persepolis." In *ABD* 5:236.

Zaccagnini, Carlo. "The Interdependence of the Great Powers." In *Amarna Diplomacy: The Beginnings of International Relations,* edited by Raymond Cohen and Raymond Westbrook, 141–53. Baltimore: Johns Hopkins, 2000.

Zakovitch, Yair. *Das Buch Rut. Ein jüdischer Kommentar.* Stuttgart: Katholisches Bibelwerk, 1999.

Zangenberg, Jürgen, et al. *Religion, Ethnicity and Identity in Ancient Galilee: A Region in Transition.* Tübingen: Mohr Siebeck, 2007.

Zaret, David. "The Use and Abuse of Textual Data." In *Weber's Protestant Ethic: Origins, Evidence, Contexts,* edited by Hartmut Lehmann and Günther Roth, 245–72. Cambridge: Cambridge University Press, 1995.

Zimmerli, Walther. *I Am Yahweh.* Atlanta: John Knox, 1982.

———. "Promise and Fulfillment." In *Essays on Old Testament Hermeneutics,* edited by Claus Westermann, 89–122. Richmond: John Knox, 1963.

Zimmern, Heinrich. *Keilinschriftliche Bibliothek.* Berlin: Reuther and Reichard, 1915.

Zucker, David. *The Torah: An Introduction for Christians and Jews.* New York: Paulist, 2005.

Zuhur, Sherifa. "Honor, Middle Eastern Notions of." In *NDHI* 3:1011–13.

Subject Index

Author Index